GRANT MORRISON   DAN MORA

ROSS RICHIE CEO & Founder
MATT GAGNON Editor-in-Chief
FILIP SABLIK President of Publishing & Marketing
STEPHEN CHRISTY President of Development
LANCE KREITER VP of Licensing & Merchandising
PHIL BARBARO VP of Finance
BRYCE CARLSON Managing Editor
MEL CAYLO Marketing Manager
SCOTT NEWMAN Production Design Manager
IRENE BRADISH Operations Manager
SIERRA HAHN Senior Editor
DAFNA PLEBAN Editor, Talent Development
SHANNON WATTERS Editor
ERIC HARBURN Editor
WHITNEY LEOPARD Associate Editor
JASMINE AMIRI Associate Editor
CHRIS ROSA Associate Editor
ALEX GALER Associate Editor
CAMERON CHITTOCK Associate Editor
MATTHEW LEVINE Assistant Editor
KELSEY DIETERICH Production Designer
JILLIAN CRAB Production Designer
MICHELLE ANKLEY Production Designer
GRACE PARK Production Design Assistant
AARON FERRARA Operations Coordinator
ELIZABETH LOUGHRIDGE Accounting Coordinator
STEPHANIE HOCUTT Social Media Coordinator
JOSÉ MEZA Sales Assistant
JAMES ARRIOLA Mailroom Assistant
HOLLY AITCHISON Operations Assistant
SAM KUSEK Direct Market Representative
AMBER PARKER Administrative Assistant

BOOM! STUDIOS

KLAUS, November 2016. Published by BOOM! Studios, a division of Boom Entertainment, Inc. Klaus is ™ & © 2016 Grant Morrison. Originally published in single magazine form as KLAUS No. 1-7. ™ & © 2015, 2016 Grant Morrison. All rights reserved. BOOM! Studios™ and the BOOM! Studios logo are trademarks of Boom Entertainment, Inc., registered in various countries and categories. All characters, events, and institutions depicted herein are fictional. Any similarity between any of the names, characters, persons, events, and/or institutions in this publication to actual names, characters, and persons, whether living or dead, events, and/or institutions is unintended and purely coincidental. BOOM! Studios does not read or accept unsolicited submissions of ideas, stories, or artwork.

A catalog record of this book is available from OCLC and from the BOOM! Studios website, www.boom-studios.com, on the Librarians Page.

BOOM! Studios, 5670 Wilshire Boulevard, Suite 450, Los Angeles, CA 90036-5679. Printed in USA. First Printing.

ISBN: 978-1-60886-903-9, eISBN: 978-1-61398-574-8

Local Comic Shop Day Limited Edition
ISBN: 978-1-68415-046-5 , eISBN: 978-1-61398-723-0

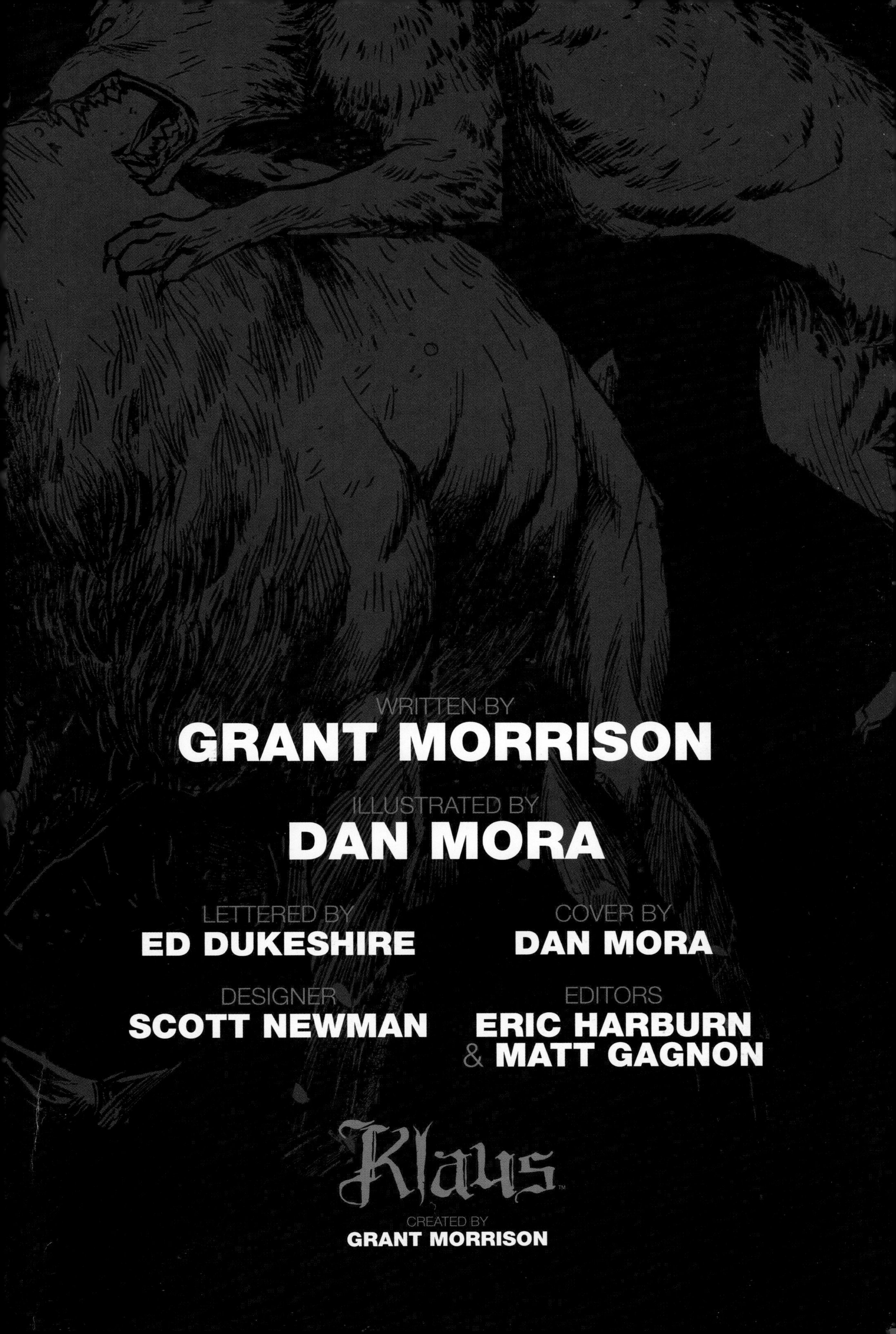

WRITTEN BY
GRANT MORRISON

ILLUSTRATED BY
DAN MORA

LETTERED BY
ED DUKESHIRE

COVER BY
DAN MORA

DESIGNER
SCOTT NEWMAN

EDITORS
ERIC HARBURN
& **MATT GAGNON**

Klaus™

CREATED BY
GRANT MORRISON

CHAPTER
ONE

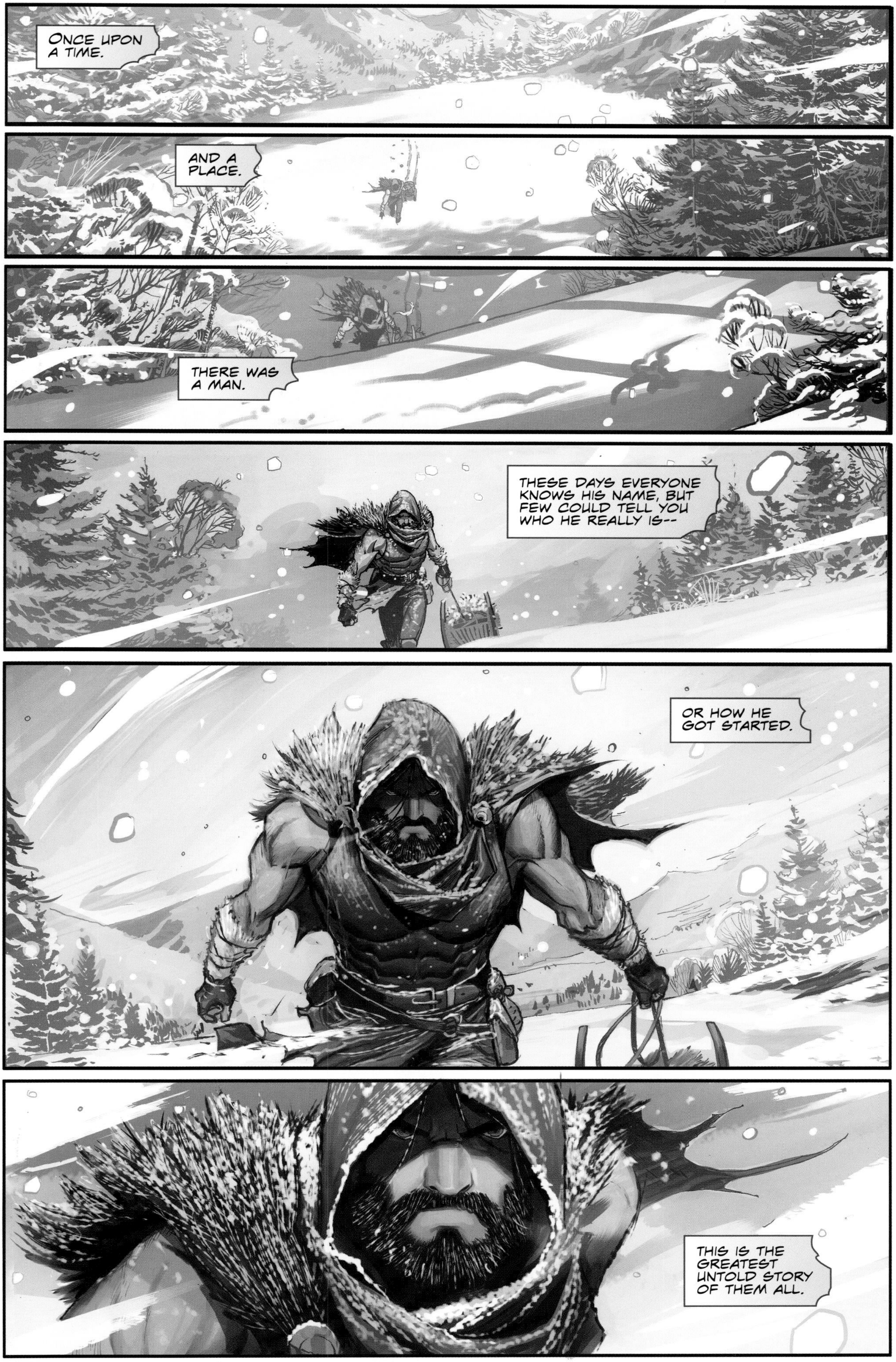
ONCE UPON A TIME.
AND A PLACE.
THERE WAS A MAN.
THESE DAYS EVERYONE KNOWS HIS NAME, BUT FEW COULD TELL YOU WHO HE REALLY IS--
OR HOW HE GOT STARTED.
THIS IS THE GREATEST UNTOLD STORY OF THEM ALL.

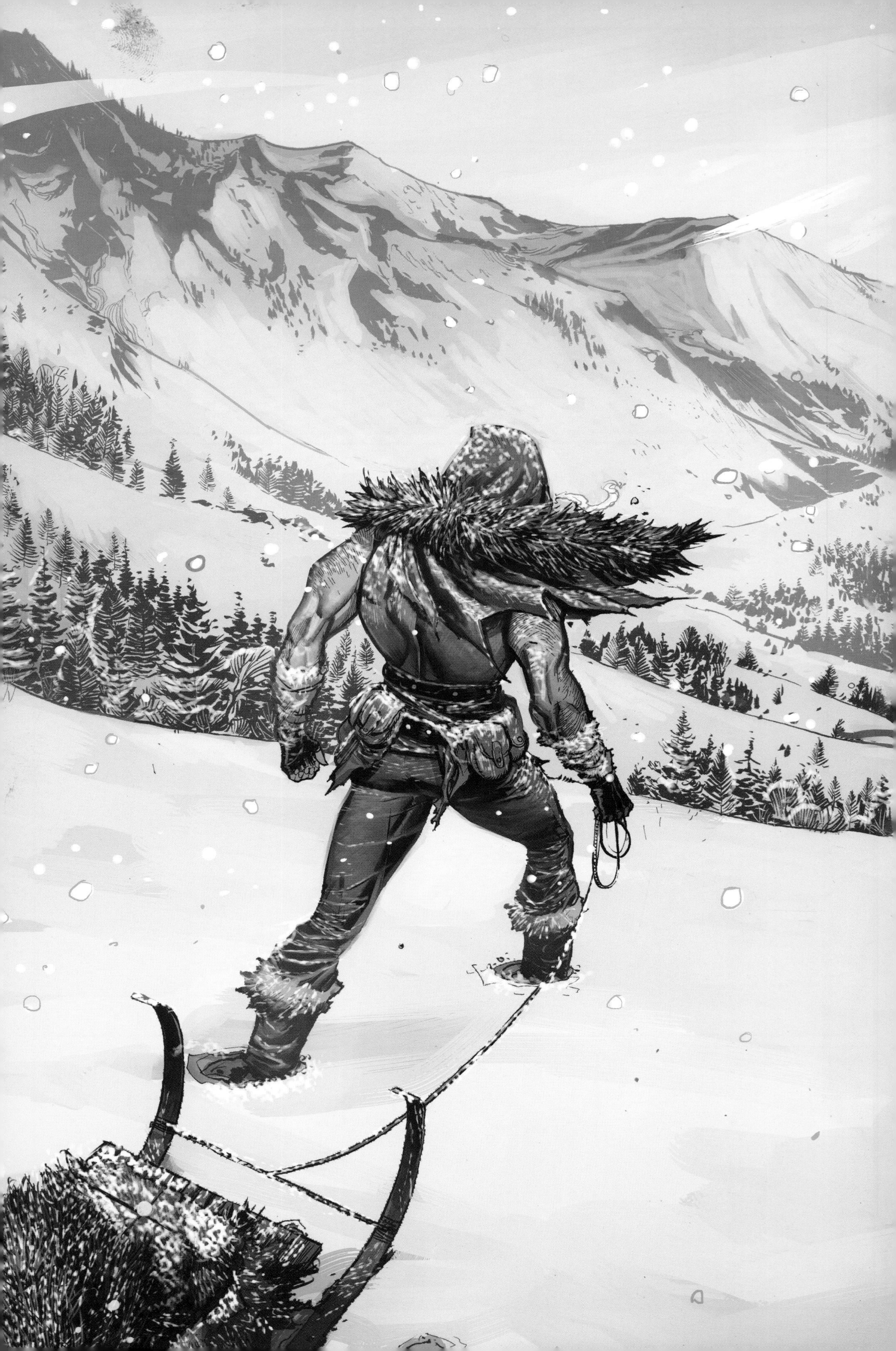

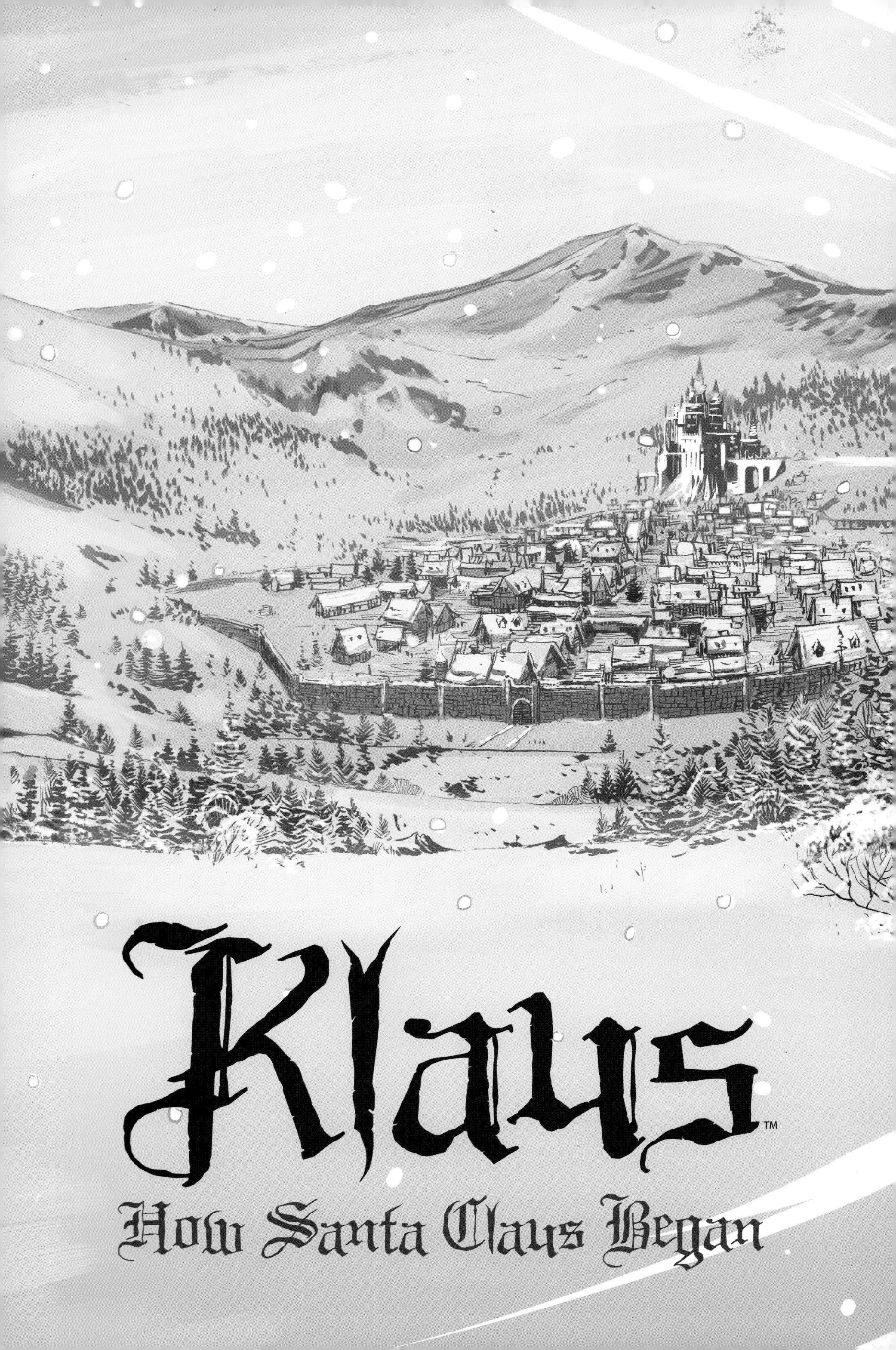

Klaus™

How Santa Claus Began

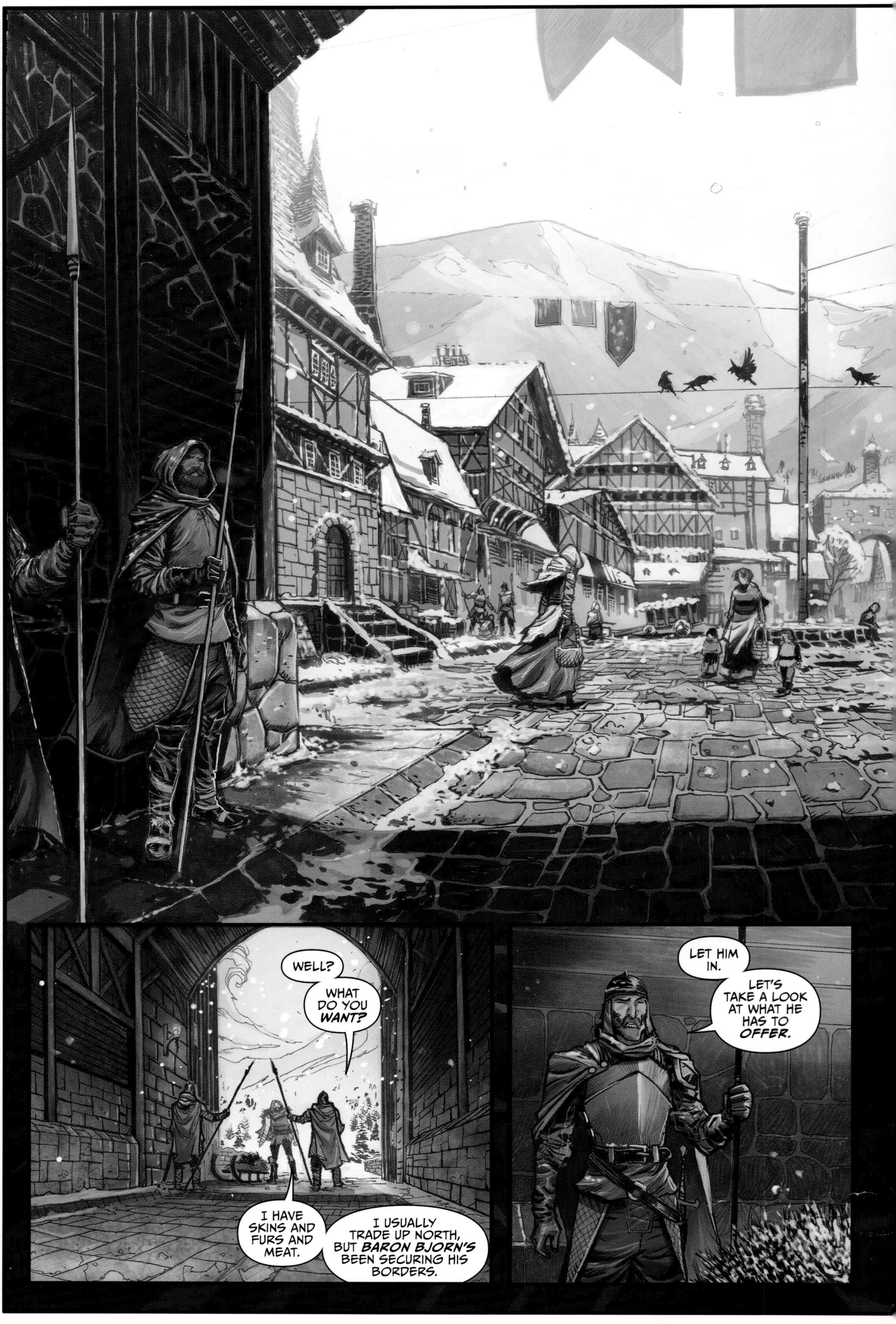
WELL?
WHAT DO YOU WANT?
I HAVE SKINS AND FURS AND MEAT.
I USUALLY TRADE UP NORTH, BUT BARON BJORN'S BEEN SECURING HIS BORDERS.
LET HIM IN.
LET'S TAKE A LOOK AT WHAT HE HAS TO OFFER.

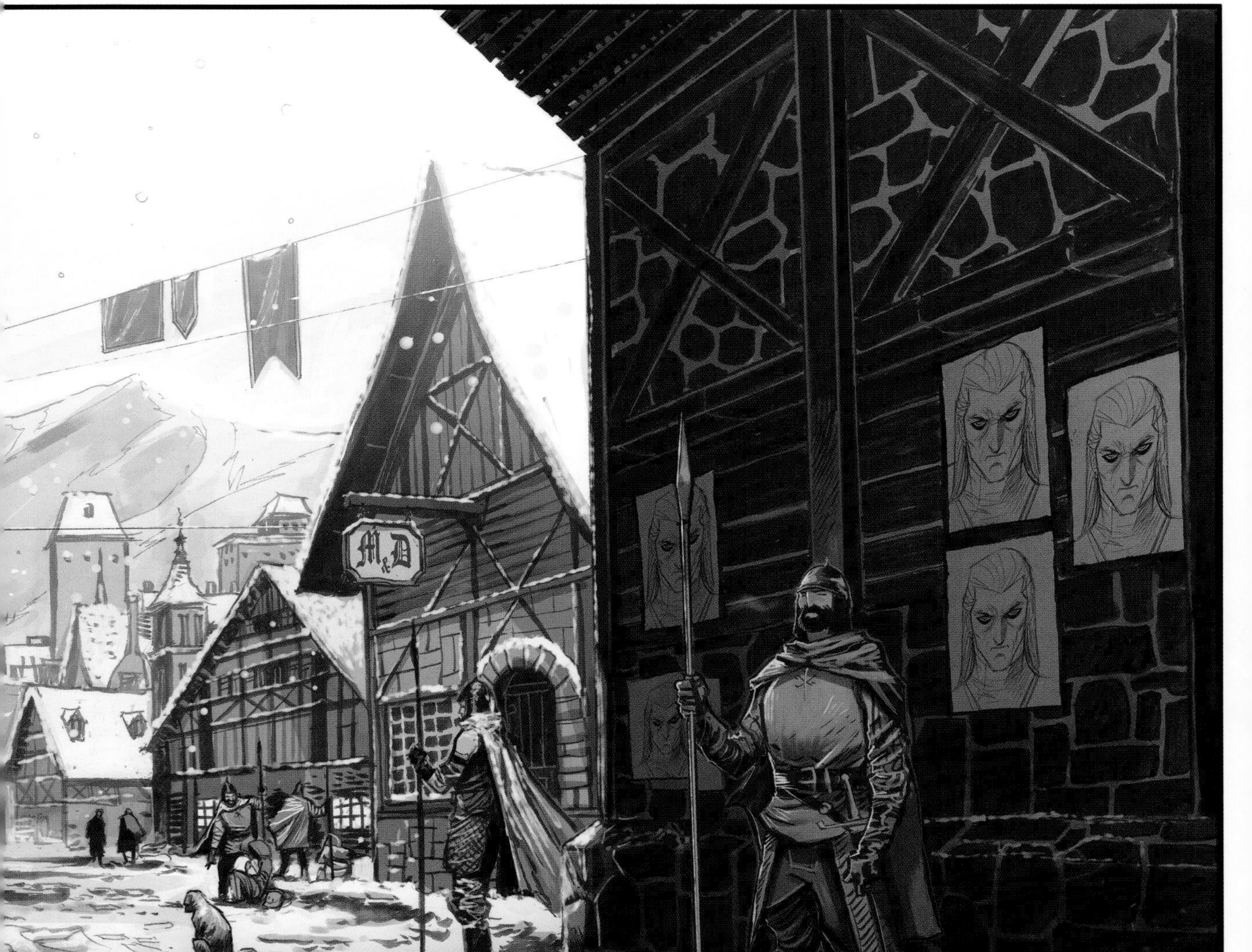
M&D

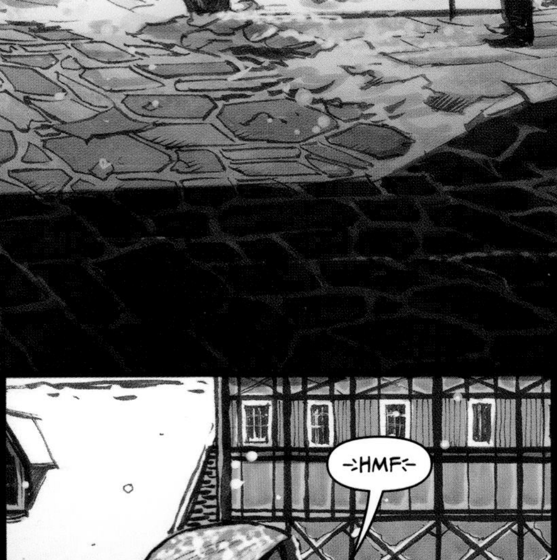
-HMF-

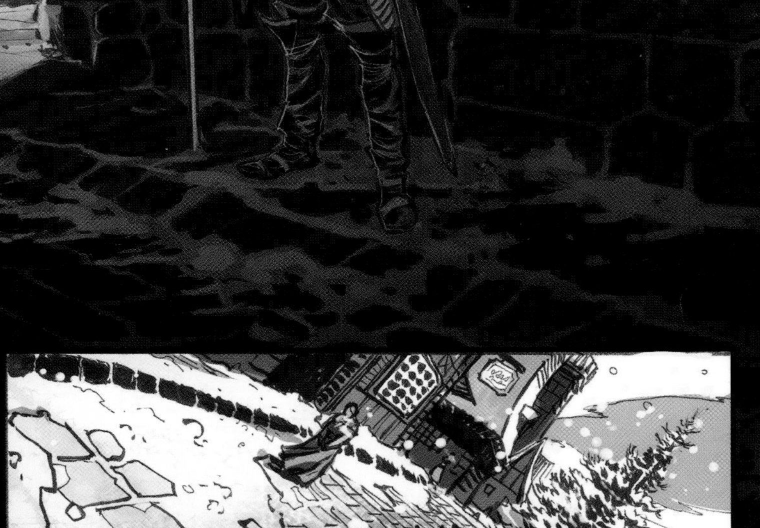
GRIMSVIG.

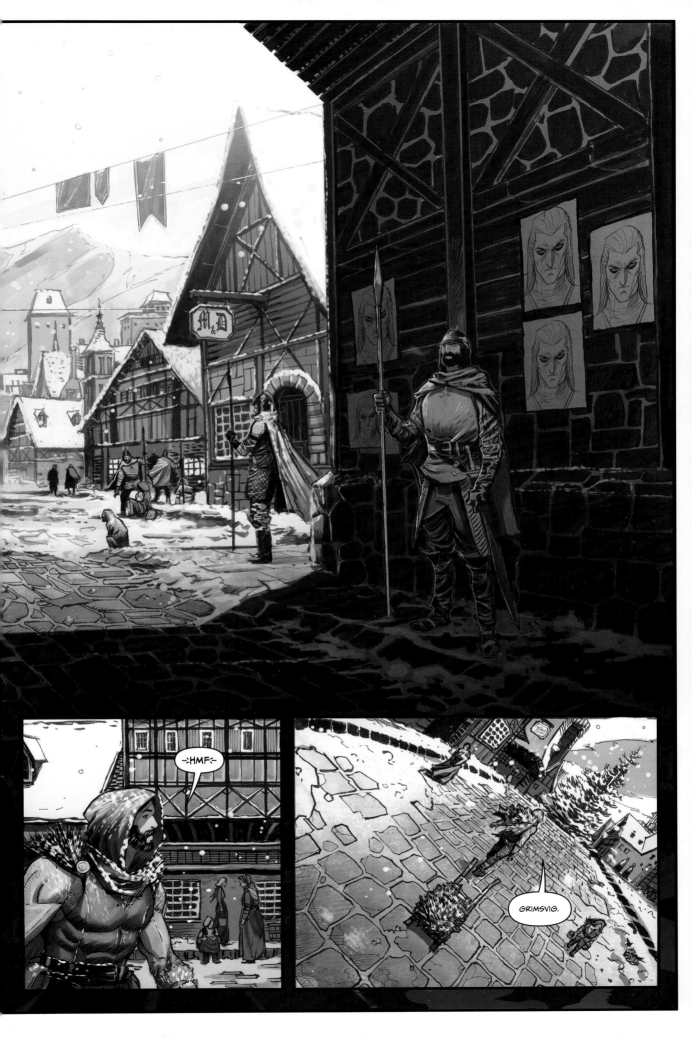

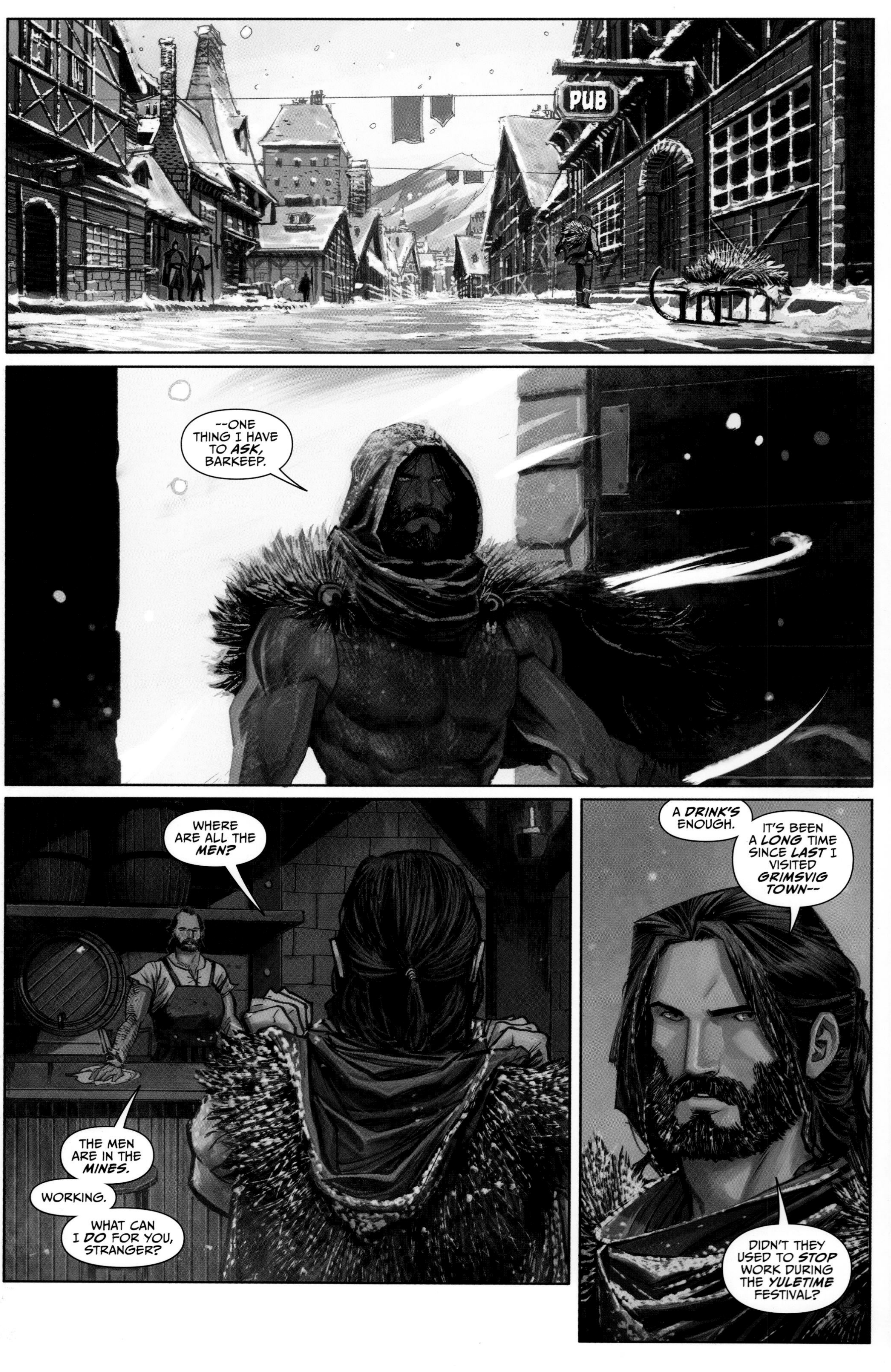
PUB
--ONE THING I HAVE TO ASK, BARKEEP.
WHERE ARE ALL THE MEN?
THE MEN ARE IN THE MINES.
WORKING.
WHAT CAN I DO FOR YOU, STRANGER?
A DRINK'S ENOUGH.
IT'S BEEN A LONG TIME SINCE LAST I VISITED GRIMSVIG TOWN--
DIDN'T THEY USED TO STOP WORK DURING THE YULETIME FESTIVAL?

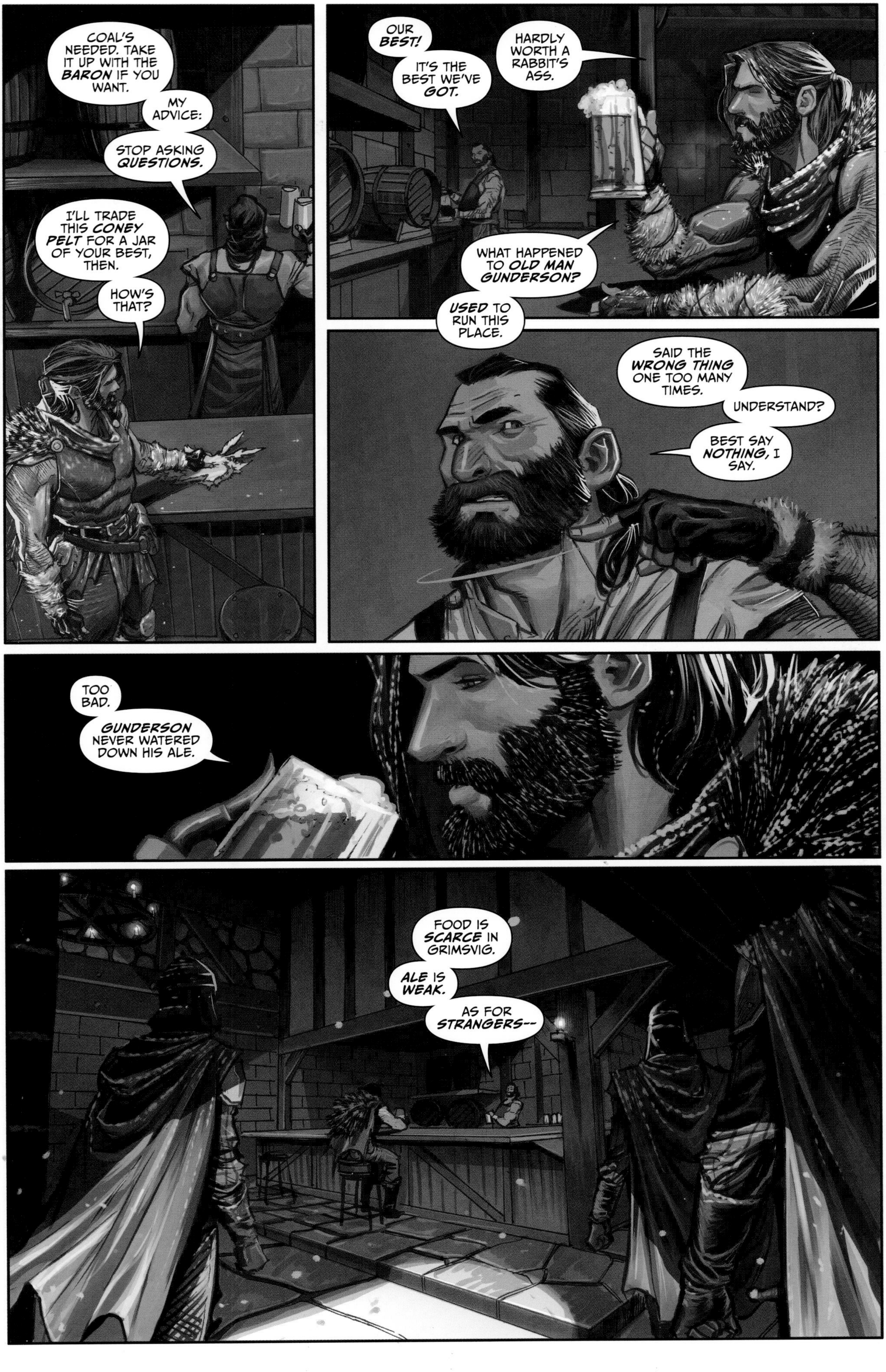
COAL'S NEEDED. TAKE IT UP WITH THE BARON IF YOU WANT.
MY ADVICE:
STOP ASKING QUESTIONS.
I'LL TRADE THIS CONEY PELT FOR A JAR OF YOUR BEST, THEN.
HOW'S THAT?
OUR BEST!
IT'S THE BEST WE'VE GOT.
HARDLY WORTH A RABBIT'S ASS.
WHAT HAPPENED TO OLD MAN GUNDERSON?
USED TO RUN THIS PLACE.
SAID THE WRONG THING ONE TOO MANY TIMES.
UNDERSTAND?
BEST SAY NOTHING, I SAY.
TOO BAD.
GUNDERSON NEVER WATERED DOWN HIS ALE.
FOOD IS SCARCE IN GRIMSVIG.
ALE IS WEAK.
AS FOR STRANGERS--

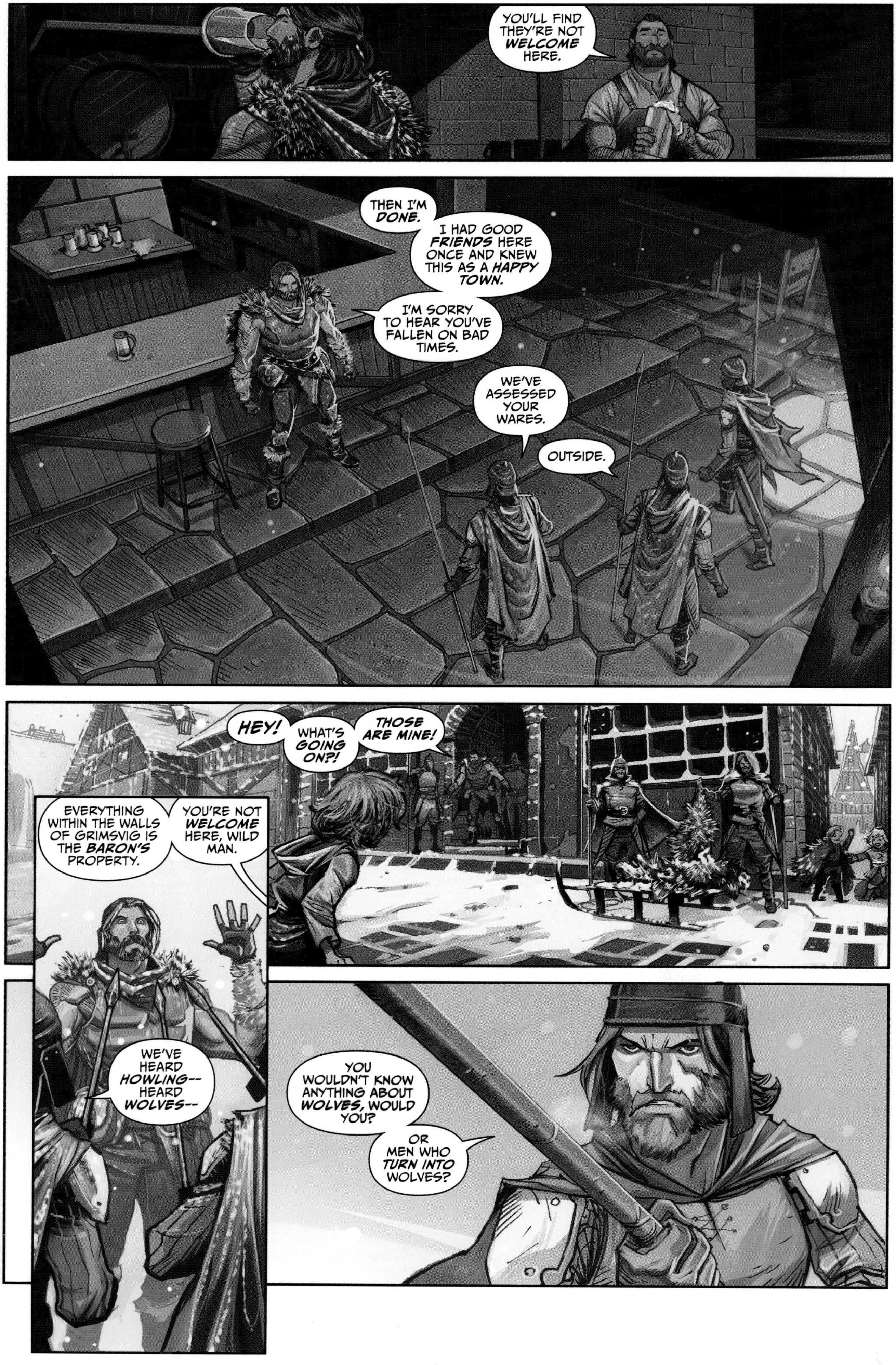
YOU'LL FIND THEY'RE NOT WELCOME HERE.
THEN I'M DONE.
I HAD GOOD FRIENDS HERE ONCE AND KNEW THIS AS A HAPPY TOWN.
I'M SORRY TO HEAR YOU'VE FALLEN ON BAD TIMES.
WE'VE ASSESSED YOUR WARES.
OUTSIDE.
HEY!
WHAT'S GOING ON?!
THOSE ARE MINE!
EVERYTHING WITHIN THE WALLS OF GRIMSVIG IS THE BARON'S PROPERTY.
YOU'RE NOT WELCOME HERE, WILD MAN.
WE'VE HEARD HOWLING-- HEARD WOLVES--
YOU WOULDN'T KNOW ANYTHING ABOUT WOLVES, WOULD YOU?
OR MEN WHO TURN INTO WOLVES?

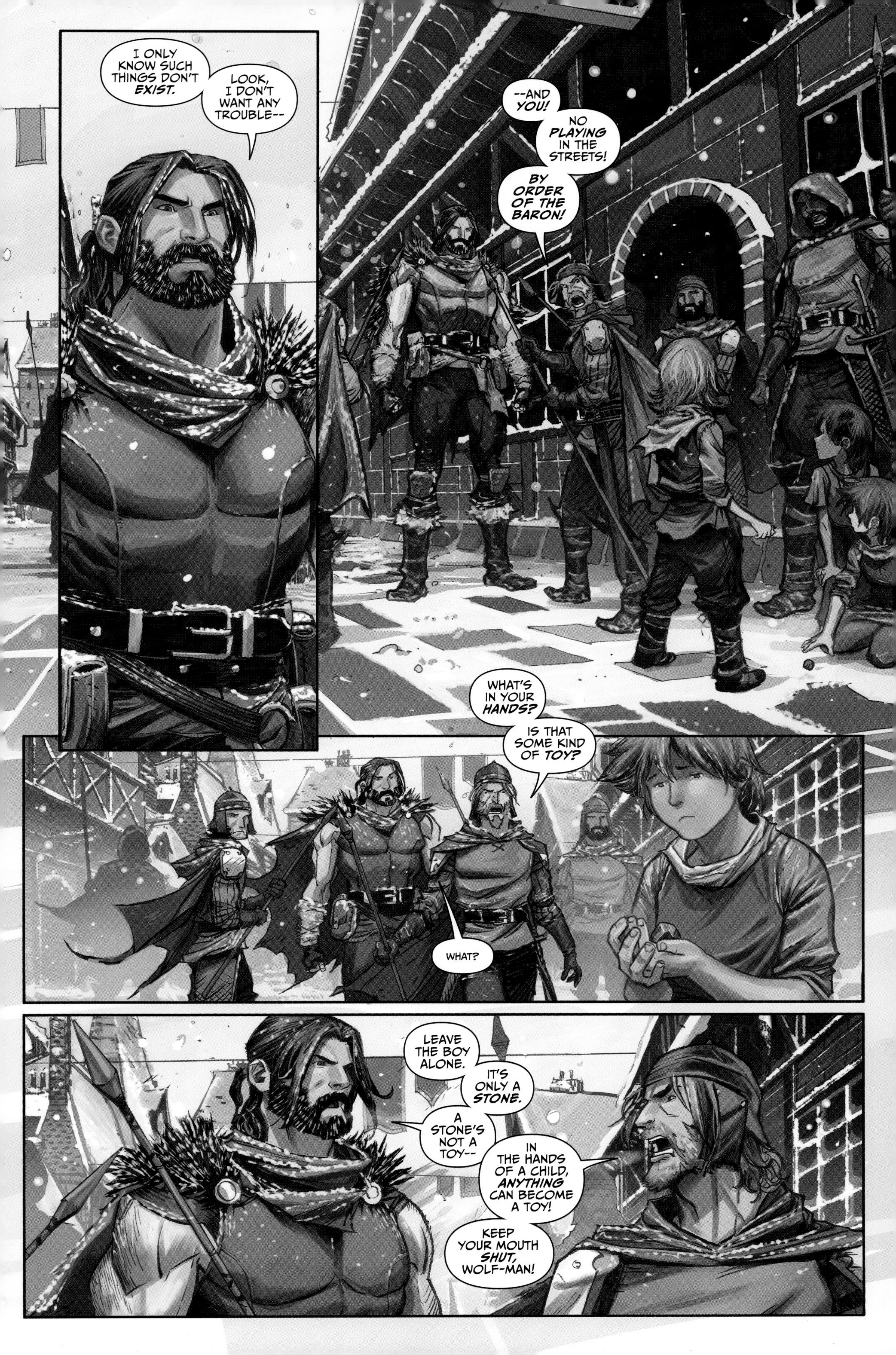
I ONLY KNOW SUCH THINGS DON'T *EXIST.*
LOOK, I DON'T WANT ANY TROUBLE--
--AND *YOU!*
NO *PLAYING* IN THE STREETS!
BY ORDER OF THE BARON!
WHAT'S IN YOUR ***HANDS?***
IS THAT SOME KIND OF ***TOY?***
WHAT?
LEAVE THE BOY ALONE.
IT'S ONLY A ***STONE.***
A STONE'S NOT A TOY--
IN THE HANDS OF A CHILD, ***ANYTHING*** CAN BECOME A TOY!
KEEP YOUR MOUTH ***SHUT,*** WOLF-MAN!

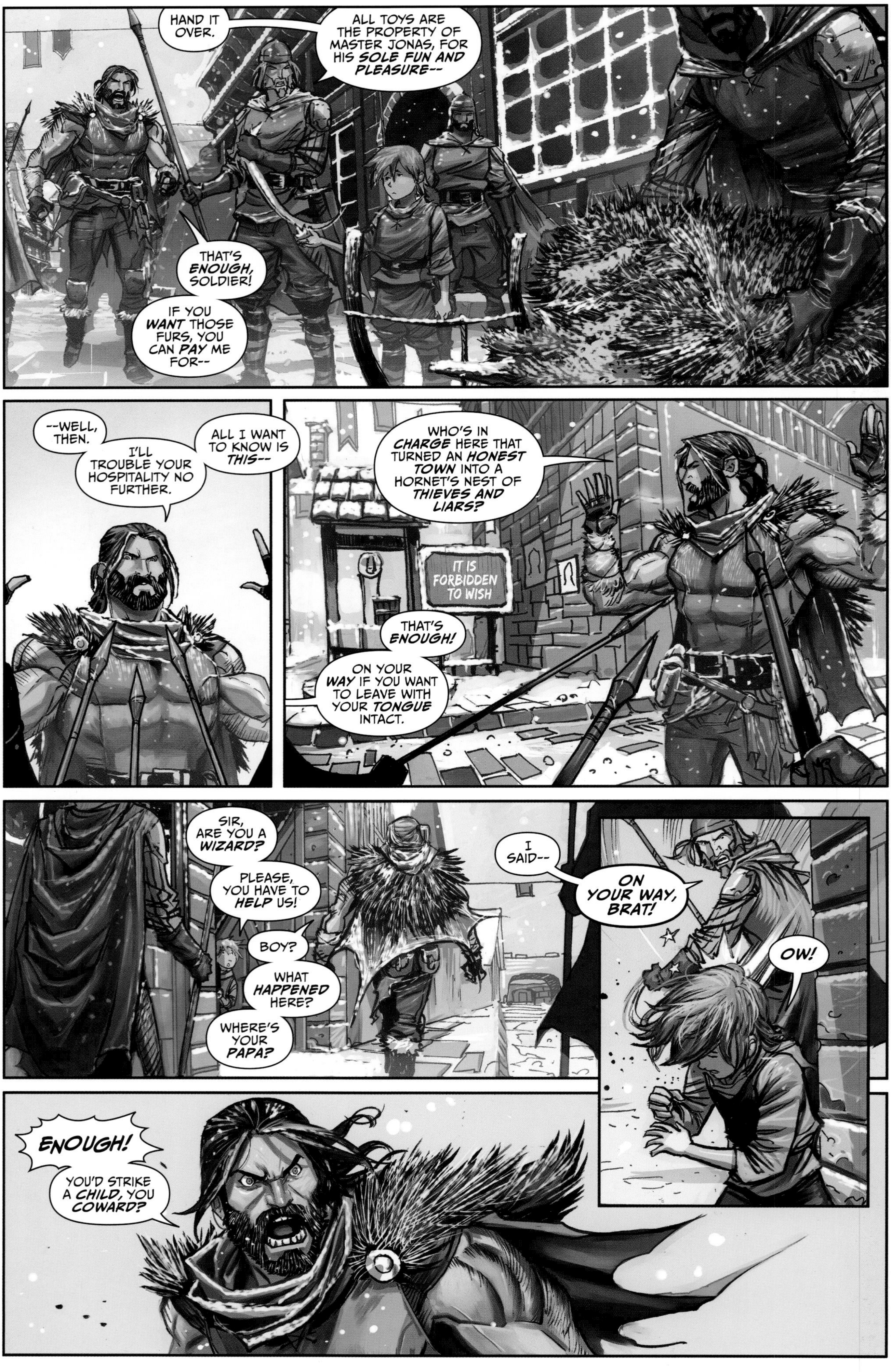

HAND IT OVER.
ALL TOYS ARE THE PROPERTY OF MASTER JONAS, FOR HIS SOLE FUN AND PLEASURE--
THAT'S ENOUGH, SOLDIER!
IF YOU WANT THOSE FURS, YOU CAN PAY ME FOR--
--WELL, THEN.
I'LL TROUBLE YOUR HOSPITALITY NO FURTHER.
ALL I WANT TO KNOW IS THIS--
WHO'S IN CHARGE HERE THAT TURNED AN HONEST TOWN INTO A HORNET'S NEST OF THIEVES AND LIARS?
IT IS FORBIDDEN TO WISH
THAT'S ENOUGH!
ON YOUR WAY IF YOU WANT TO LEAVE WITH YOUR TONGUE INTACT.
SIR, ARE YOU A WIZARD?
PLEASE, YOU HAVE TO HELP US!
BOY?
WHAT HAPPENED HERE?
WHERE'S YOUR PAPA?
I SAID--
ON YOUR WAY, BRAT!
OW!
ENOUGH!
YOU'D STRIKE A CHILD, YOU COWARD?

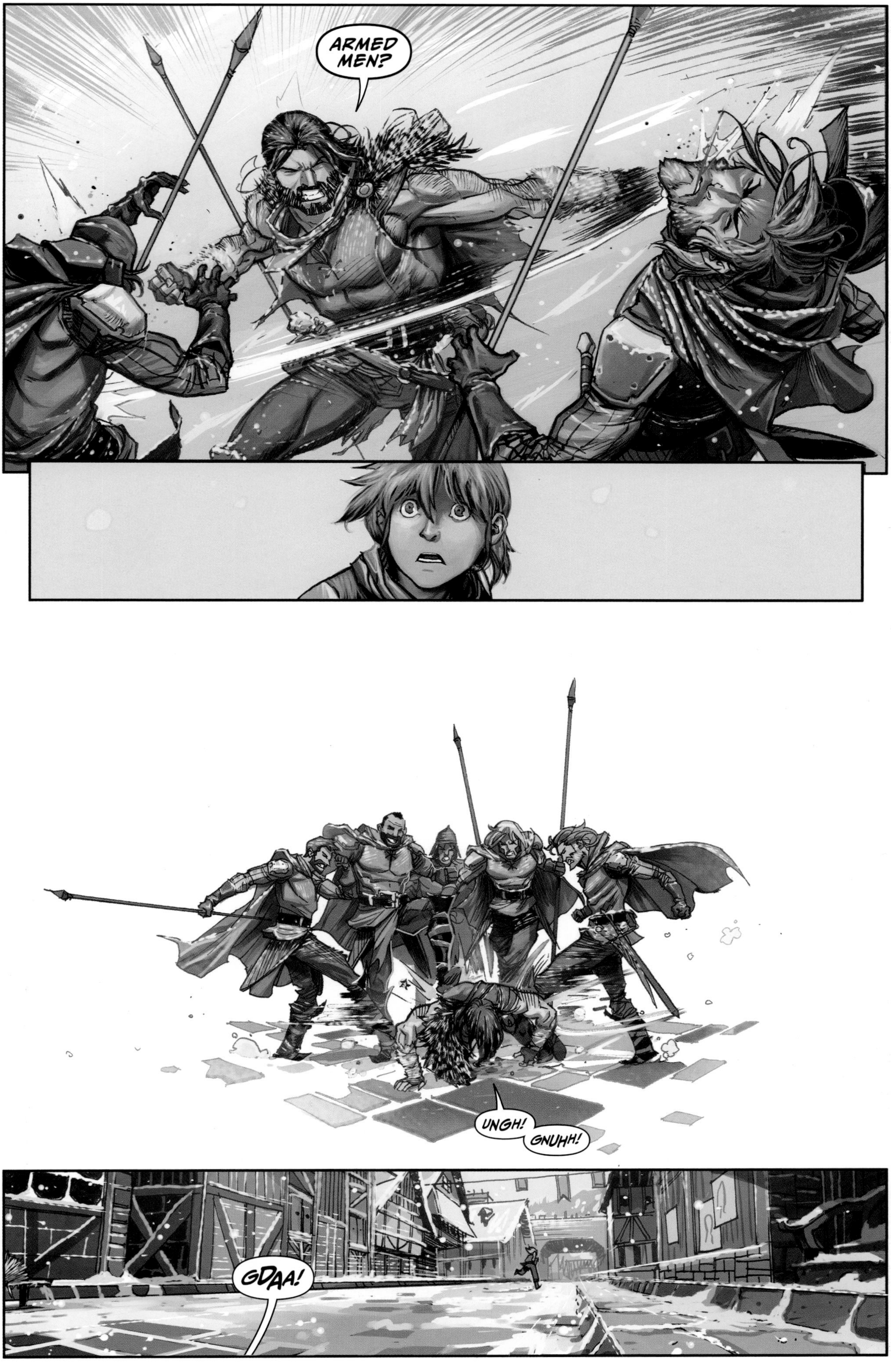
ARMED MEN?
UNGH!
GNUHH!
GDAA!

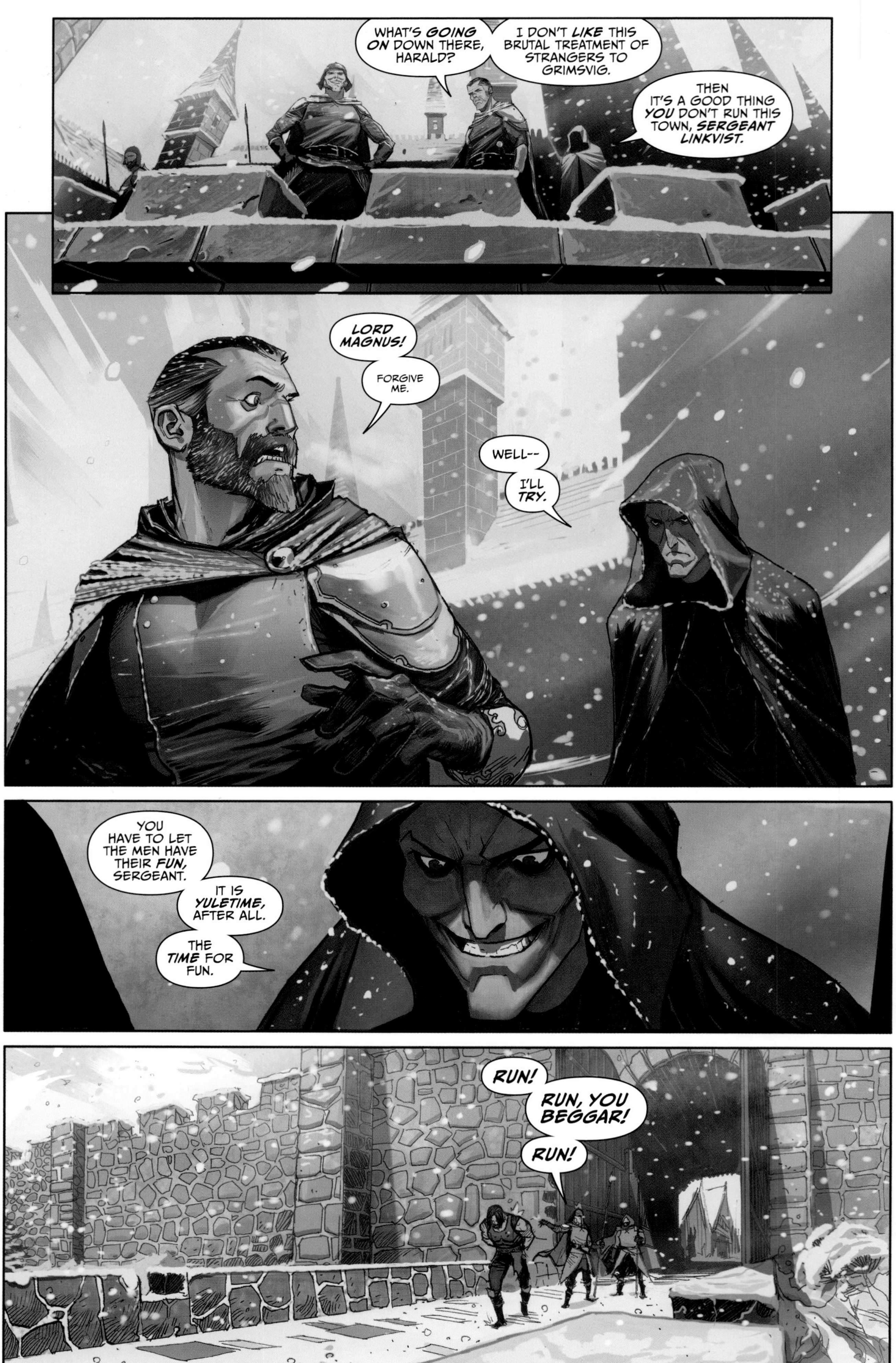
WHAT'S GOING ON DOWN THERE, HARALD?
I DON'T LIKE THIS BRUTAL TREATMENT OF STRANGERS TO GRIMSVIG.
THEN IT'S A GOOD THING YOU DON'T RUN THIS TOWN, SERGEANT LINKVIST.
LORD MAGNUS!
FORGIVE ME.
WELL--
I'LL TRY.
YOU HAVE TO LET THE MEN HAVE THEIR FUN, SERGEANT.
IT IS YULETIME, AFTER ALL.
THE TIME FOR FUN.
RUN!
RUN, YOU BEGGAR!
RUN!

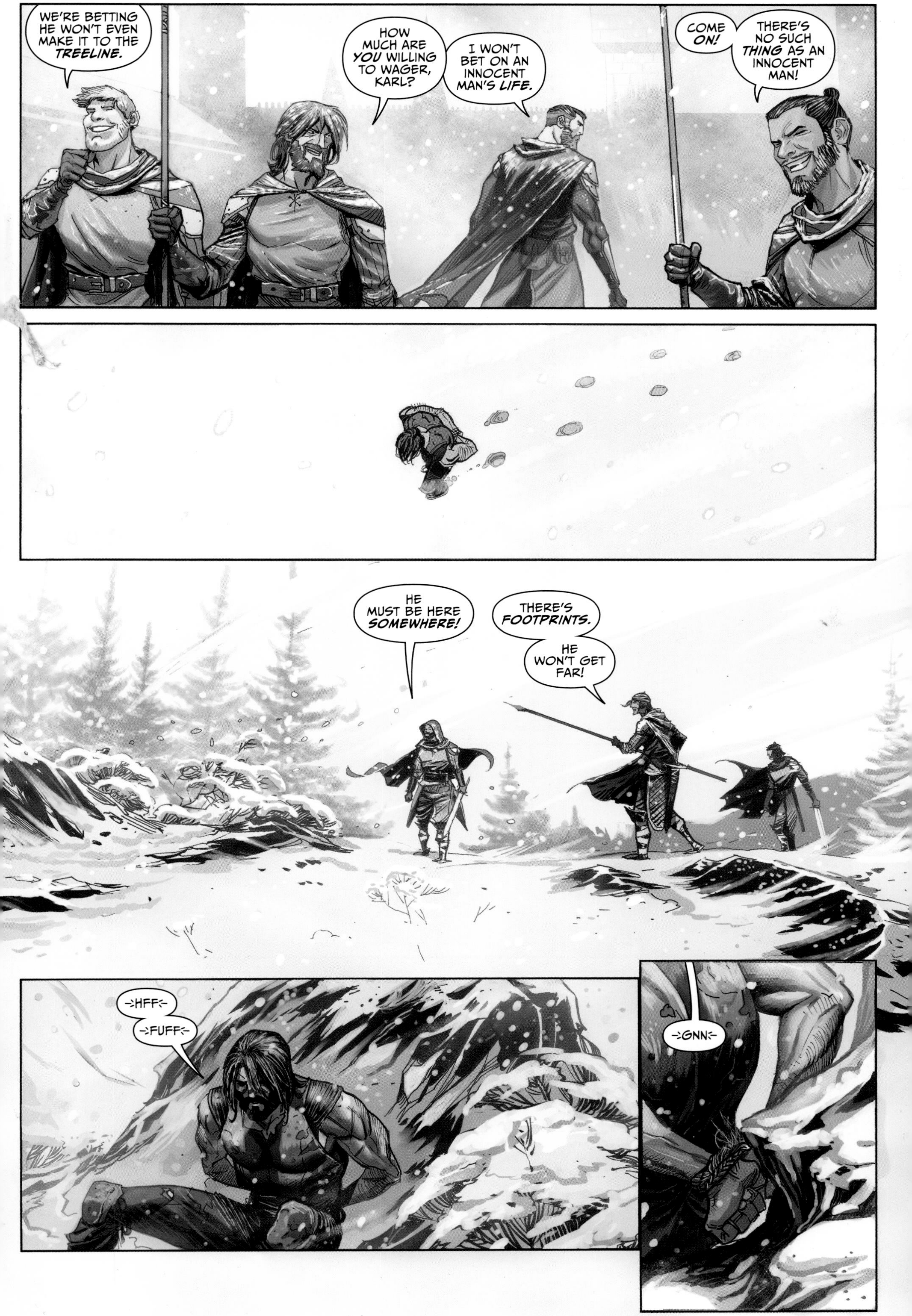
WE'RE BETTING HE WON'T EVEN MAKE IT TO THE TREELINE.
HOW MUCH ARE YOU WILLING TO WAGER, KARL?
I WON'T BET ON AN INNOCENT MAN'S LIFE.
COME ON!
THERE'S NO SUCH THING AS AN INNOCENT MAN!
HE MUST BE HERE SOMEWHERE!
THERE'S FOOTPRINTS.
HE WON'T GET FAR!
-HFF-
-FUFF-
-GNN-

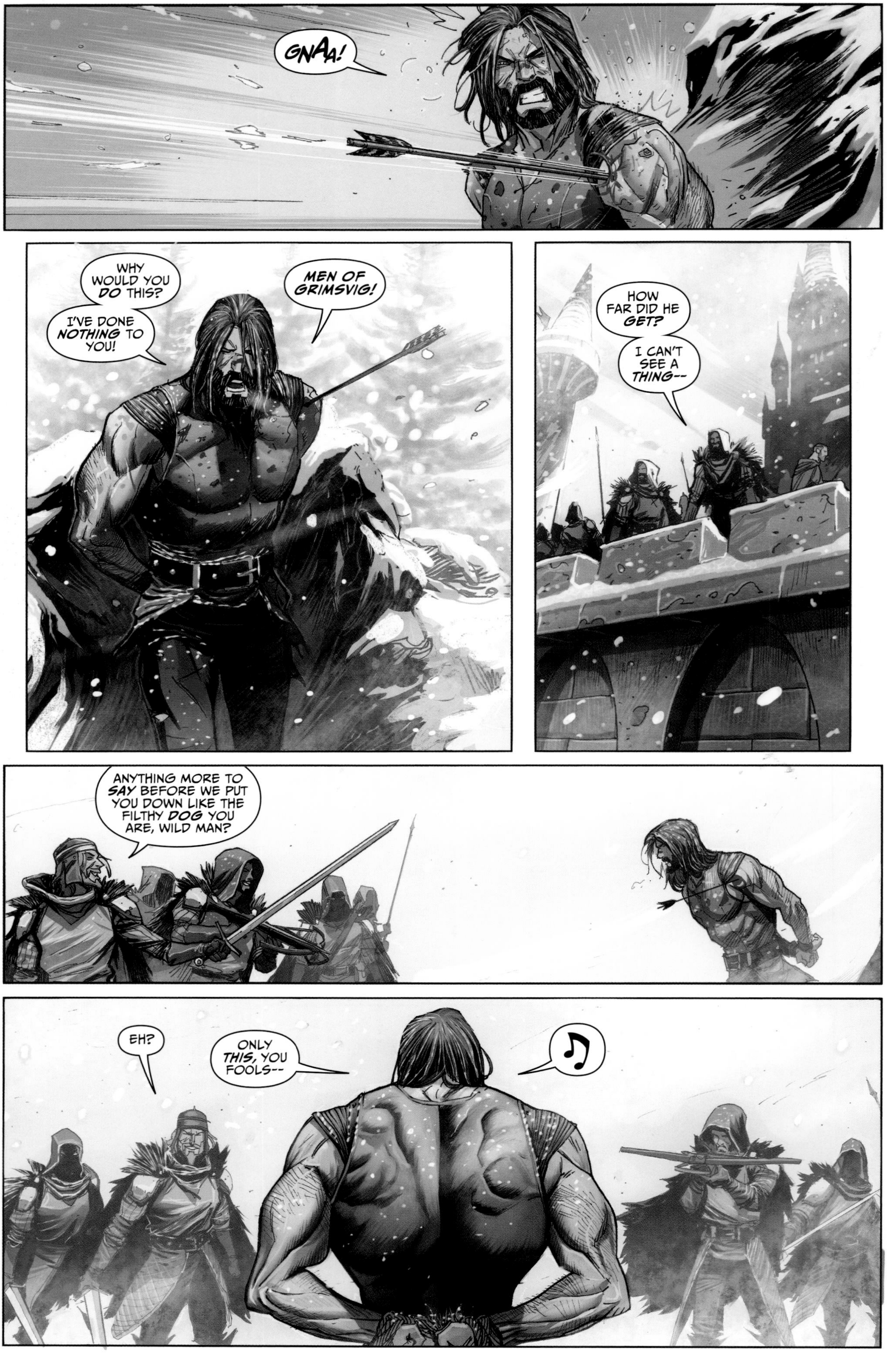
GNAA!
WHY WOULD YOU DO THIS?
I'VE DONE NOTHING TO YOU!
MEN OF GRIMSVIG!
HOW FAR DID HE GET?
I CAN'T SEE A THING--
ANYTHING MORE TO SAY BEFORE WE PUT YOU DOWN LIKE THE FILTHY DOG YOU ARE, WILD MAN?
EH?
ONLY THIS, YOU FOOLS--
♪

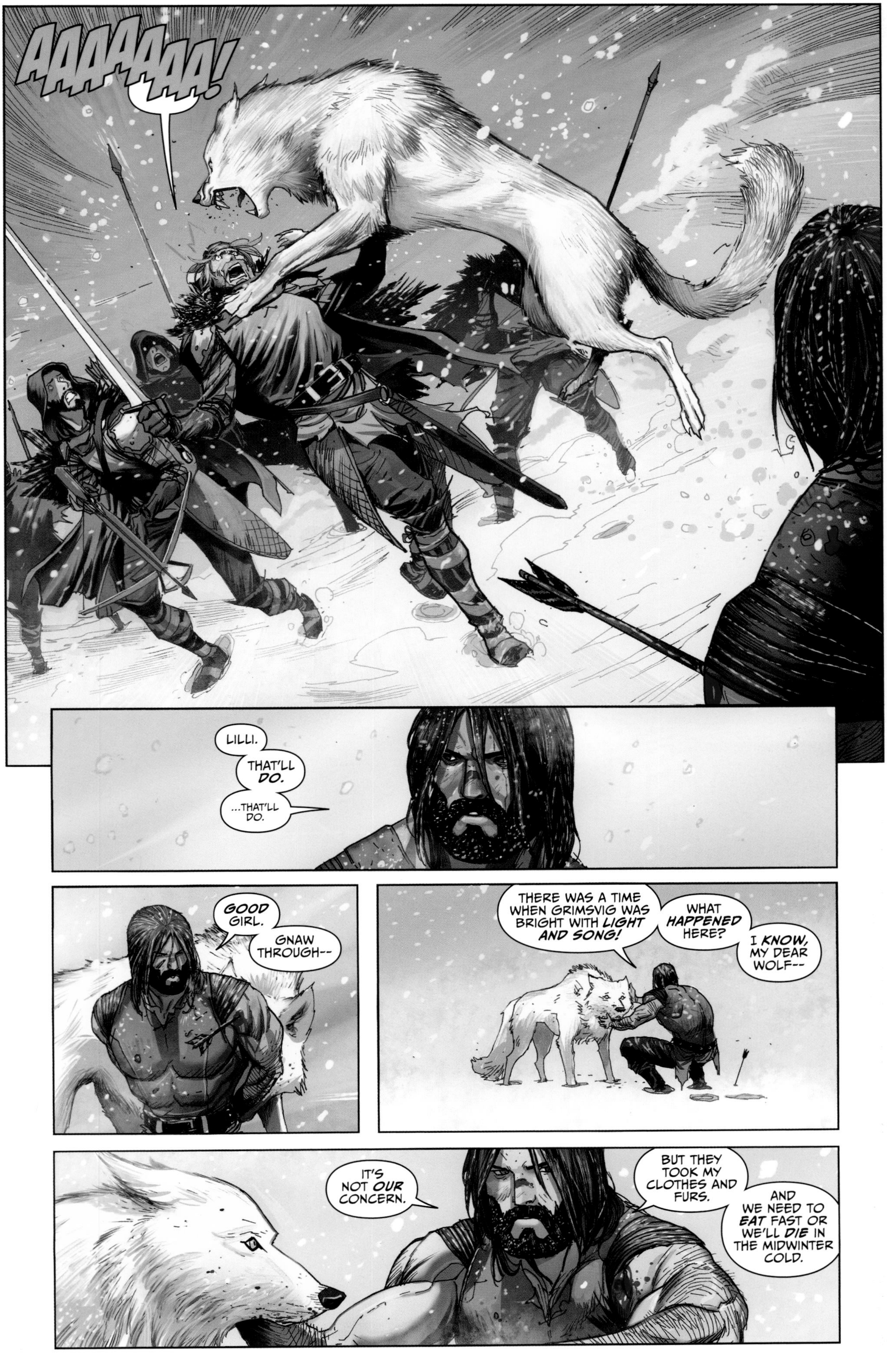
AAAAAAA!
LILLI.
THAT'LL DO.
...THAT'LL DO.
GOOD GIRL.
GNAW THROUGH--
THERE WAS A TIME WHEN GRIMSVIG WAS BRIGHT WITH LIGHT AND SONG!
WHAT HAPPENED HERE?
I KNOW, MY DEAR WOLF--
IT'S NOT OUR CONCERN.
BUT THEY TOOK MY CLOTHES AND FURS.
AND WE NEED TO EAT FAST OR WE'LL DIE IN THE MIDWINTER COLD.

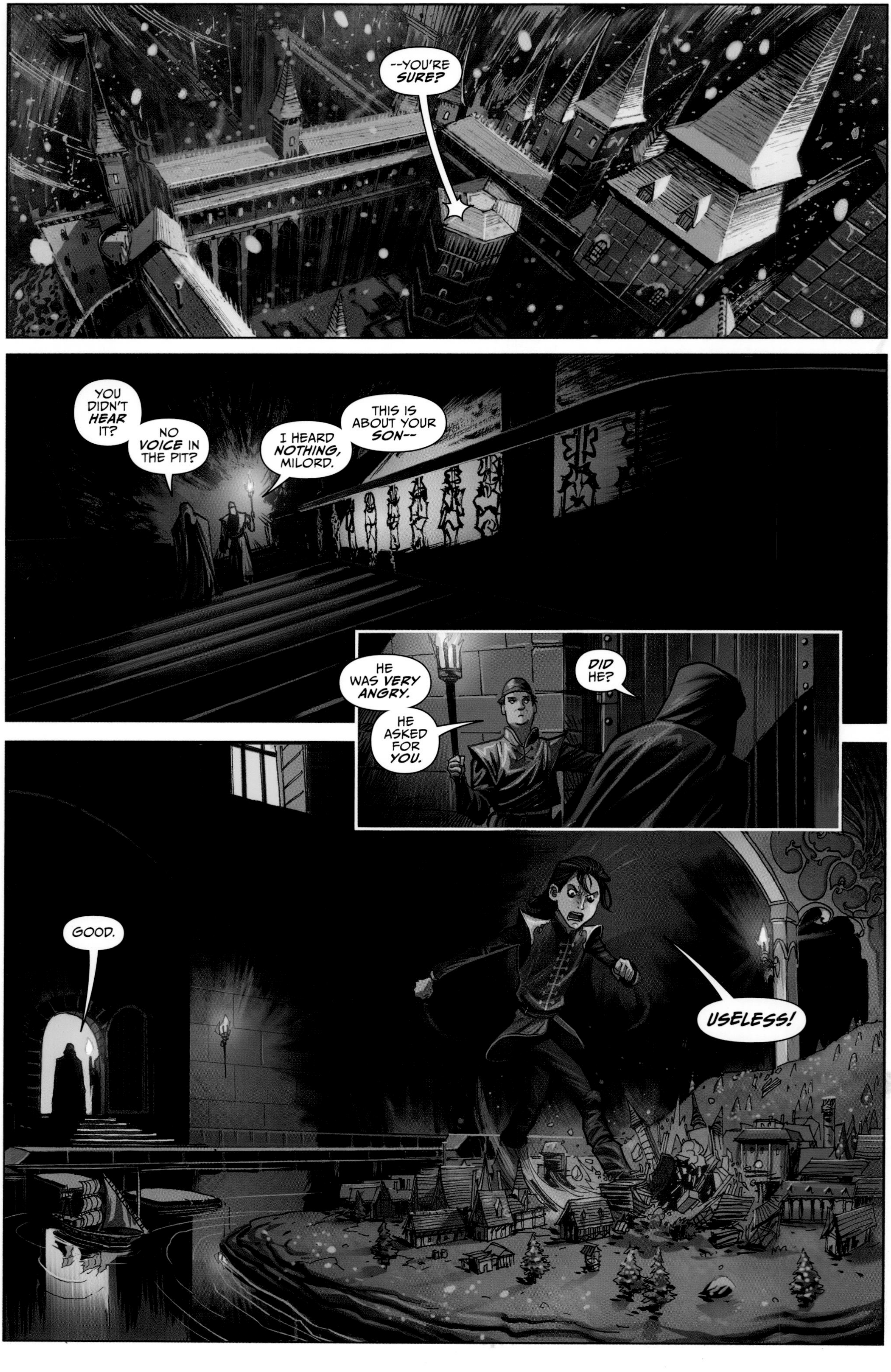
--YOU'RE SURE?
YOU DIDN'T HEAR IT?
NO VOICE IN THE PIT?
I HEARD NOTHING, MILORD.
THIS IS ABOUT YOUR SON--
HE WAS VERY ANGRY.
HE ASKED FOR YOU.
DID HE?
GOOD.
USELESS!

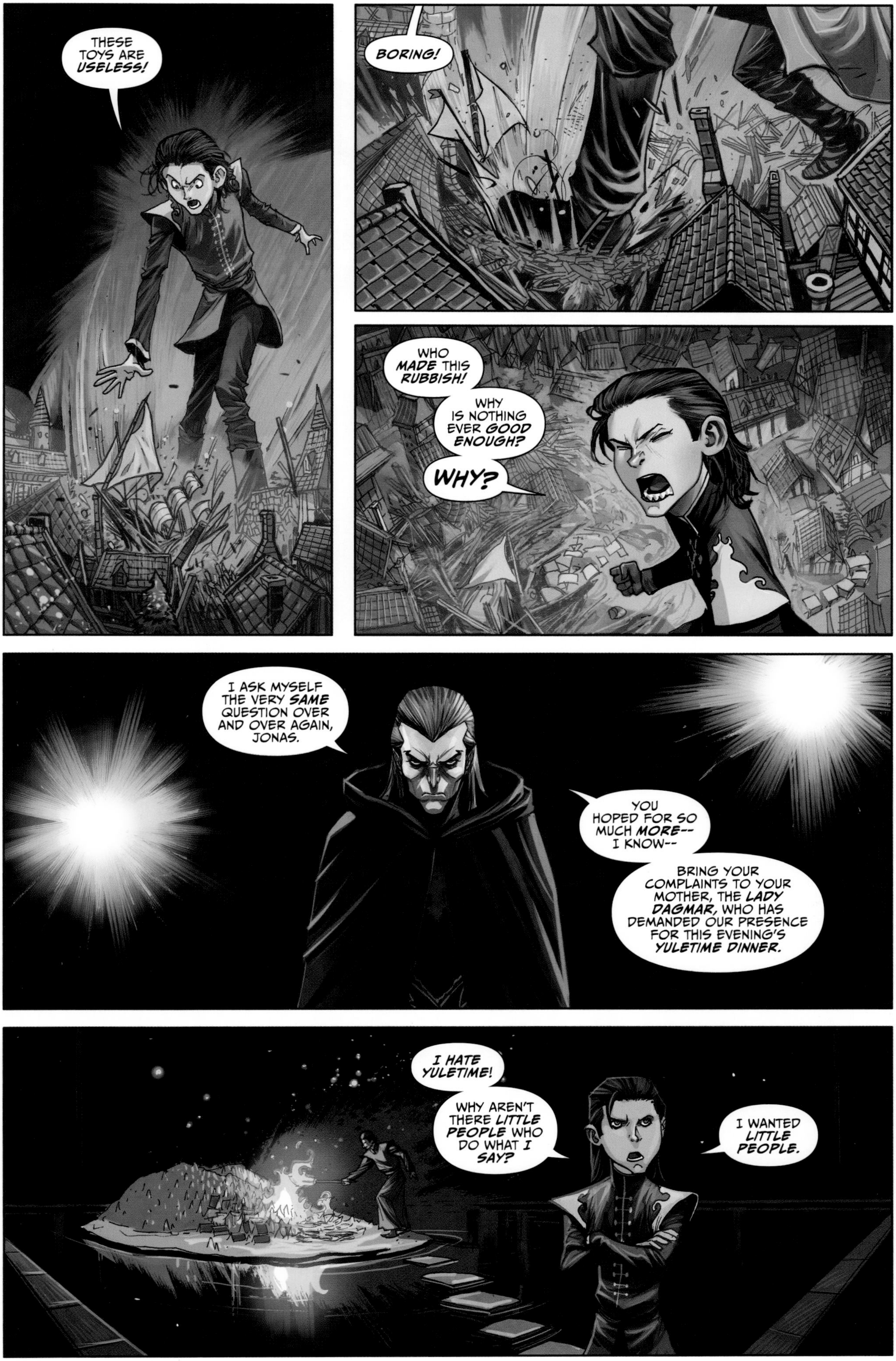
THESE TOYS ARE USELESS!
BORING!
WHO MADE THIS RUBBISH!
WHY IS NOTHING EVER GOOD ENOUGH?
WHY?
I ASK MYSELF THE VERY SAME QUESTION OVER AND OVER AGAIN, JONAS.
YOU HOPED FOR SO MUCH MORE-- I KNOW--
BRING YOUR COMPLAINTS TO YOUR MOTHER, THE LADY DAGMAR, WHO HAS DEMANDED OUR PRESENCE FOR THIS EVENING'S YULETIME DINNER.
I HATE YULETIME!
WHY AREN'T THERE LITTLE PEOPLE WHO DO WHAT I SAY?
I WANTED LITTLE PEOPLE.

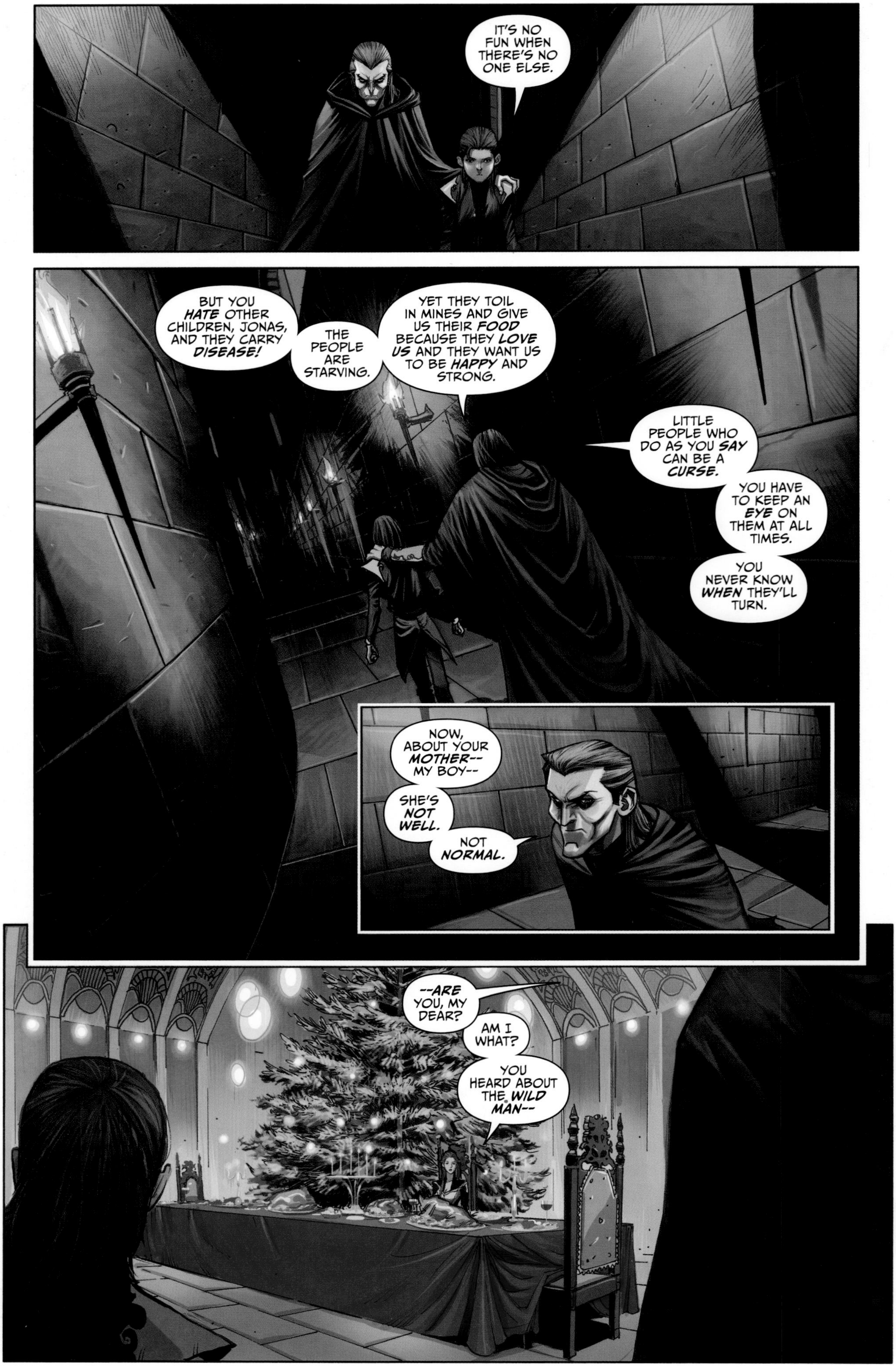
IT'S NO FUN WHEN THERE'S NO ONE ELSE.
BUT YOU *HATE* OTHER CHILDREN, JONAS, AND THEY CARRY *DISEASE!*
THE PEOPLE ARE STARVING.
YET THEY TOIL IN MINES AND GIVE US THEIR *FOOD* BECAUSE THEY *LOVE US* AND THEY WANT US TO BE *HAPPY* AND STRONG.
LITTLE PEOPLE WHO DO AS YOU *SAY* CAN BE A *CURSE.*
YOU HAVE TO KEEP AN *EYE* ON THEM AT ALL TIMES.
YOU NEVER KNOW *WHEN* THEY'LL TURN.
NOW, ABOUT YOUR *MOTHER--* MY BOY--
SHE'S *NOT WELL.*
NOT *NORMAL.*
--ARE YOU, MY DEAR?
AM I WHAT?
YOU HEARD ABOUT THE *WILD MAN--*

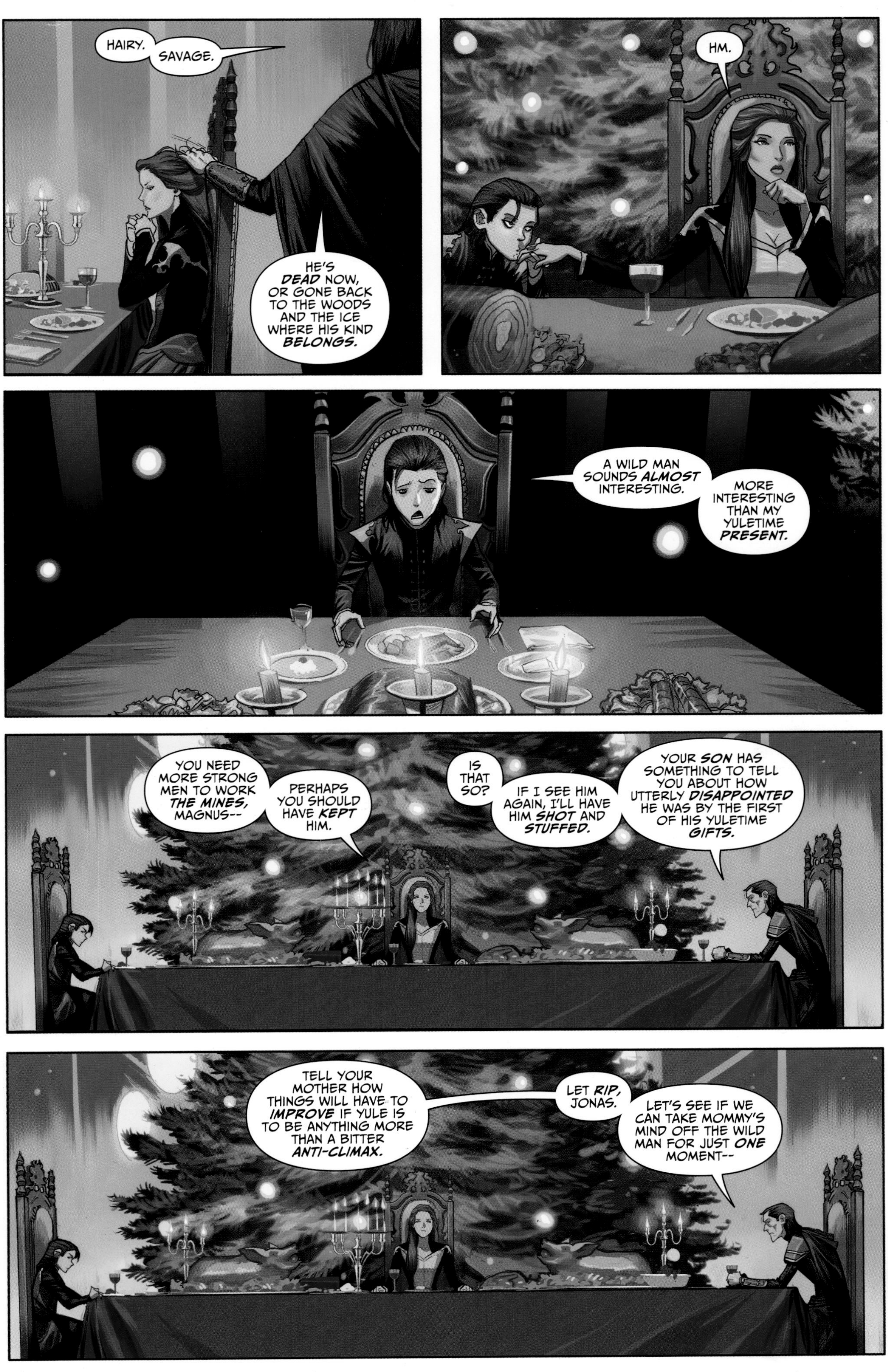
HAIRY.
SAVAGE.
HE'S DEAD NOW, OR GONE BACK TO THE WOODS AND THE ICE WHERE HIS KIND BELONGS.
HM.
A WILD MAN SOUNDS ALMOST INTERESTING.
MORE INTERESTING THAN MY YULETIME PRESENT.
YOU NEED MORE STRONG MEN TO WORK THE MINES, MAGNUS--
PERHAPS YOU SHOULD HAVE KEPT HIM.
IS THAT SO?
IF I SEE HIM AGAIN, I'LL HAVE HIM SHOT AND STUFFED.
YOUR SON HAS SOMETHING TO TELL YOU ABOUT HOW UTTERLY DISAPPOINTED HE WAS BY THE FIRST OF HIS YULETIME GIFTS.
TELL YOUR MOTHER HOW THINGS WILL HAVE TO IMPROVE IF YULE IS TO BE ANYTHING MORE THAN A BITTER ANTI-CLIMAX.
LET RIP, JONAS.
LET'S SEE IF WE CAN TAKE MOMMY'S MIND OFF THE WILD MAN FOR JUST ONE MOMENT--

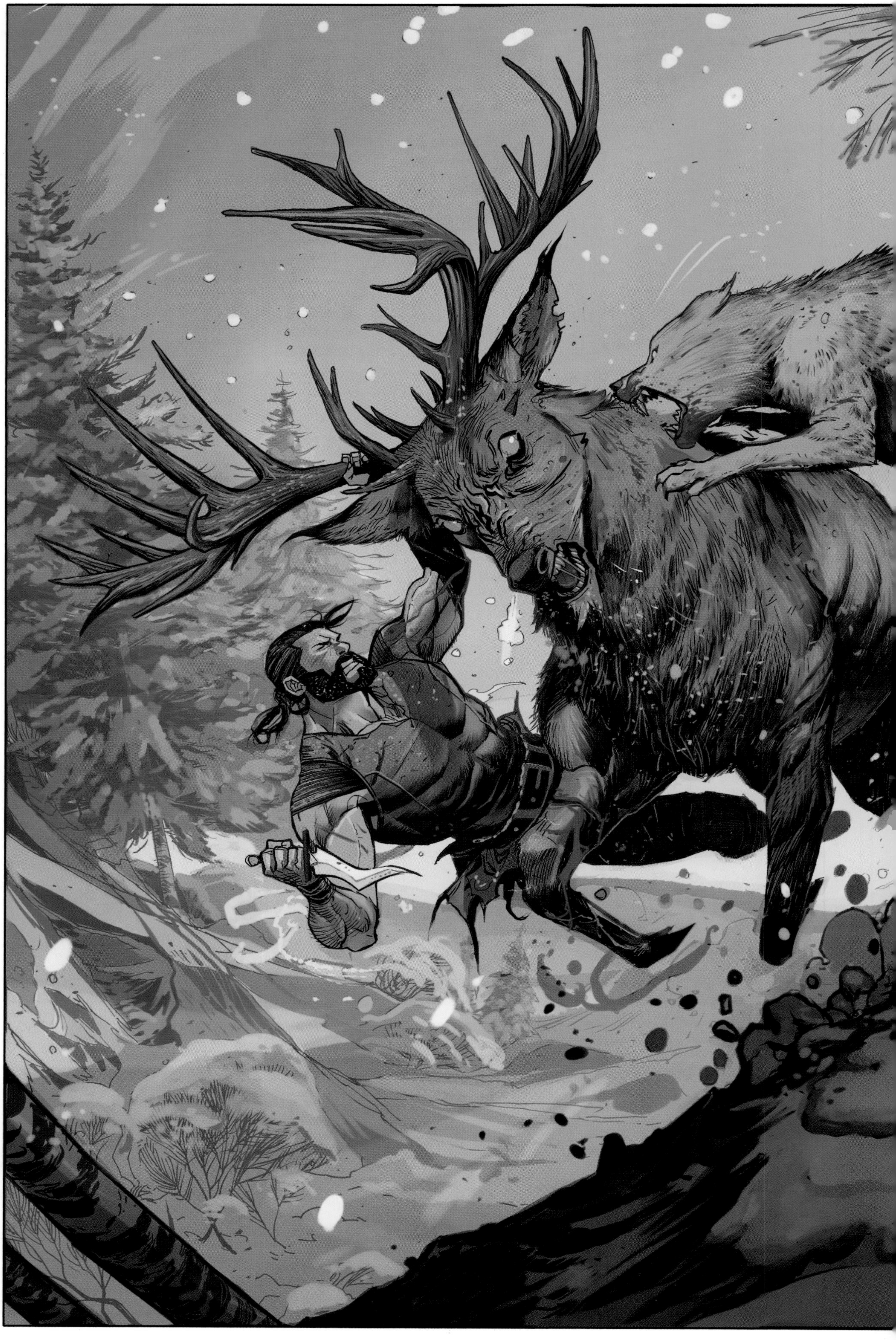

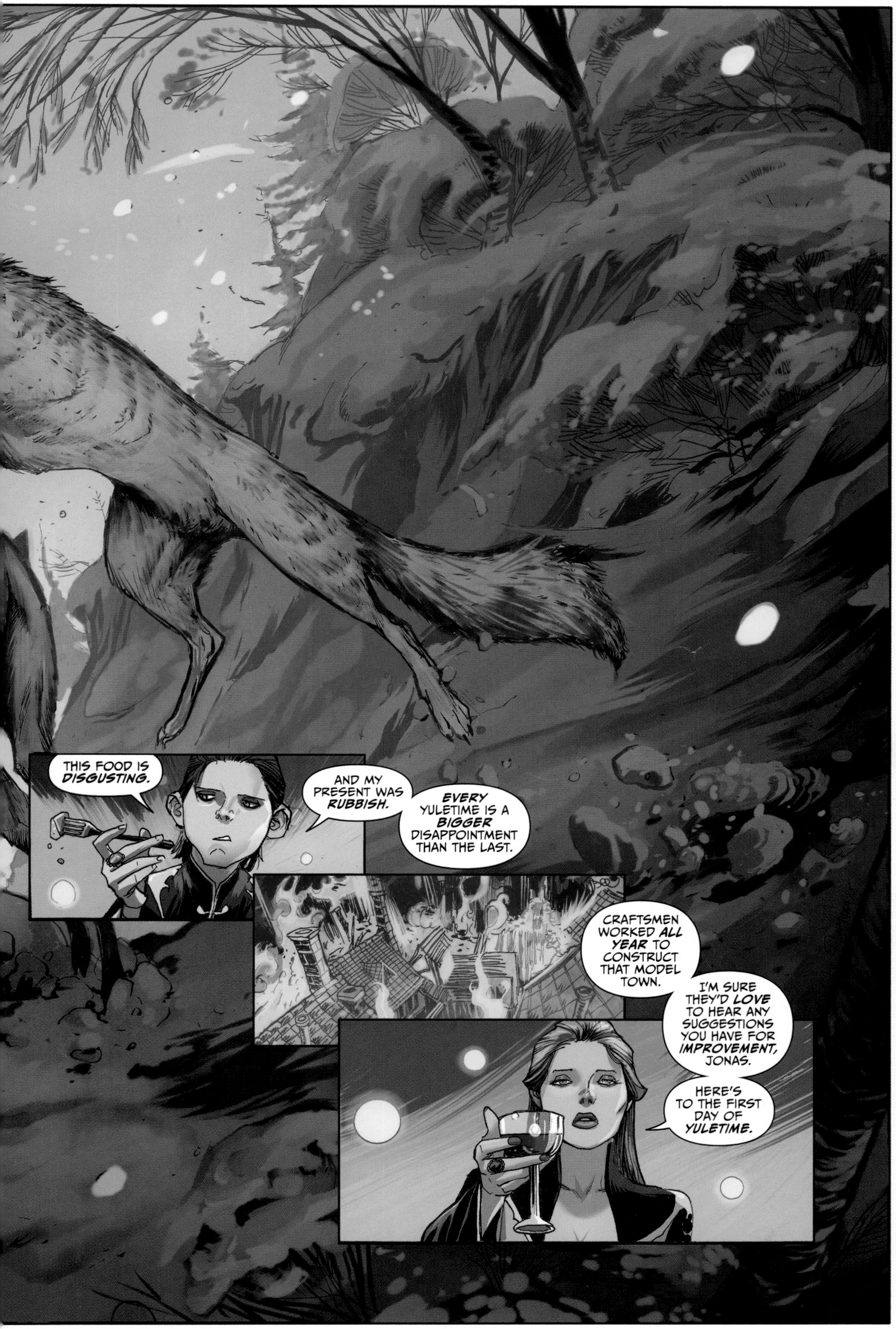
THIS FOOD IS *DISGUSTING.*
AND MY PRESENT WAS *RUBBISH.*
EVERY YULETIME IS A *BIGGER* DISAPPOINTMENT THAN THE LAST.
CRAFTSMEN WORKED *ALL YEAR* TO CONSTRUCT THAT MODEL TOWN.
I'M SURE THEY'D *LOVE* TO HEAR ANY SUGGESTIONS YOU HAVE FOR *IMPROVEMENT,* JONAS.
HERE'S TO THE FIRST DAY OF *YULETIME.*

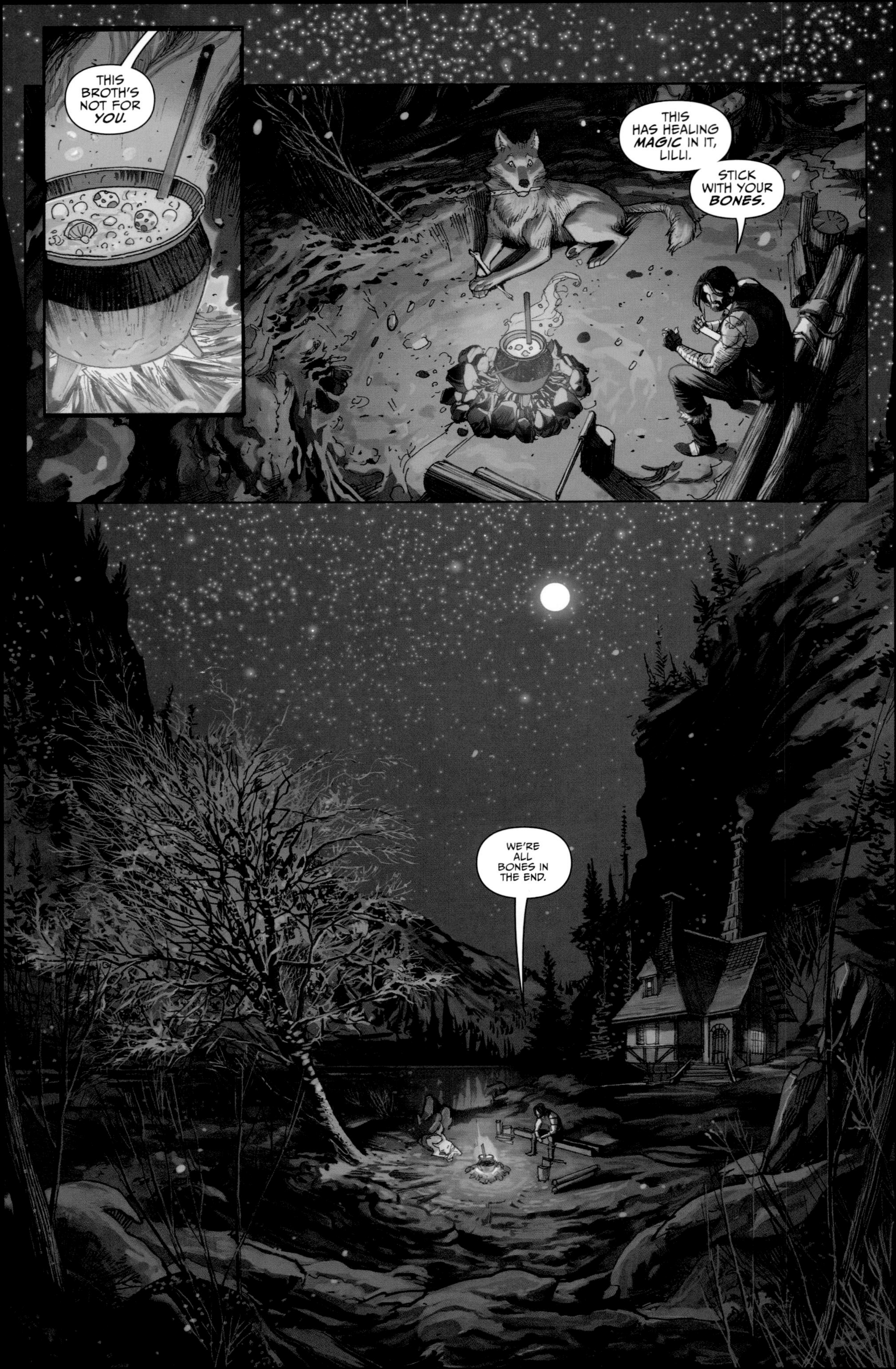
THIS BROTH'S NOT FOR *YOU.*
THIS HAS HEALING *MAGIC* IN IT, LILLI.
STICK WITH YOUR *BONES.*
WE'RE ALL BONES IN THE END.

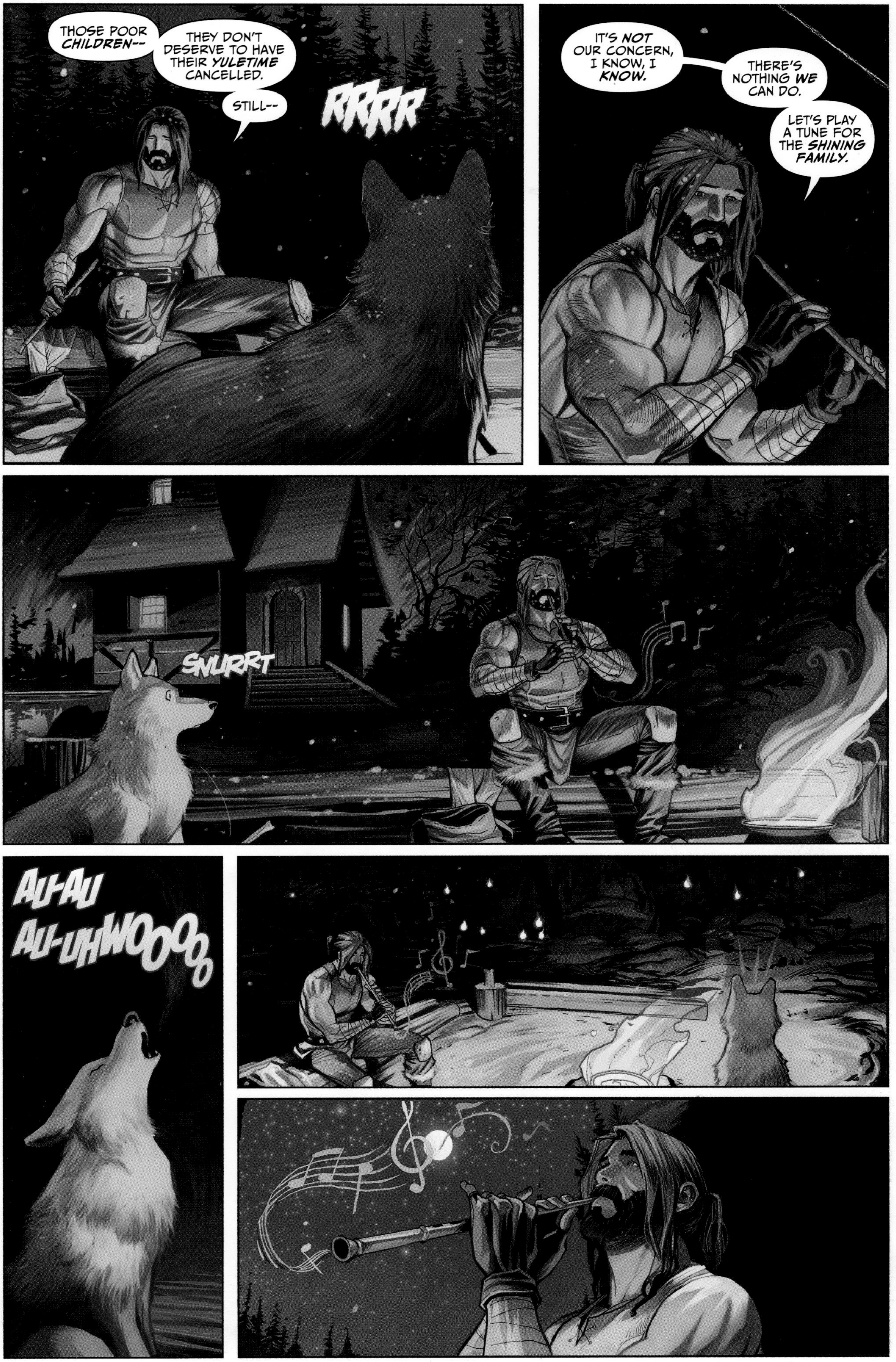
THOSE POOR CHILDREN--
THEY DON'T DESERVE TO HAVE THEIR YULETIME CANCELLED.
STILL--
RRRR
IT'S NOT OUR CONCERN, I KNOW, I KNOW.
THERE'S NOTHING WE CAN DO.
LET'S PLAY A TUNE FOR THE SHINING FAMILY.
SNURRT
AU-AU AU-UHWOOOOO

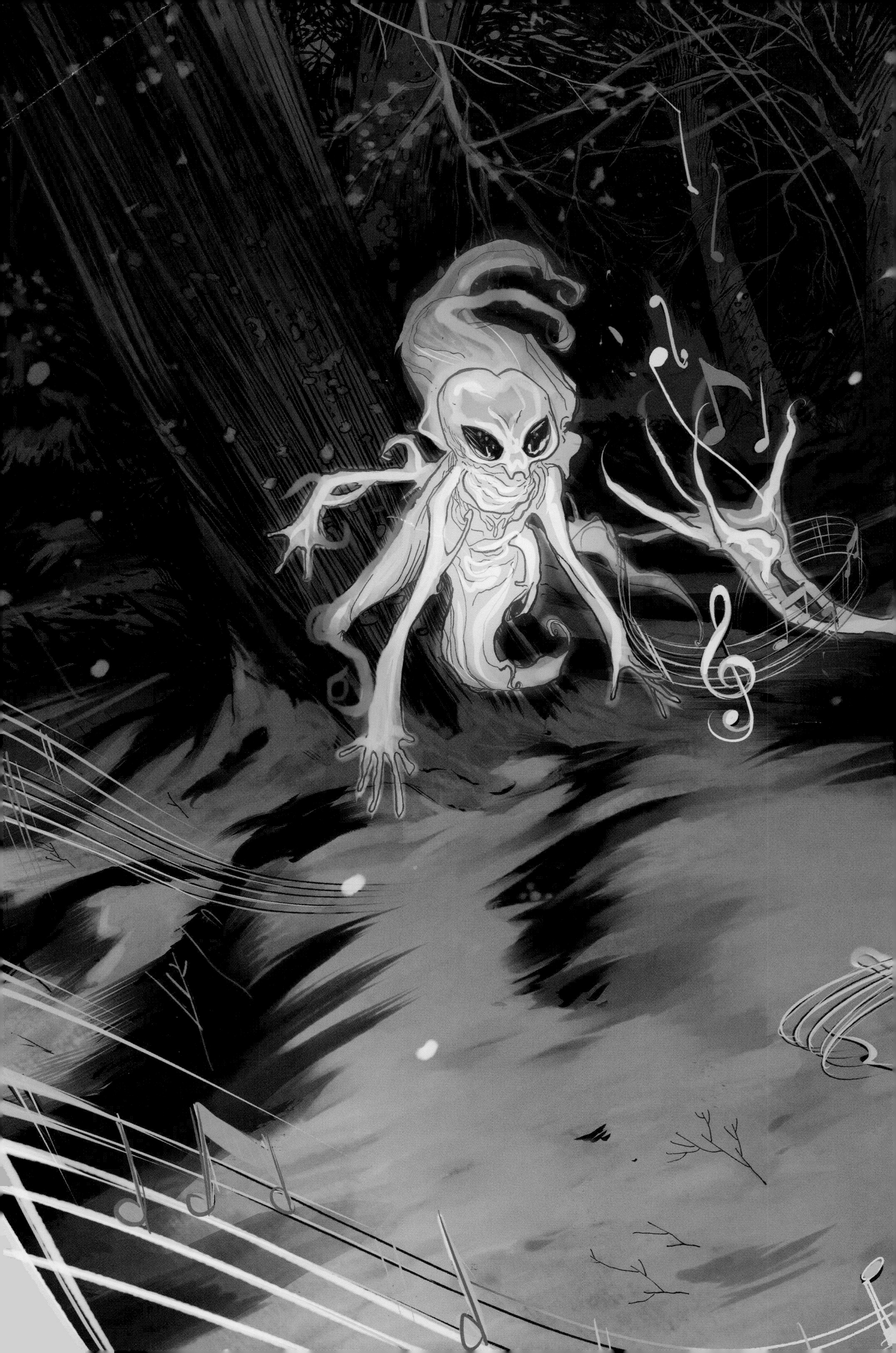

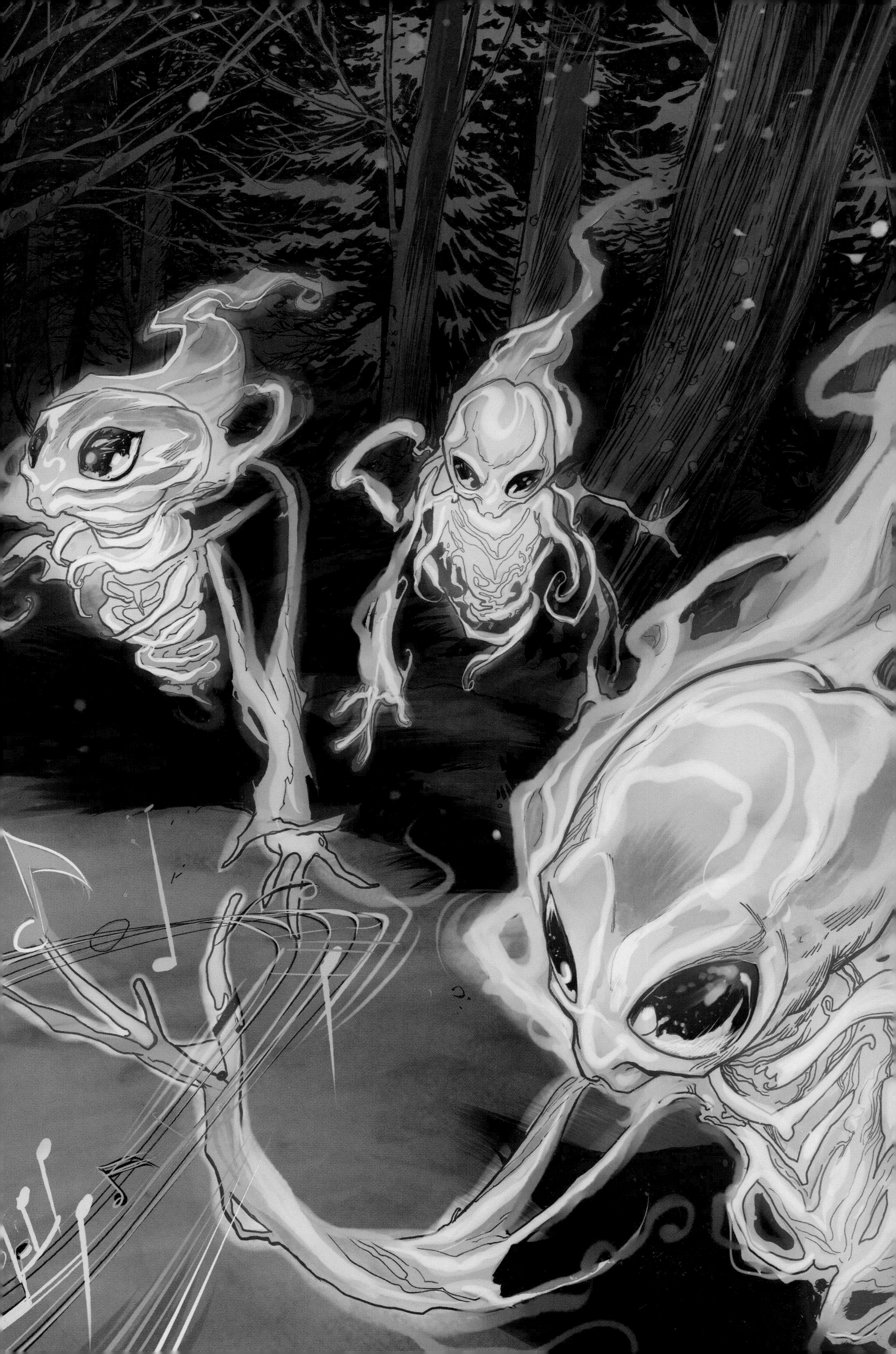

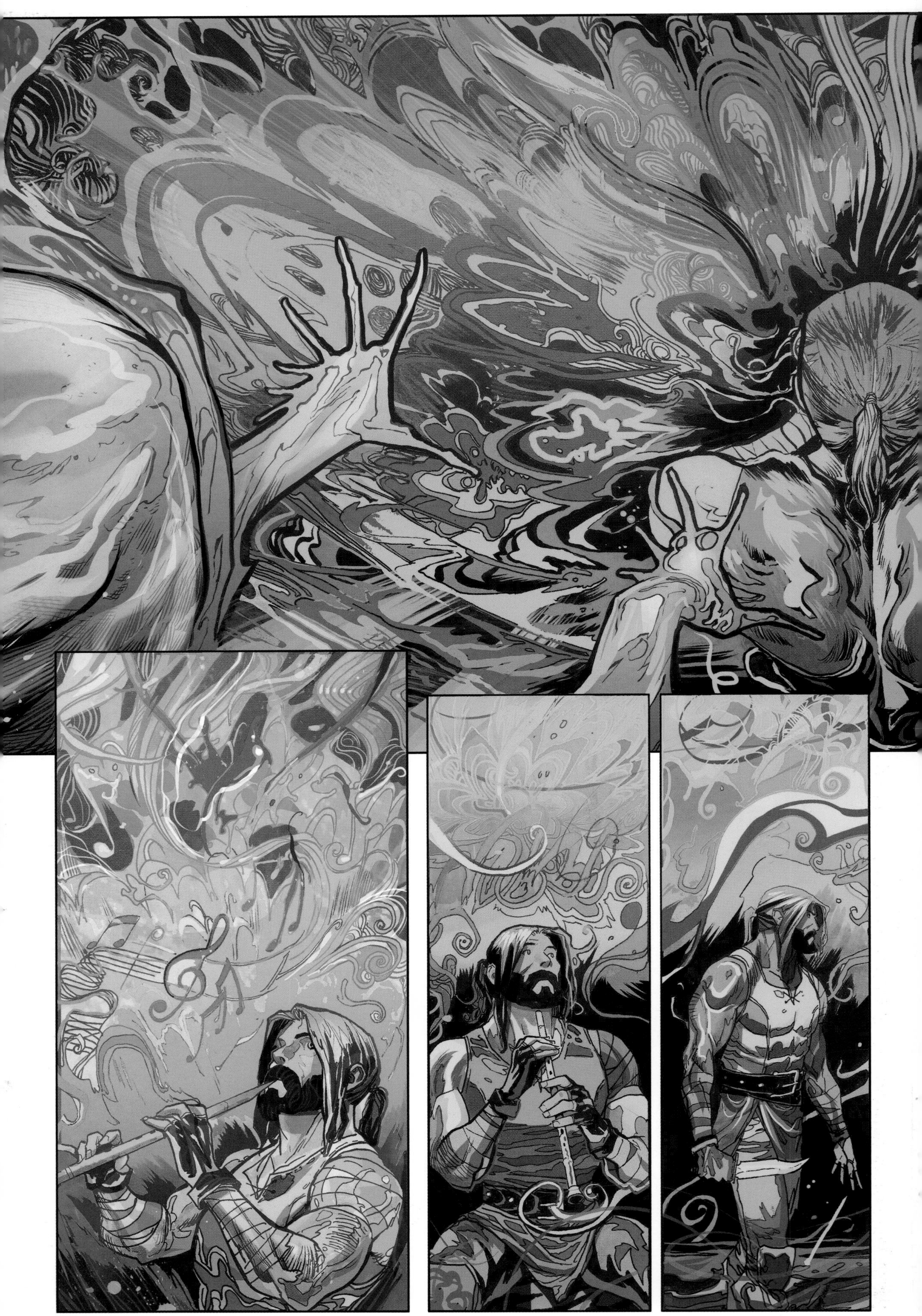

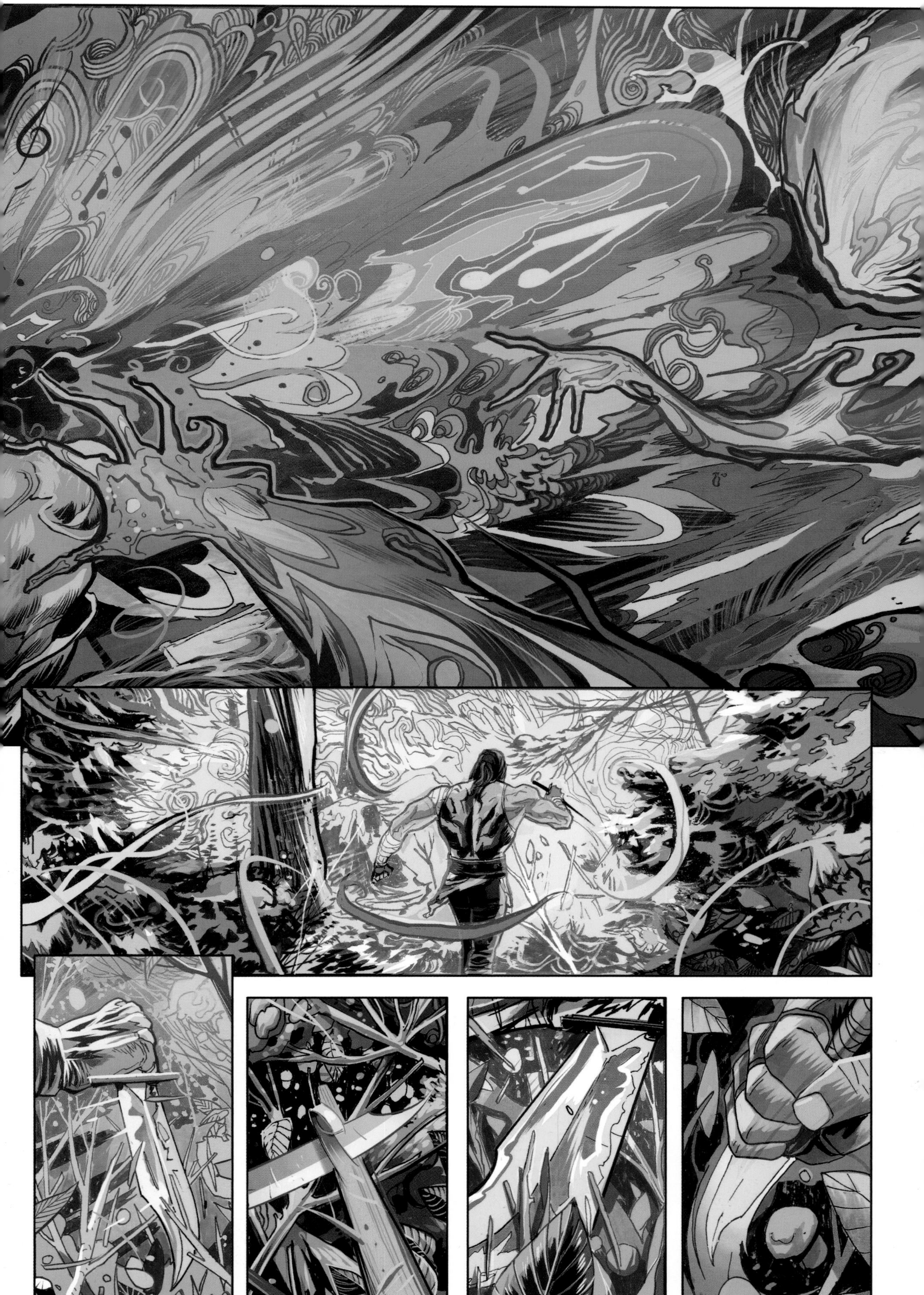

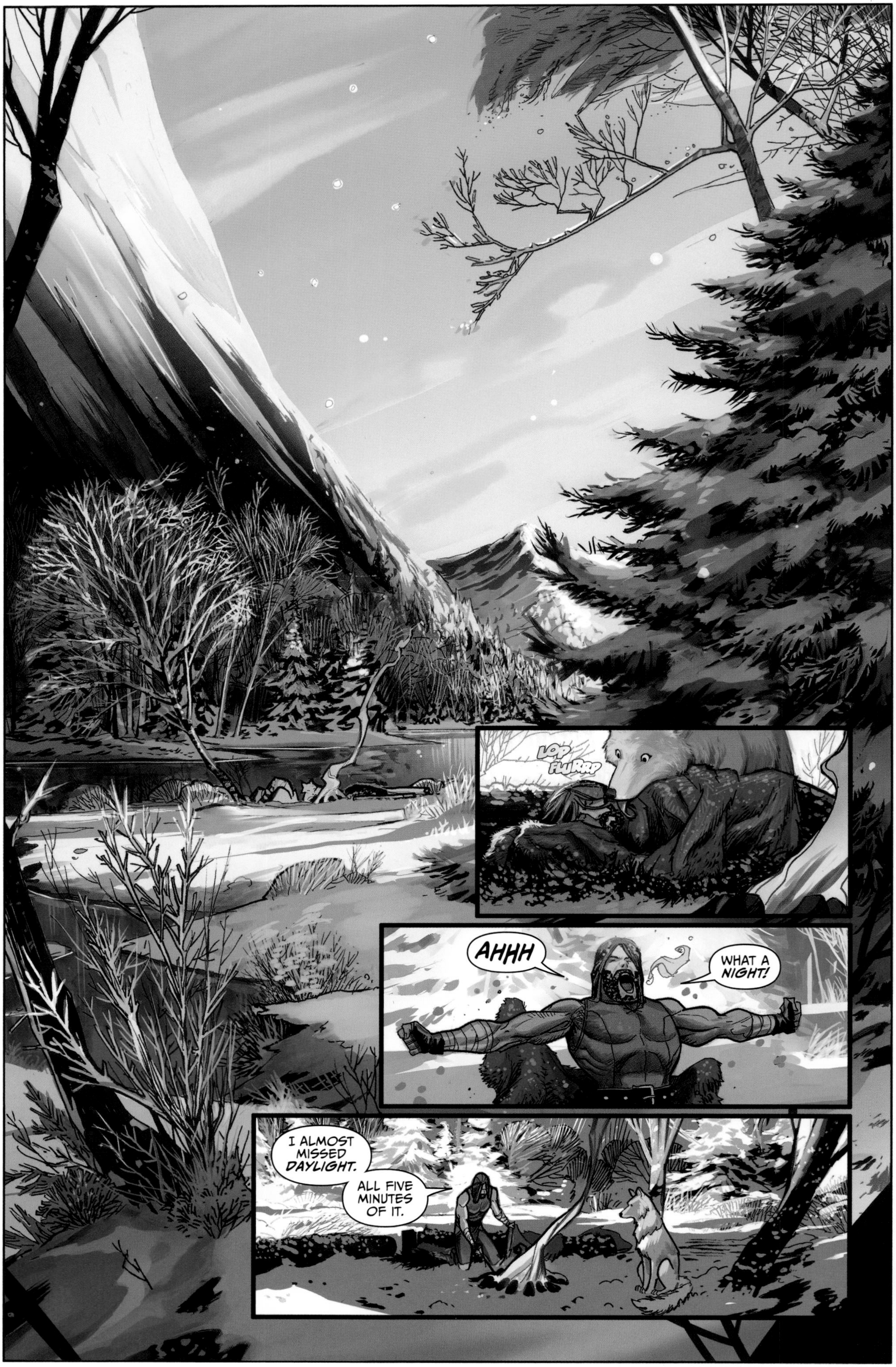
LOP
FLURRP
AHHH
WHAT A NIGHT!
I ALMOST MISSED DAYLIGHT.
ALL FIVE MINUTES OF IT.

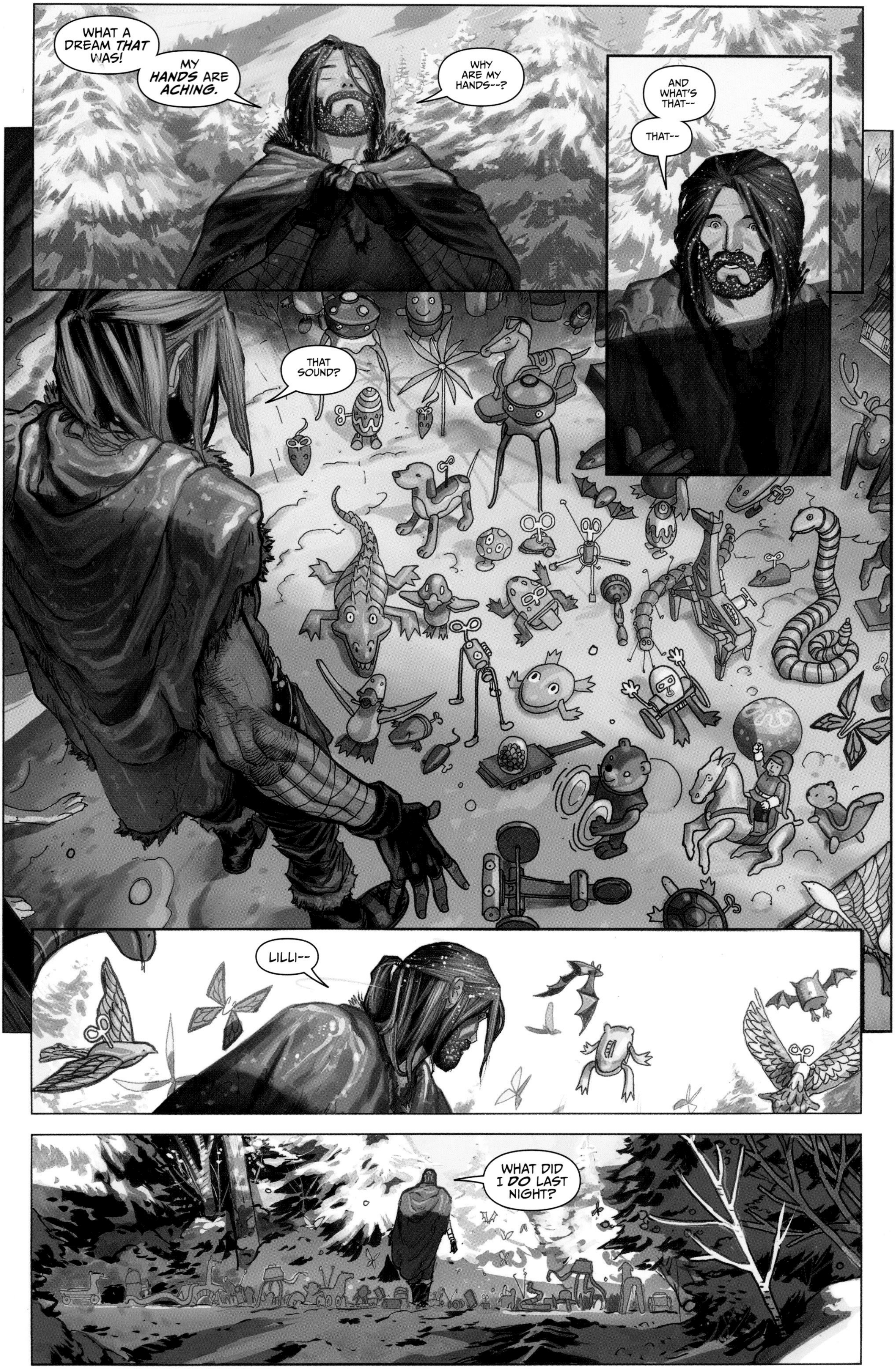
WHAT A DREAM THAT WAS!
MY HANDS ARE ACHING.
WHY ARE MY HANDS--?
AND WHAT'S THAT--
THAT--
THAT SOUND?
LILLI--
WHAT DID I DO LAST NIGHT?

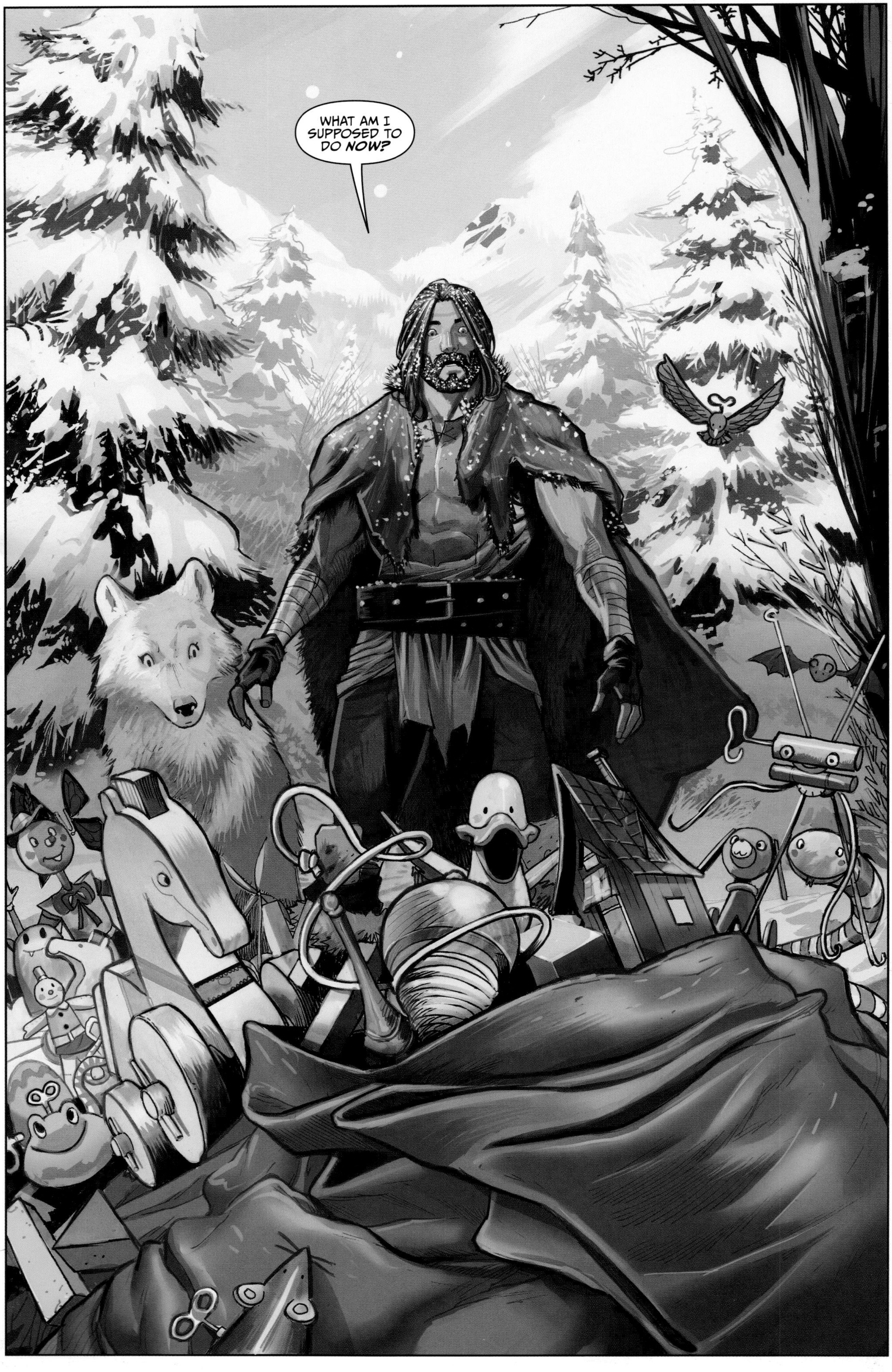
WHAT AM I SUPPOSED TO DO NOW?

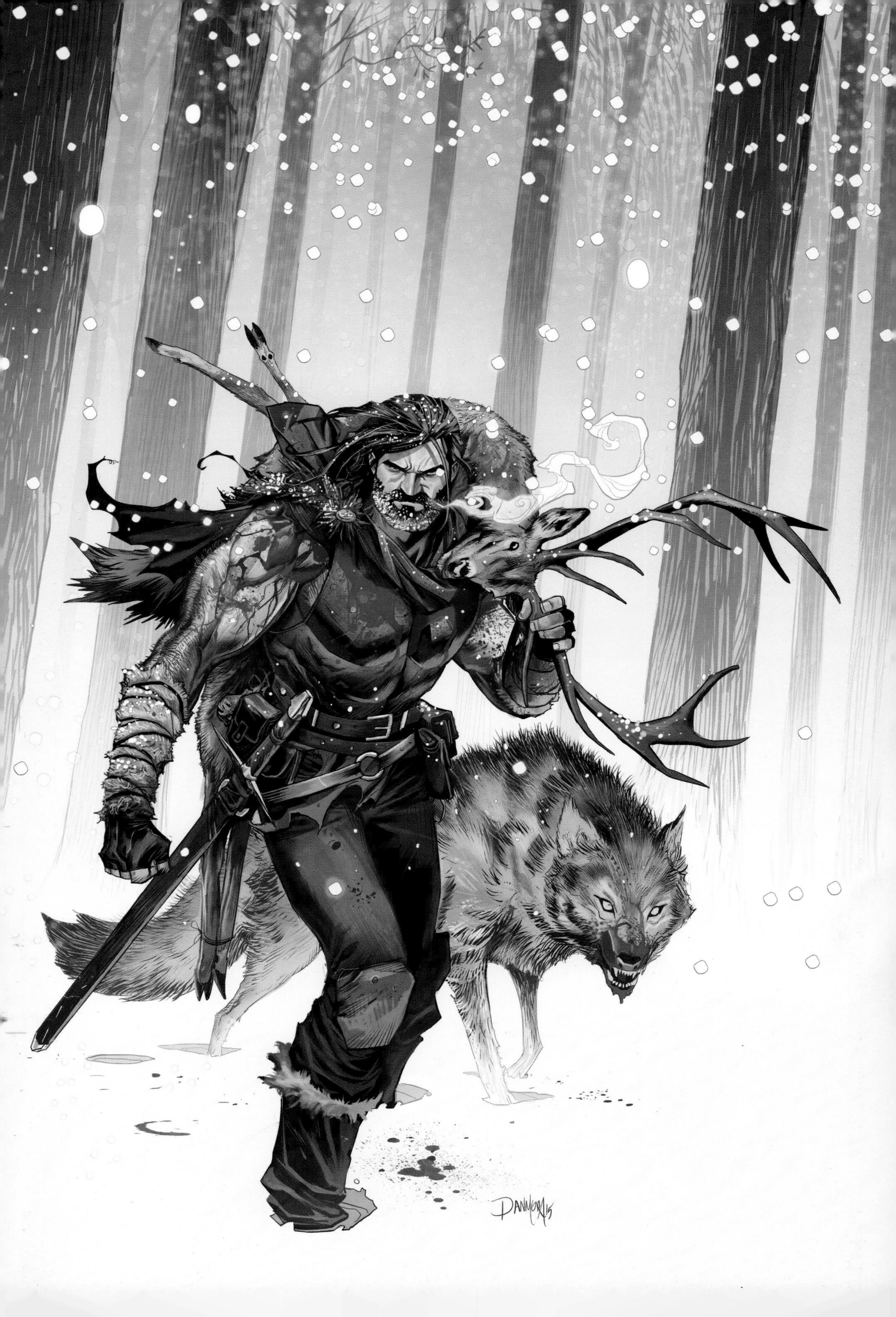

CHAPTER
TWO

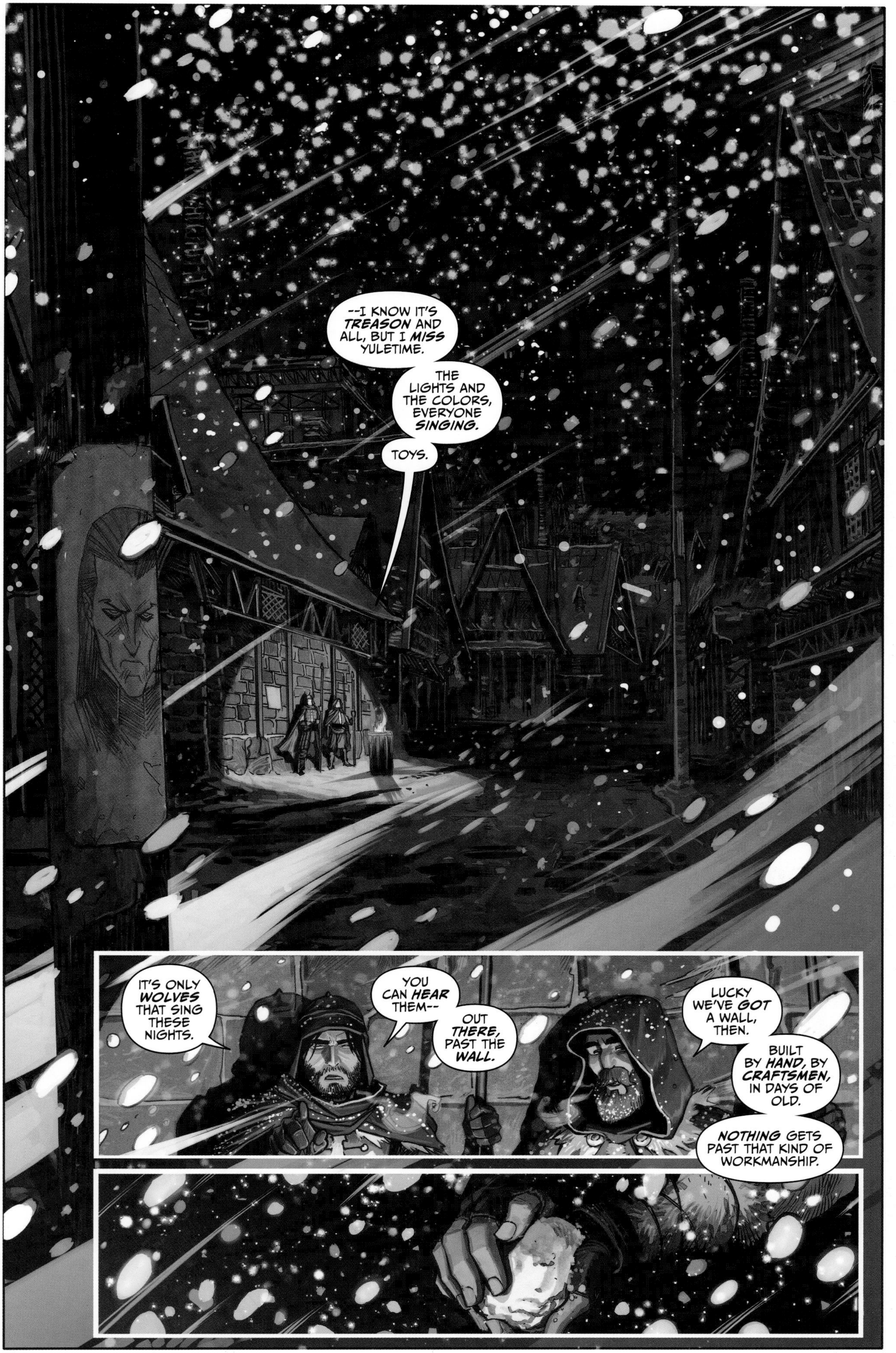
--I KNOW IT'S TREASON AND ALL, BUT I MISS YULETIME.
THE LIGHTS AND THE COLORS, EVERYONE SINGING.
TOYS.
IT'S ONLY WOLVES THAT SING THESE NIGHTS.
YOU CAN HEAR THEM--
OUT THERE, PAST THE WALL.
LUCKY WE'VE GOT A WALL, THEN.
BUILT BY HAND, BY CRAFTSMEN, IN DAYS OF OLD.
NOTHING GETS PAST THAT KIND OF WORKMANSHIP.

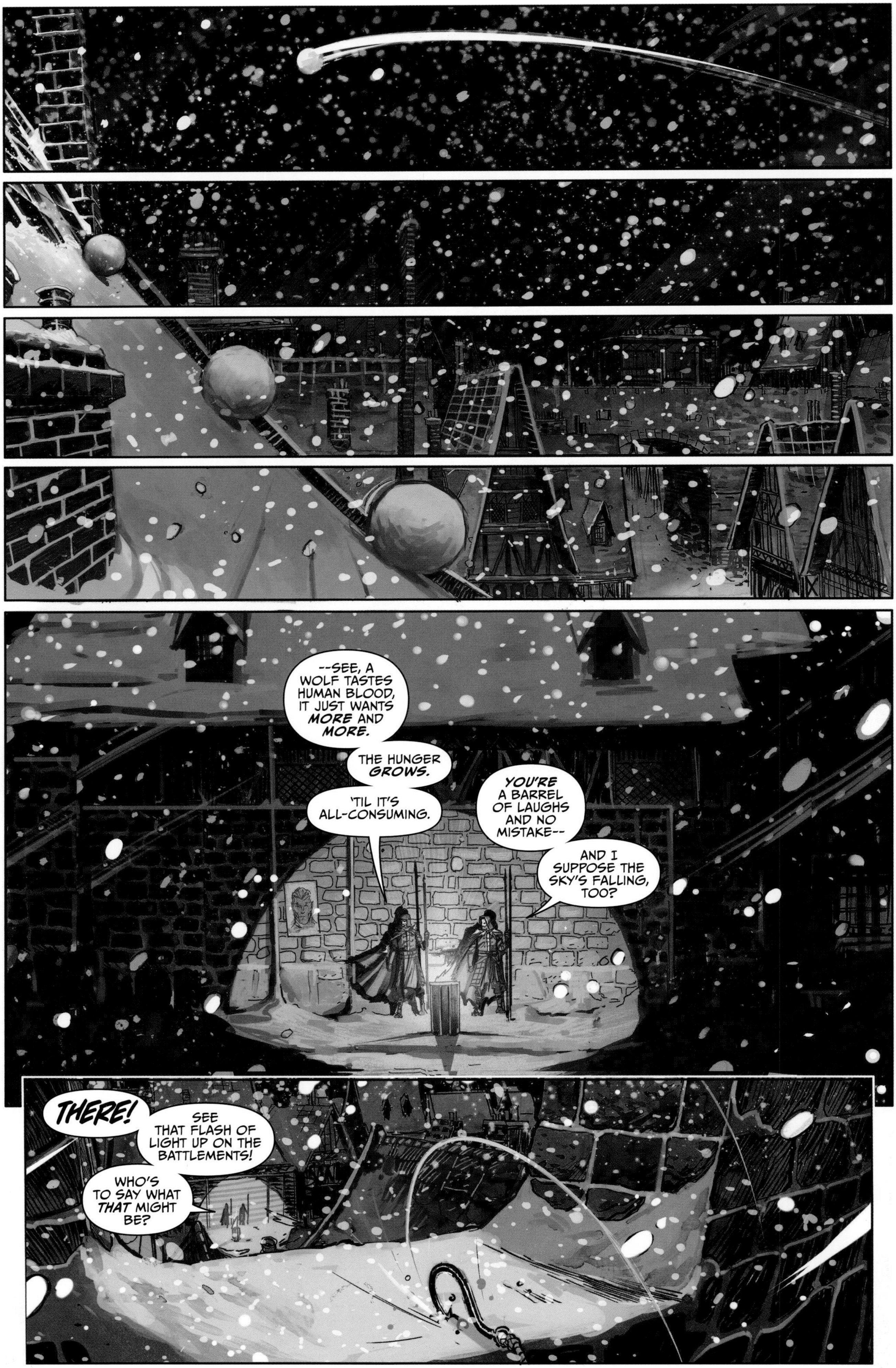
--SEE, A WOLF TASTES HUMAN BLOOD, IT JUST WANTS *MORE* AND *MORE.*
THE HUNGER *GROWS.*
'TIL IT'S ALL-CONSUMING.
YOU'RE A BARREL OF LAUGHS AND NO MISTAKE--
AND I SUPPOSE THE SKY'S FALLING, TOO?
THERE!
SEE THAT FLASH OF LIGHT UP ON THE BATTLEMENTS!
WHO'S TO SAY WHAT *THAT* MIGHT BE?

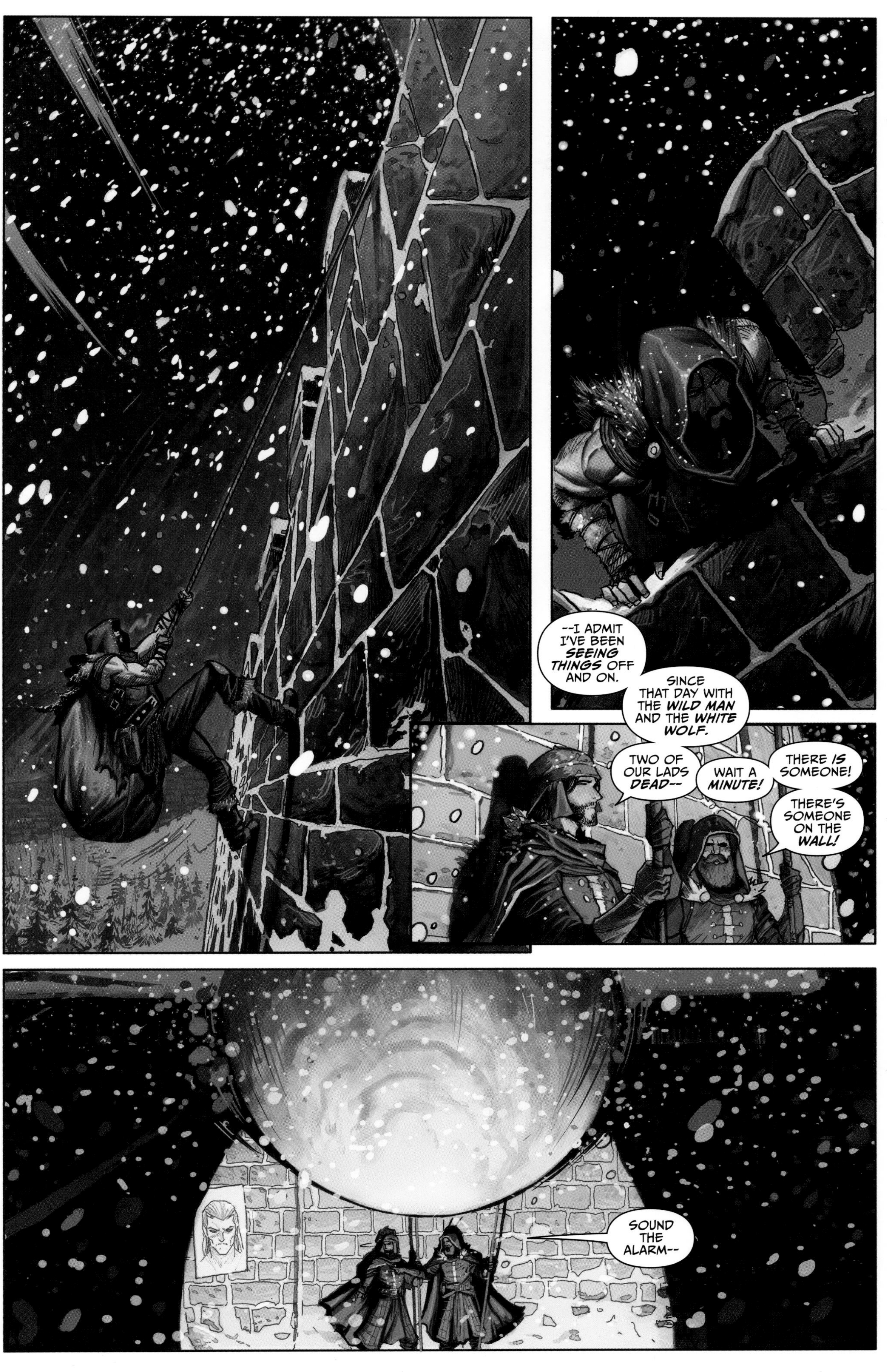
--I ADMIT I'VE BEEN SEEING THINGS OFF AND ON.
SINCE THAT DAY WITH THE WILD MAN AND THE WHITE WOLF.
TWO OF OUR LADS DEAD--
WAIT A MINUTE!
THERE IS SOMEONE!
THERE'S SOMEONE ON THE WALL!
SOUND THE ALARM--

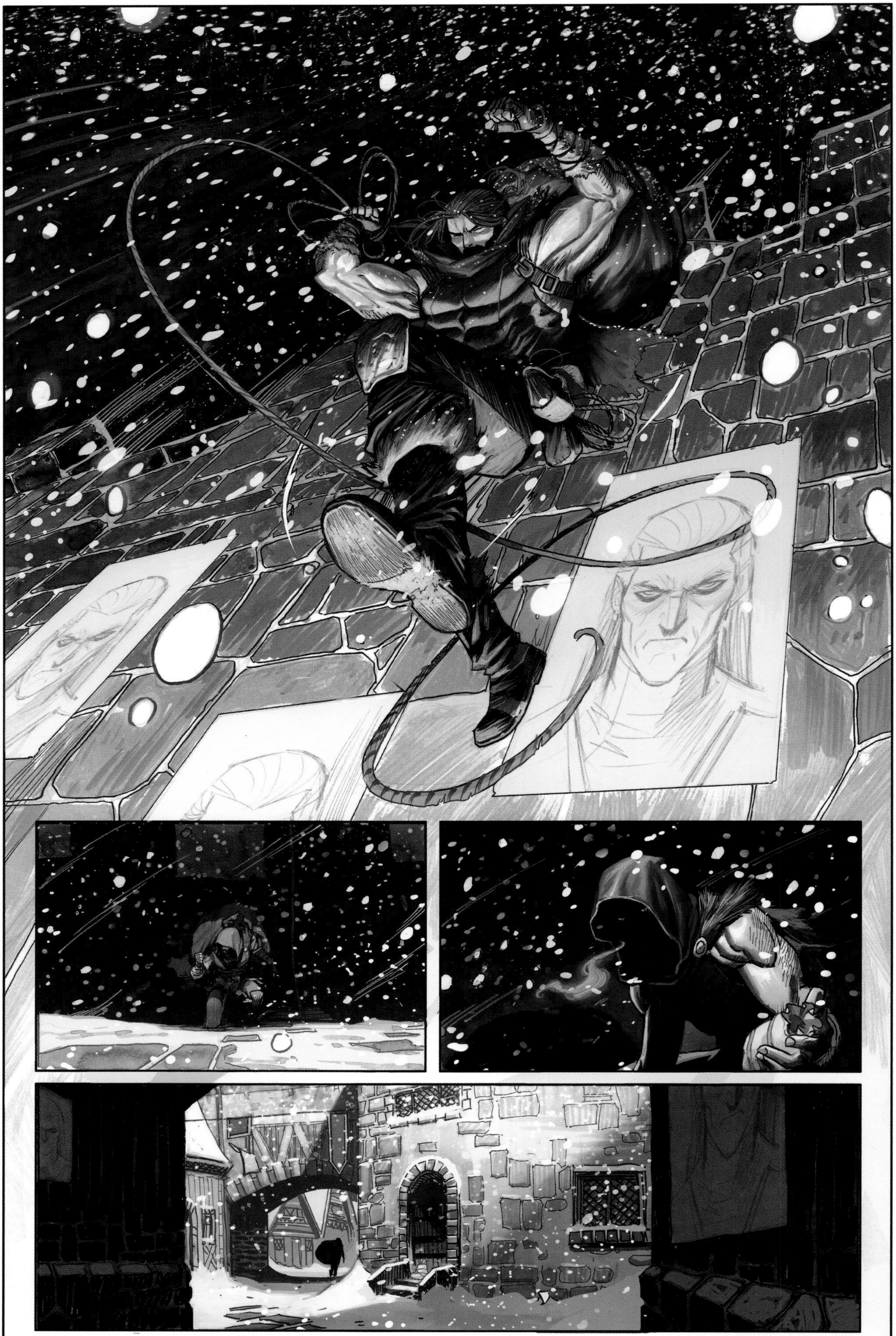

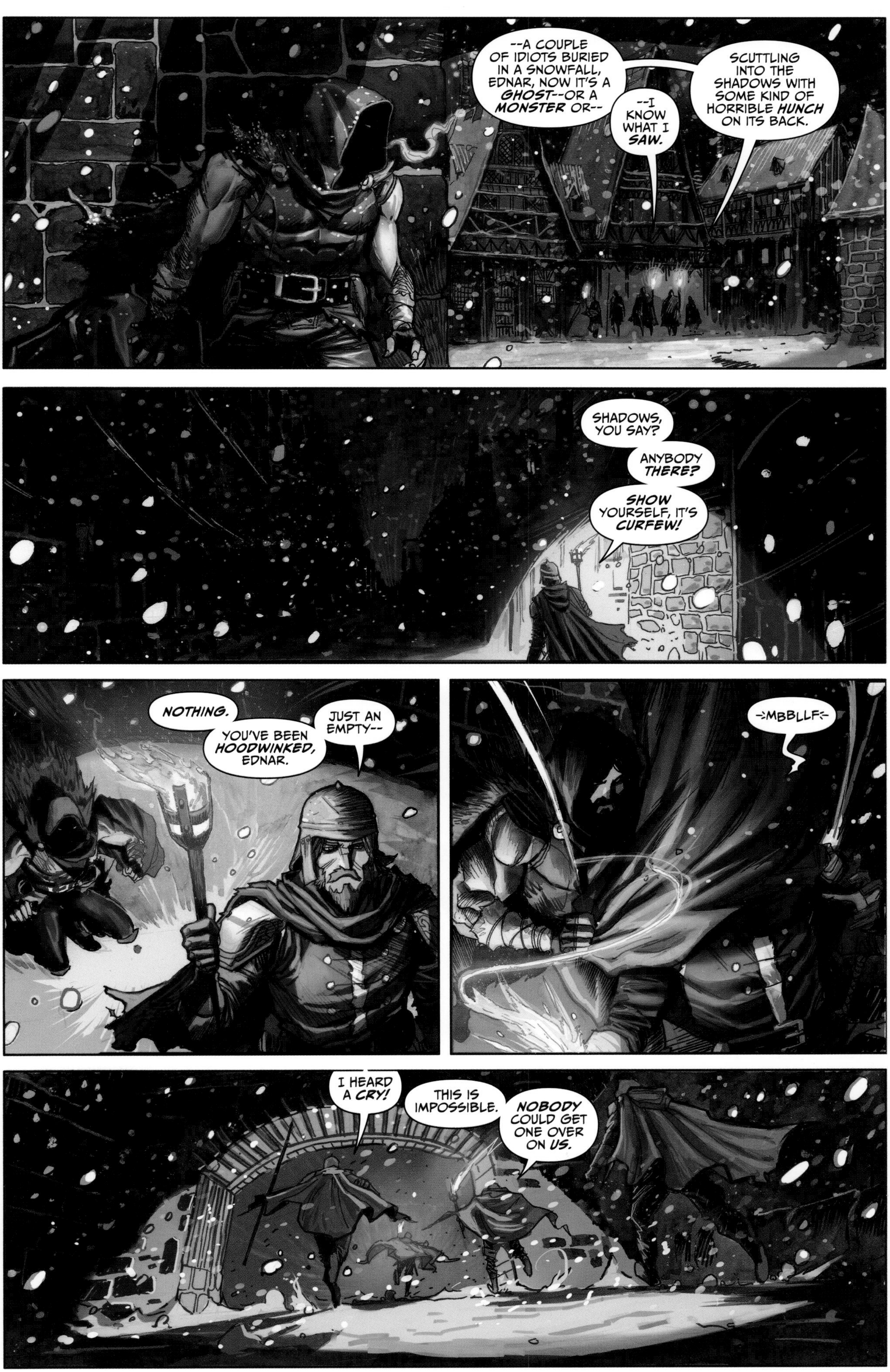
--A COUPLE OF IDIOTS BURIED IN A SNOWFALL, EDNAR, NOW IT'S A GHOST--OR A MONSTER OR--
--I KNOW WHAT I SAW.
SCUTTLING INTO THE SHADOWS WITH SOME KIND OF HORRIBLE HUNCH ON ITS BACK.
SHADOWS, YOU SAY?
ANYBODY THERE?
SHOW YOURSELF, IT'S CURFEW!
NOTHING.
YOU'VE BEEN HOODWINKED, EDNAR.
JUST AN EMPTY--
-MBBLLF-
I HEARD A CRY!
THIS IS IMPOSSIBLE.
NOBODY COULD GET ONE OVER ON US.

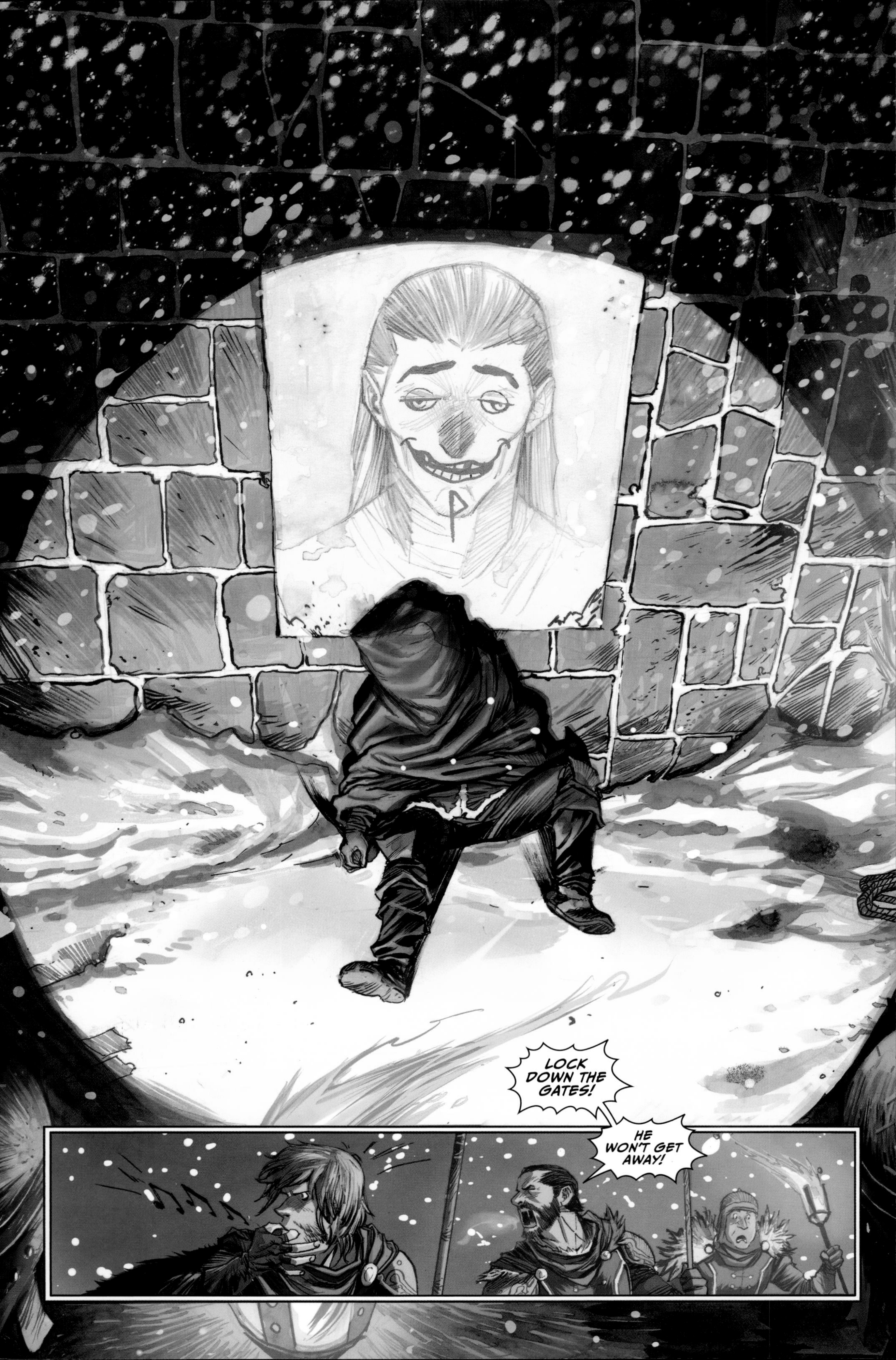
LOCK DOWN THE GATES!
HE WON'T GET AWAY!

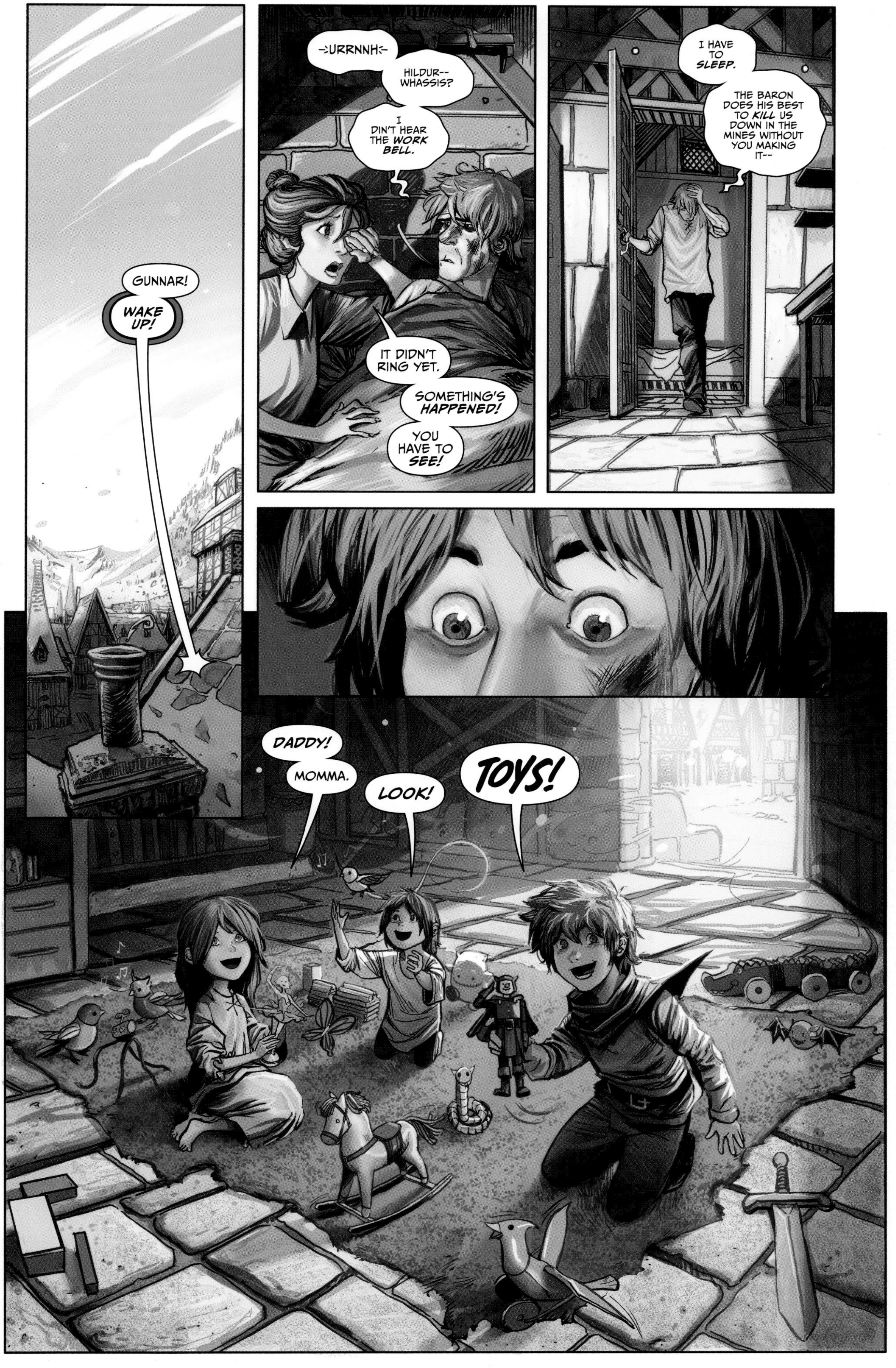
GUNNAR!
WAKE UP!
-URRNNH-
HILDUR-- WHASSIS?
I DIN'T HEAR THE WORK BELL.
IT DIDN'T RING YET.
SOMETHING'S HAPPENED!
YOU HAVE TO SEE!
I HAVE TO SLEEP.
THE BARON DOES HIS BEST TO KILL US DOWN IN THE MINES WITHOUT YOU MAKING IT--
DADDY!
MOMMA.
LOOK!
TOYS!

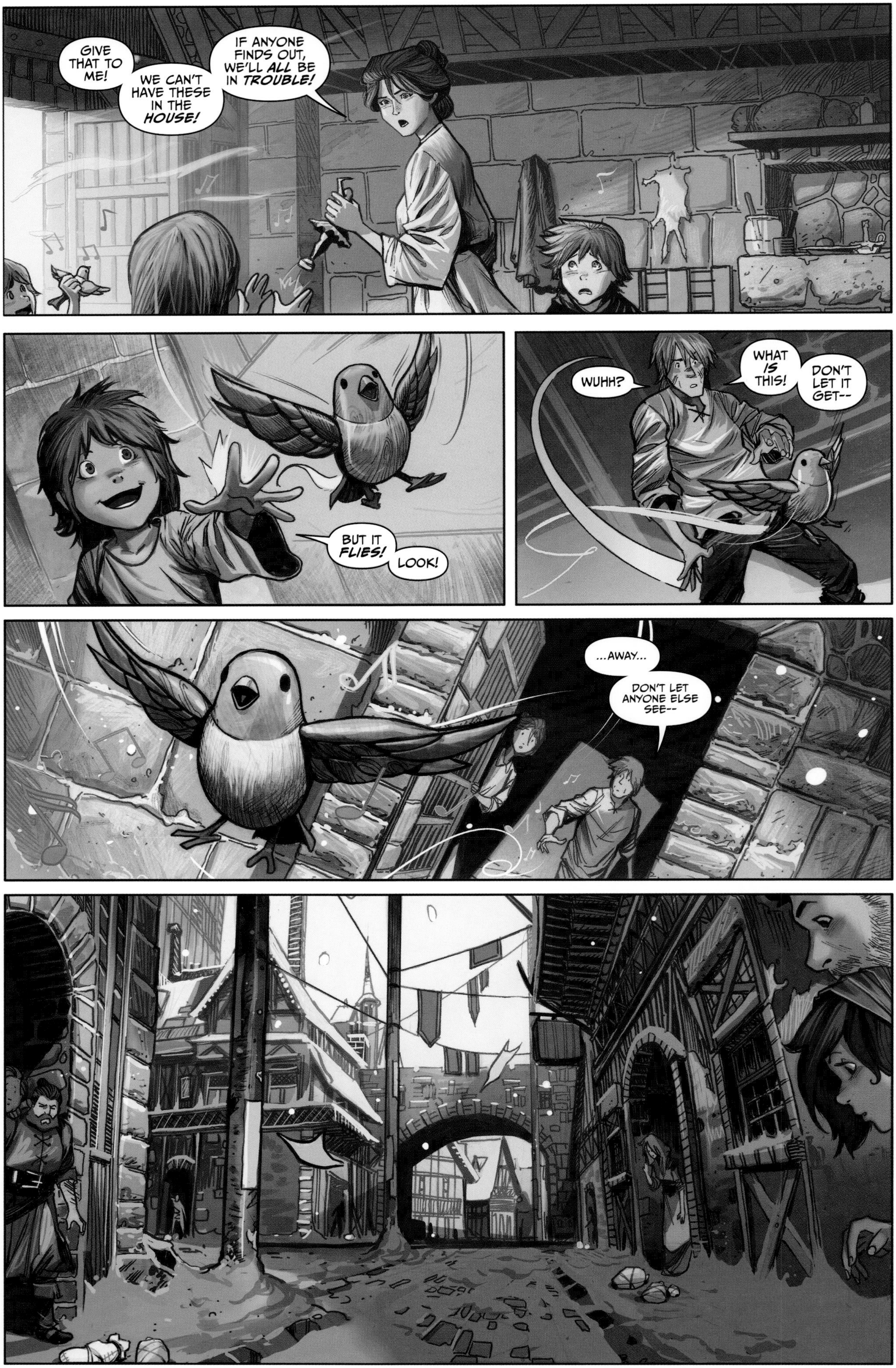
GIVE THAT TO ME!
WE CAN'T HAVE THESE IN THE HOUSE!
IF ANYONE FINDS OUT, WE'LL ALL BE IN TROUBLE!
BUT IT FLIES!
LOOK!
WUHH?
WHAT IS THIS!
DON'T LET IT GET--
...AWAY...
DON'T LET ANYONE ELSE SEE--

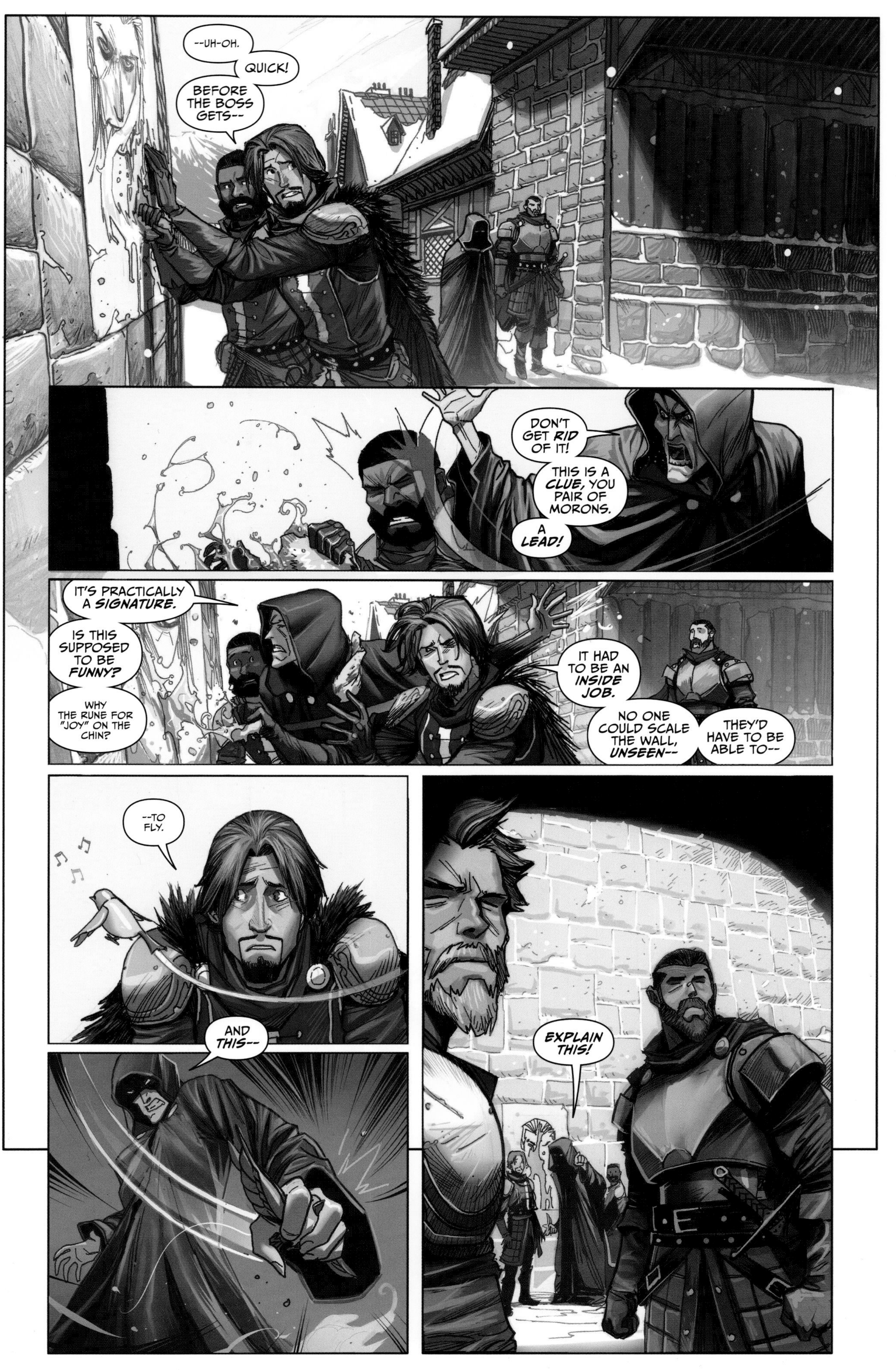

--UH-OH.
QUICK!
BEFORE THE BOSS GETS--
DON'T GET RID OF IT!
THIS IS A CLUE, YOU PAIR OF MORONS.
A LEAD!
IT'S PRACTICALLY A SIGNATURE.
IS THIS SUPPOSED TO BE FUNNY?
WHY THE RUNE FOR "JOY" ON THE CHIN?
IT HAD TO BE AN INSIDE JOB.
NO ONE COULD SCALE THE WALL, UNSEEN--
THEY'D HAVE TO BE ABLE TO--
--TO FLY.
AND THIS--
EXPLAIN THIS!

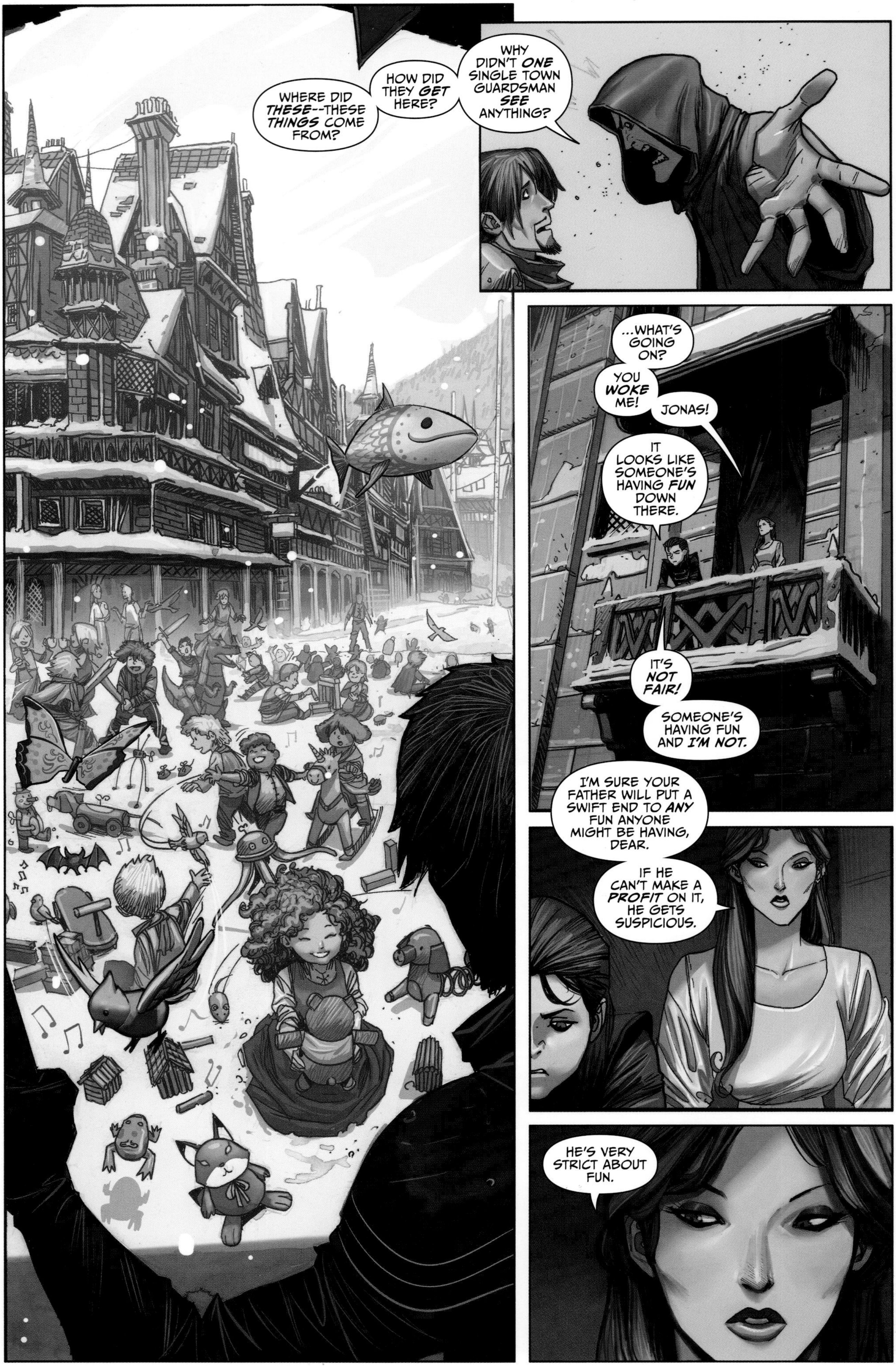
WHERE DID THESE--THESE THINGS COME FROM?
HOW DID THEY GET HERE?
WHY DIDN'T ONE SINGLE TOWN GUARDSMAN SEE ANYTHING?
...WHAT'S GOING ON?
YOU WOKE ME!
JONAS!
IT LOOKS LIKE SOMEONE'S HAVING FUN DOWN THERE.
IT'S NOT FAIR!
SOMEONE'S HAVING FUN AND I'M NOT.
I'M SURE YOUR FATHER WILL PUT A SWIFT END TO ANY FUN ANYONE MIGHT BE HAVING, DEAR.
IF HE CAN'T MAKE A PROFIT ON IT, HE GETS SUSPICIOUS.
HE'S VERY STRICT ABOUT FUN.

YOU KNOW THE RULES.

WHAT ABOUT OUR *CHILDREN,* LORD MAGNUS?

WE *ALWAYS* GIVE TOYS AT YULETIME!

HAVE *MERCY!*

...YULETIME...

YULETIME IS *CANCELLED* THIS YEAR.

UNTIL THE *MINERS* REACH THEIR *QUOTA.*

UNTIL THE *KING HIMSELF* ARRIVES IN *THREE DAYS'* TIME FOR THE *FEAST.*

AS FOR *MY SON,* WELL...

THE POOR CHILD'S *MEDICAL CONDITION* PROHIBITS HIM FROM *LEAVING* THE SAFETY OF THE CASTLE.

CONDEMNED TO A *SOLITARY LIFE,* THESE TOYS, GRATEFULLY DONATED BY THE CHILDREN OF GRIMSVIG, ARE *ALL* HE HAS.

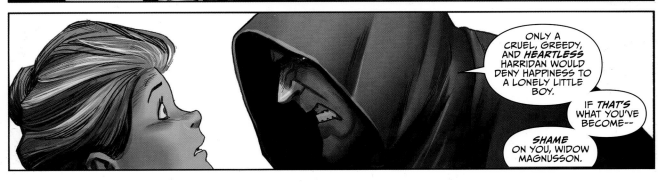

ONLY A CRUEL, GREEDY, AND *HEARTLESS* HARRIDAN WOULD DENY HAPPINESS TO A LONELY LITTLE BOY.

IF *THAT'S* WHAT YOU'VE BECOME--

SHAME ON YOU, WIDOW MAGNUSSON.

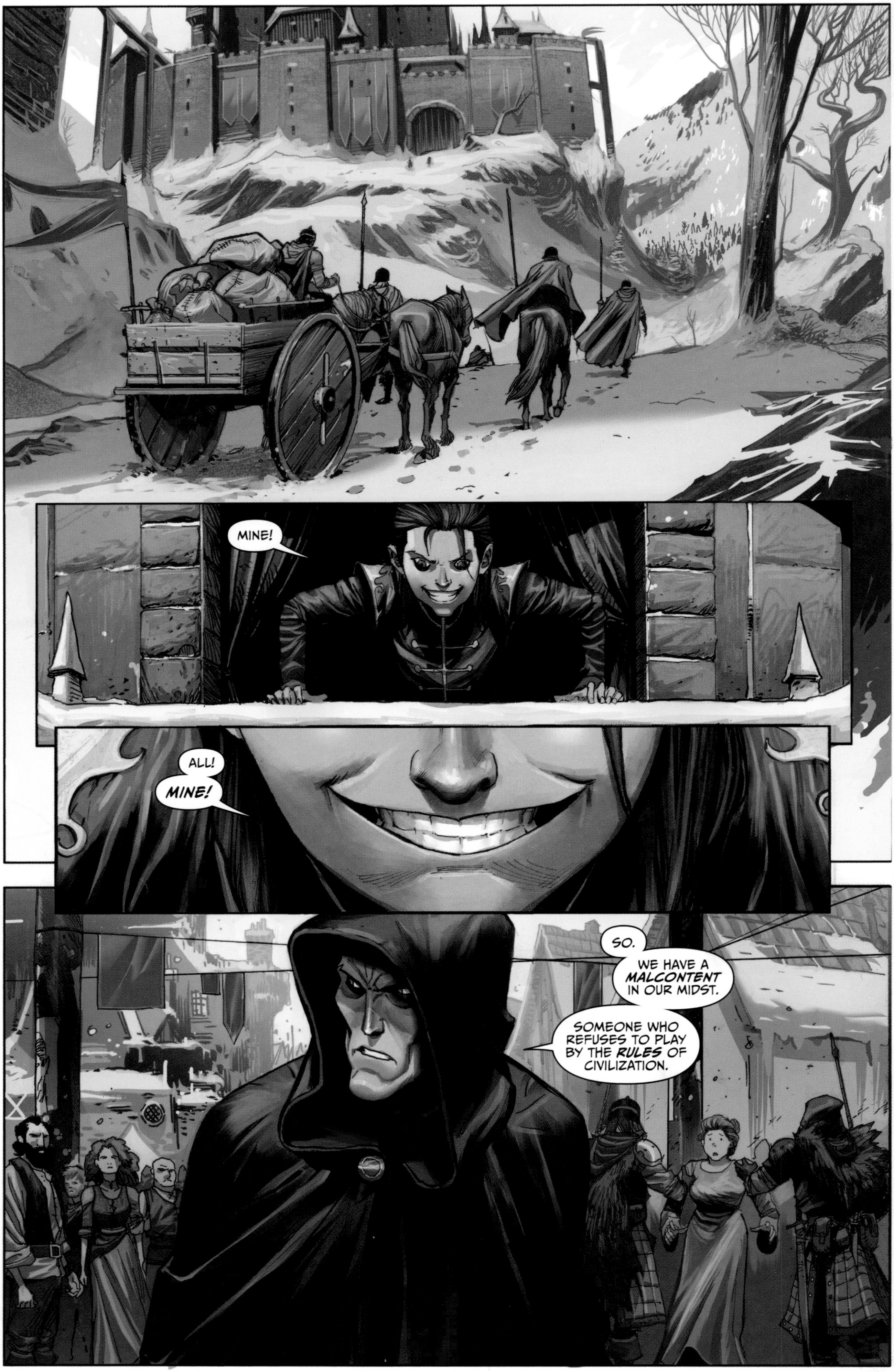
MINE!
ALL!
MINE!
SO.
WE HAVE A MALCONTENT IN OUR MIDST.
SOMEONE WHO REFUSES TO PLAY BY THE RULES OF CIVILIZATION.

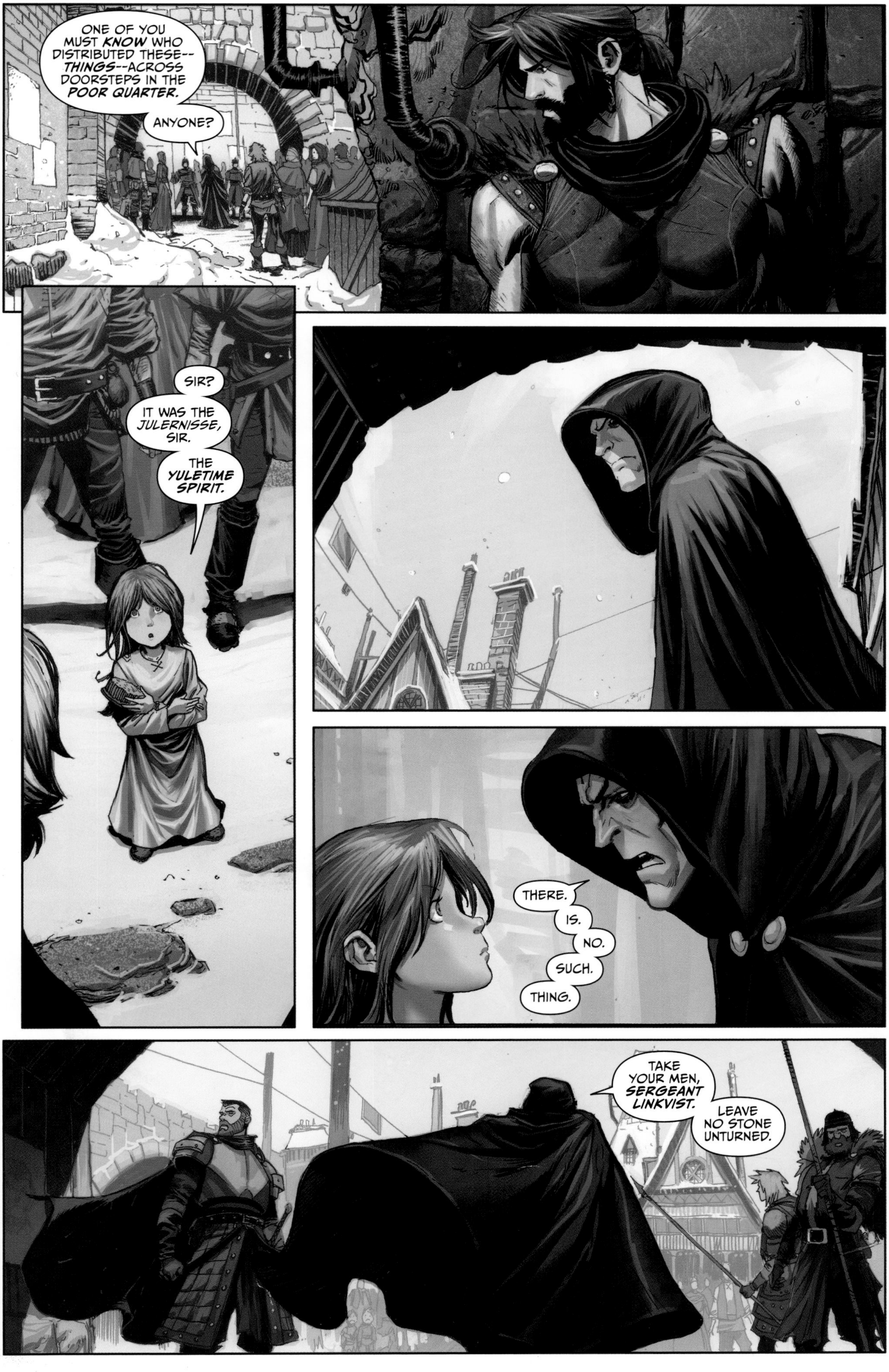
ONE OF YOU MUST **KNOW** WHO DISTRIBUTED THESE--***THINGS***--ACROSS DOORSTEPS IN THE ***POOR QUARTER.***
ANYONE?
SIR?
IT WAS THE ***JULERNISSE,*** SIR.
THE ***YULETIME SPIRIT.***
THERE.
IS.
NO.
SUCH.
THING.
TAKE YOUR MEN, ***SERGEANT LINKVIST.***
LEAVE NO STONE UNTURNED.

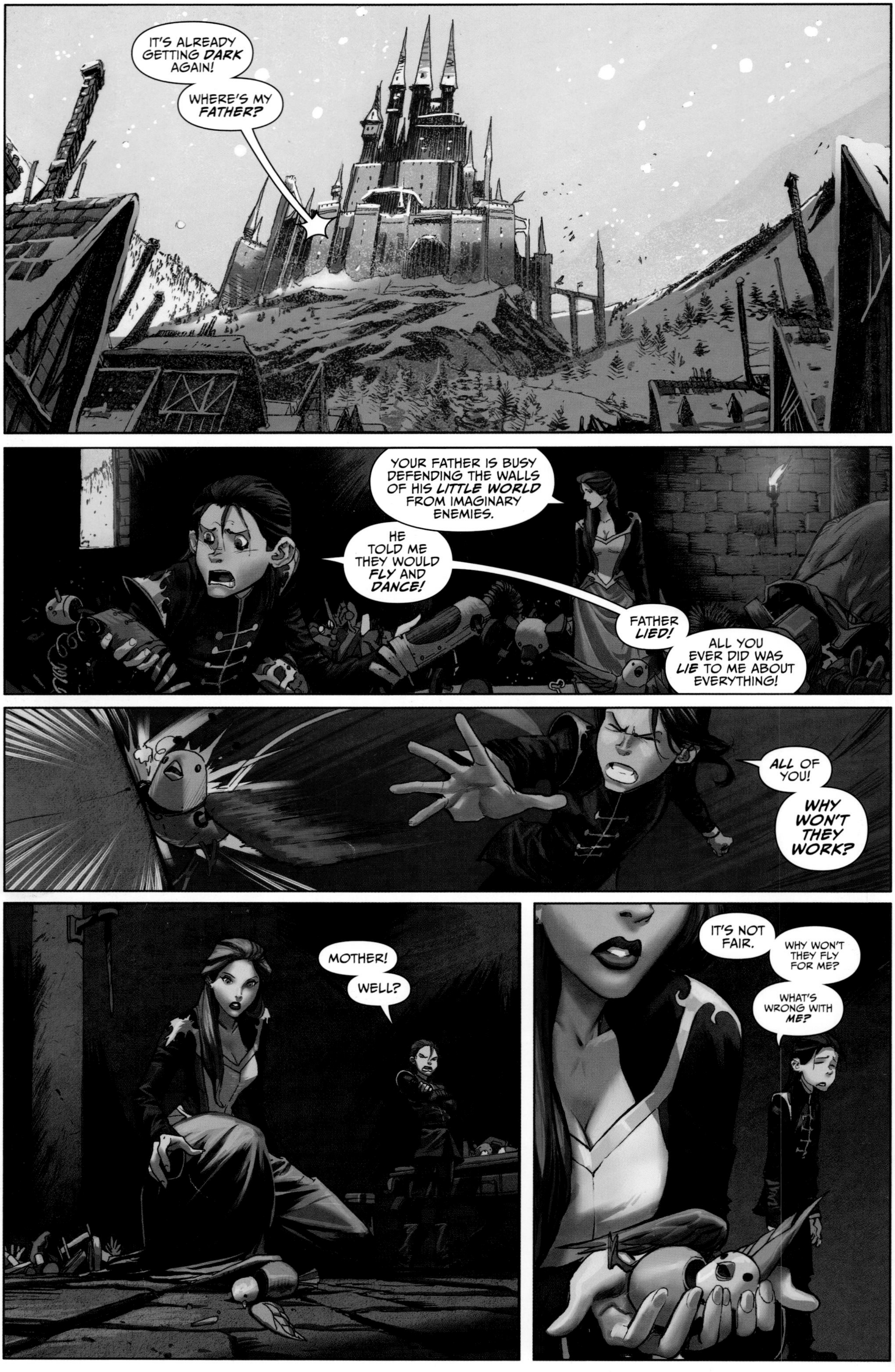

IT'S ALREADY GETTING DARK AGAIN!
WHERE'S MY FATHER?
YOUR FATHER IS BUSY DEFENDING THE WALLS OF HIS LITTLE WORLD FROM IMAGINARY ENEMIES.
HE TOLD ME THEY WOULD FLY AND DANCE!
FATHER LIED!
ALL YOU EVER DID WAS LIE TO ME ABOUT EVERYTHING!
ALL OF YOU!
WHY WON'T THEY WORK?
MOTHER!
WELL?
IT'S NOT FAIR.
WHY WON'T THEY FLY FOR ME?
WHAT'S WRONG WITH ME?

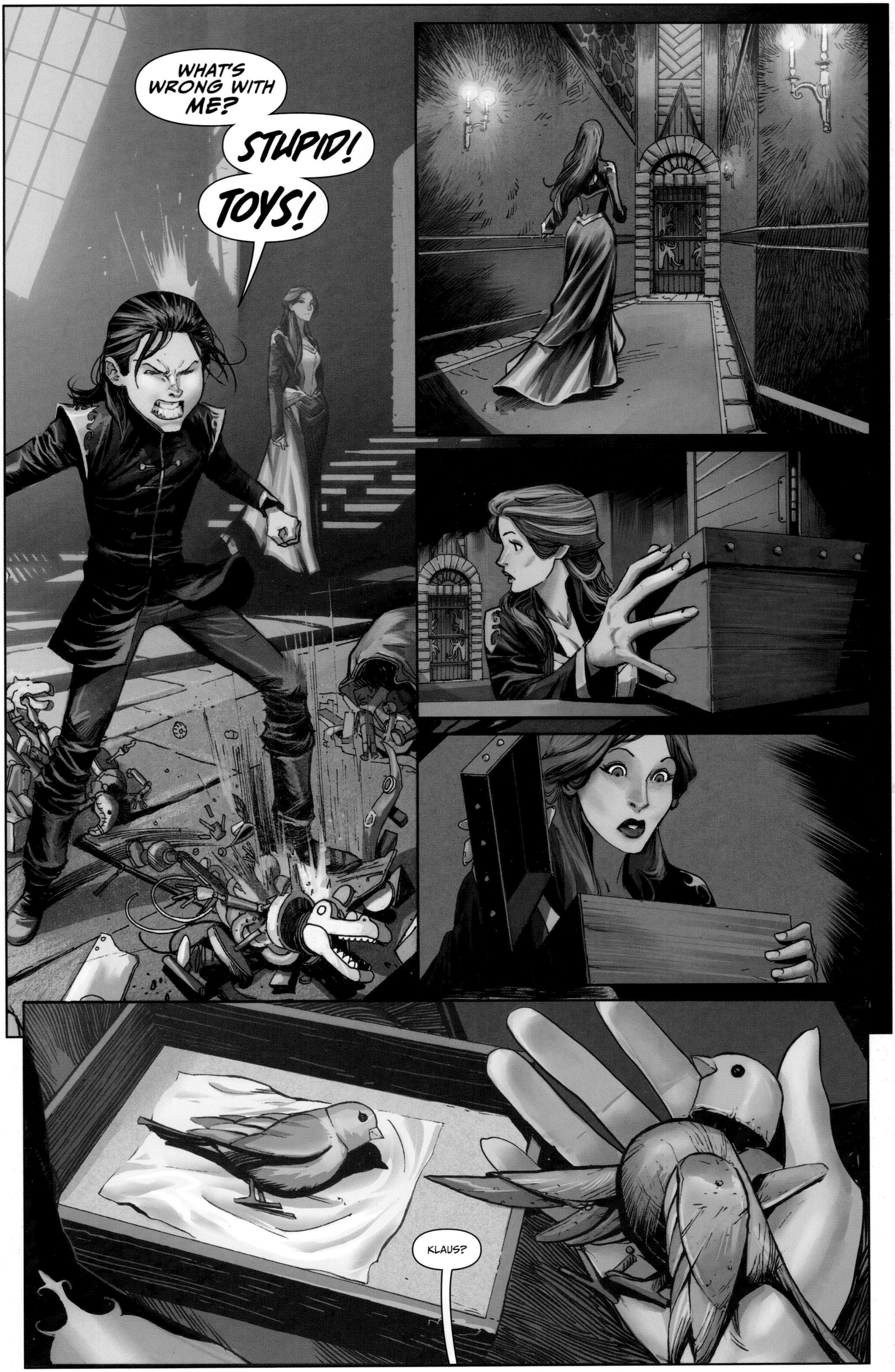
WHAT'S WRONG WITH ME?
STUPID!
TOYS!
KLAUS?

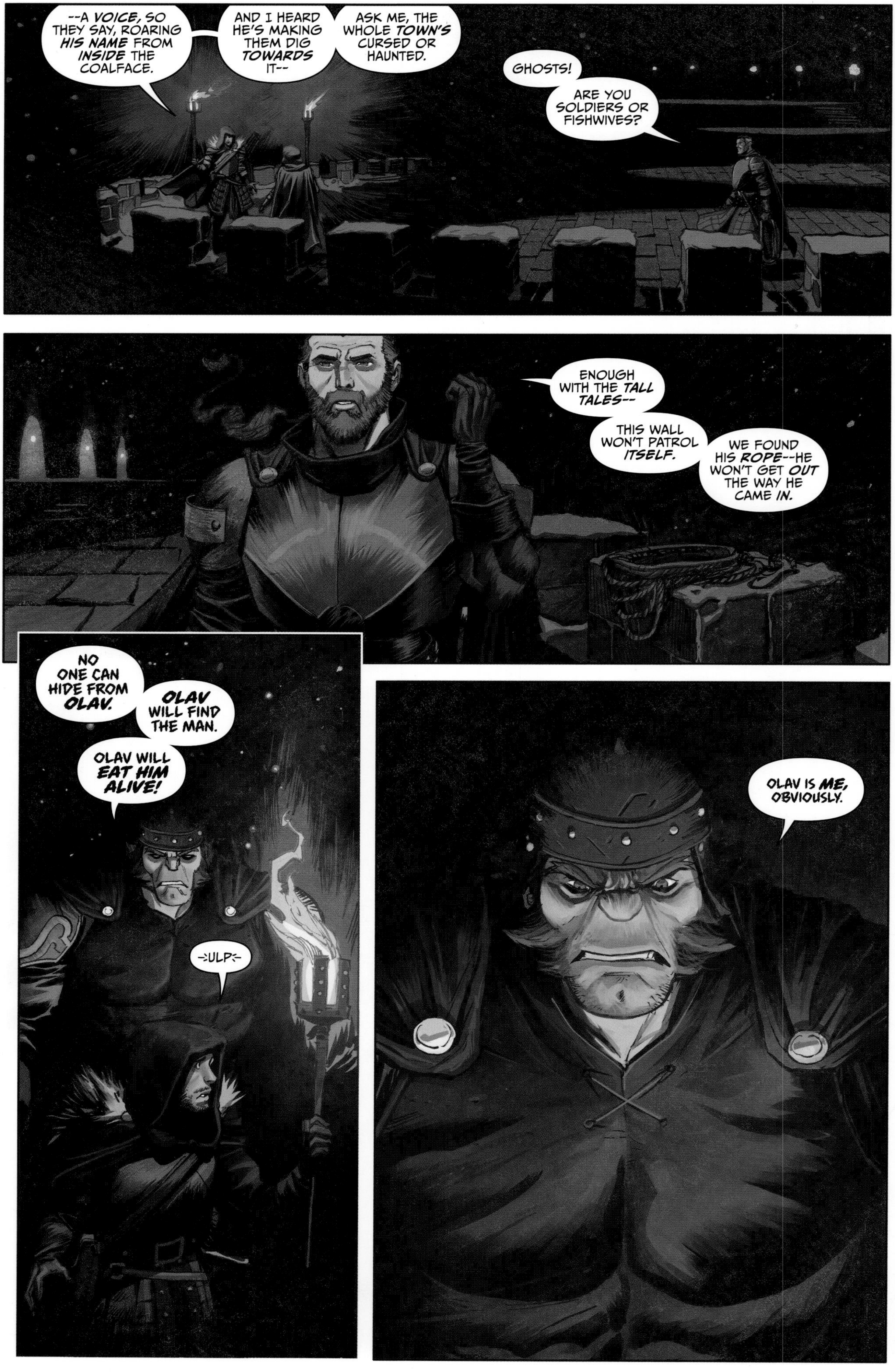
--A VOICE, SO THEY SAY, ROARING HIS NAME FROM INSIDE THE COALFACE.
AND I HEARD HE'S MAKING THEM DIG TOWARDS IT--
ASK ME, THE WHOLE TOWN'S CURSED OR HAUNTED.
GHOSTS!
ARE YOU SOLDIERS OR FISHWIVES?
ENOUGH WITH THE TALL TALES--
THIS WALL WON'T PATROL ITSELF.
WE FOUND HIS ROPE--HE WON'T GET OUT THE WAY HE CAME IN.
NO ONE CAN HIDE FROM OLAV.
OLAV WILL FIND THE MAN.
OLAV WILL EAT HIM ALIVE!
-ULP-
OLAV IS ME, OBVIOUSLY.

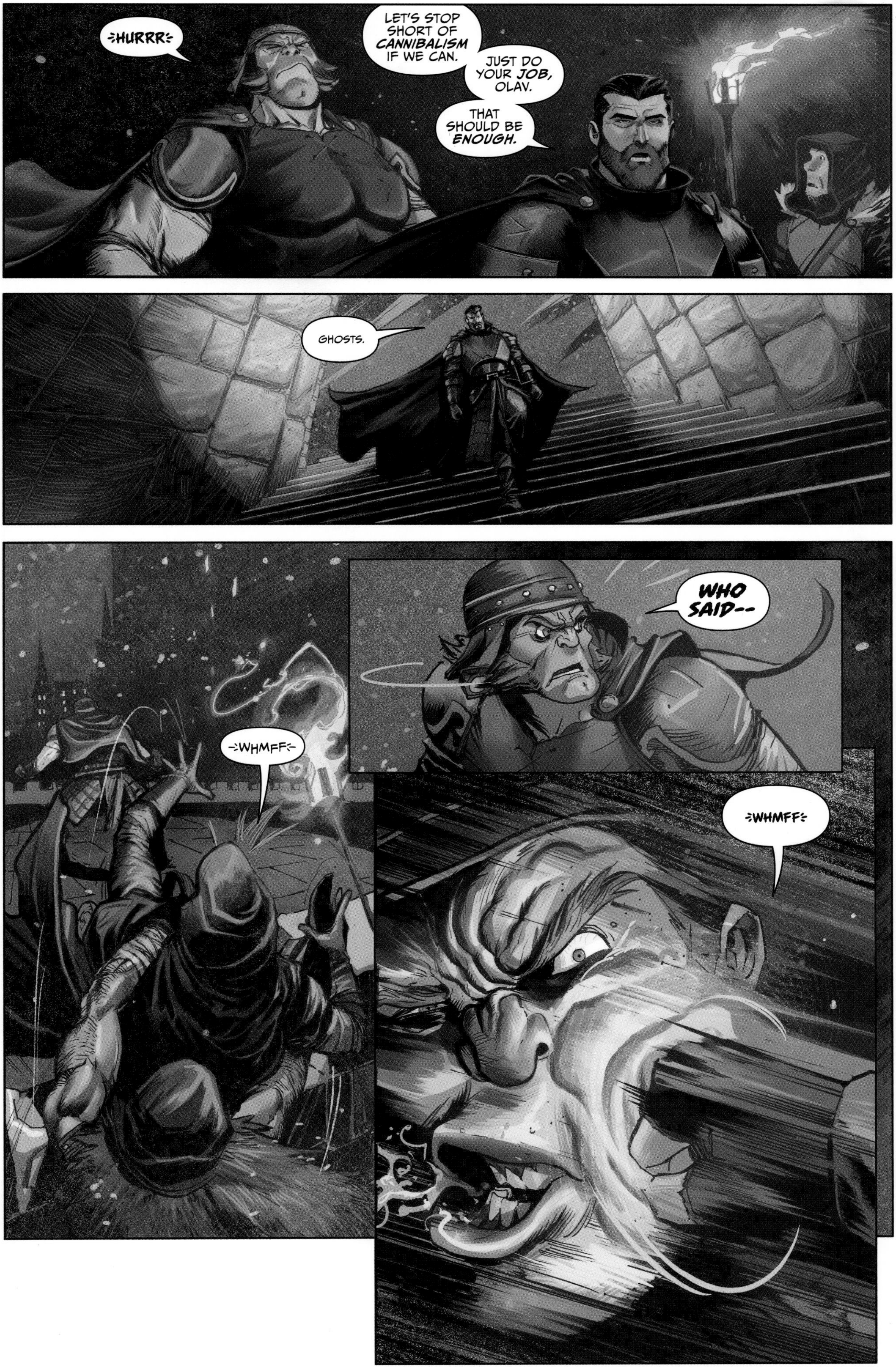
-HURRR-
LET'S STOP SHORT OF CANNIBALISM IF WE CAN.
JUST DO YOUR JOB, OLAV.
THAT SHOULD BE ENOUGH.
GHOSTS.
WHO SAID--
-WHMFF-
-WHMFF-

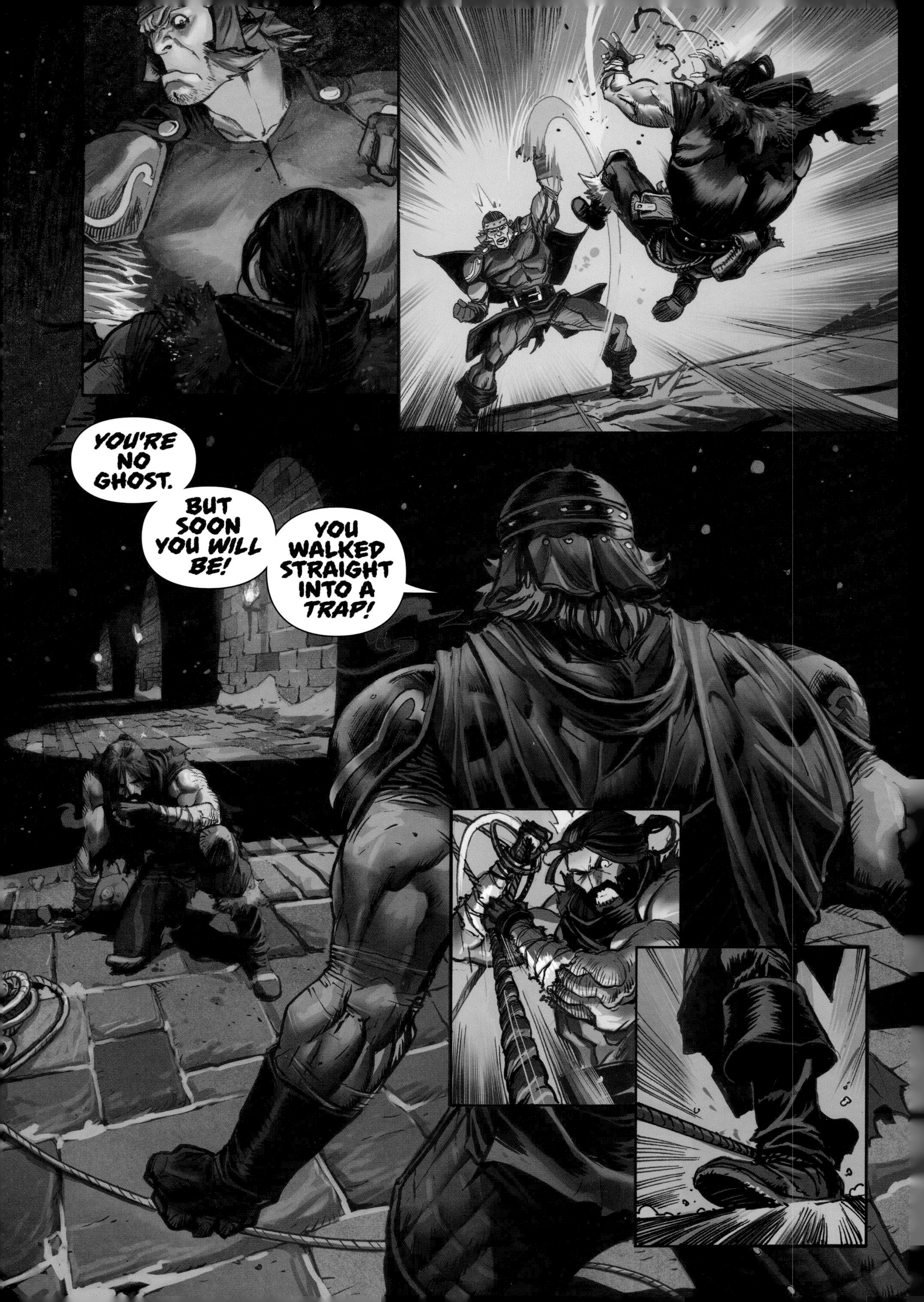
YOU'RE NO GHOST.
BUT SOON YOU WILL BE!
YOU WALKED STRAIGHT INTO A TRAP!

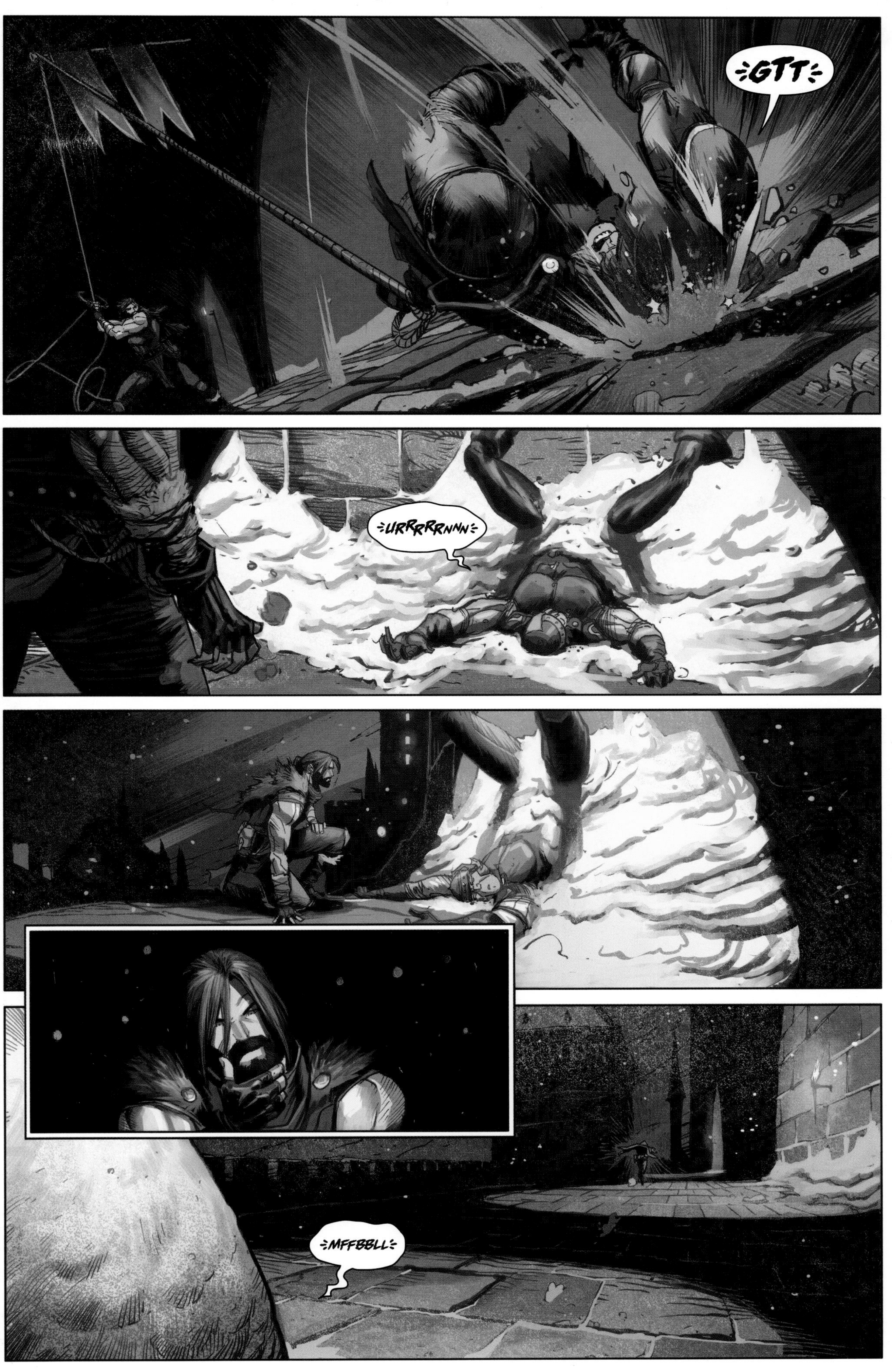
GTT
URRRRRNNN
MFFBBLL

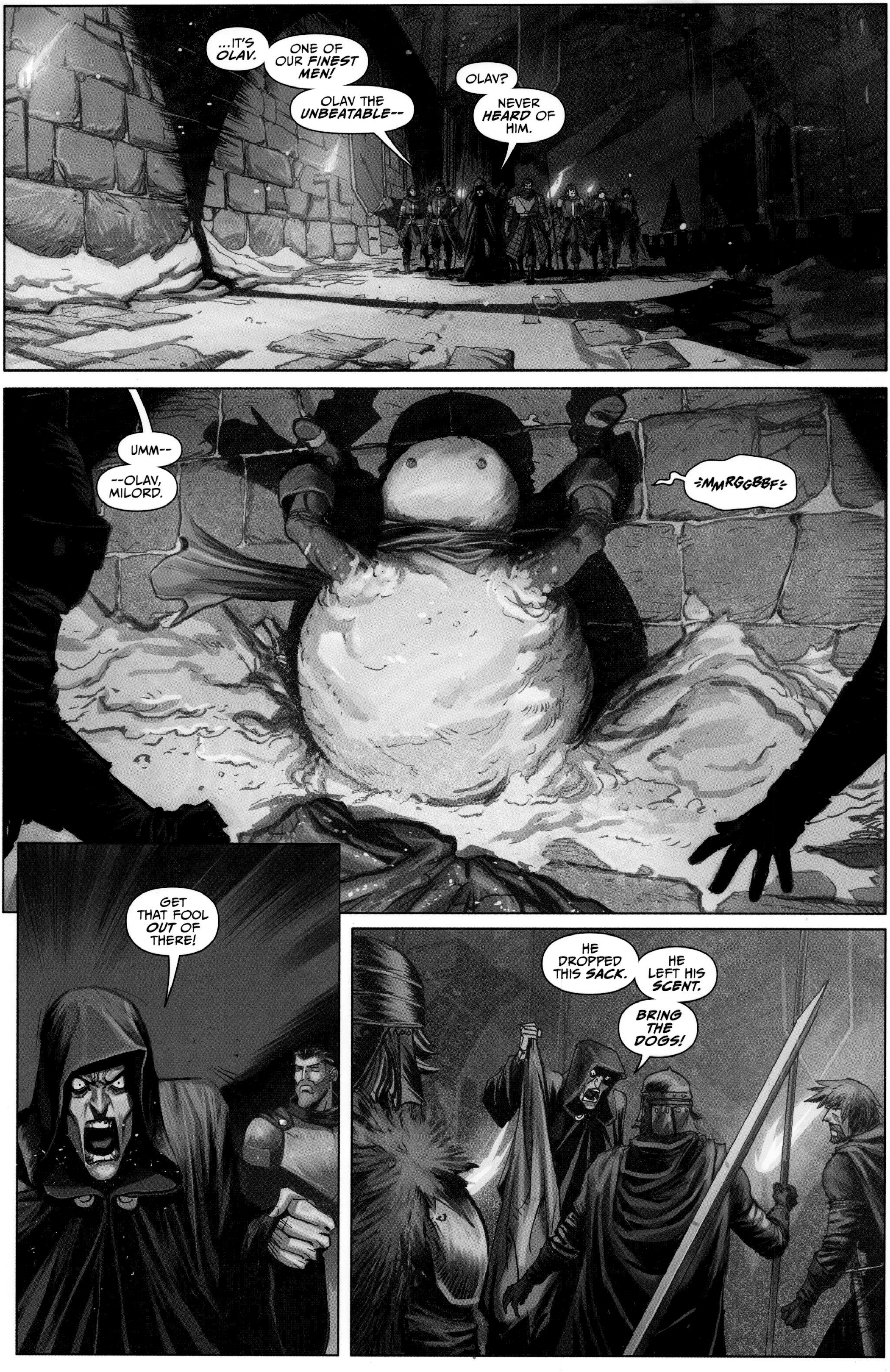
...IT'S OLAV.
ONE OF OUR FINEST MEN!
OLAV THE UNBEATABLE--
OLAV?
NEVER HEARD OF HIM.
UMM--
--OLAV, MILORD.
MMRGGBBF
GET THAT FOOL OUT OF THERE!
HE DROPPED THIS SACK.
HE LEFT HIS SCENT.
BRING THE DOGS!

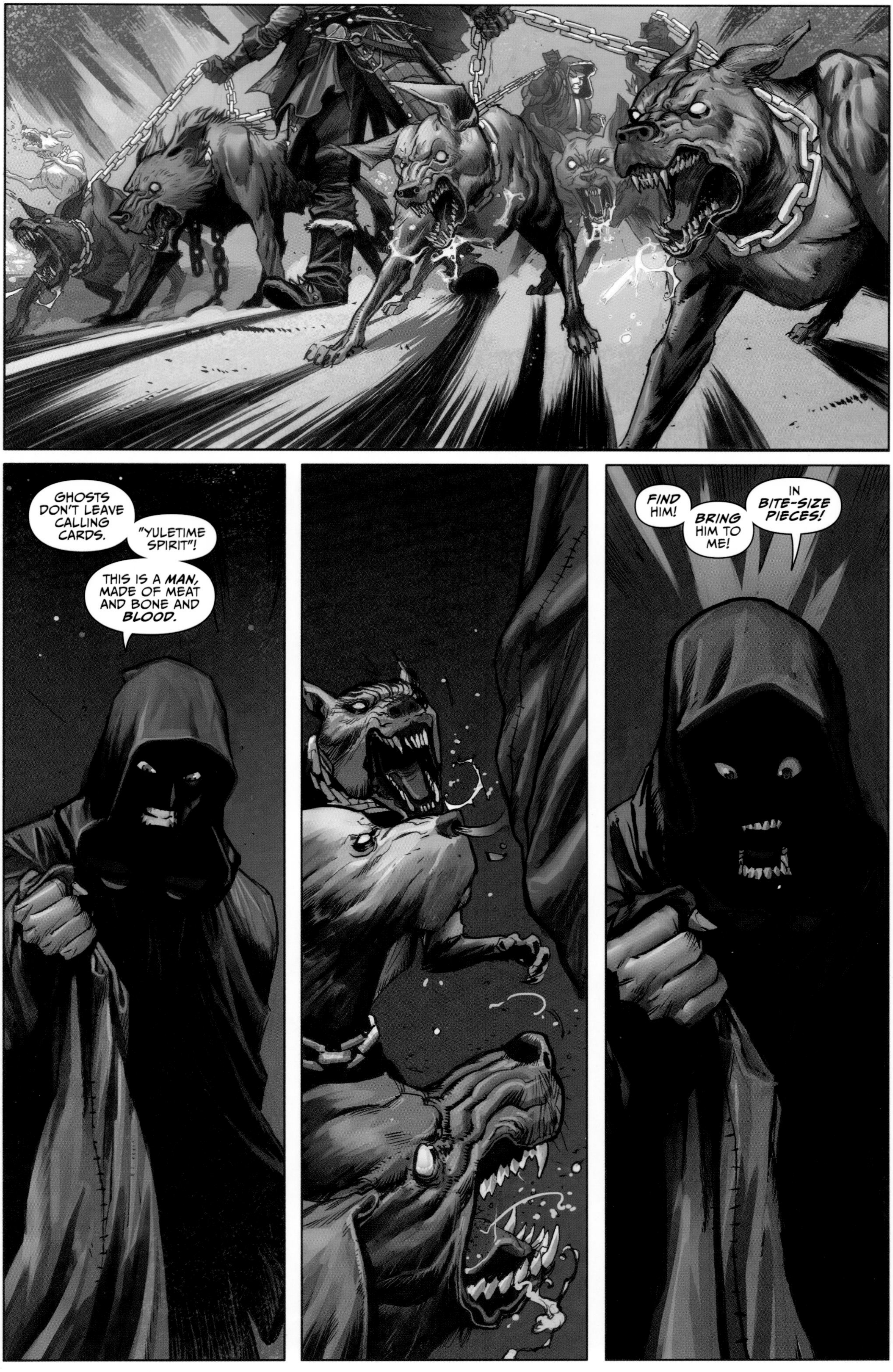
GHOSTS DON'T LEAVE CALLING CARDS.
"YULETIME SPIRIT"!
THIS IS A *MAN*, MADE OF MEAT AND BONE AND *BLOOD.*
FIND HIM!
BRING HIM TO ME!
IN *BITE-SIZE PIECES!*

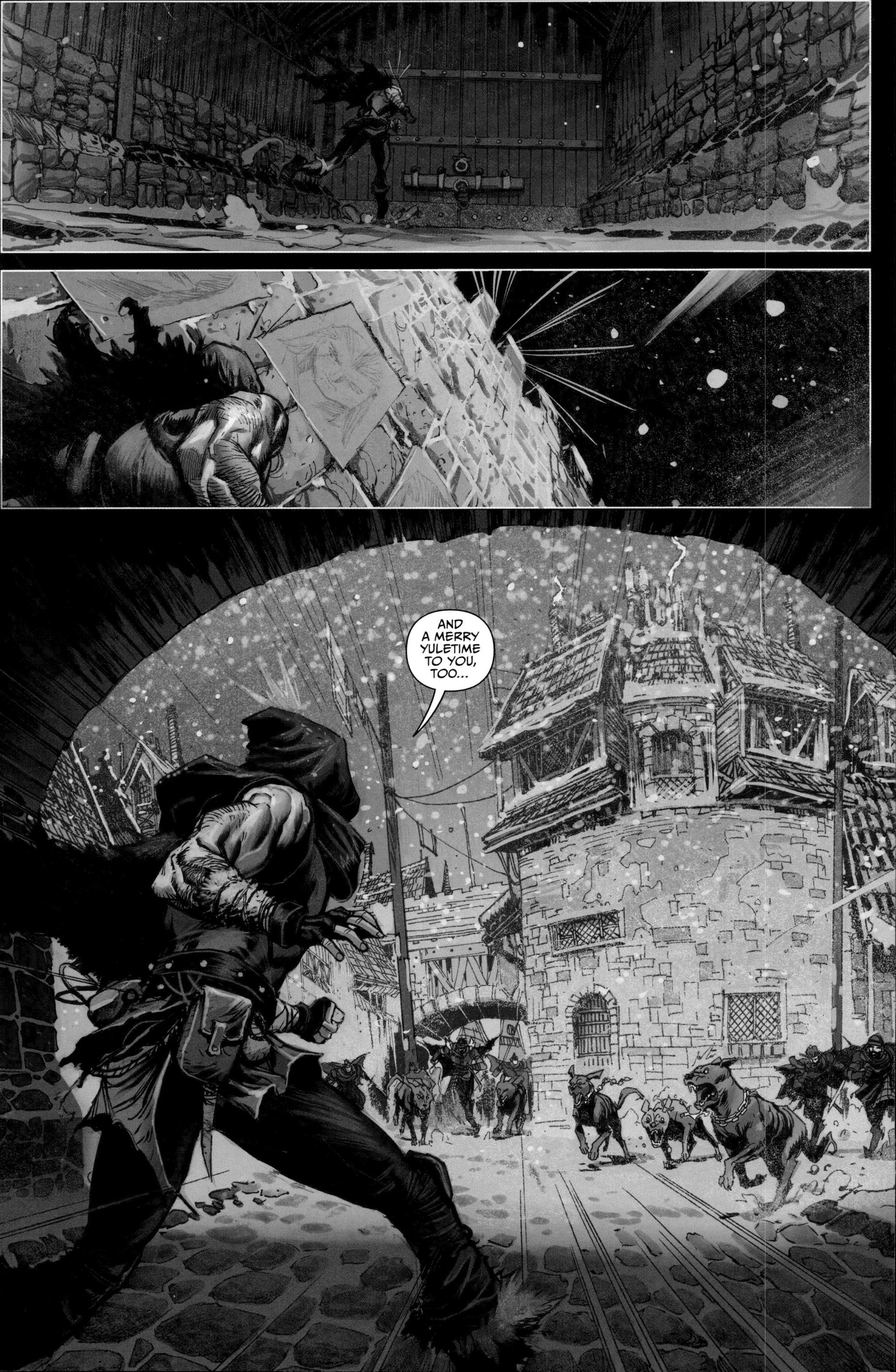
AND A MERRY YULETIME TO YOU, TOO...

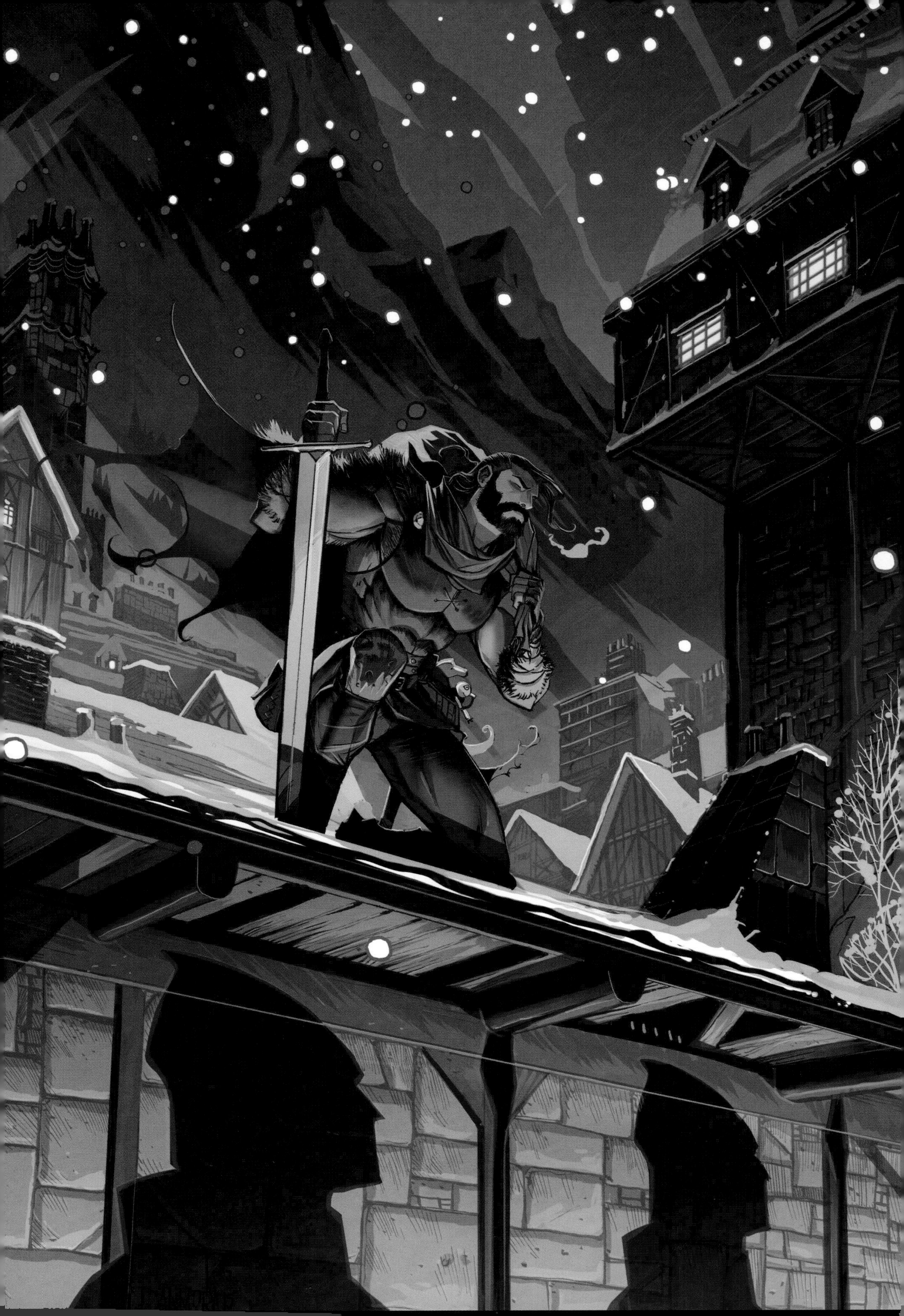

CHAPTER

THREE

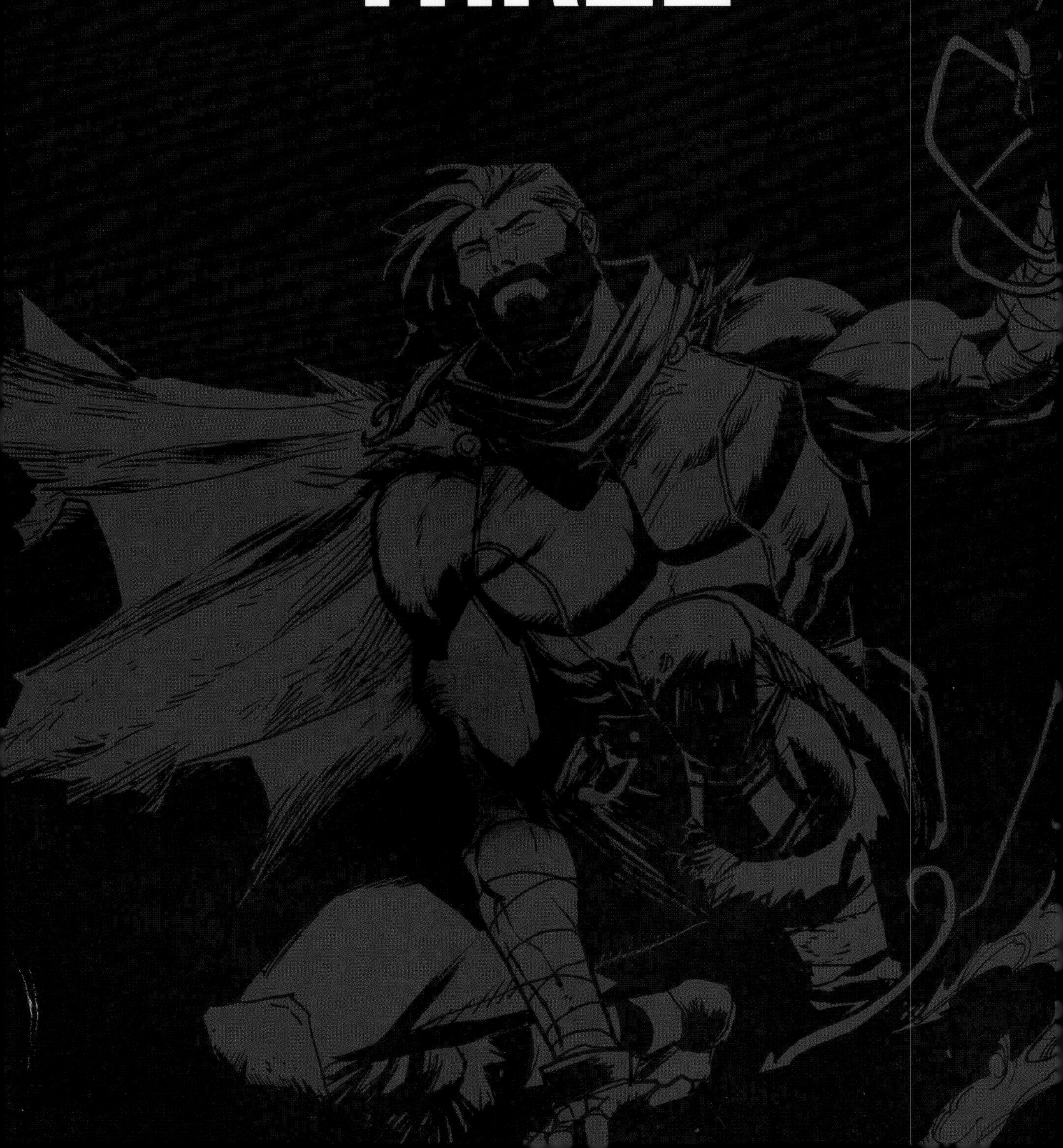

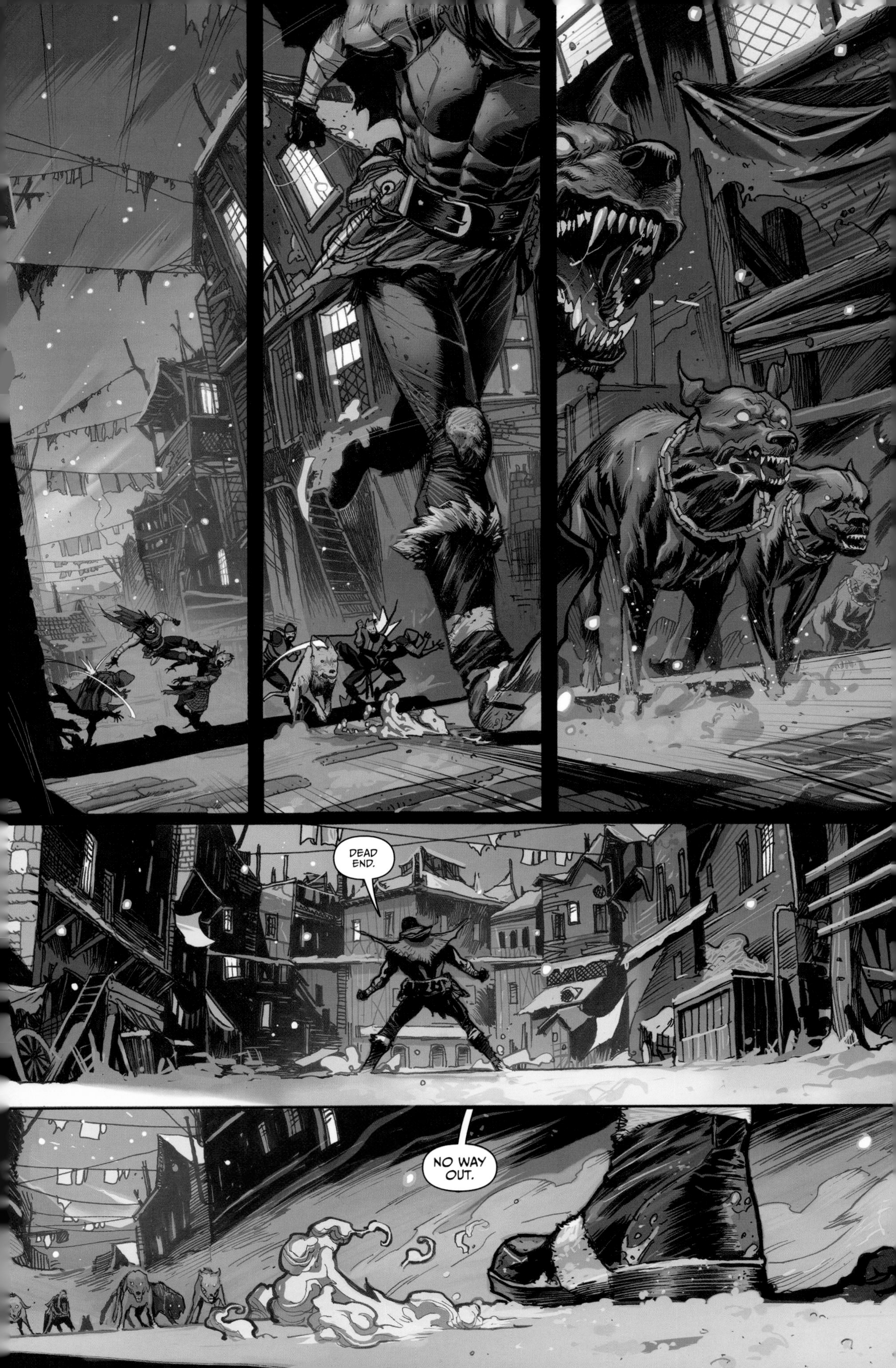
DEAD END.
NO WAY OUT.

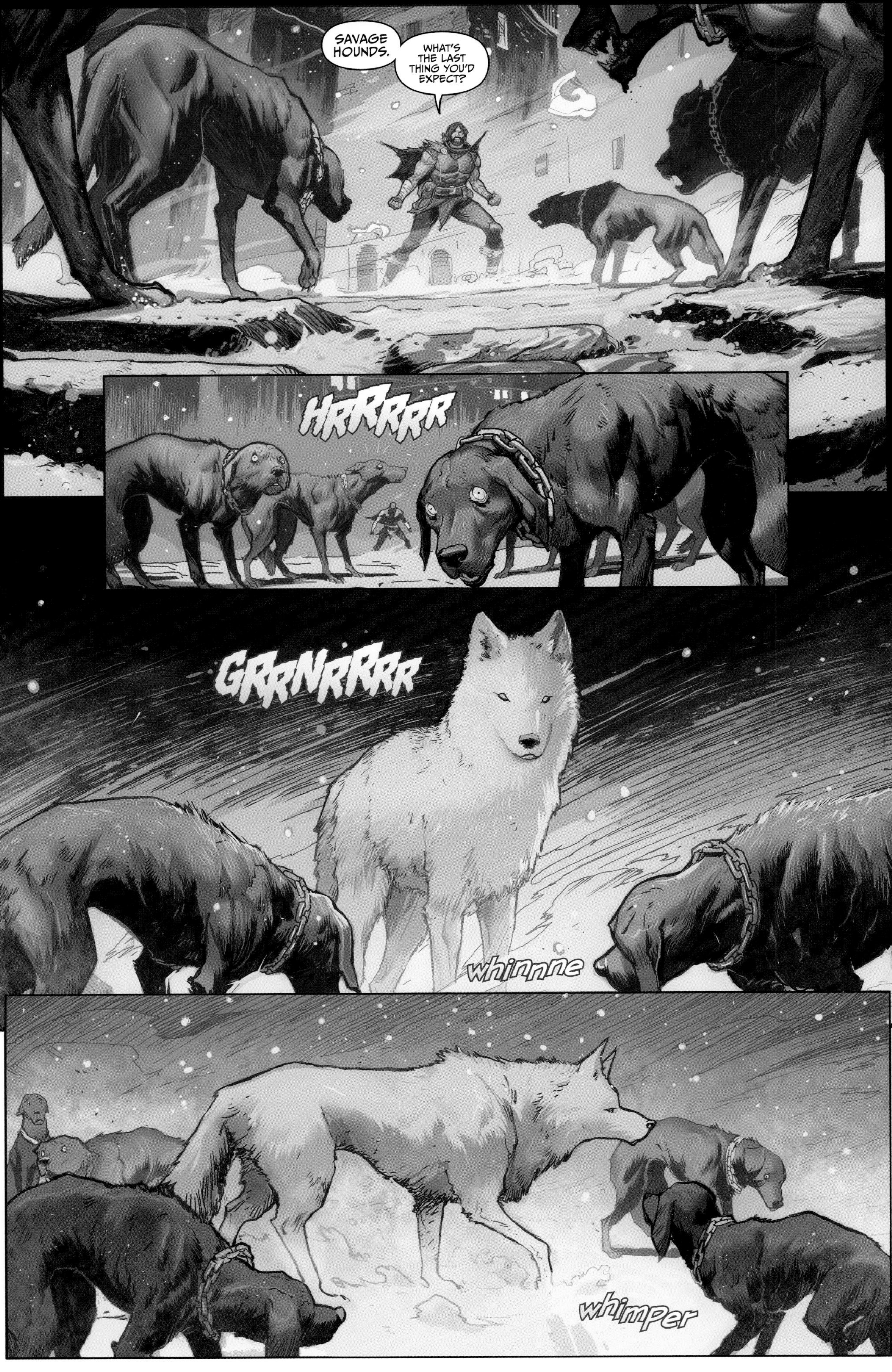
SAVAGE HOUNDS.
WHAT'S THE LAST THING YOU'D EXPECT?
HRRRRR
GRRNRRRR
whinnne
whimper

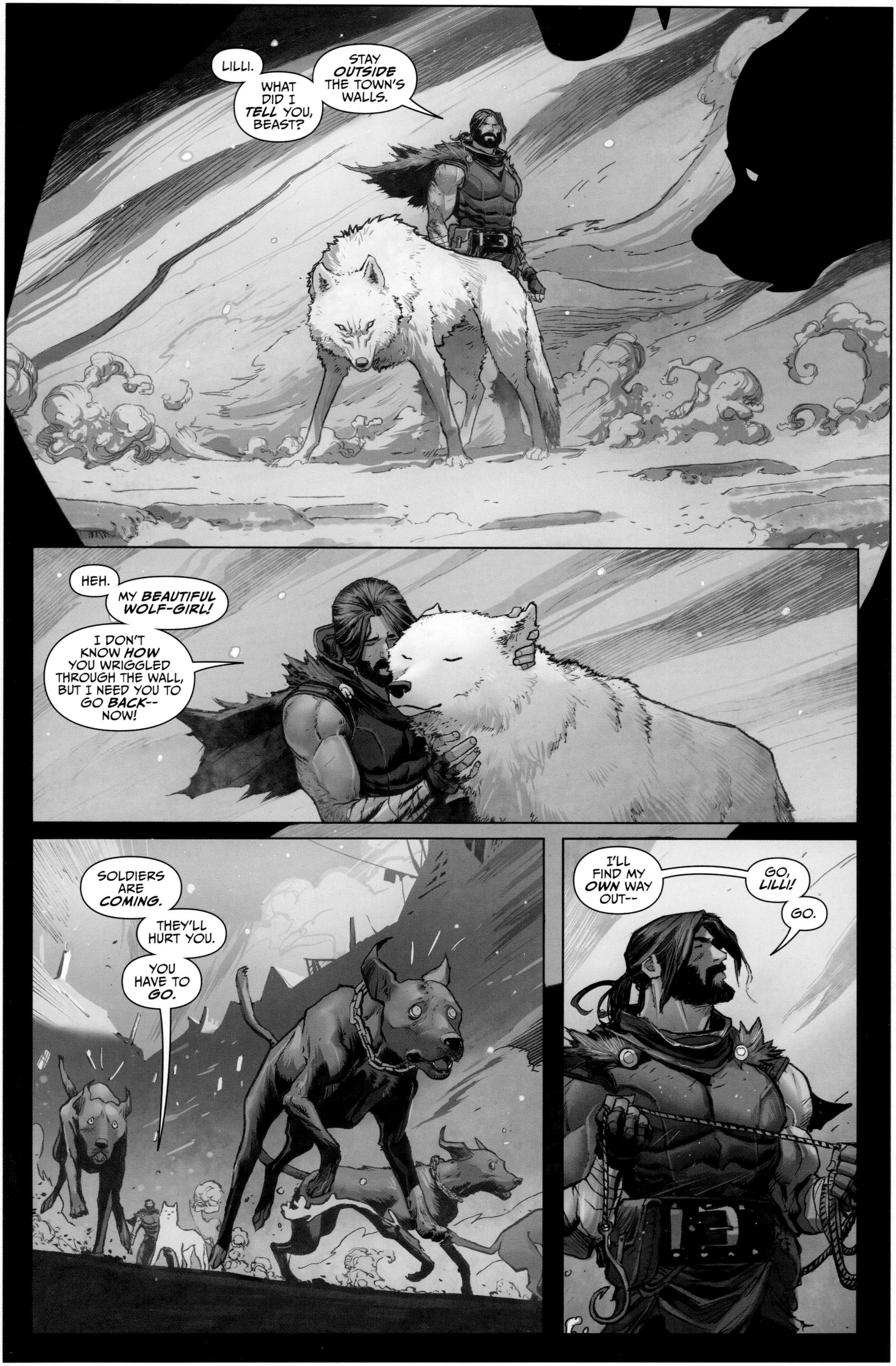
LILLI.
WHAT DID I TELL YOU, BEAST?
STAY OUTSIDE THE TOWN'S WALLS.
HEH.
MY BEAUTIFUL WOLF-GIRL!
I DON'T KNOW HOW YOU WRIGGLED THROUGH THE WALL, BUT I NEED YOU TO GO BACK-- NOW!
SOLDIERS ARE COMING.
THEY'LL HURT YOU.
YOU HAVE TO GO.
I'LL FIND MY OWN WAY OUT--
GO, LILLI!
GO.

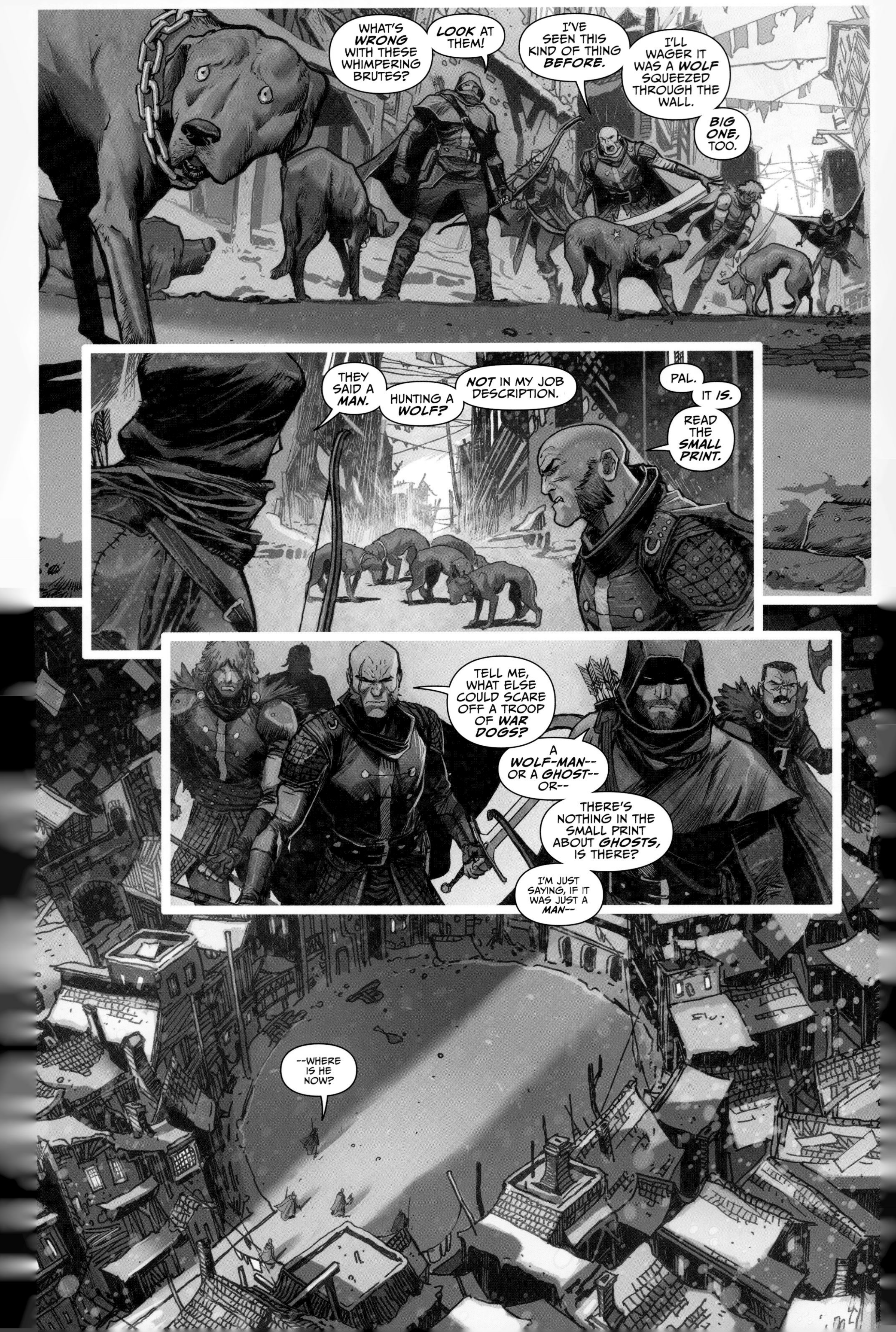

WHAT'S WRONG WITH THESE WHIMPERING BRUTES?
LOOK AT THEM!
I'VE SEEN THIS KIND OF THING BEFORE.
I'LL WAGER IT WAS A WOLF SQUEEZED THROUGH THE WALL.
BIG ONE, TOO.
THEY SAID A MAN.
HUNTING A WOLF?
NOT IN MY JOB DESCRIPTION.
PAL.
IT IS.
READ THE SMALL PRINT.
TELL ME, WHAT ELSE COULD SCARE OFF A TROOP OF WAR DOGS?
A WOLF-MAN-- OR A GHOST-- OR--
THERE'S NOTHING IN THE SMALL PRINT ABOUT GHOSTS, IS THERE?
I'M JUST SAYING, IF IT WAS JUST A MAN--
--WHERE IS HE NOW?

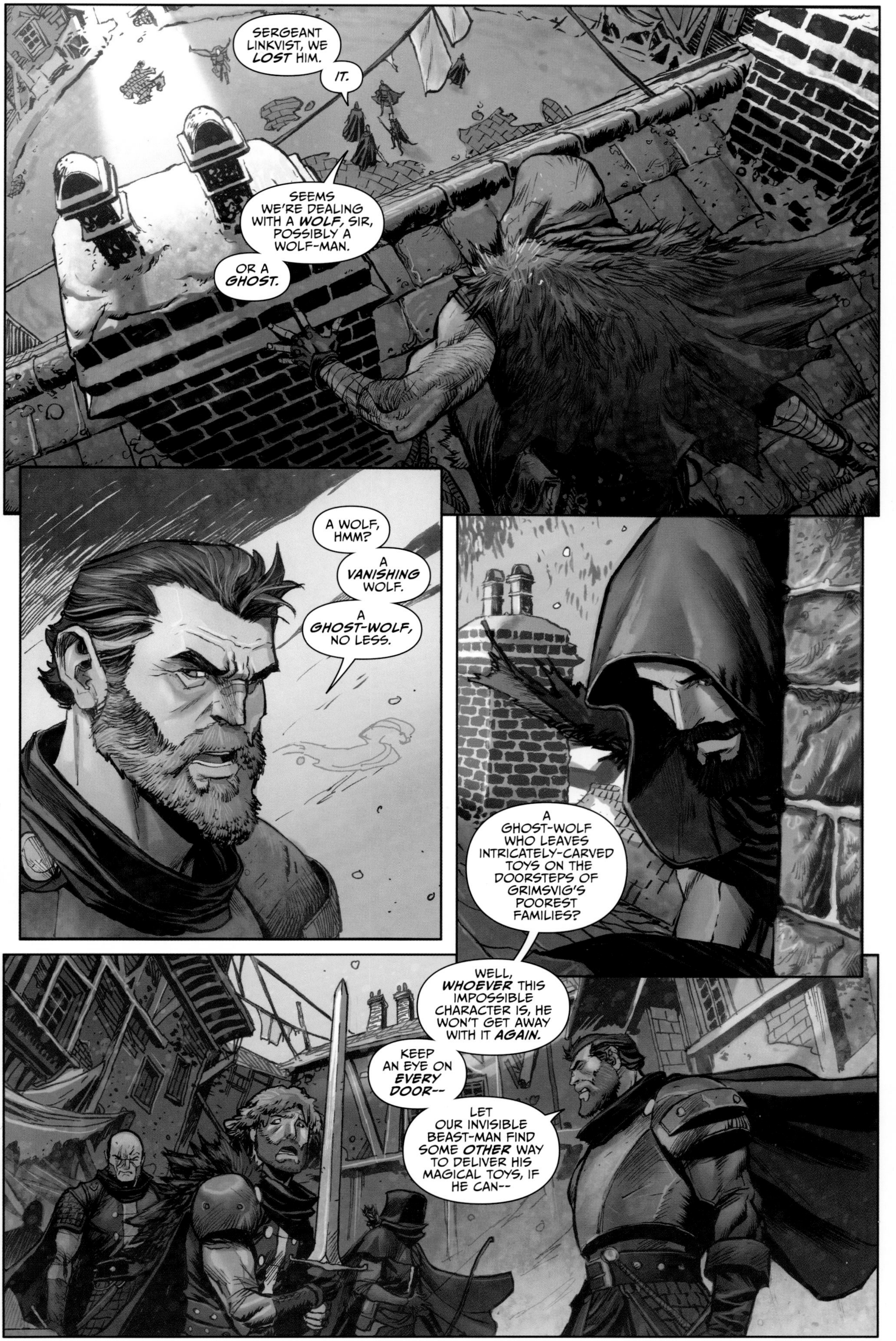
SERGEANT LINKVIST, WE *LOST* HIM.
IT.
SEEMS WE'RE DEALING WITH A *WOLF,* SIR, POSSIBLY A WOLF-MAN.
OR A *GHOST.*
A WOLF, HMM?
A *VANISHING* WOLF.
A *GHOST-WOLF,* NO LESS.
A GHOST-WOLF WHO LEAVES INTRICATELY-CARVED TOYS ON THE DOORSTEPS OF GRIMSVIG'S POOREST FAMILIES?
WELL, *WHOEVER* THIS IMPOSSIBLE CHARACTER IS, HE WON'T GET AWAY WITH IT *AGAIN.*
KEEP AN EYE ON *EVERY DOOR*--
LET OUR INVISIBLE BEAST-MAN FIND SOME *OTHER* WAY TO DELIVER HIS MAGICAL TOYS, IF HE CAN--

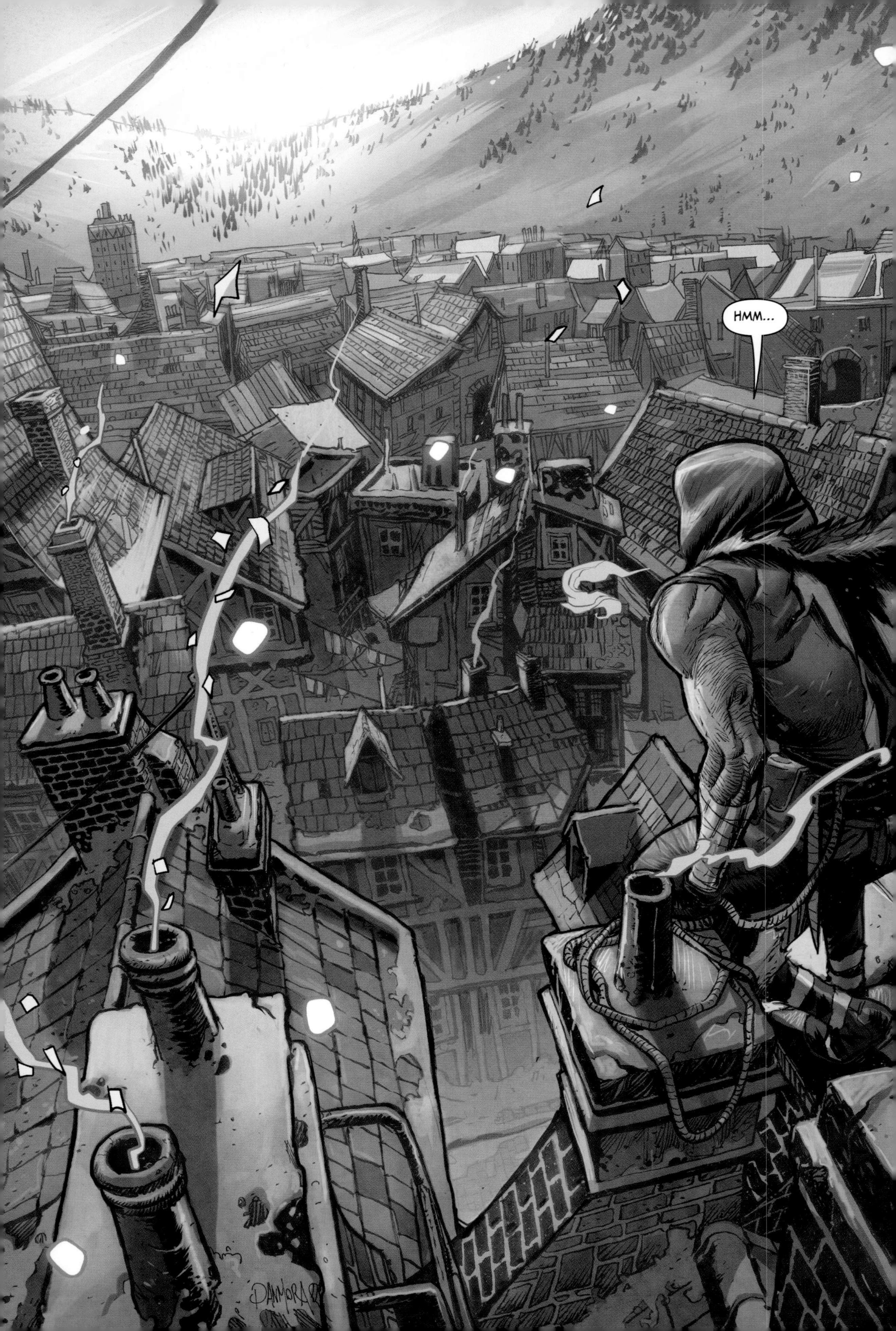
HMM...
DANMORA 08

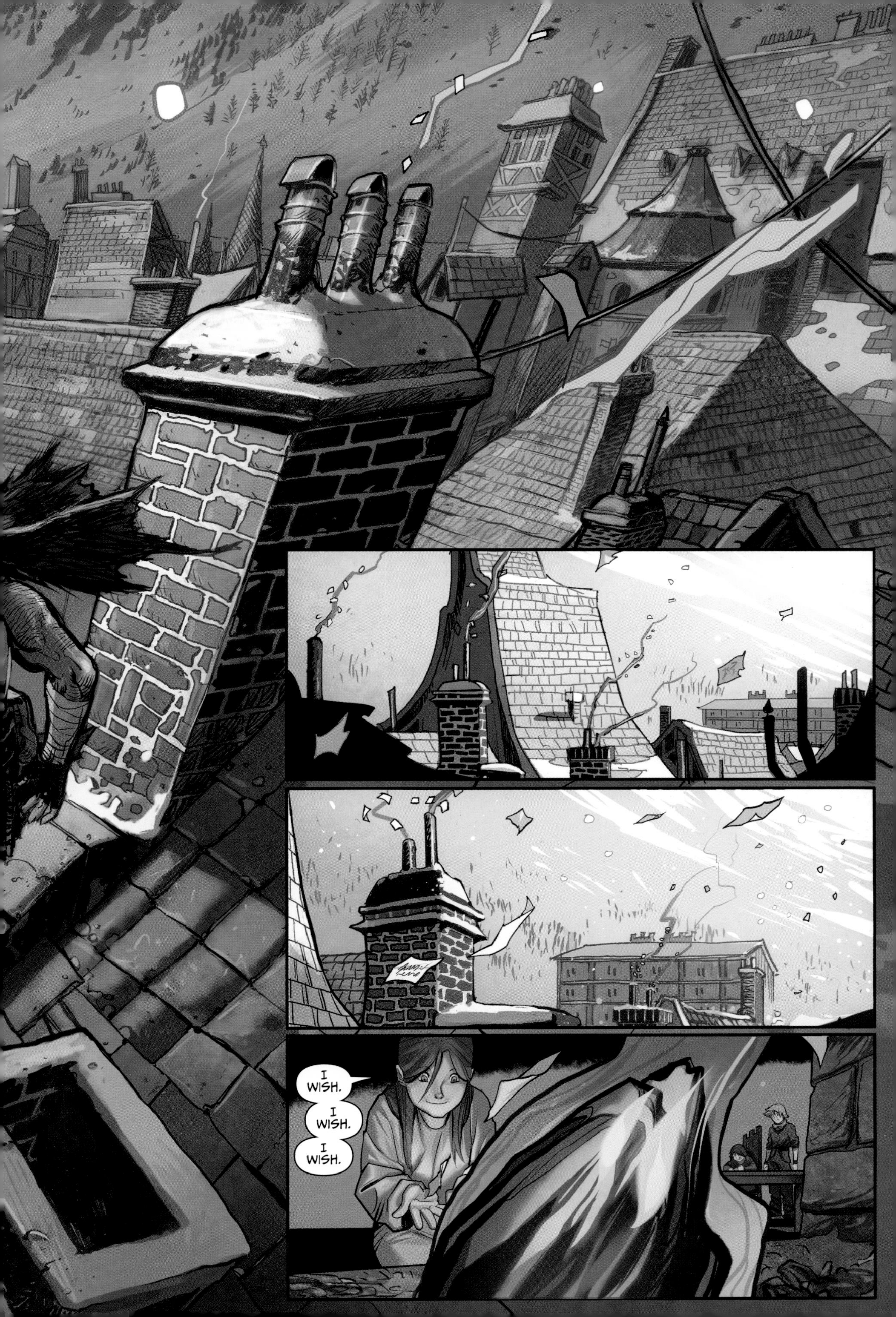
I WISH.
I WISH.
I WISH.

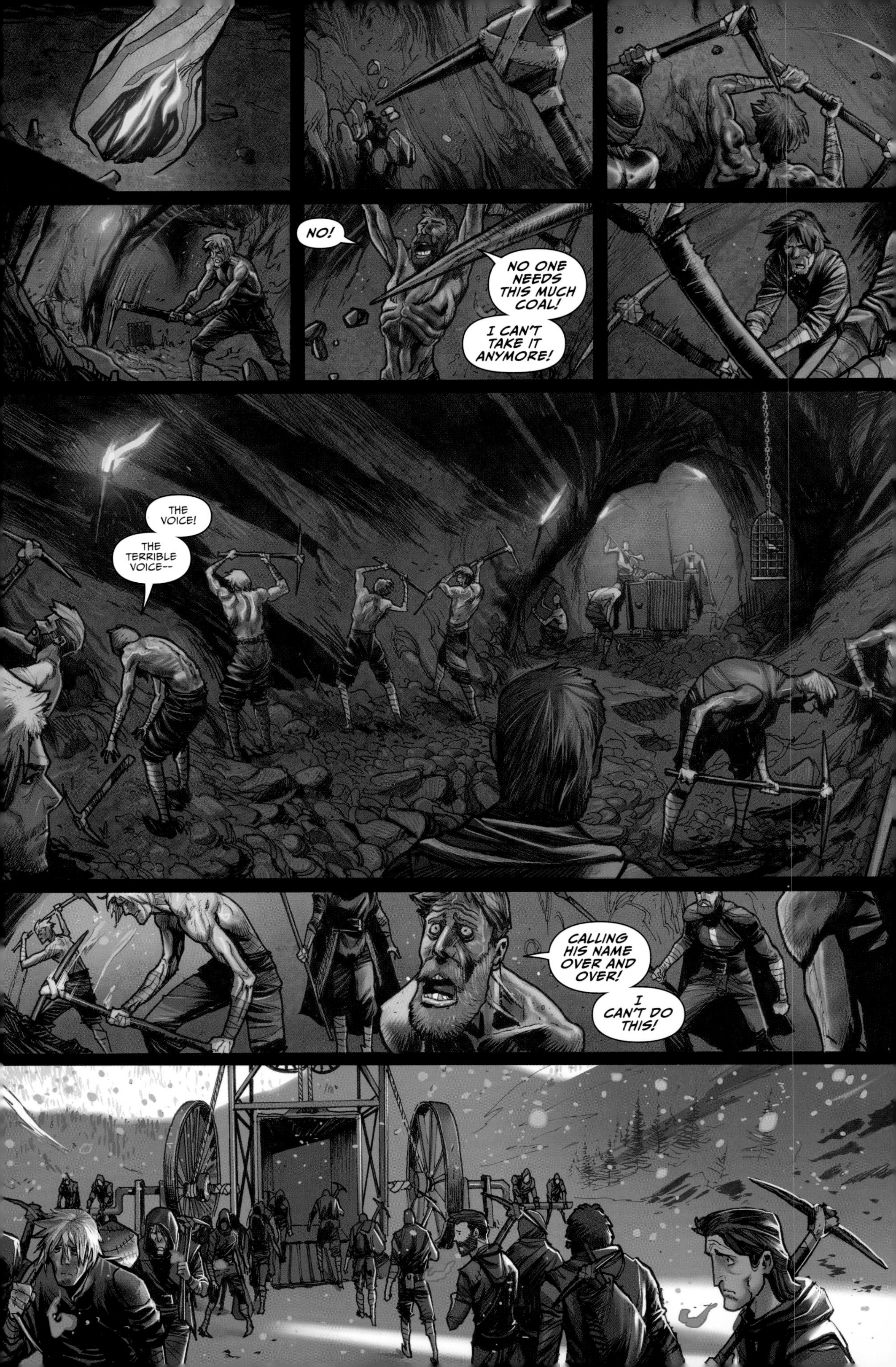
NO!
NO ONE NEEDS THIS MUCH COAL!
I CAN'T TAKE IT ANYMORE!
THE VOICE!
THE TERRIBLE VOICE--
CALLING HIS NAME OVER AND OVER!
I CAN'T DO THIS!

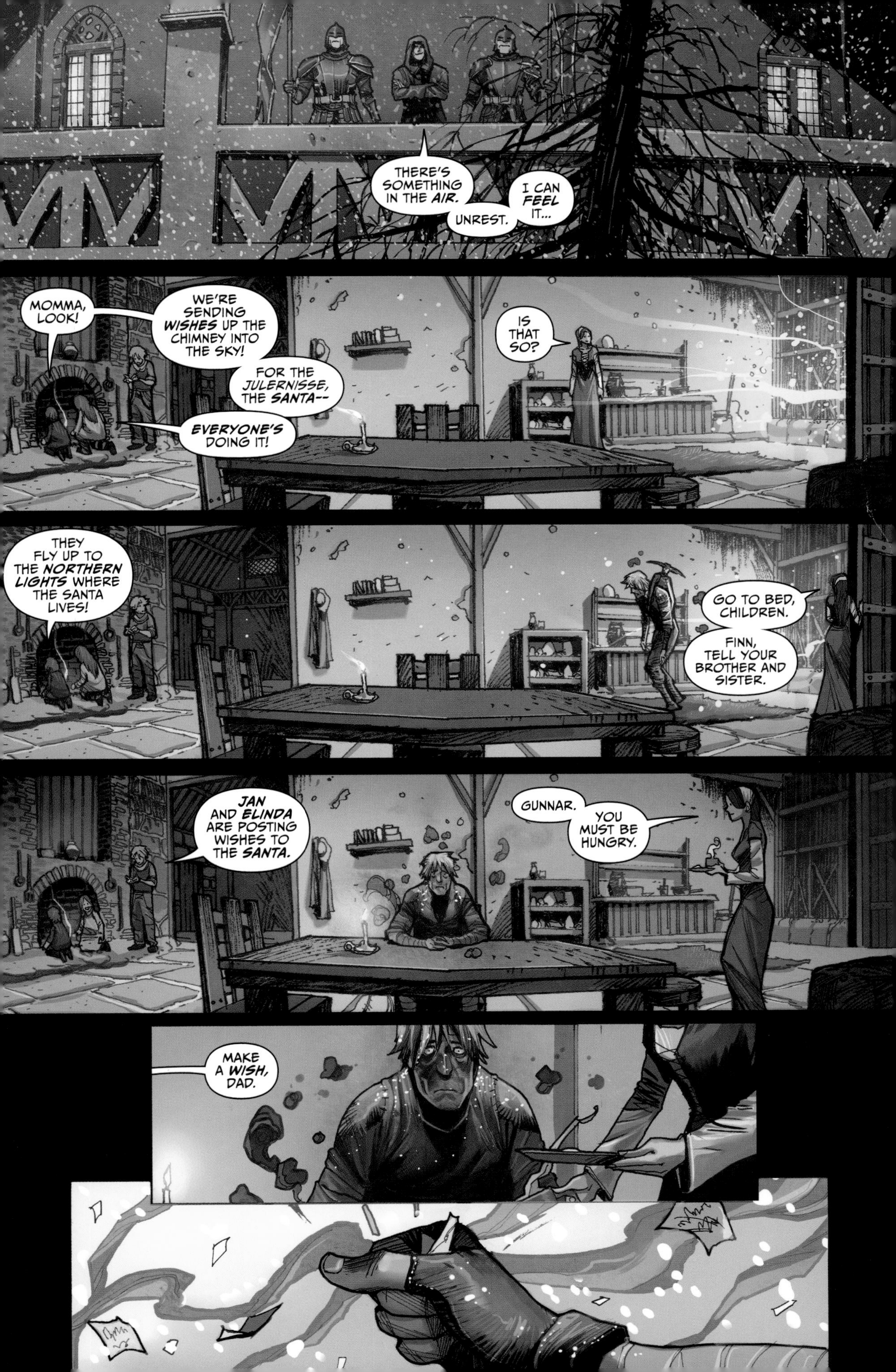
THERE'S SOMETHING IN THE AIR.
UNREST.
I CAN FEEL IT...
MOMMA, LOOK!
WE'RE SENDING WISHES UP THE CHIMNEY INTO THE SKY!
FOR THE JULERNISSE, THE SANTA--
EVERYONE'S DOING IT!
IS THAT SO?
THEY FLY UP TO THE NORTHERN LIGHTS WHERE THE SANTA LIVES!
GO TO BED, CHILDREN.
FINN, TELL YOUR BROTHER AND SISTER.
JAN AND ELINDA ARE POSTING WISHES TO THE SANTA.
GUNNAR.
YOU MUST BE HUNGRY.
MAKE A WISH, DAD.

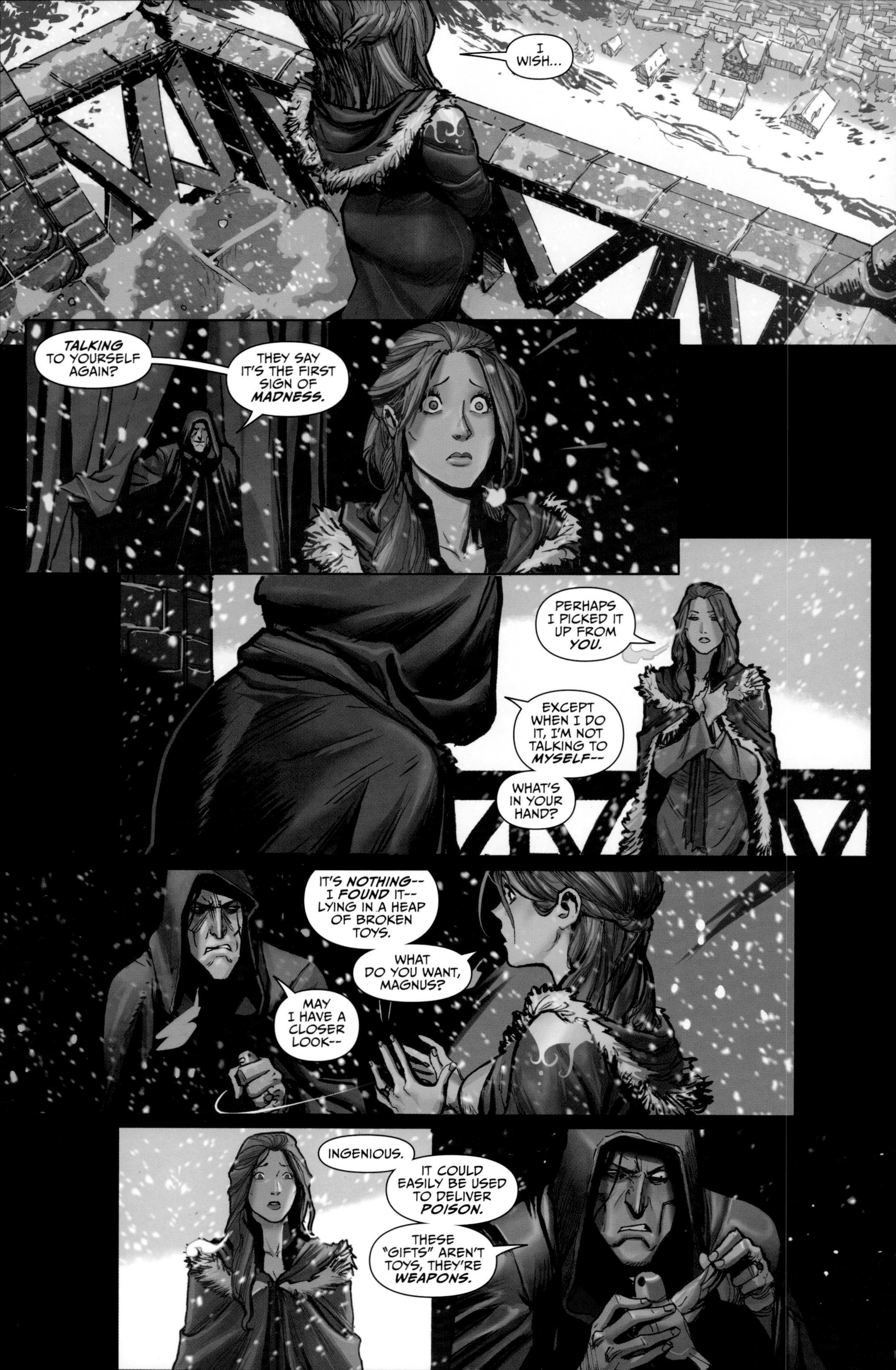
I WISH...
TALKING TO YOURSELF AGAIN?
THEY SAY IT'S THE FIRST SIGN OF MADNESS.
PERHAPS I PICKED IT UP FROM YOU.
EXCEPT WHEN I DO IT, I'M NOT TALKING TO MYSELF--
WHAT'S IN YOUR HAND?
IT'S NOTHING-- I FOUND IT-- LYING IN A HEAP OF BROKEN TOYS.
WHAT DO YOU WANT, MAGNUS?
MAY I HAVE A CLOSER LOOK--
INGENIOUS.
IT COULD EASILY BE USED TO DELIVER POISON.
THESE "GIFTS" AREN'T TOYS, THEY'RE WEAPONS.

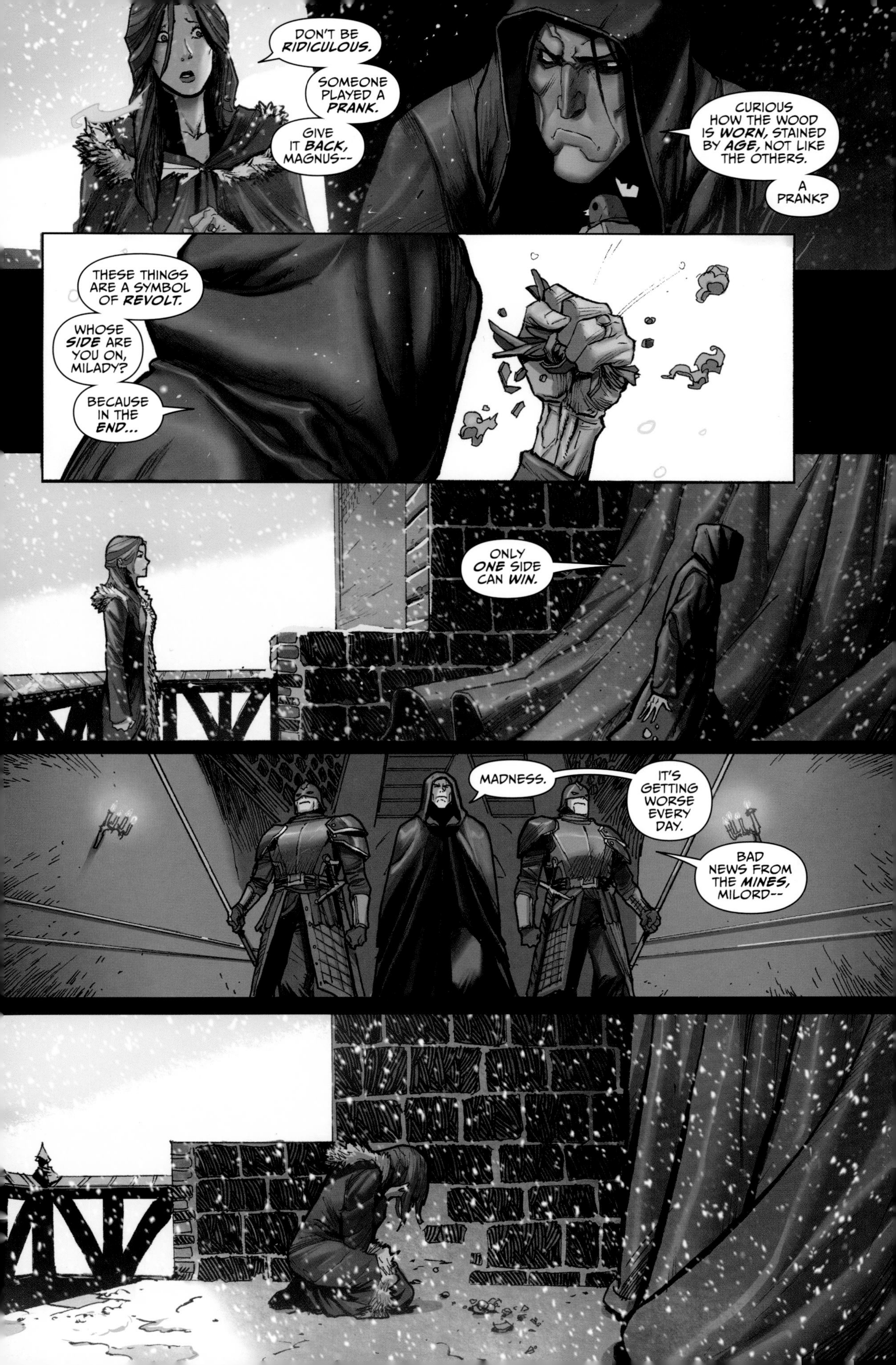
DON'T BE RIDICULOUS.
SOMEONE PLAYED A PRANK.
GIVE IT BACK, MAGNUS--
CURIOUS HOW THE WOOD IS WORN, STAINED BY AGE, NOT LIKE THE OTHERS.
A PRANK?
THESE THINGS ARE A SYMBOL OF REVOLT.
WHOSE SIDE ARE YOU ON, MILADY?
BECAUSE IN THE END...
ONLY ONE SIDE CAN WIN.
MADNESS.
IT'S GETTING WORSE EVERY DAY.
BAD NEWS FROM THE MINES, MILORD--

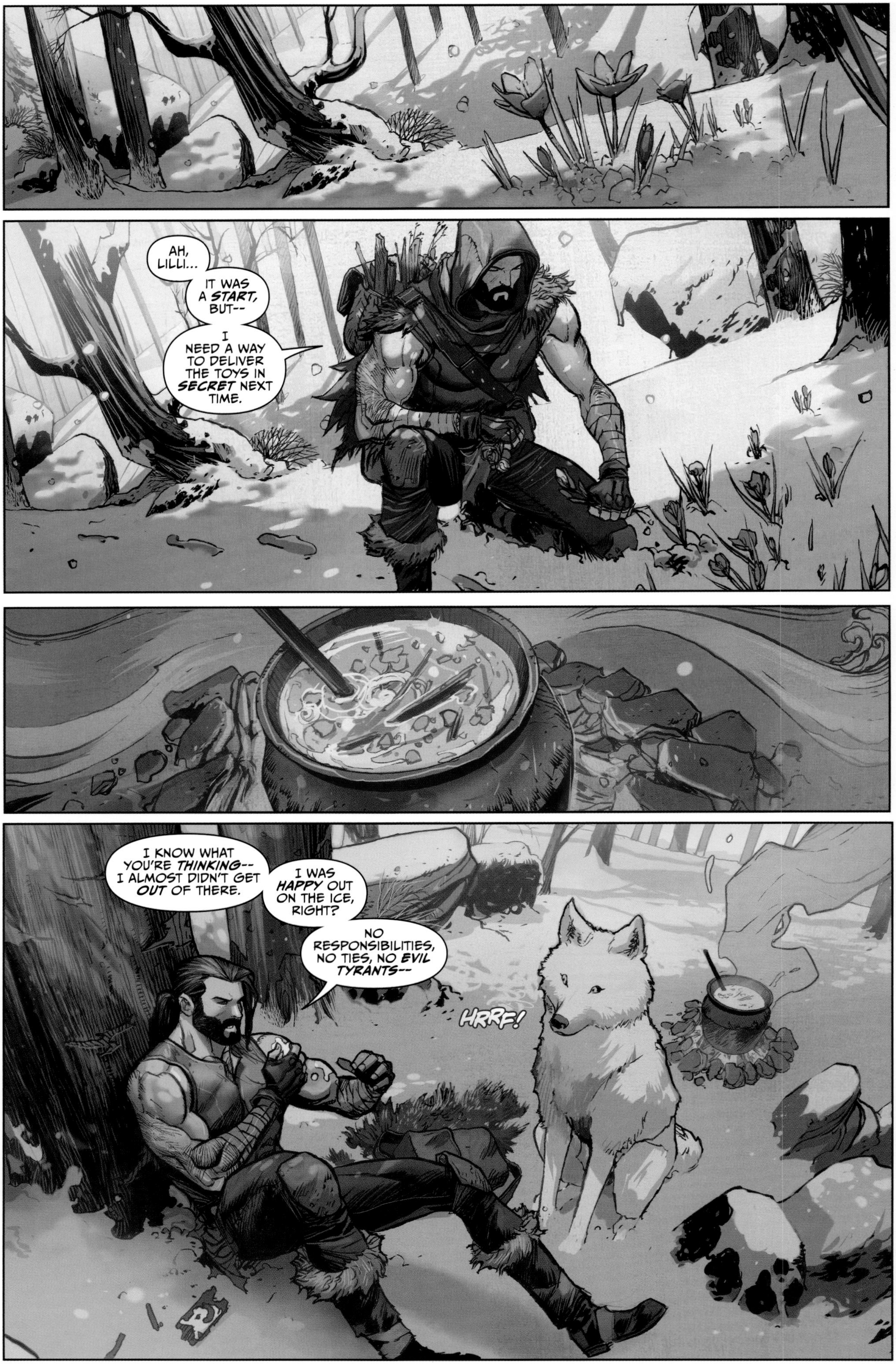
AH, LILLI...
IT WAS A START, BUT--
I NEED A WAY TO DELIVER THE TOYS IN SECRET NEXT TIME.
I KNOW WHAT YOU'RE THINKING-- I ALMOST DIDN'T GET OUT OF THERE.
I WAS HAPPY OUT ON THE ICE, RIGHT?
NO RESPONSIBILITIES, NO TIES, NO EVIL TYRANTS--
HRRF!

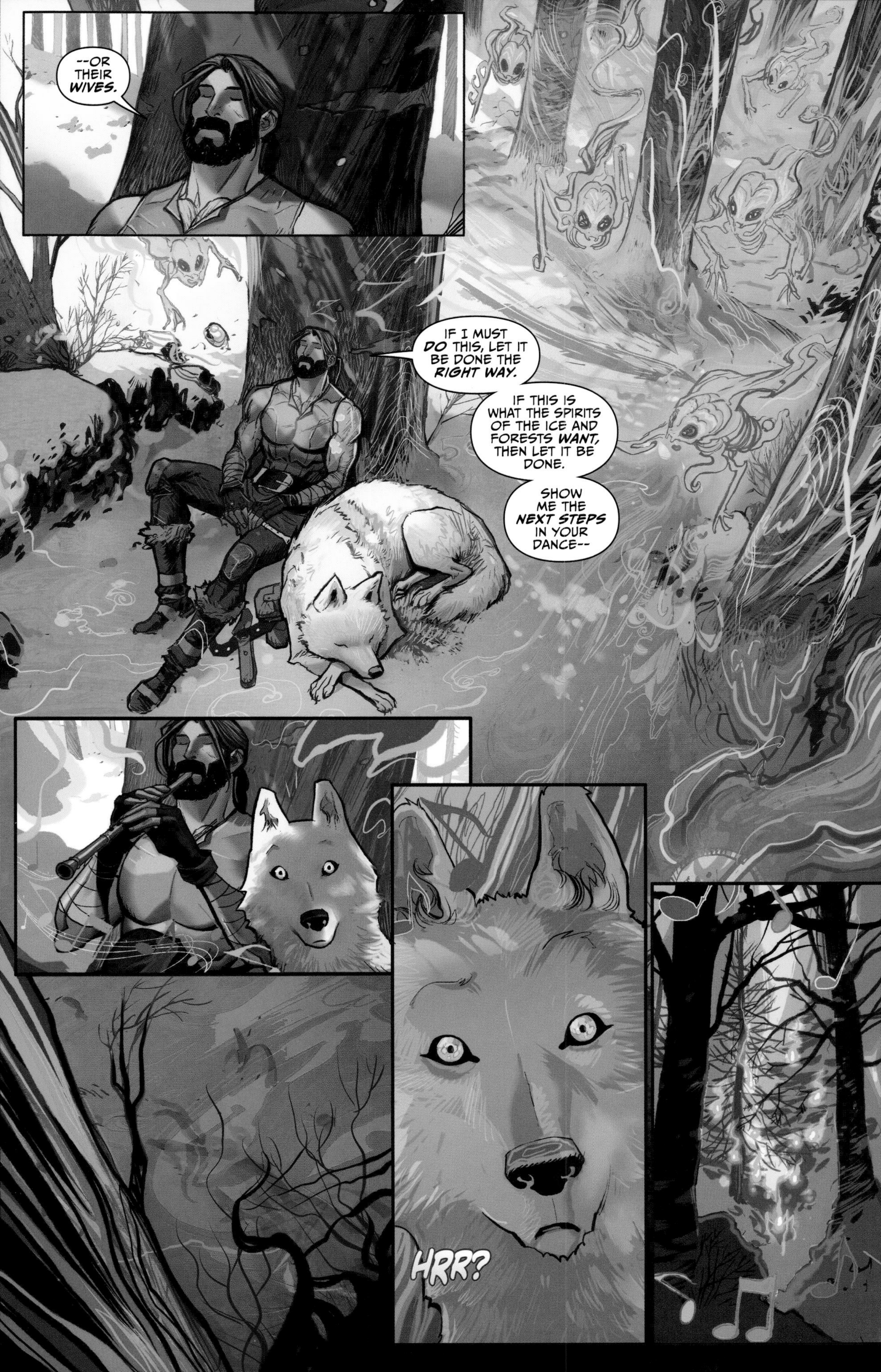
--OR THEIR *WIVES.*
IF I MUST *DO* THIS, LET IT BE DONE THE *RIGHT WAY.*
IF THIS IS WHAT THE SPIRITS OF THE ICE AND FORESTS *WANT,* THEN LET IT BE DONE.
SHOW ME THE *NEXT STEPS* IN YOUR DANCE--
HRR?

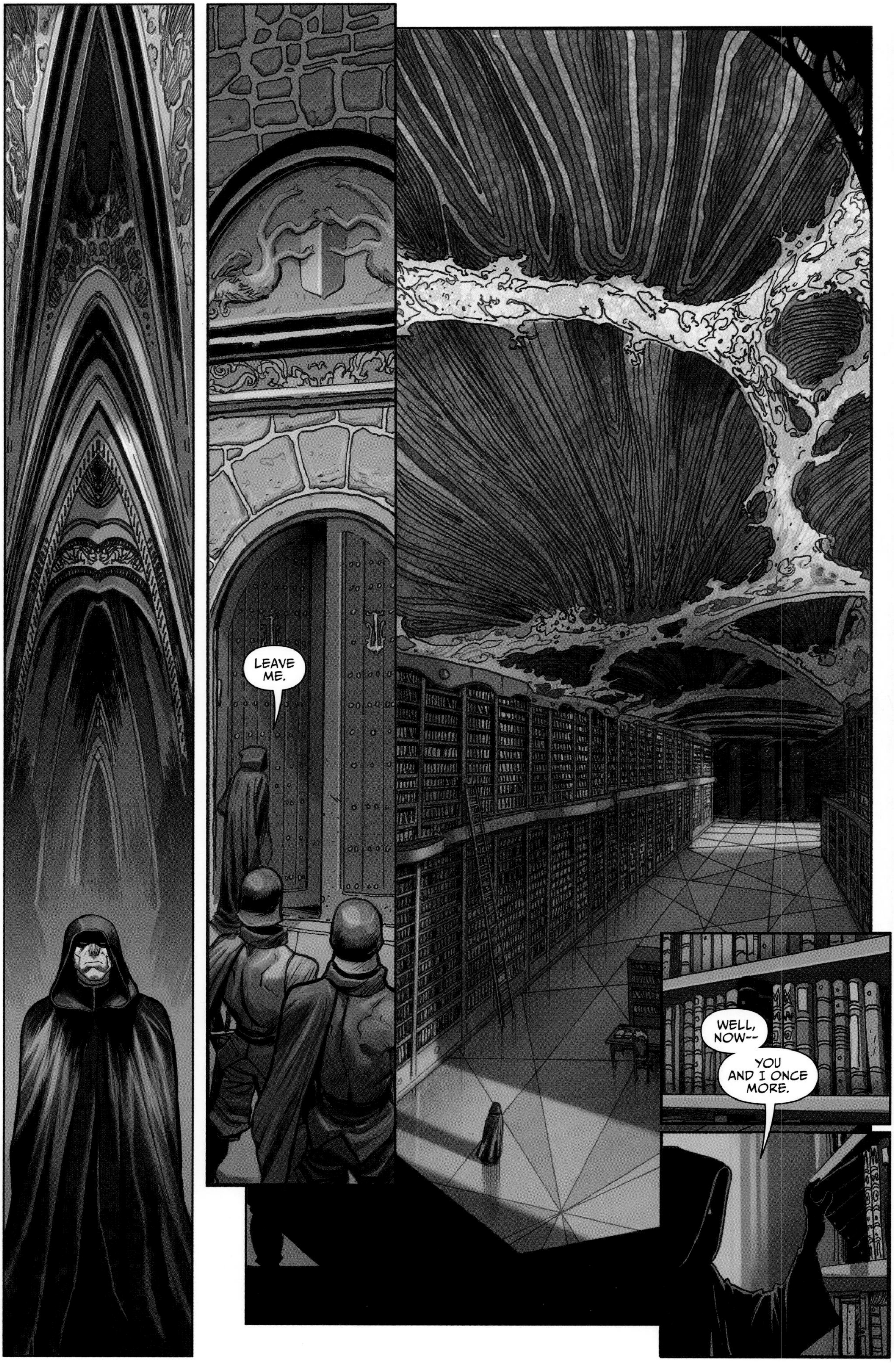
LEAVE ME.
WELL, NOW--
YOU AND I ONCE MORE.

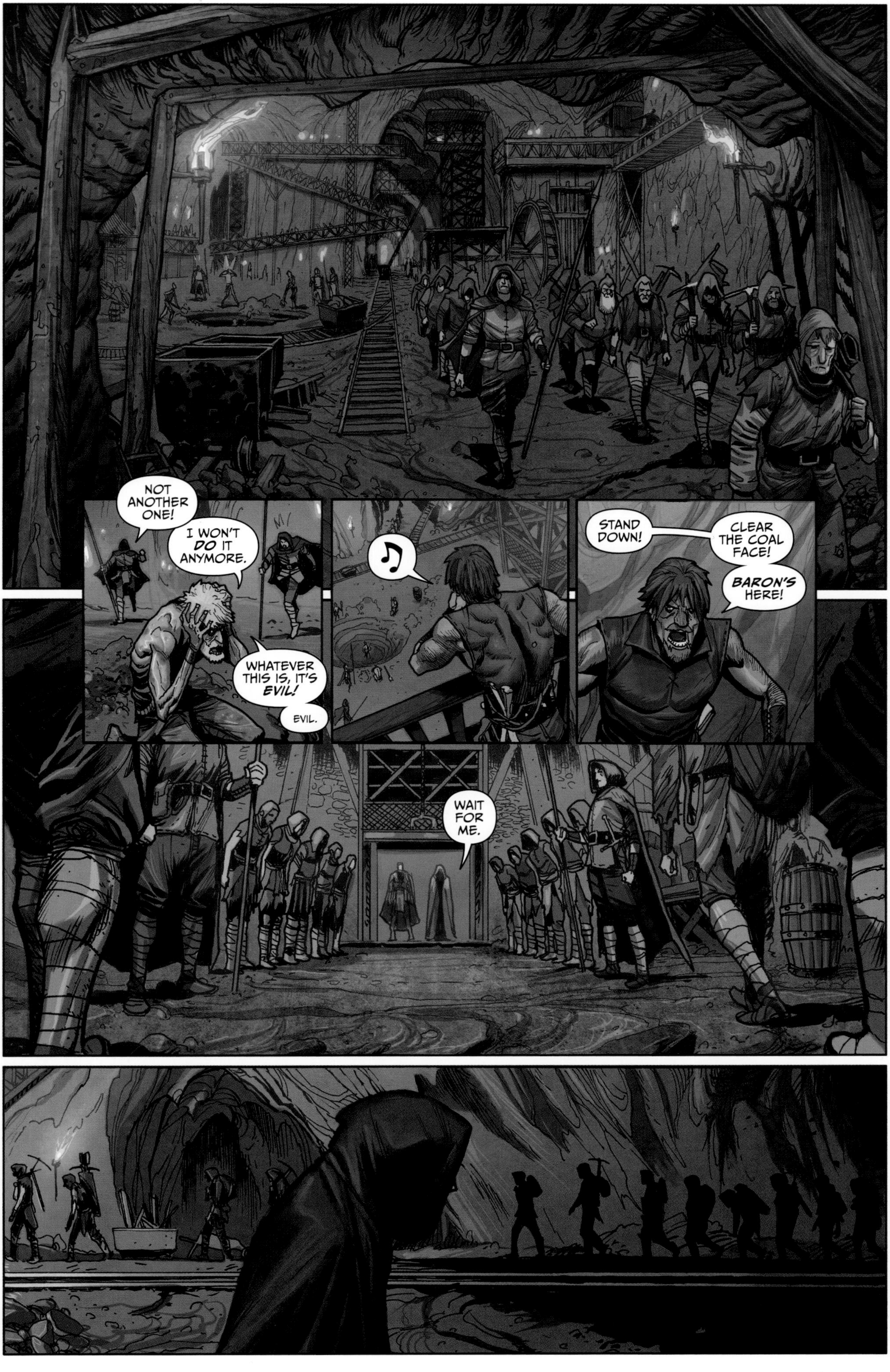
NOT ANOTHER ONE!
I WON'T DO IT ANYMORE.
WHATEVER THIS IS, IT'S EVIL!
EVIL.
♫
STAND DOWN!
CLEAR THE COAL FACE!
BARON'S HERE!
WAIT FOR ME.

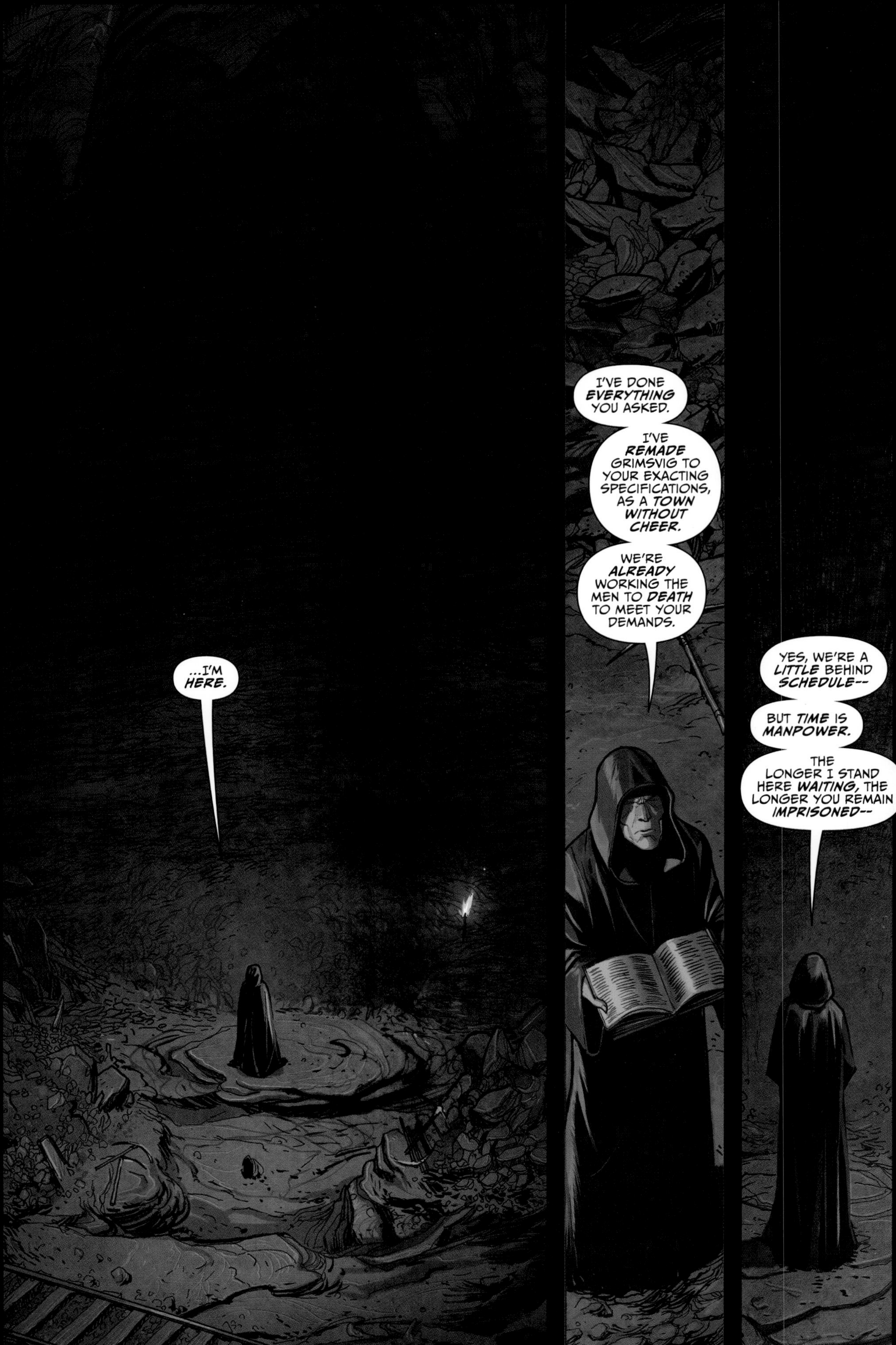
...I'M HERE.
I'VE DONE EVERYTHING YOU ASKED.
I'VE REMADE GRIMSVIG TO YOUR EXACTING SPECIFICATIONS, AS A TOWN WITHOUT CHEER.
WE'RE ALREADY WORKING THE MEN TO DEATH TO MEET YOUR DEMANDS.
YES, WE'RE A LITTLE BEHIND SCHEDULE--
BUT TIME IS MANPOWER.
THE LONGER I STAND HERE WAITING, THE LONGER YOU REMAIN IMPRISONED--

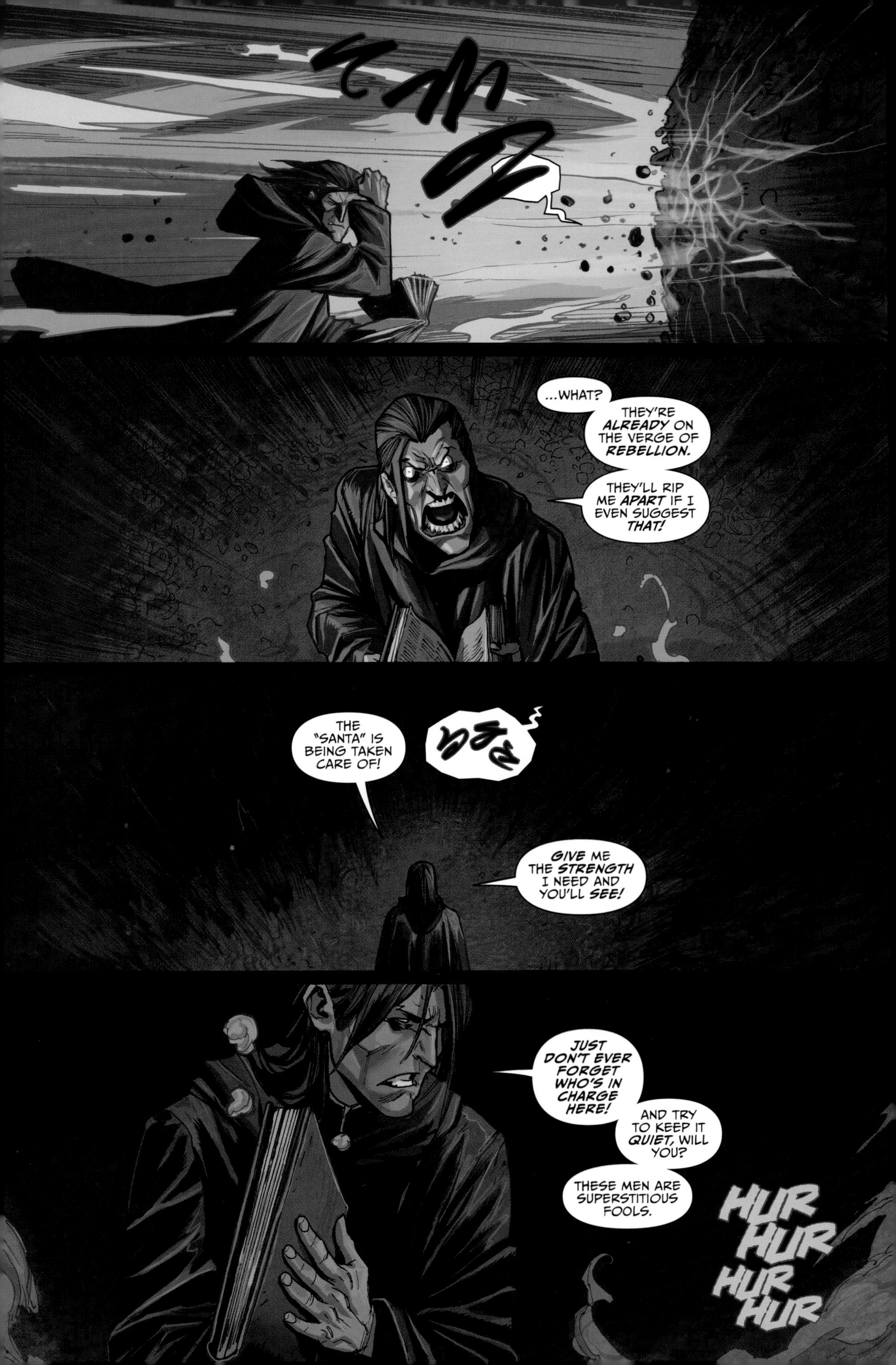
...WHAT?
THEY'RE ALREADY ON THE VERGE OF REBELLION.
THEY'LL RIP ME APART IF I EVEN SUGGEST THAT!
THE "SANTA" IS BEING TAKEN CARE OF!
GIVE ME THE STRENGTH I NEED AND YOU'LL SEE!
JUST DON'T EVER FORGET WHO'S IN CHARGE HERE!
AND TRY TO KEEP IT QUIET, WILL YOU?
THESE MEN ARE SUPERSTITIOUS FOOLS.
HUR HUR HUR HUR

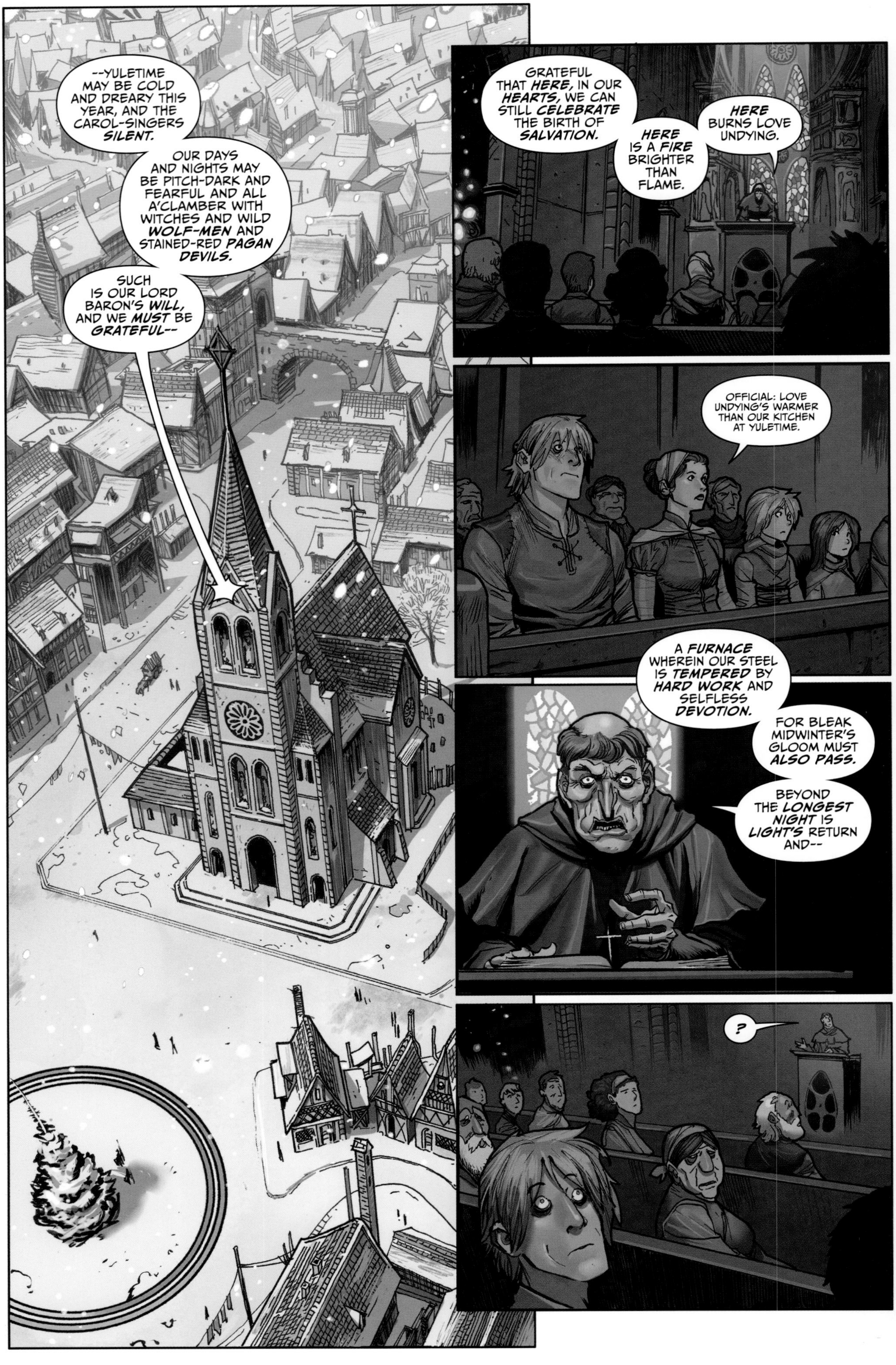
--YULETIME MAY BE COLD AND DREARY THIS YEAR, AND THE CAROL-SINGERS SILENT.
OUR DAYS AND NIGHTS MAY BE PITCH-DARK AND FEARFUL AND ALL A'CLAMBER WITH WITCHES AND WILD WOLF-MEN AND STAINED-RED PAGAN DEVILS.
SUCH IS OUR LORD BARON'S WILL, AND WE MUST BE GRATEFUL--
GRATEFUL THAT HERE, IN OUR HEARTS, WE CAN STILL CELEBRATE THE BIRTH OF SALVATION.
HERE IS A FIRE BRIGHTER THAN FLAME.
HERE BURNS LOVE UNDYING.
OFFICIAL: LOVE UNDYING'S WARMER THAN OUR KITCHEN AT YULETIME.
A FURNACE WHEREIN OUR STEEL IS TEMPERED BY HARD WORK AND SELFLESS DEVOTION.
FOR BLEAK MIDWINTER'S GLOOM MUST ALSO PASS.
BEYOND THE LONGEST NIGHT IS LIGHT'S RETURN AND--
?

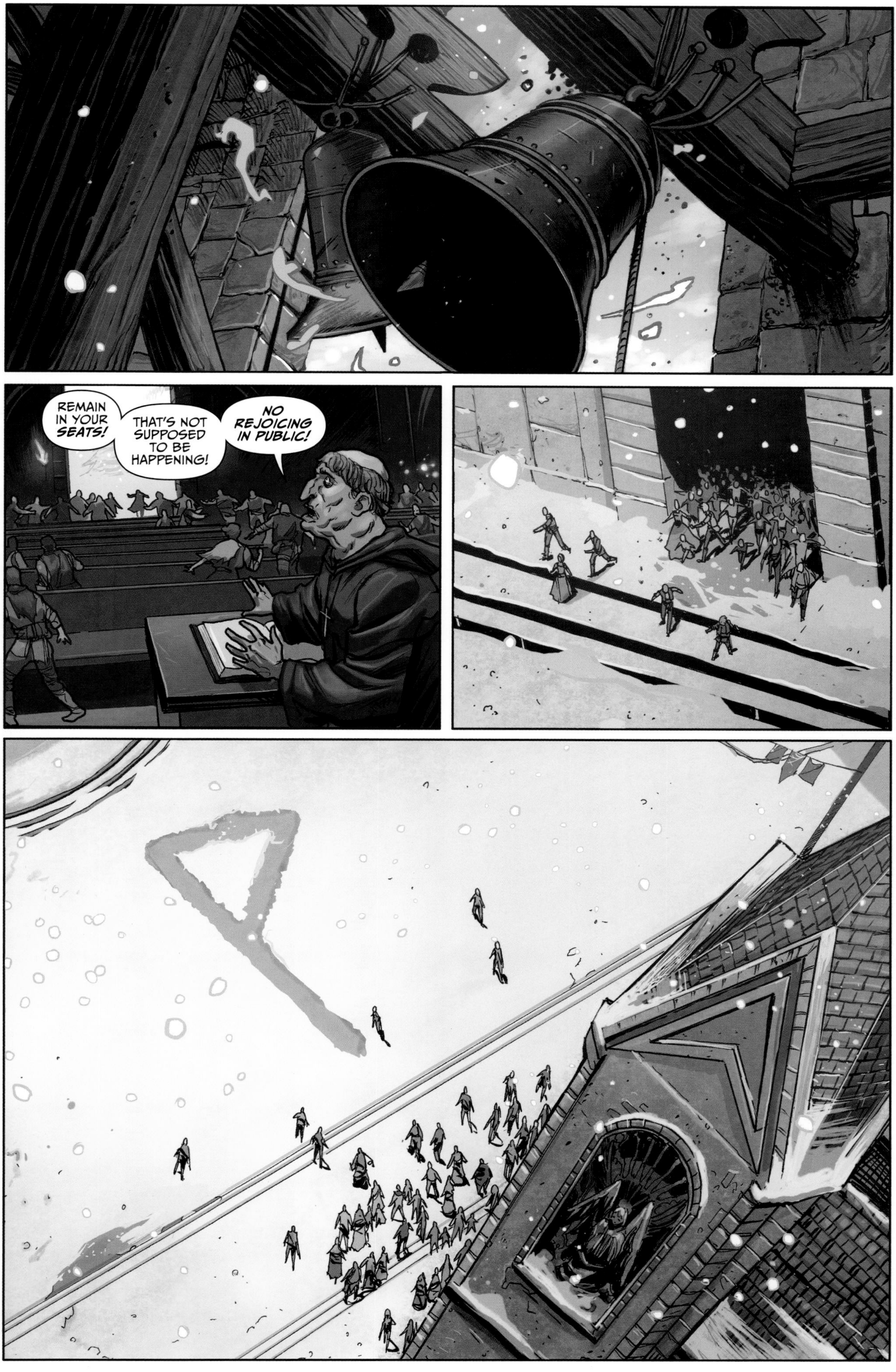
REMAIN IN YOUR SEATS!
THAT'S NOT SUPPOSED TO BE HAPPENING!
NO REJOICING IN PUBLIC!

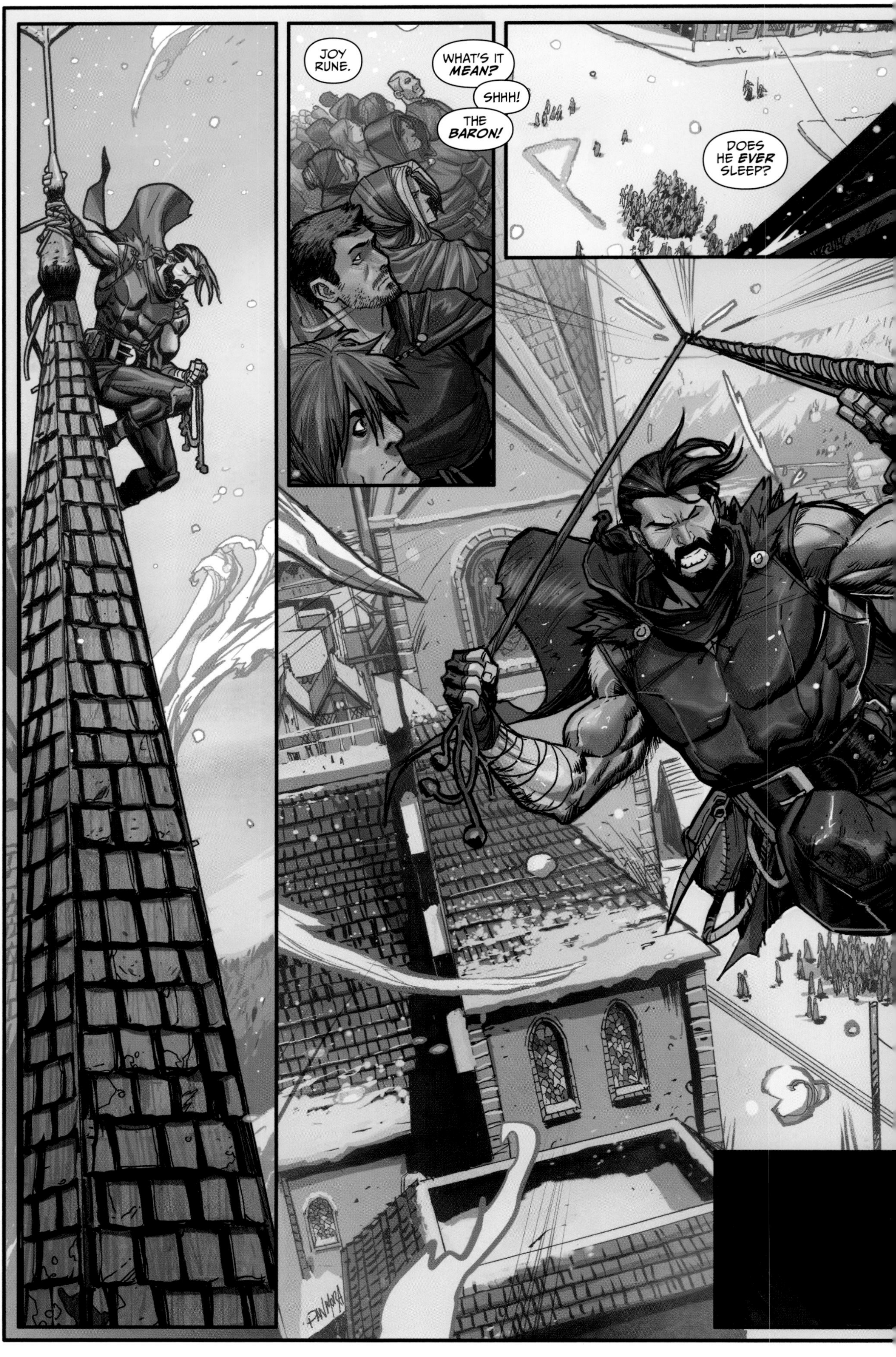
JOY RUNE.
WHAT'S IT *MEAN?*
SHHH!
THE *BARON!*
DOES HE *EVER* SLEEP?

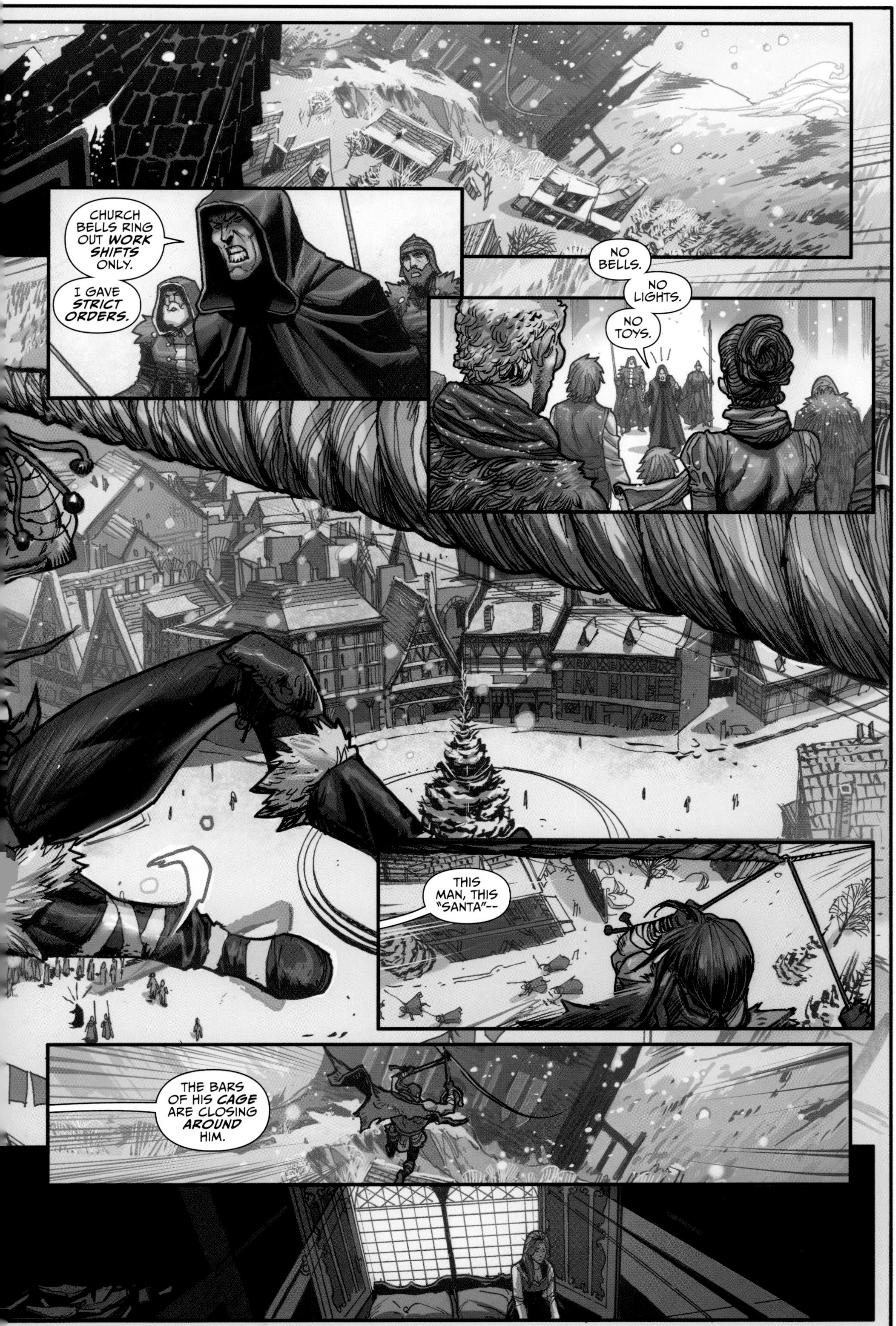
CHURCH BELLS RING OUT WORK SHIFTS ONLY.
I GAVE STRICT ORDERS.
NO BELLS.
NO LIGHTS.
NO TOYS.
THIS MAN, THIS "SANTA"--
THE BARS OF HIS CAGE ARE CLOSING AROUND HIM.

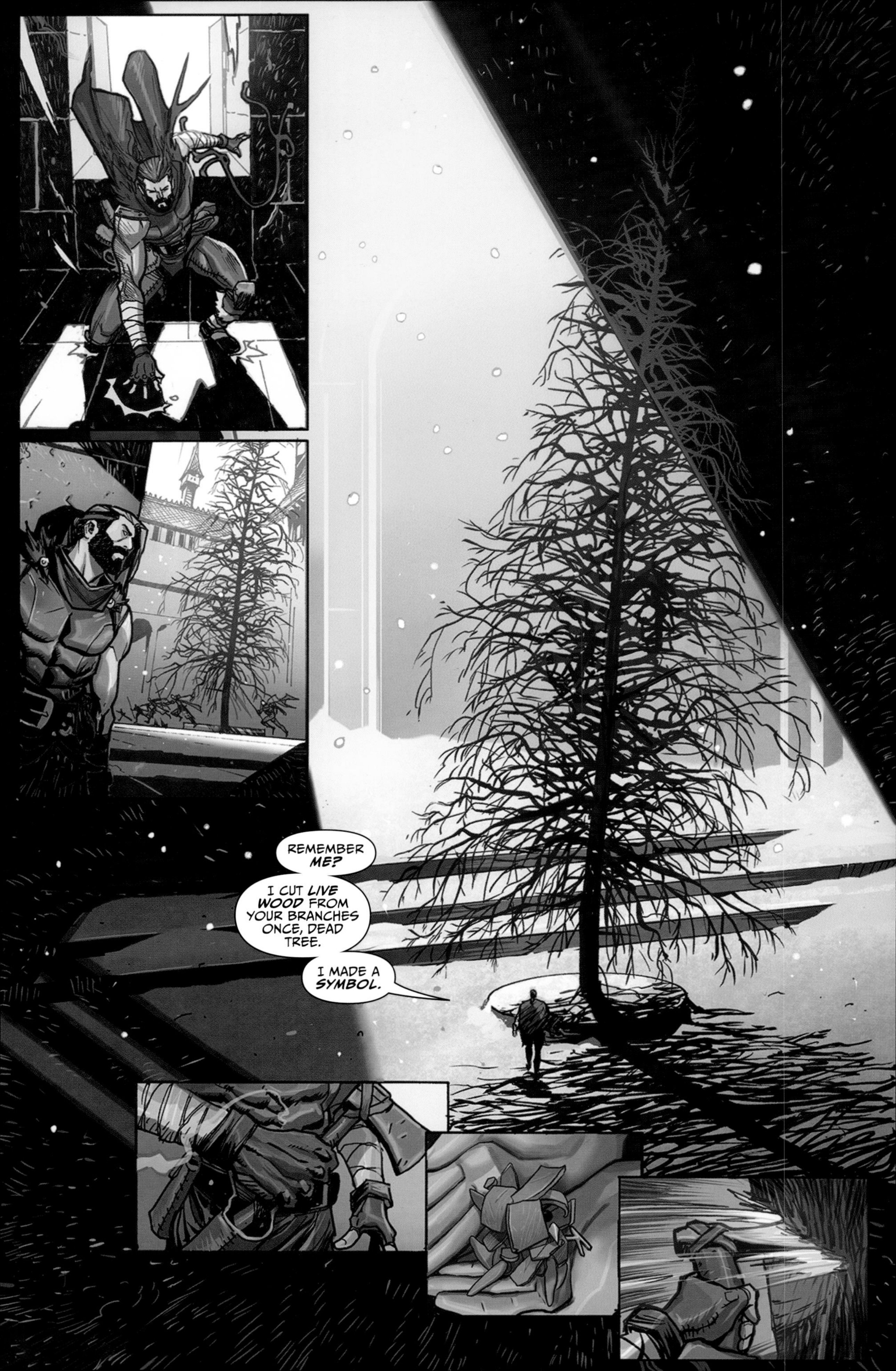
REMEMBER ME?
I CUT LIVE WOOD FROM YOUR BRANCHES ONCE, DEAD TREE.
I MADE A SYMBOL.

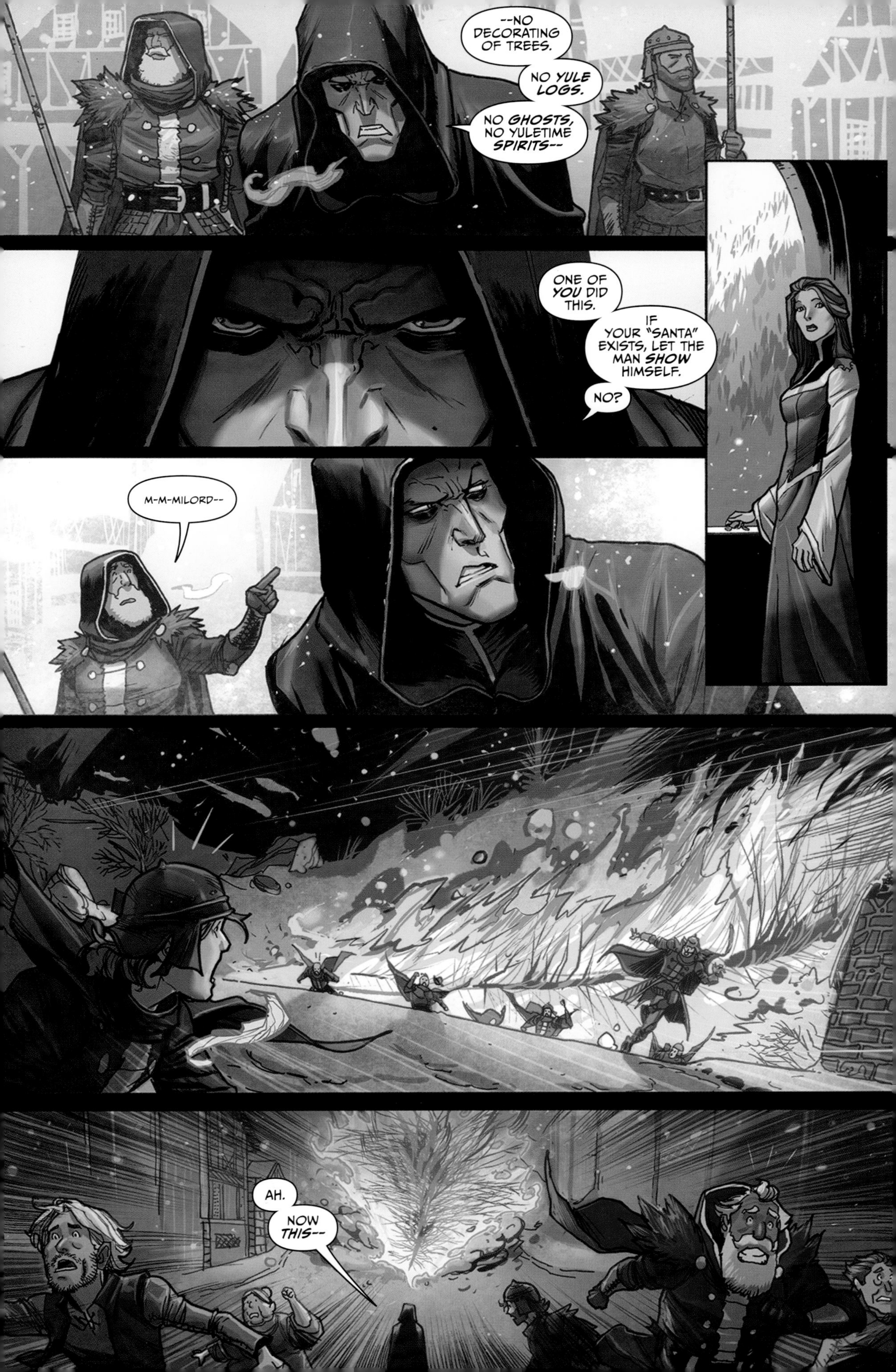
--NO DECORATING OF TREES.
NO YULE LOGS.
NO GHOSTS, NO YULETIME SPIRITS--
ONE OF YOU DID THIS.
IF YOUR "SANTA" EXISTS, LET THE MAN SHOW HIMSELF.
NO?
M-M-MILORD--
AH.
NOW THIS--

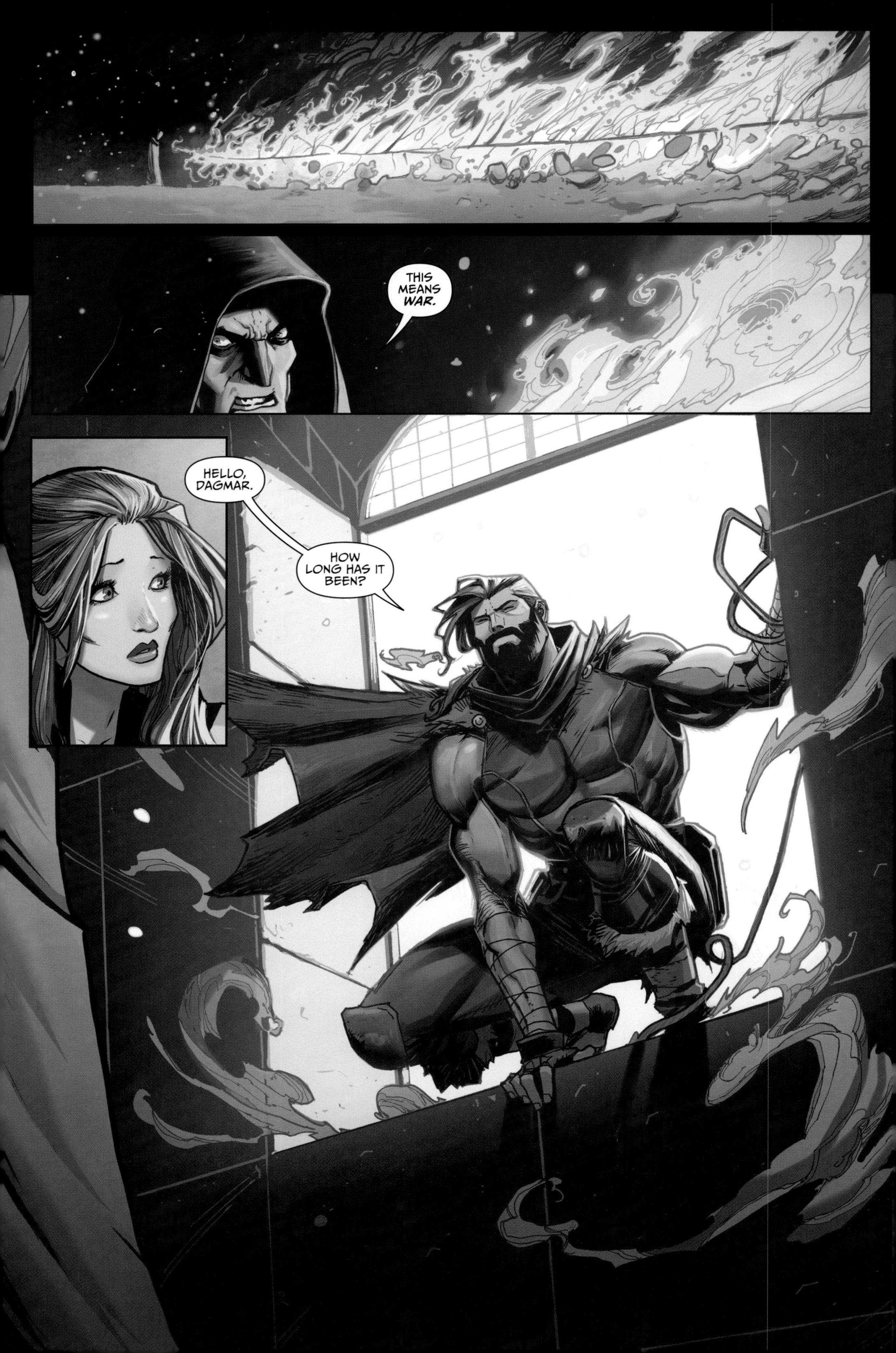
THIS MEANS WAR.
HELLO, DAGMAR.
HOW LONG HAS IT BEEN?

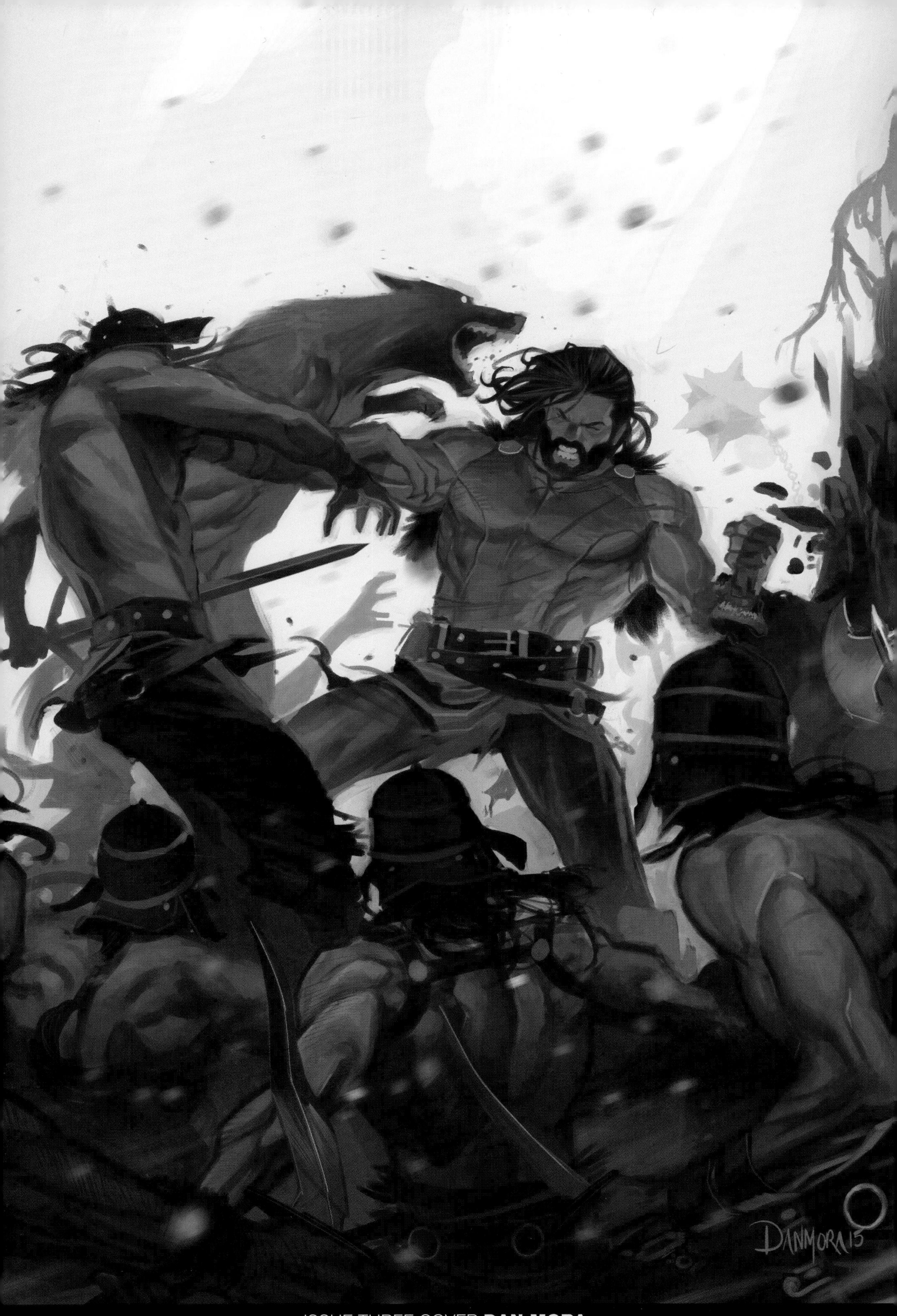
DANMORA 15
ISSUE THREE COVER **DAN MORA**

CHAPTER
FOUR

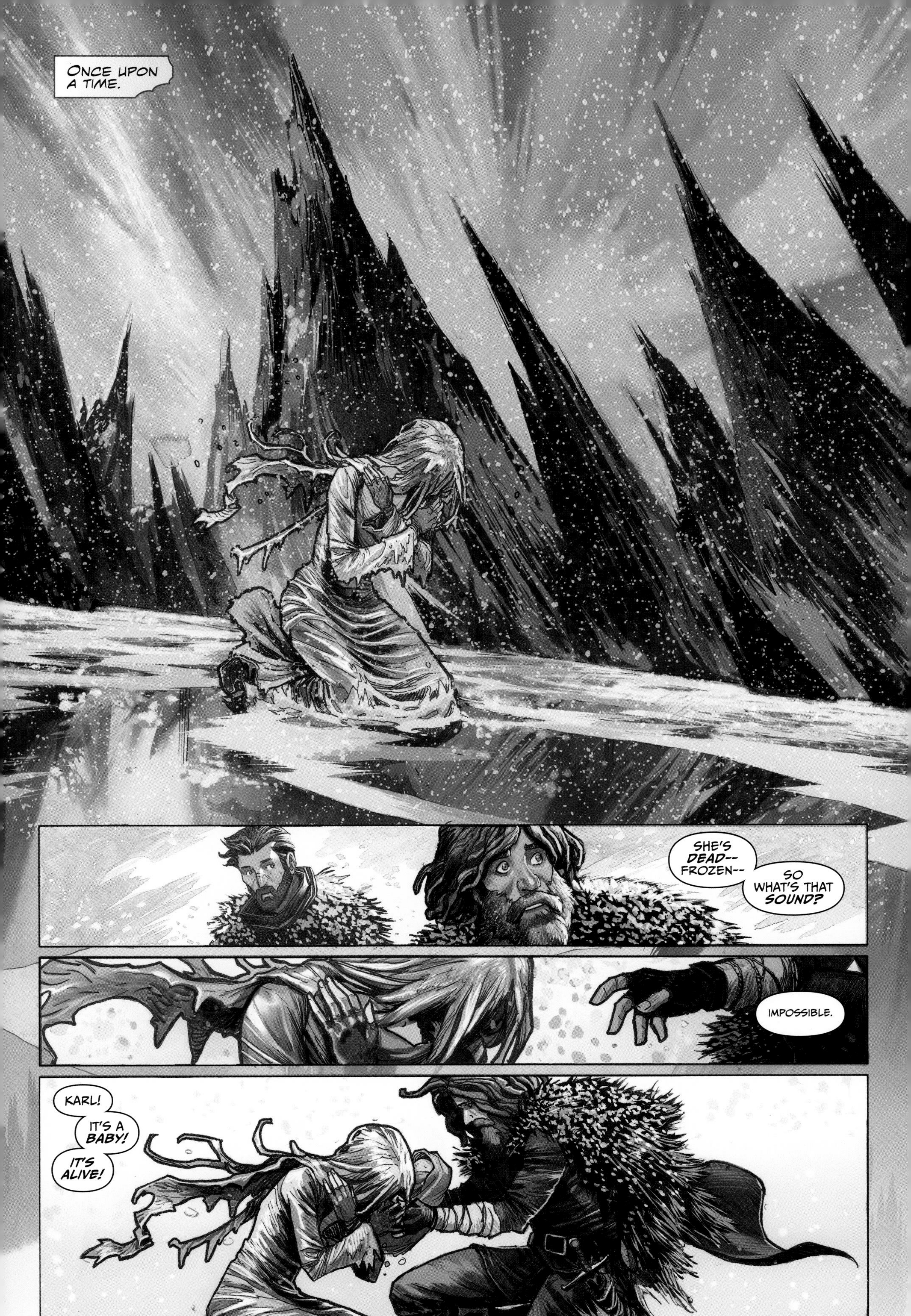

ONCE UPON A TIME.
SHE'S *DEAD*-- FROZEN--
SO WHAT'S THAT *SOUND?*
IMPOSSIBLE.
KARL!
IT'S A *BABY!*
IT'S ALIVE!

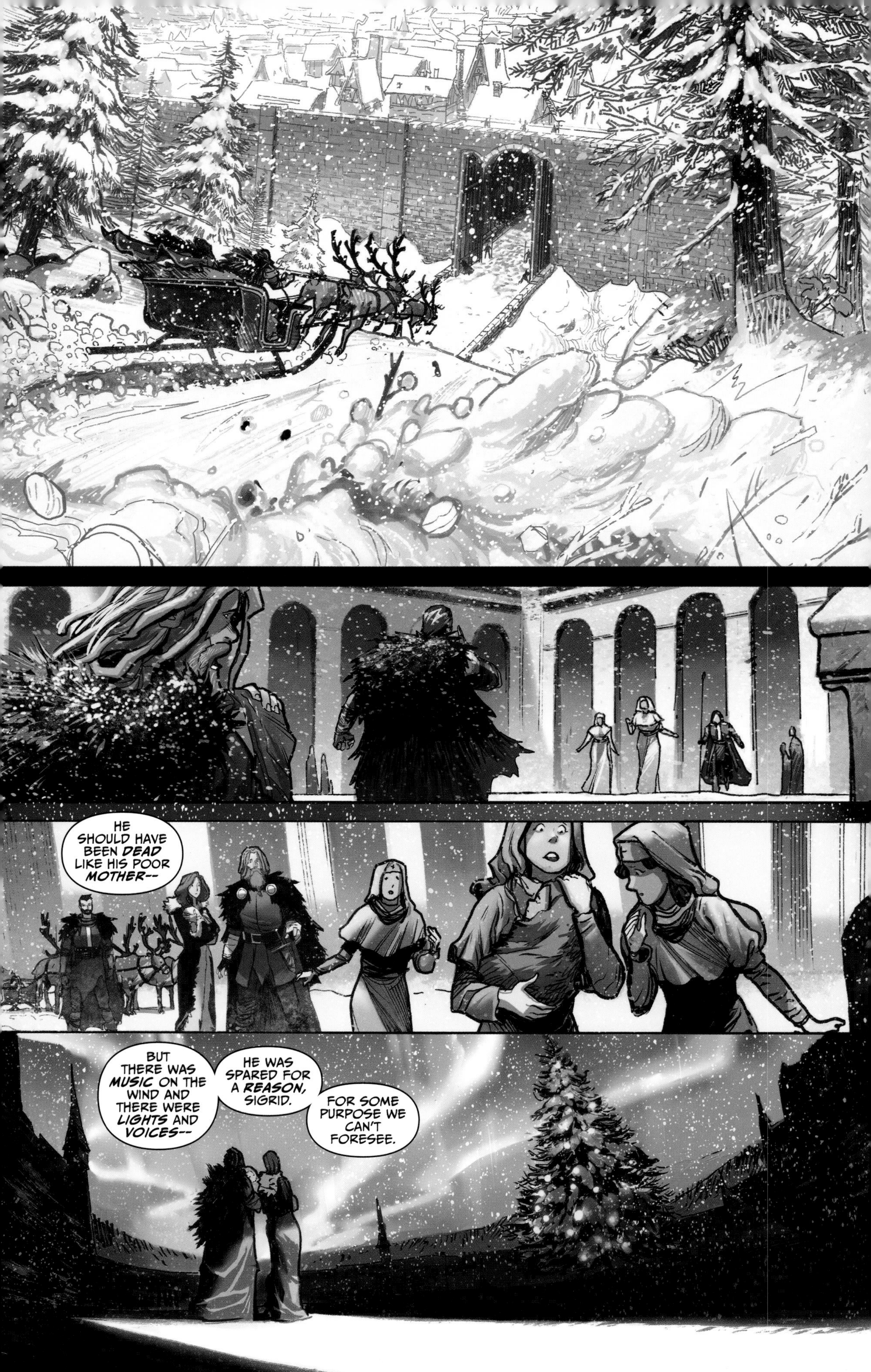
HE SHOULD HAVE BEEN *DEAD* LIKE HIS POOR *MOTHER*--
BUT THERE WAS *MUSIC* ON THE WIND AND THERE WERE *LIGHTS* AND *VOICES*--
HE WAS SPARED FOR A *REASON*, SIGRID.
FOR SOME PURPOSE WE CAN'T FORESEE.

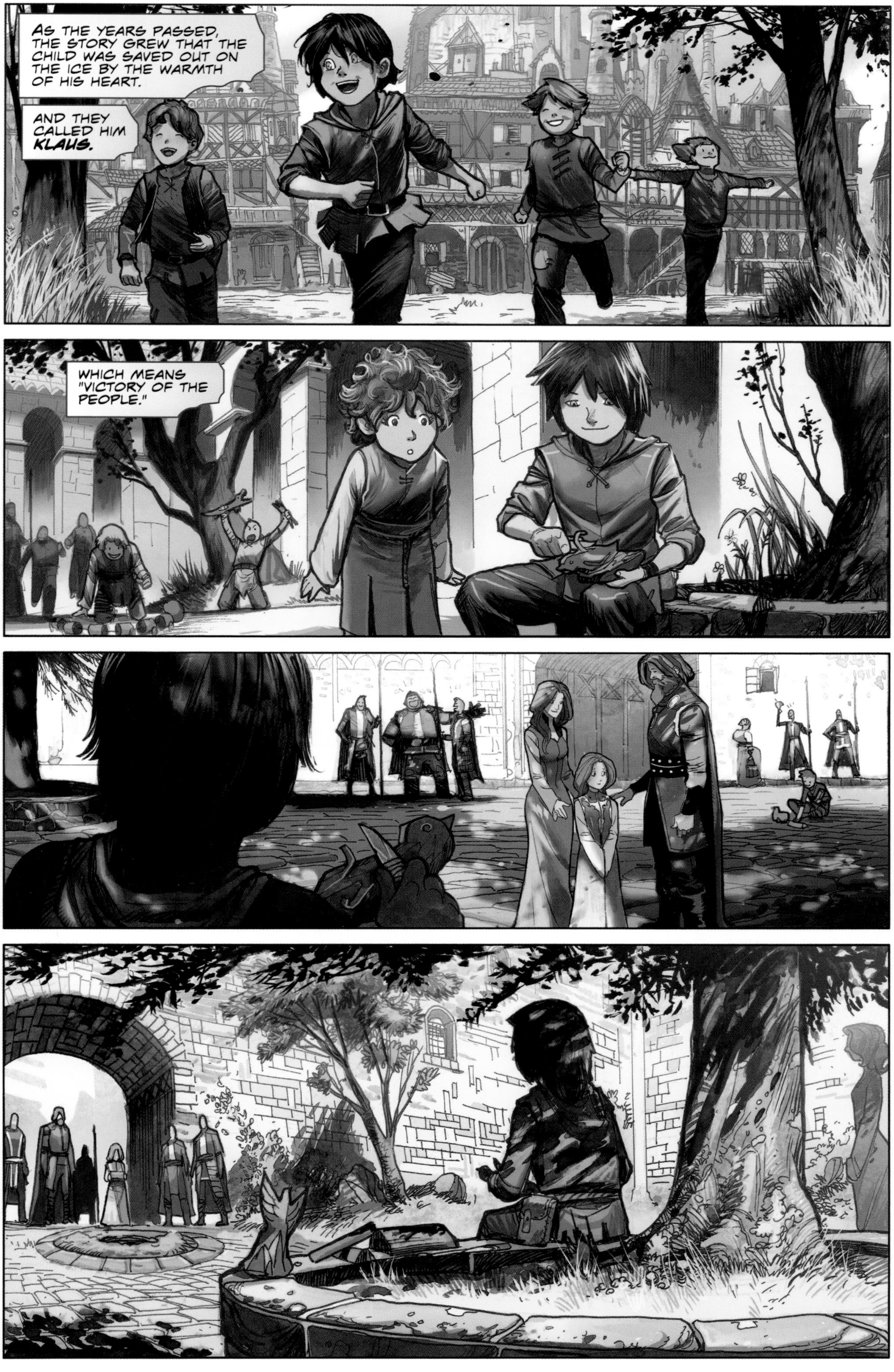
AS THE YEARS PASSED, THE STORY GREW THAT THE CHILD WAS SAVED OUT ON THE ICE BY THE WARMTH OF HIS HEART.
AND THEY CALLED HIM **KLAUS.**
WHICH MEANS "VICTORY OF THE PEOPLE."

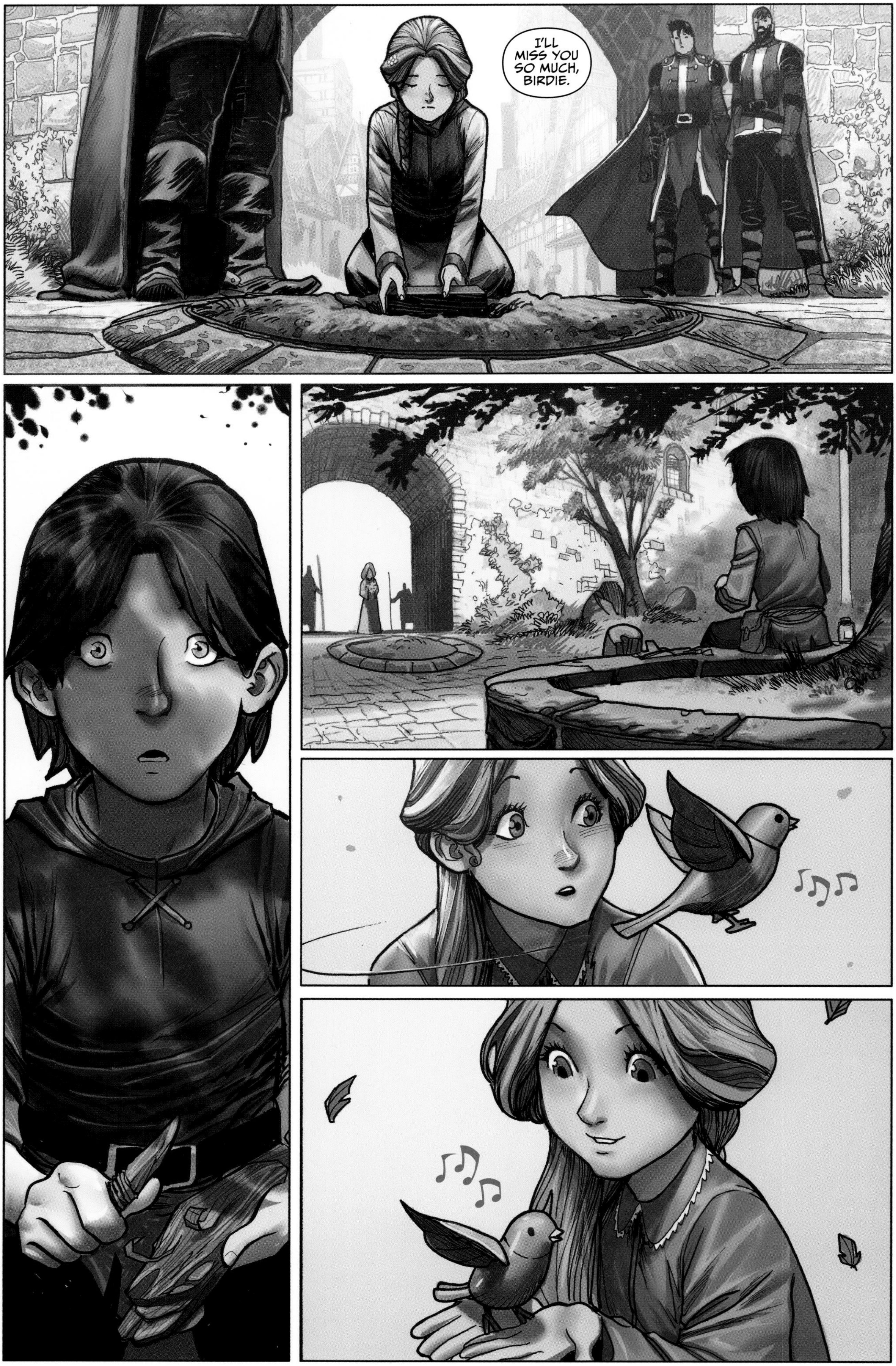
I'LL MISS YOU SO MUCH, BIRDIE.

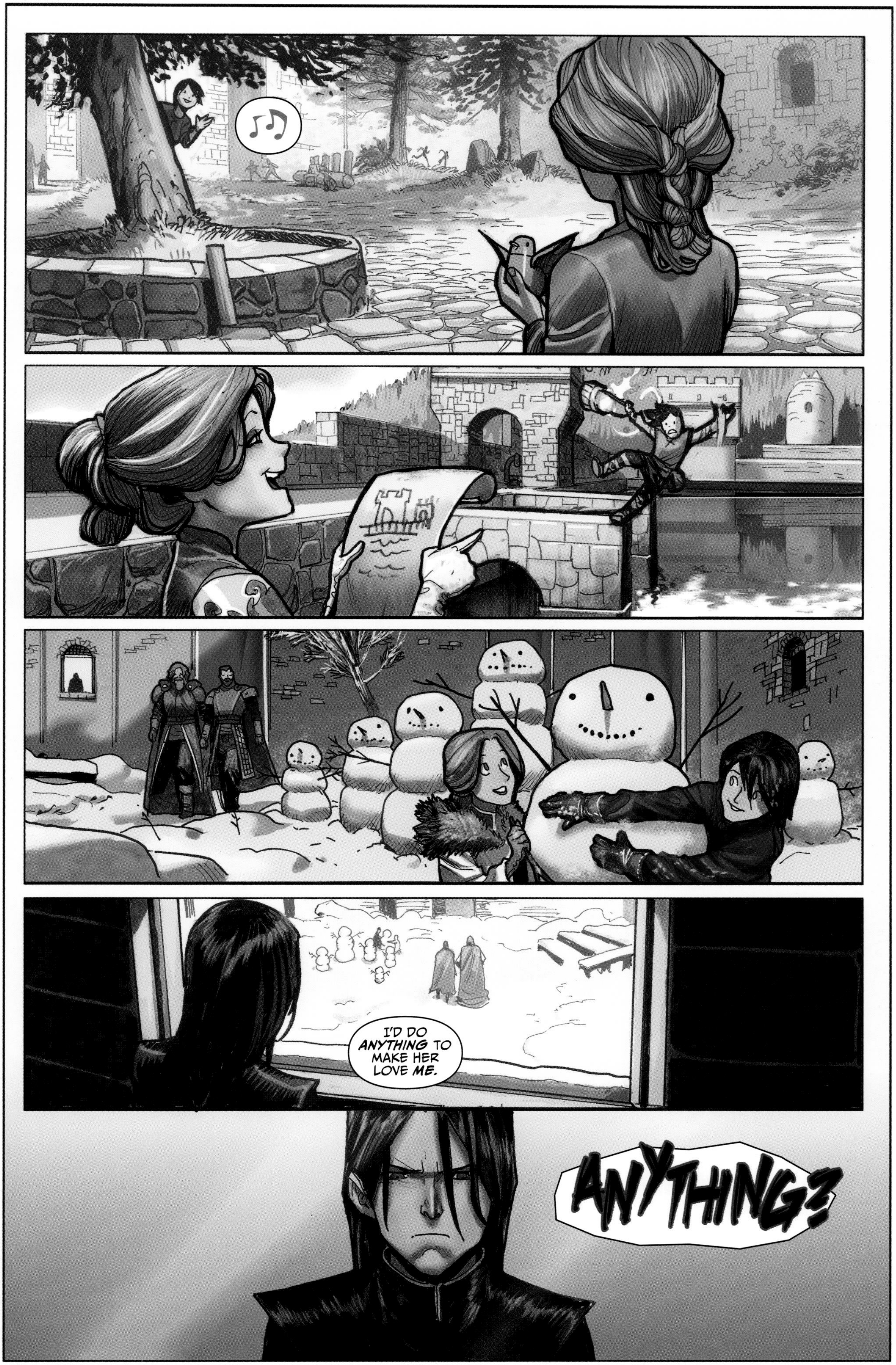
♫
I'D DO ANYTHING TO MAKE HER LOVE ME.
ANYTHING?

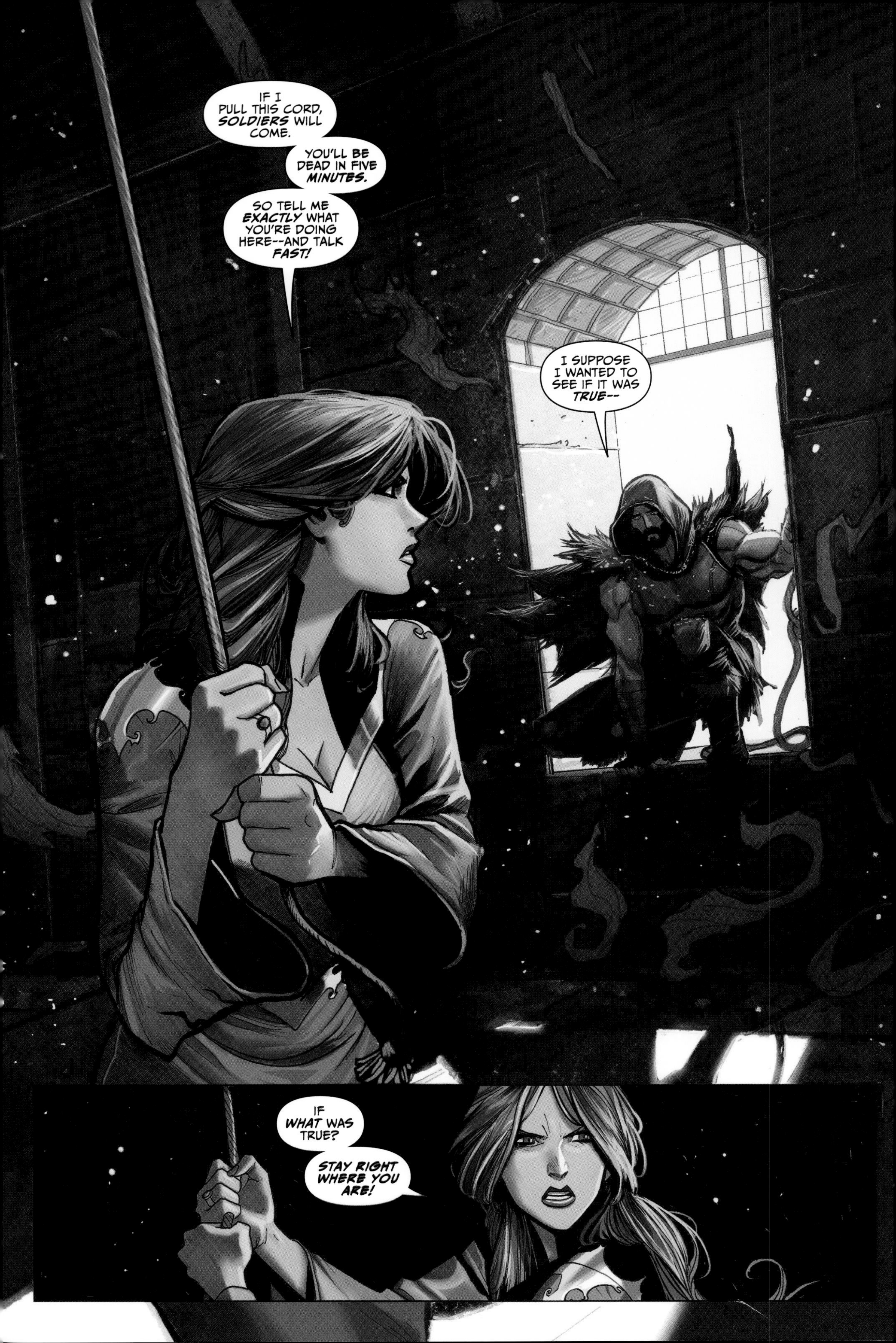
IF I PULL THIS CORD, SOLDIERS WILL COME.
YOU'LL BE DEAD IN FIVE MINUTES.
SO TELL ME EXACTLY WHAT YOU'RE DOING HERE--AND TALK FAST!
I SUPPOSE I WANTED TO SEE IF IT WAS TRUE--
IF WHAT WAS TRUE?
STAY RIGHT WHERE YOU ARE!

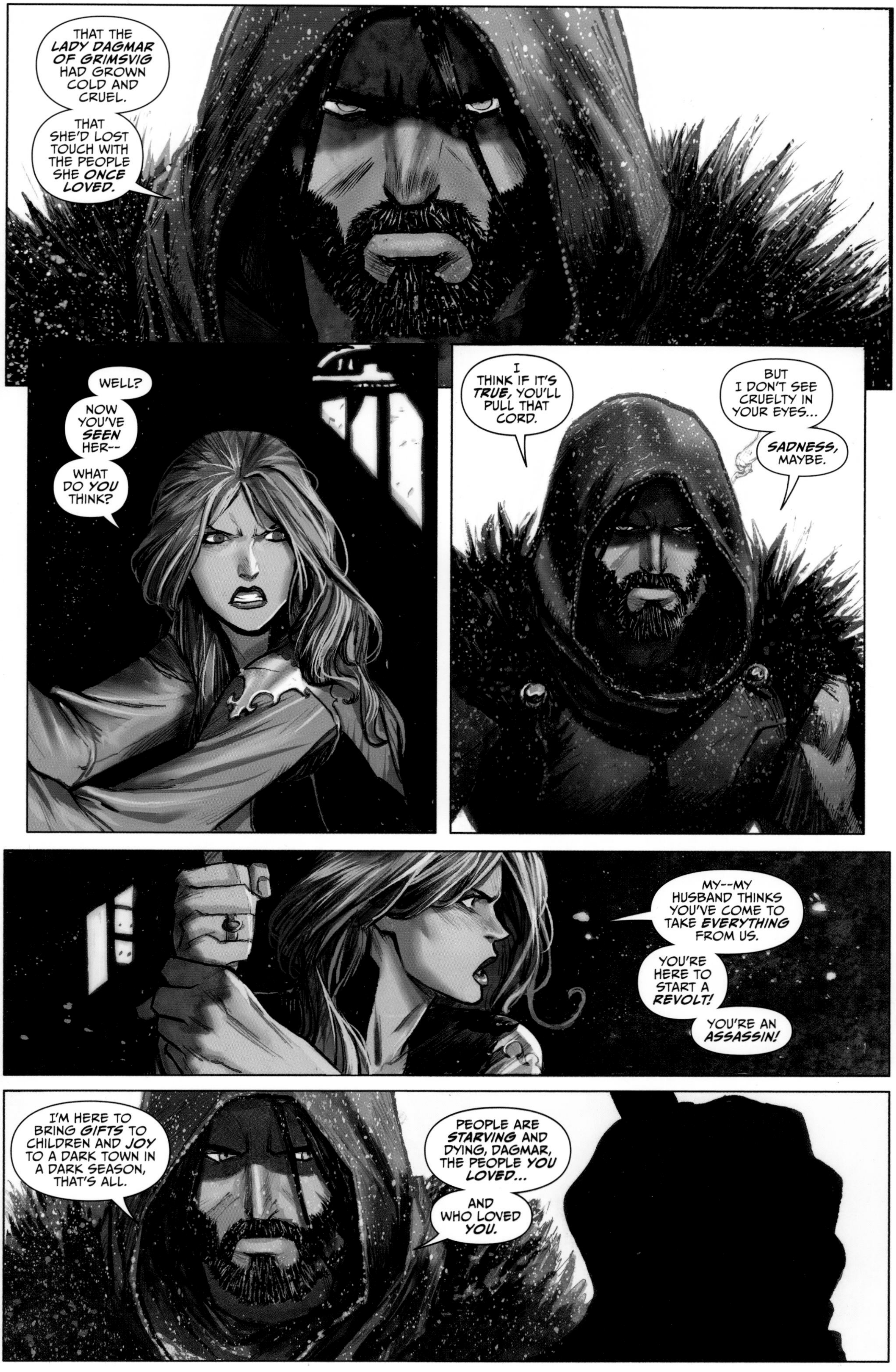
THAT THE LADY DAGMAR OF GRIMSVIG HAD GROWN COLD AND CRUEL.
THAT SHE'D LOST TOUCH WITH THE PEOPLE SHE ONCE LOVED.
WELL?
NOW YOU'VE SEEN HER--
WHAT DO YOU THINK?
I THINK IF IT'S TRUE, YOU'LL PULL THAT CORD.
BUT I DON'T SEE CRUELTY IN YOUR EYES...
SADNESS, MAYBE.
MY--MY HUSBAND THINKS YOU'VE COME TO TAKE EVERYTHING FROM US.
YOU'RE HERE TO START A REVOLT!
YOU'RE AN ASSASSIN!
I'M HERE TO BRING GIFTS TO CHILDREN AND JOY TO A DARK TOWN IN A DARK SEASON, THAT'S ALL.
PEOPLE ARE STARVING AND DYING, DAGMAR, THE PEOPLE YOU LOVED...
AND WHO LOVED YOU.

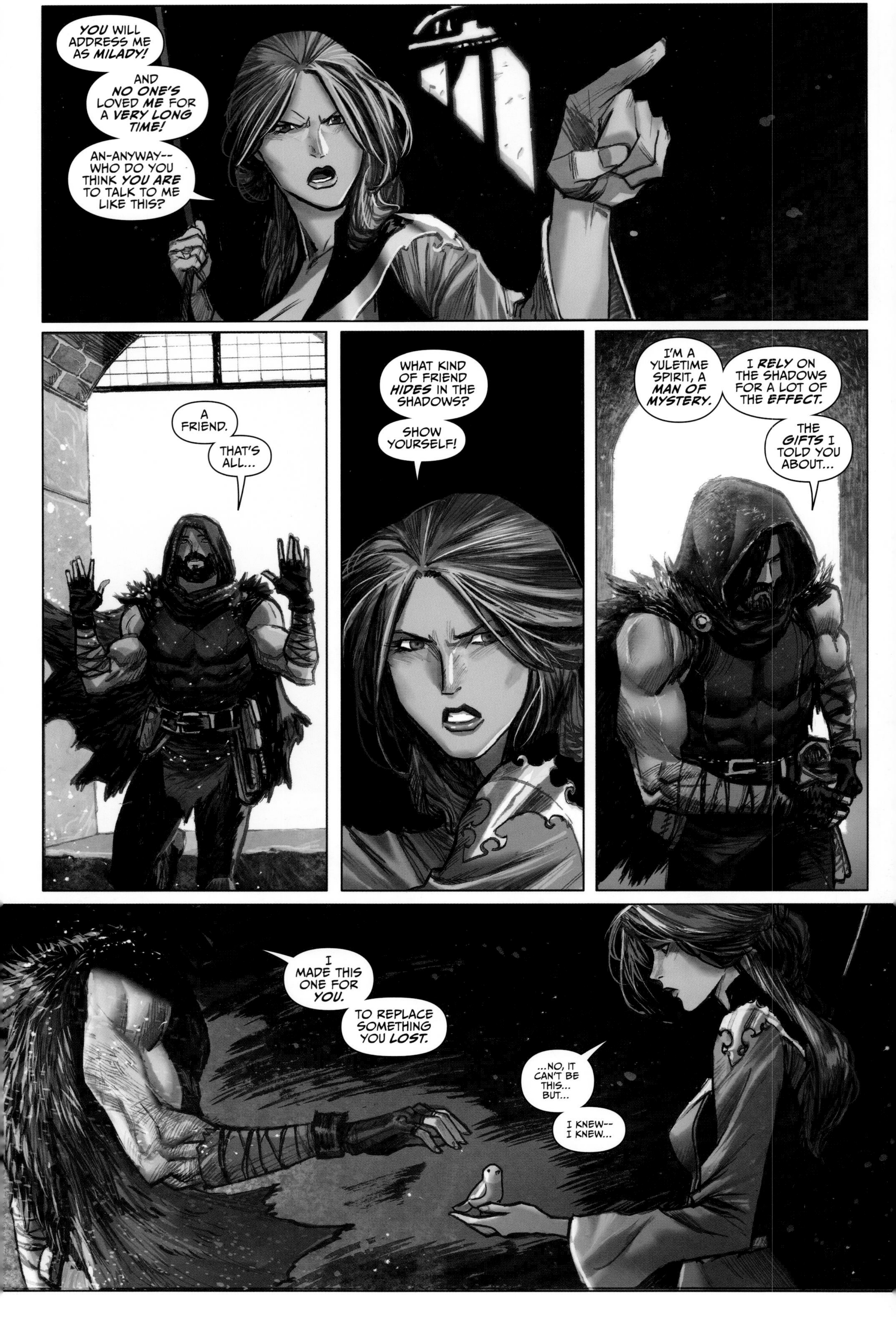
YOU WILL ADDRESS ME AS MILADY!
AND NO ONE'S LOVED ME FOR A VERY LONG TIME!
AN-ANYWAY-- WHO DO YOU THINK YOU ARE TO TALK TO ME LIKE THIS?
A FRIEND.
THAT'S ALL...
WHAT KIND OF FRIEND HIDES IN THE SHADOWS?
SHOW YOURSELF!
I'M A YULETIME SPIRIT, A MAN OF MYSTERY.
I RELY ON THE SHADOWS FOR A LOT OF THE EFFECT.
THE GIFTS I TOLD YOU ABOUT...
I MADE THIS ONE FOR YOU.
TO REPLACE SOMETHING YOU LOST.
...NO, IT CAN'T BE THIS... BUT...
I KNEW-- I KNEW...

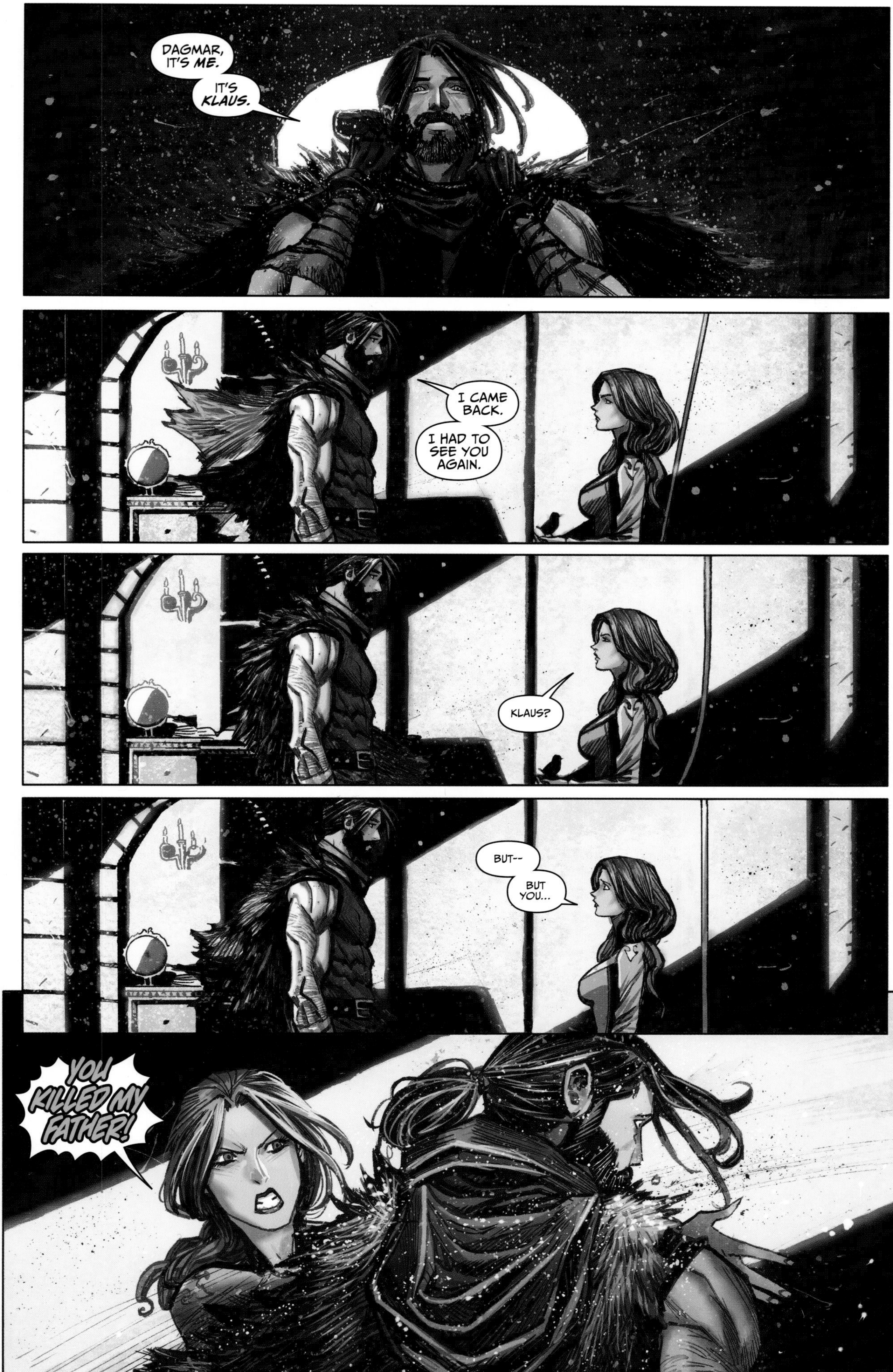
DAGMAR, IT'S ME.
IT'S KLAUS.
I CAME BACK.
I HAD TO SEE YOU AGAIN.
KLAUS?
BUT--
BUT YOU...
YOU KILLED MY FATHER!

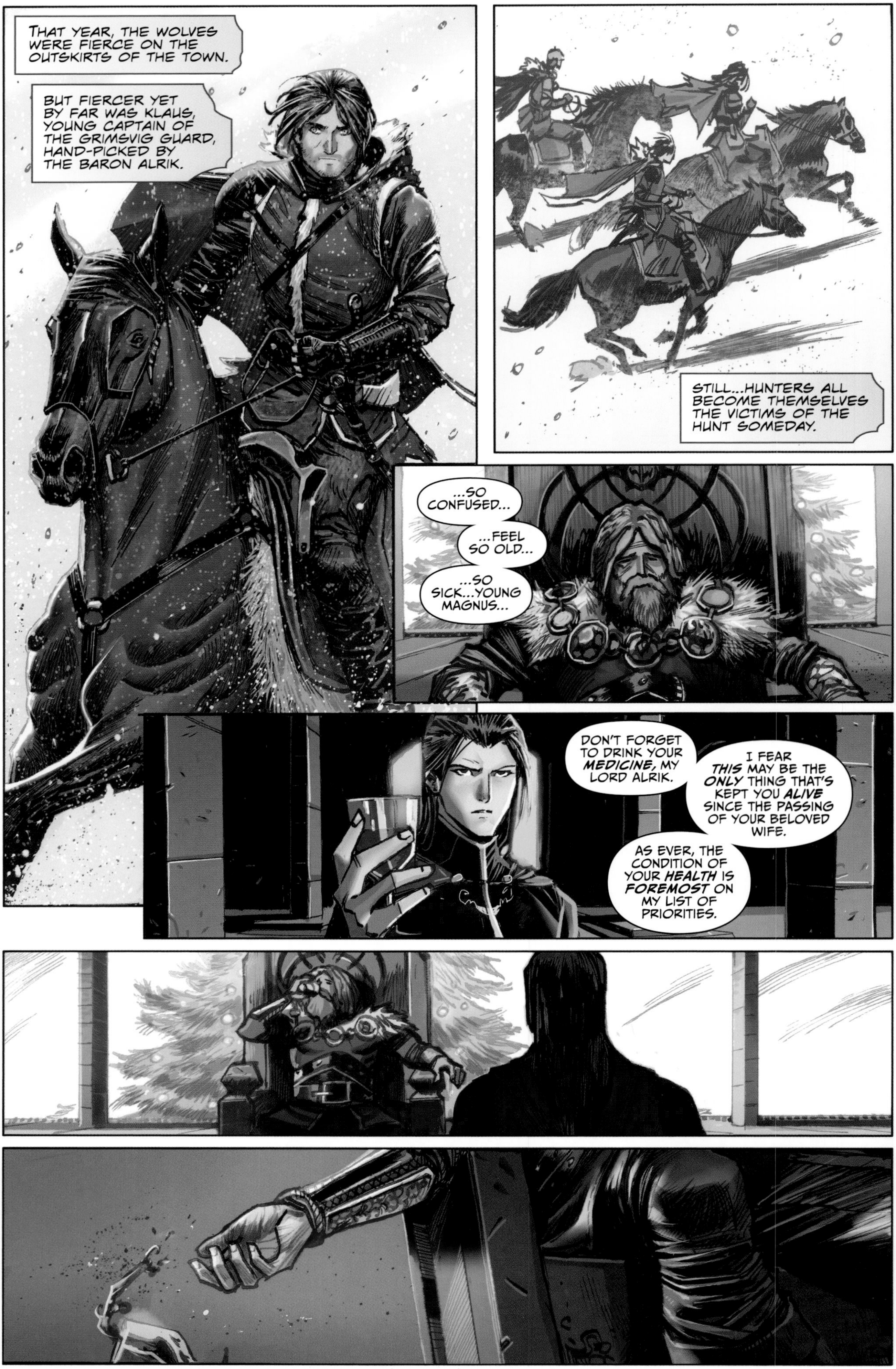

THAT YEAR, THE WOLVES WERE FIERCE ON THE OUTSKIRTS OF THE TOWN.
BUT FIERCER YET BY FAR WAS KLAUS, YOUNG CAPTAIN OF THE GRIMSVIG GUARD, HAND-PICKED BY THE BARON ALRIK.
STILL...HUNTERS ALL BECOME THEMSELVES THE VICTIMS OF THE HUNT SOMEDAY.
...SO CONFUSED...
...FEEL SO OLD...
...SO SICK...YOUNG MAGNUS...
DON'T FORGET TO DRINK YOUR *MEDICINE,* MY LORD ALRIK.
I FEAR *THIS* MAY BE THE *ONLY* THING THAT'S KEPT YOU *ALIVE* SINCE THE PASSING OF YOUR BELOVED WIFE.
AS EVER, THE CONDITION OF YOUR *HEALTH* IS *FOREMOST* ON MY LIST OF PRIORITIES.

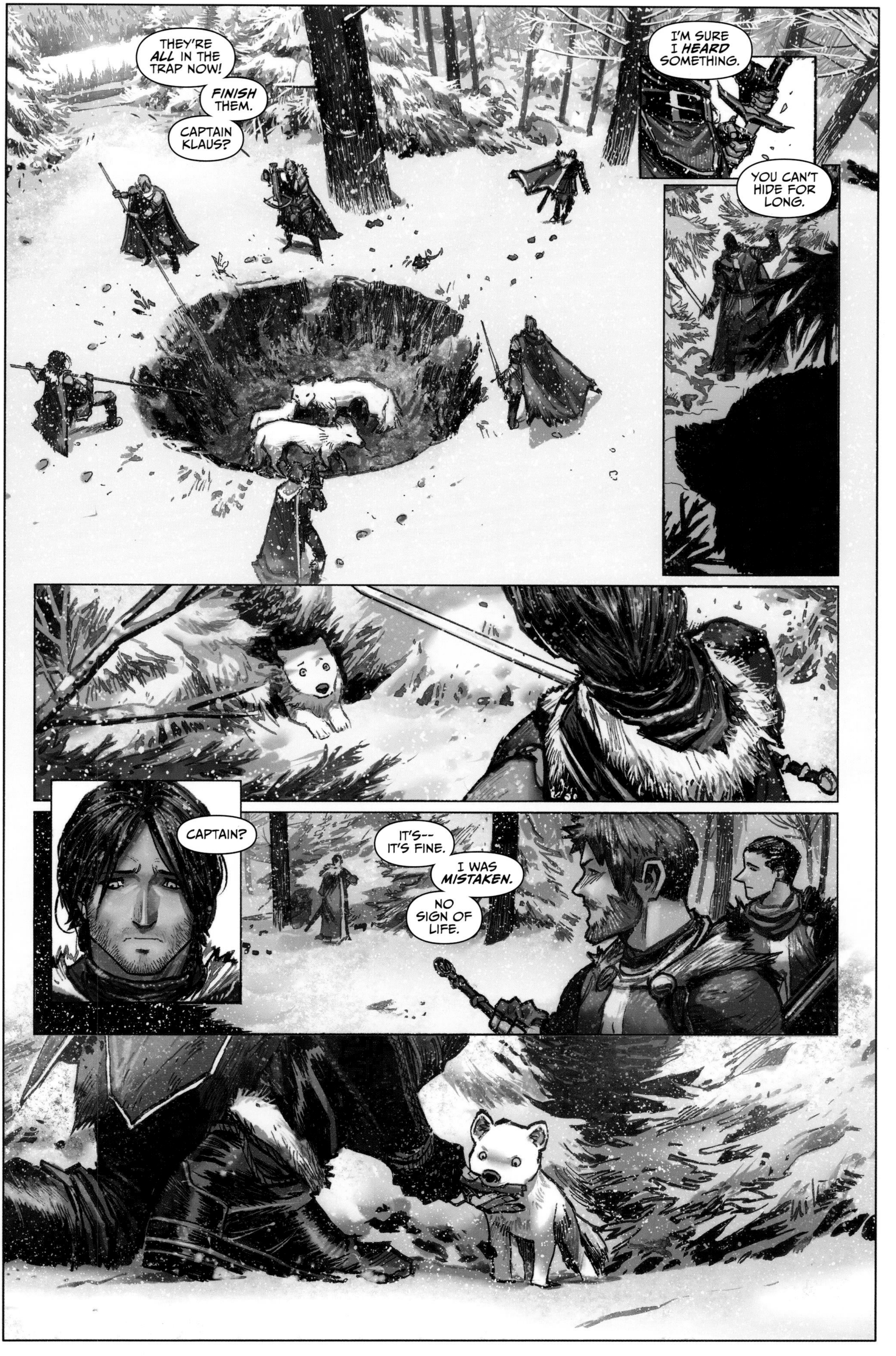
THEY'RE *ALL* IN THE TRAP NOW!
FINISH THEM.
CAPTAIN KLAUS?
I'M SURE I *HEARD* SOMETHING.
YOU CAN'T HIDE FOR LONG.
CAPTAIN?
IT'S-- IT'S FINE.
I WAS *MISTAKEN.*
NO SIGN OF LIFE.

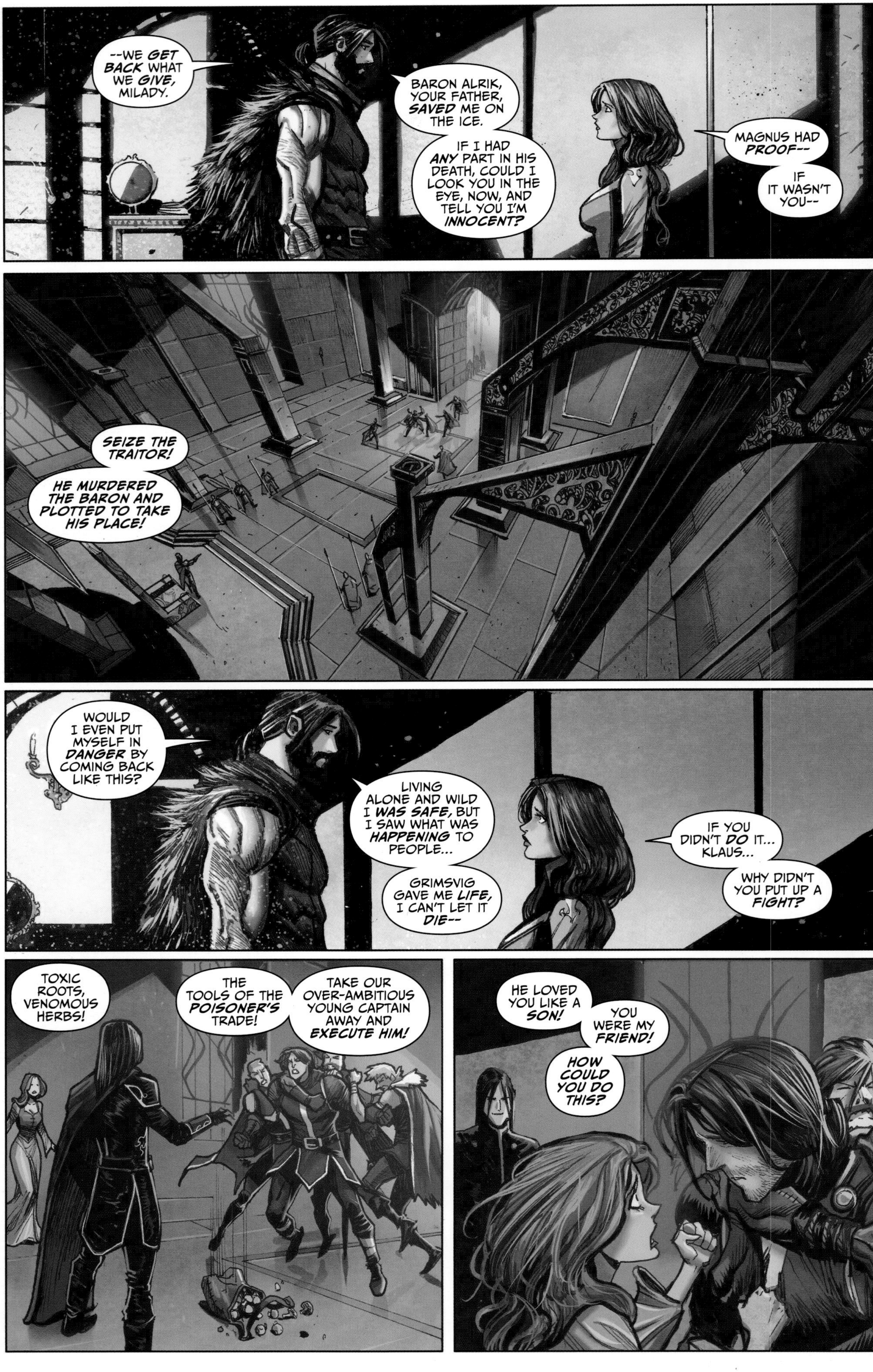
--WE GET BACK WHAT WE GIVE, MILADY.
BARON ALRIK, YOUR FATHER, SAVED ME ON THE ICE.
IF I HAD ANY PART IN HIS DEATH, COULD I LOOK YOU IN THE EYE, NOW, AND TELL YOU I'M INNOCENT?
MAGNUS HAD PROOF--
IF IT WASN'T YOU--
SEIZE THE TRAITOR!
HE MURDERED THE BARON AND PLOTTED TO TAKE HIS PLACE!
WOULD I EVEN PUT MYSELF IN DANGER BY COMING BACK LIKE THIS?
LIVING ALONE AND WILD I WAS SAFE, BUT I SAW WHAT WAS HAPPENING TO PEOPLE...
GRIMSVIG GAVE ME LIFE, I CAN'T LET IT DIE--
IF YOU DIDN'T DO IT... KLAUS...
WHY DIDN'T YOU PUT UP A FIGHT?
TOXIC ROOTS, VENOMOUS HERBS!
THE TOOLS OF THE POISONER'S TRADE!
TAKE OUR OVER-AMBITIOUS YOUNG CAPTAIN AWAY AND EXECUTE HIM!
HE LOVED YOU LIKE A SON!
YOU WERE MY FRIEND!
HOW COULD YOU DO THIS?

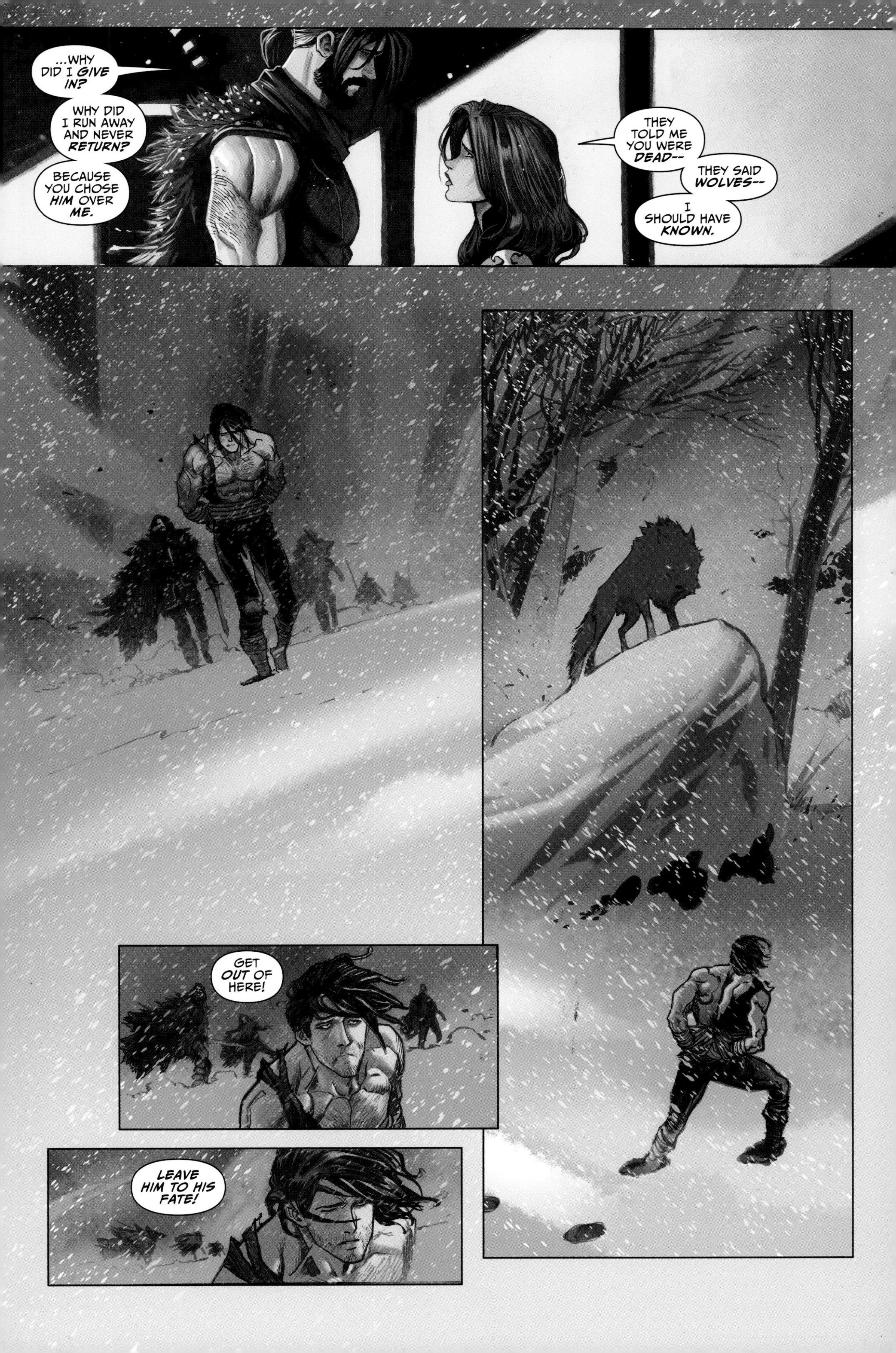
...WHY DID I GIVE IN?
WHY DID I RUN AWAY AND NEVER RETURN?
BECAUSE YOU CHOSE HIM OVER ME.
THEY TOLD ME YOU WERE DEAD--
THEY SAID WOLVES--
I SHOULD HAVE KNOWN.
GET OUT OF HERE!
LEAVE HIM TO HIS FATE!

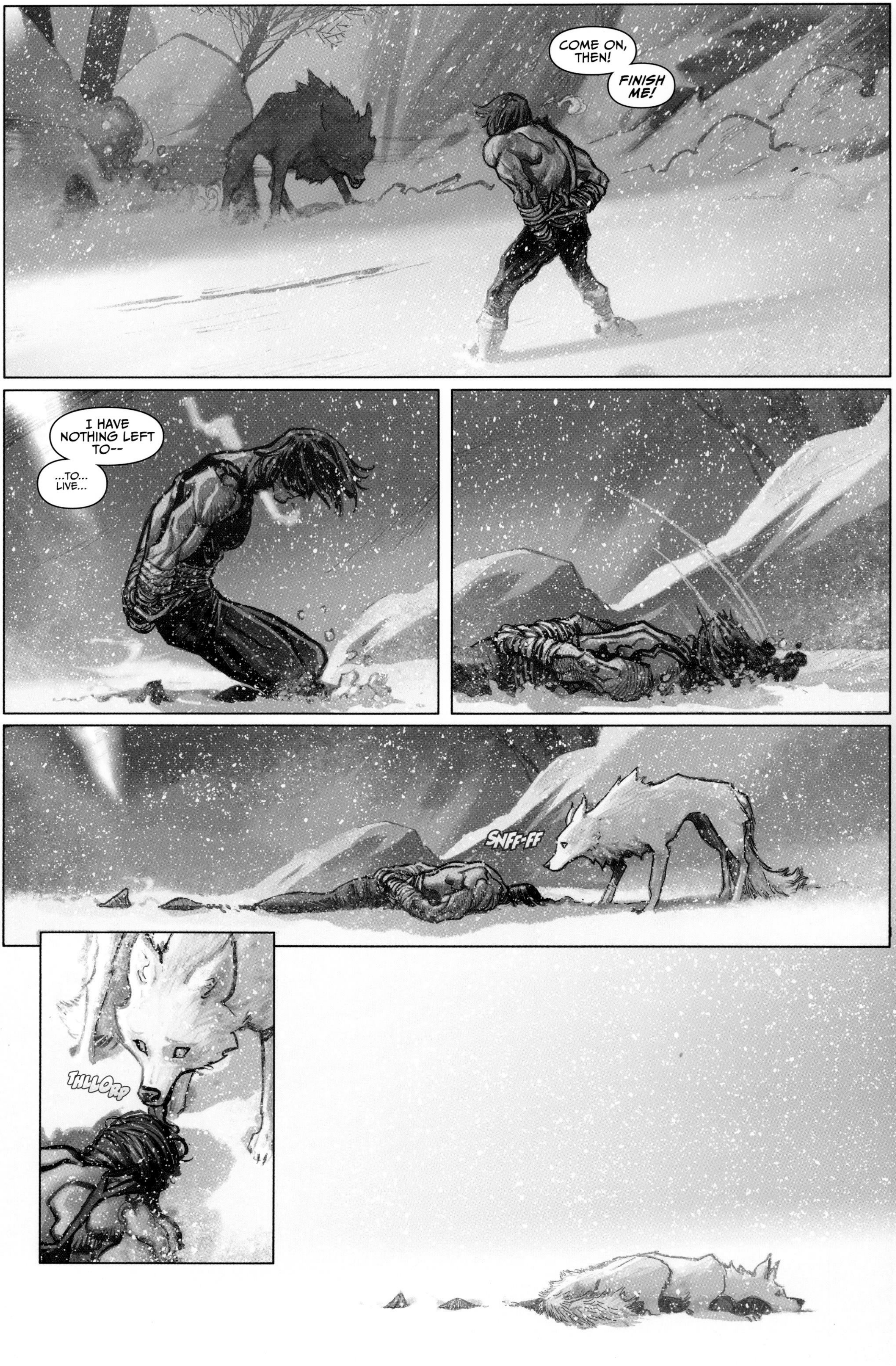
COME ON, THEN!
FINISH ME!
I HAVE NOTHING LEFT TO--
...TO... LIVE...
SNFF-FF
THLLORP

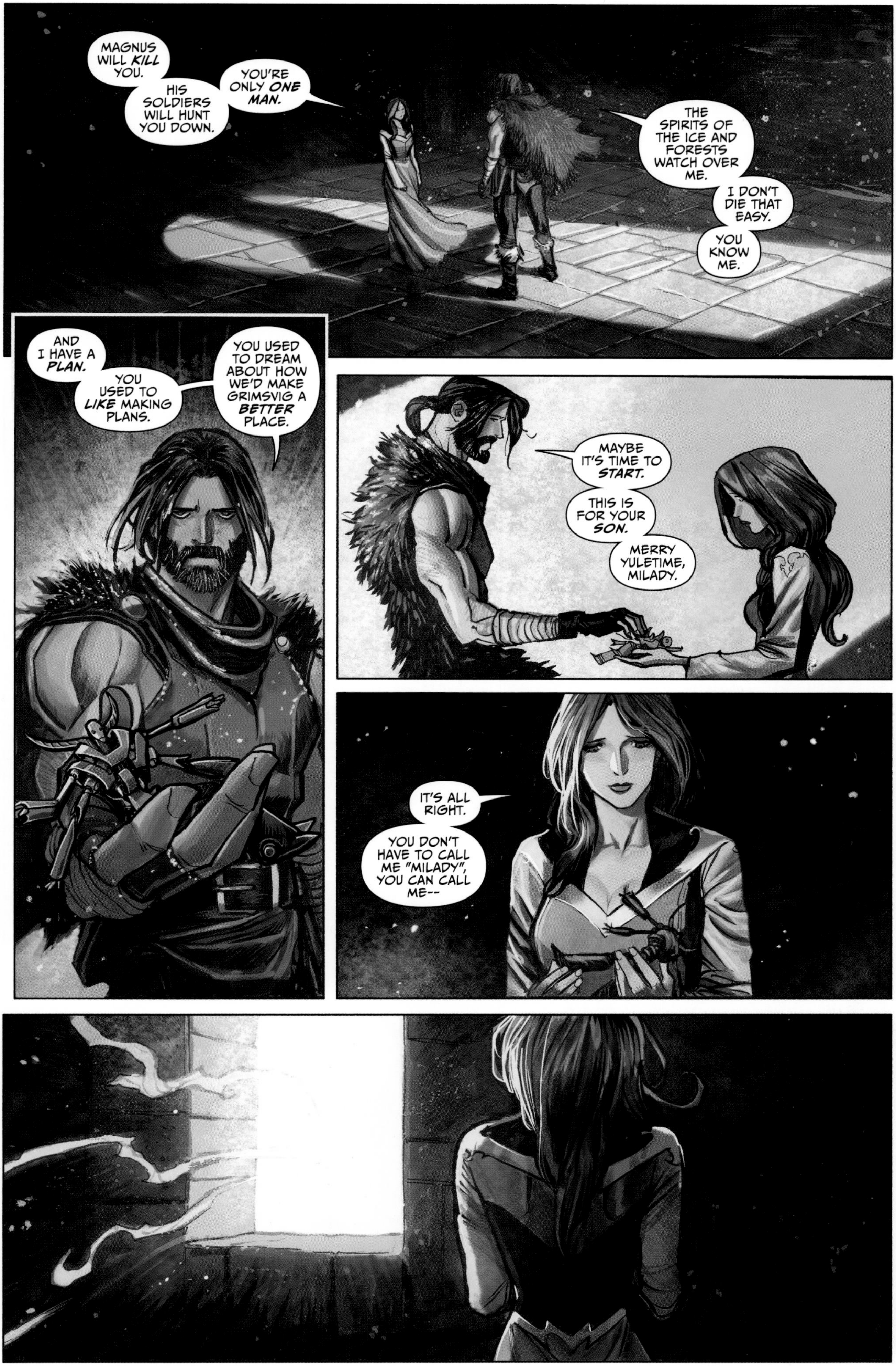

MAGNUS WILL KILL YOU.
HIS SOLDIERS WILL HUNT YOU DOWN.
YOU'RE ONLY ONE MAN.
THE SPIRITS OF THE ICE AND FORESTS WATCH OVER ME.
I DON'T DIE THAT EASY.
YOU KNOW ME.
AND I HAVE A PLAN.
YOU USED TO LIKE MAKING PLANS.
YOU USED TO DREAM ABOUT HOW WE'D MAKE GRIMSVIG A BETTER PLACE.
MAYBE IT'S TIME TO START.
THIS IS FOR YOUR SON.
MERRY YULETIME, MILADY.
IT'S ALL RIGHT.
YOU DON'T HAVE TO CALL ME "MILADY", YOU CAN CALL ME--

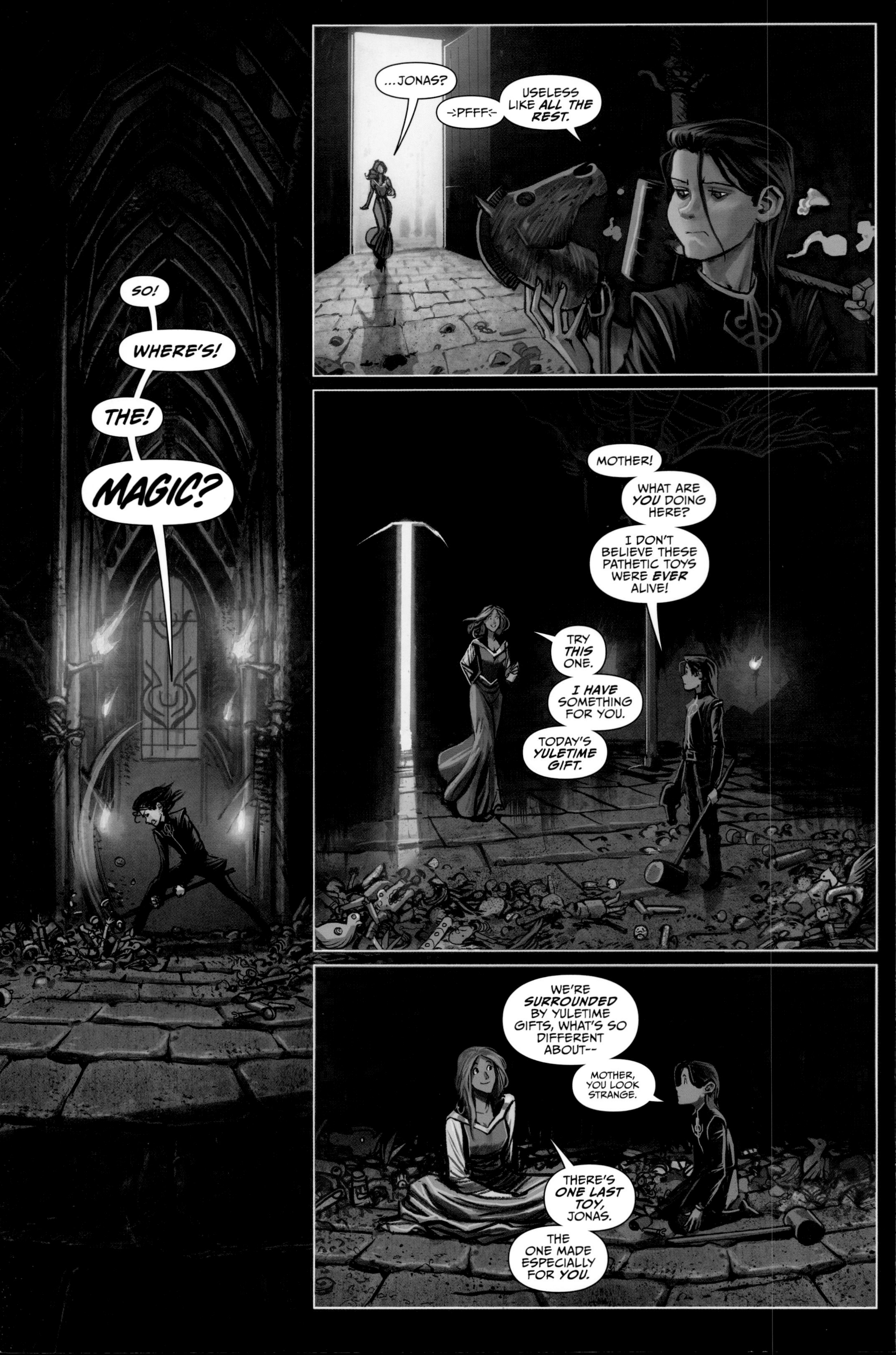
SO!
WHERE'S!
THE!
MAGIC?
...JONAS?
-PFFF-
USELESS LIKE ALL THE REST.
MOTHER!
WHAT ARE YOU DOING HERE?
I DON'T BELIEVE THESE PATHETIC TOYS WERE EVER ALIVE!
TRY THIS ONE.
I HAVE SOMETHING FOR YOU.
TODAY'S YULETIME GIFT.
WE'RE SURROUNDED BY YULETIME GIFTS, WHAT'S SO DIFFERENT ABOUT--
MOTHER, YOU LOOK STRANGE.
THERE'S ONE LAST TOY, JONAS.
THE ONE MADE ESPECIALLY FOR YOU.

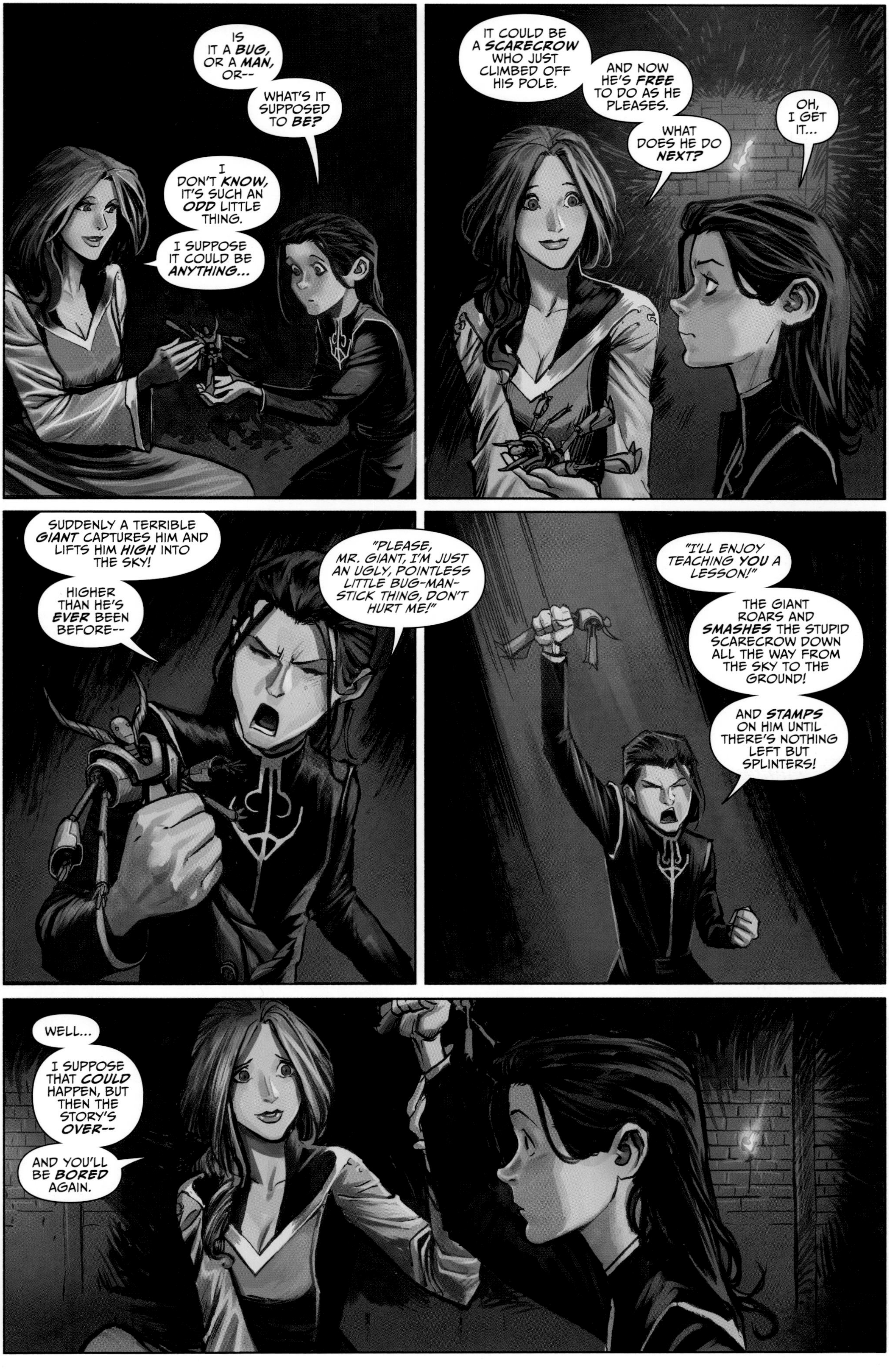
IS IT A BUG, OR A MAN, OR--
WHAT'S IT SUPPOSED TO BE?
I DON'T KNOW, IT'S SUCH AN ODD LITTLE THING.
I SUPPOSE IT COULD BE ANYTHING...
IT COULD BE A SCARECROW WHO JUST CLIMBED OFF HIS POLE.
AND NOW HE'S FREE TO DO AS HE PLEASES.
WHAT DOES HE DO NEXT?
OH, I GET IT...
SUDDENLY A TERRIBLE GIANT CAPTURES HIM AND LIFTS HIM HIGH INTO THE SKY!
HIGHER THAN HE'S EVER BEEN BEFORE--
"PLEASE, MR. GIANT, I'M JUST AN UGLY, POINTLESS LITTLE BUG-MAN-STICK THING, DON'T HURT ME!"
"I'LL ENJOY TEACHING YOU A LESSON!"
THE GIANT ROARS AND SMASHES THE STUPID SCARECROW DOWN ALL THE WAY FROM THE SKY TO THE GROUND!
AND STAMPS ON HIM UNTIL THERE'S NOTHING LEFT BUT SPLINTERS!
WELL...
I SUPPOSE THAT COULD HAPPEN, BUT THEN THE STORY'S OVER--
AND YOU'LL BE BORED AGAIN.

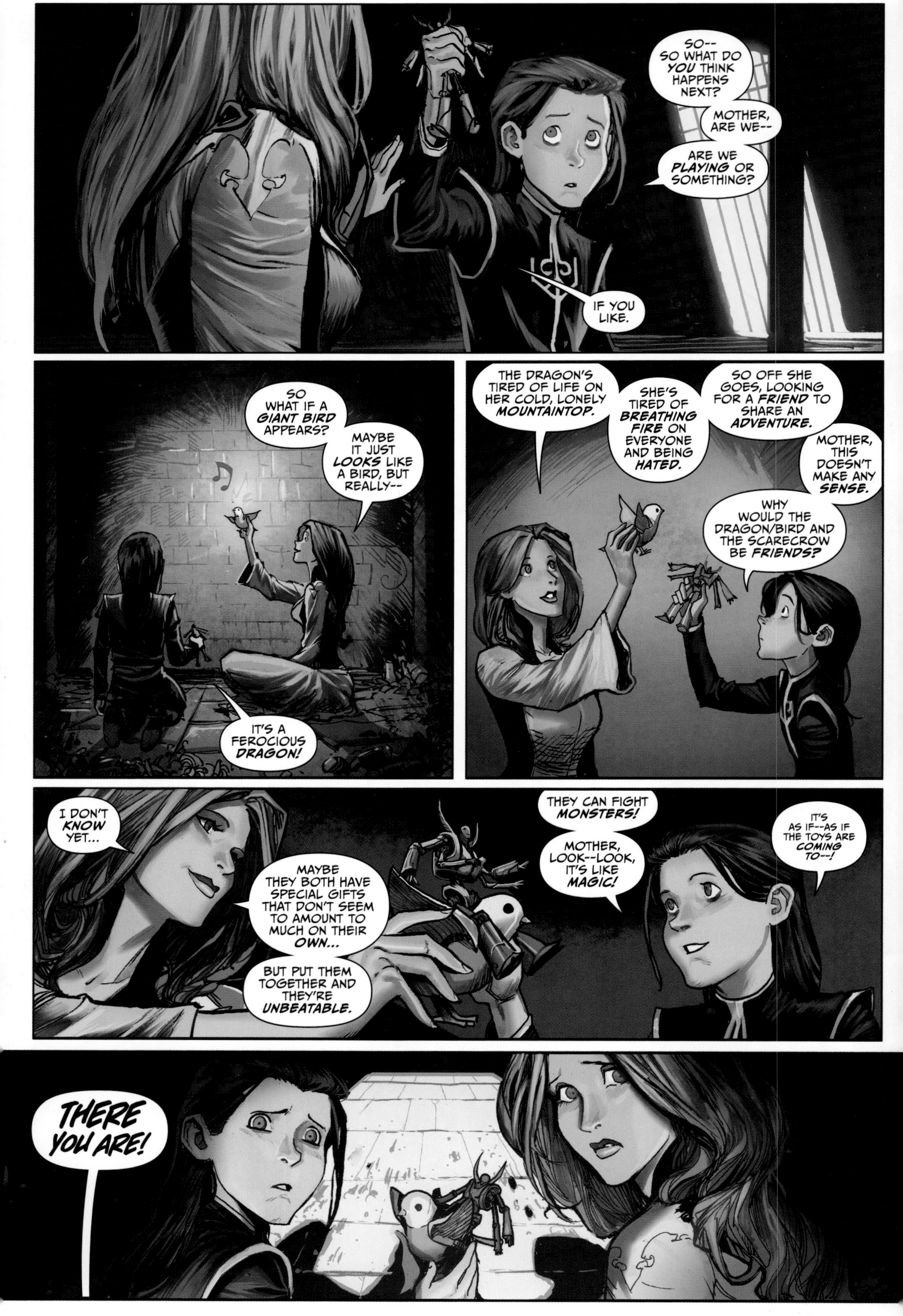
SO--
SO WHAT DO *YOU* THINK HAPPENS NEXT?
MOTHER, ARE WE--
ARE WE *PLAYING* OR SOMETHING?
IF YOU LIKE.
SO WHAT IF A *GIANT BIRD* APPEARS?
MAYBE IT JUST *LOOKS* LIKE A BIRD, BUT REALLY--
IT'S A FEROCIOUS *DRAGON!*
THE DRAGON'S TIRED OF LIFE ON HER COLD, LONELY *MOUNTAINTOP.*
SHE'S TIRED OF *BREATHING FIRE* ON EVERYONE AND BEING *HATED.*
SO OFF SHE GOES, LOOKING FOR A *FRIEND* TO SHARE AN *ADVENTURE.*
MOTHER, THIS DOESN'T MAKE ANY *SENSE.*
WHY WOULD THE DRAGON/BIRD AND THE SCARECROW BE *FRIENDS?*
I DON'T *KNOW* YET...
MAYBE THEY BOTH HAVE SPECIAL GIFTS THAT DON'T SEEM TO AMOUNT TO MUCH ON THEIR *OWN...*
BUT PUT THEM TOGETHER AND THEY'RE *UNBEATABLE.*
THEY CAN FIGHT *MONSTERS!*
MOTHER, LOOK--LOOK, IT'S LIKE *MAGIC!*
IT'S AS IF--AS IF THE TOYS ARE *COMING* TO--!
THERE YOU ARE!

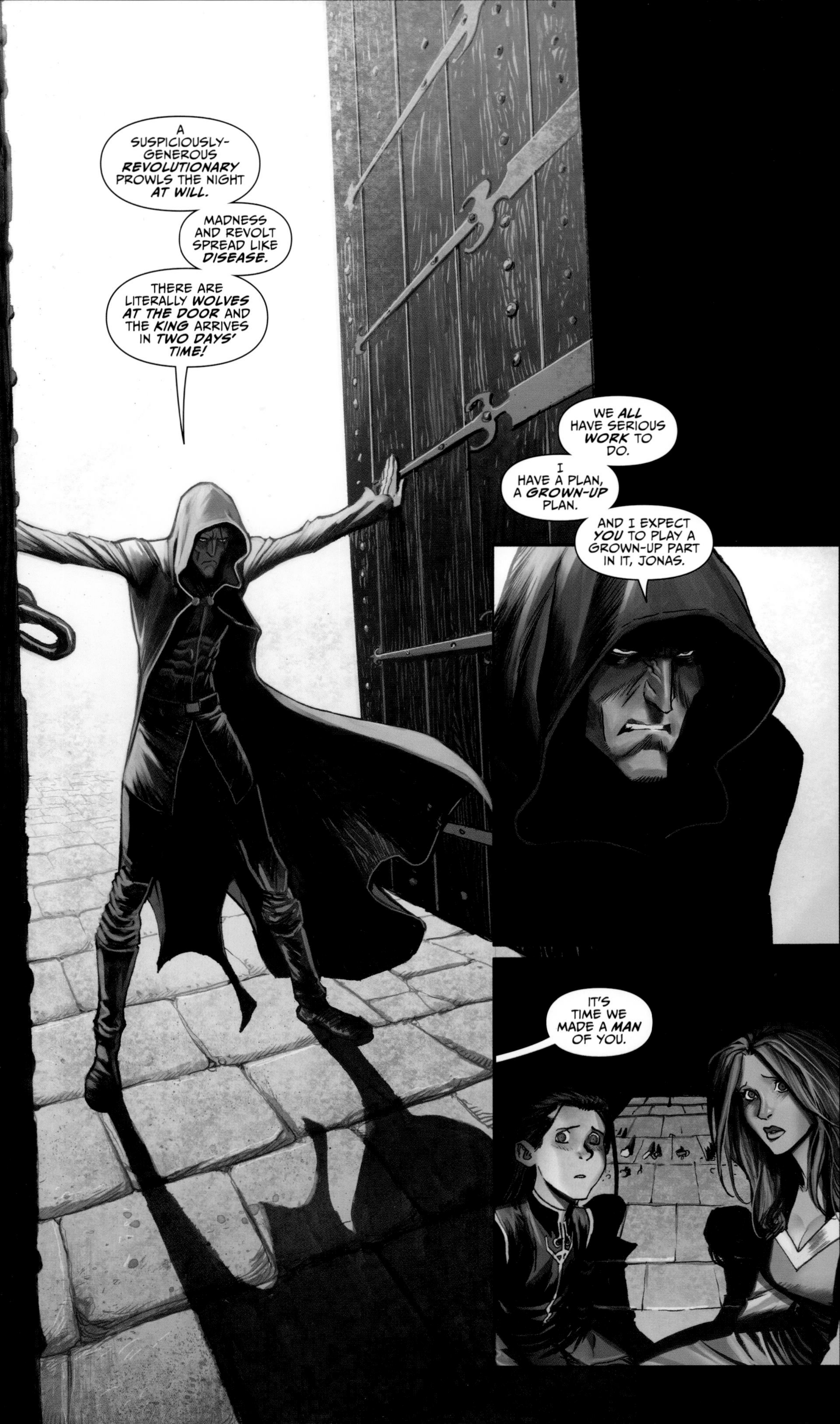
A SUSPICIOUSLY-GENEROUS ***REVOLUTIONARY*** PROWLS THE NIGHT ***AT WILL.***
MADNESS AND REVOLT SPREAD LIKE ***DISEASE.***
THERE ARE LITERALLY ***WOLVES AT THE DOOR*** AND THE ***KING*** ARRIVES IN ***TWO DAYS' TIME!***
WE ***ALL*** HAVE SERIOUS ***WORK*** TO DO.
I HAVE A PLAN, A ***GROWN-UP*** PLAN.
AND I EXPECT ***YOU*** TO PLAY A GROWN-UP PART IN IT, JONAS.
IT'S TIME WE MADE A ***MAN*** OF YOU.

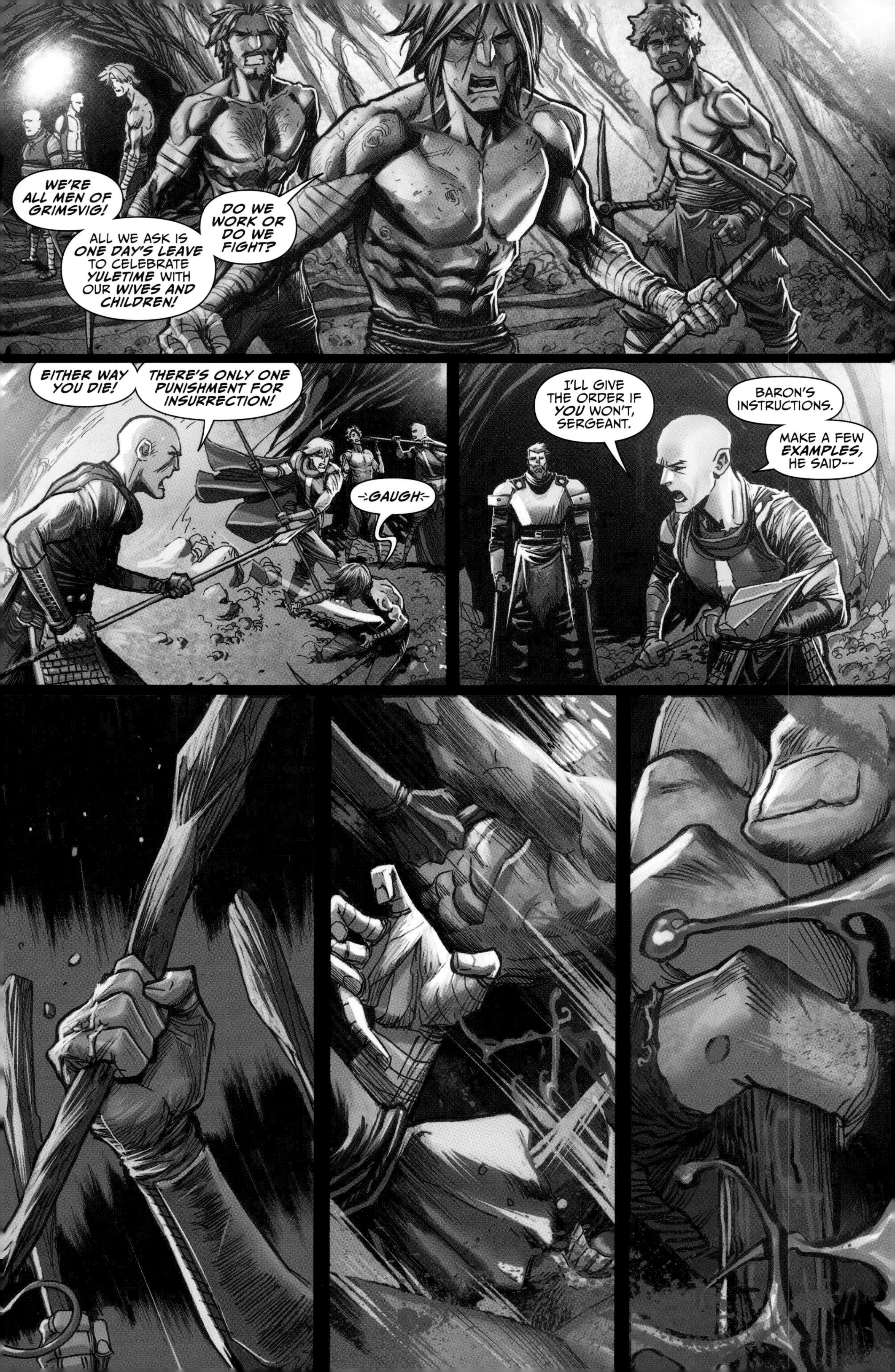
WE'RE ALL MEN OF GRIMSVIG!
ALL WE ASK IS ONE DAY'S LEAVE TO CELEBRATE YULETIME WITH OUR WIVES AND CHILDREN!
DO WE WORK OR DO WE FIGHT?
EITHER WAY YOU DIE!
THERE'S ONLY ONE PUNISHMENT FOR INSURRECTION!
-GAUGH-
I'LL GIVE THE ORDER IF YOU WON'T, SERGEANT.
BARON'S INSTRUCTIONS.
MAKE A FEW EXAMPLES, HE SAID--

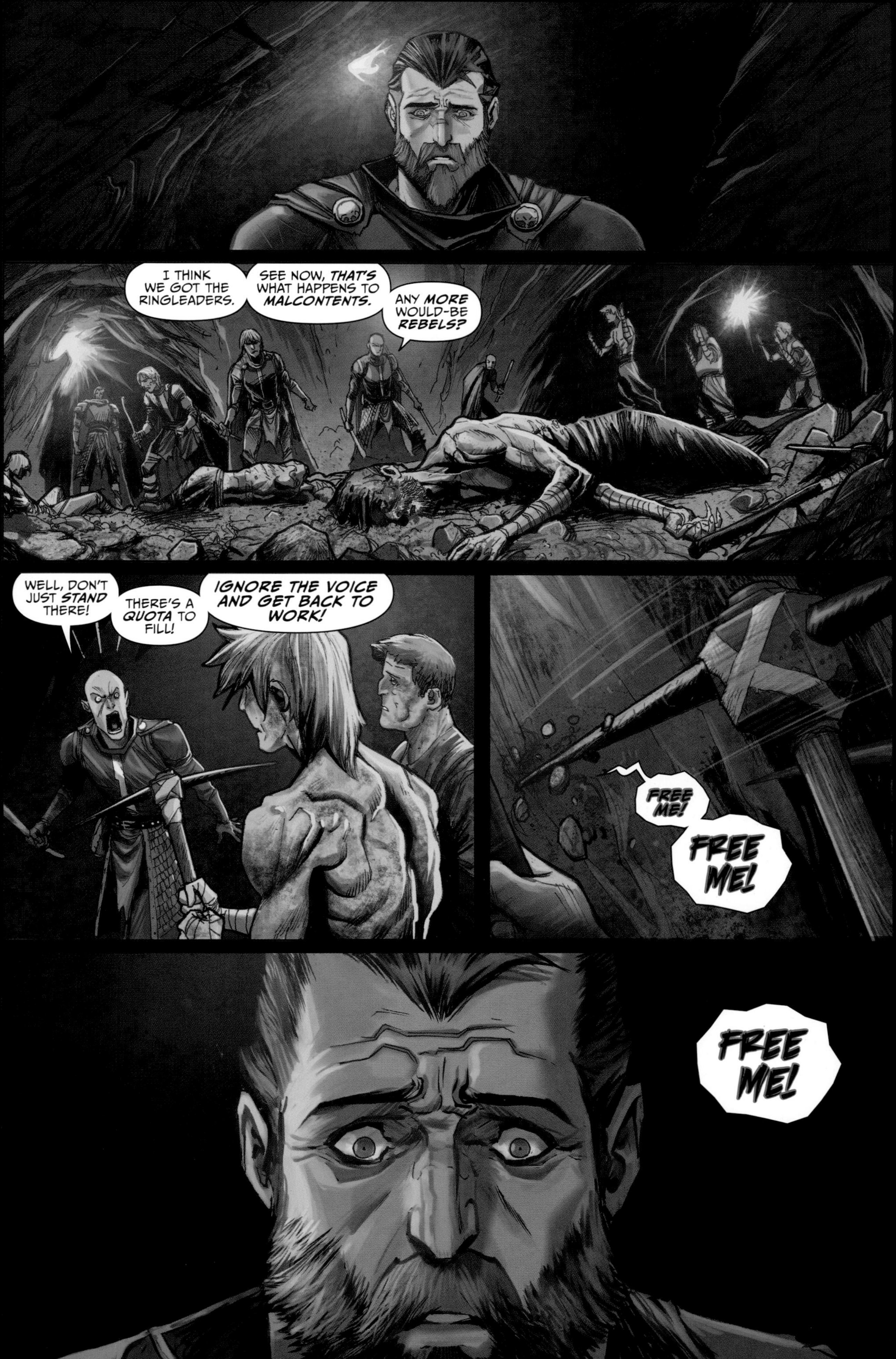
I THINK WE GOT THE RINGLEADERS.
SEE NOW, THAT'S WHAT HAPPENS TO MALCONTENTS.
ANY MORE WOULD-BE REBELS?
WELL, DON'T JUST STAND THERE!
THERE'S A QUOTA TO FILL!
IGNORE THE VOICE AND GET BACK TO WORK!
FREE ME!
FREE ME!
FREE ME!

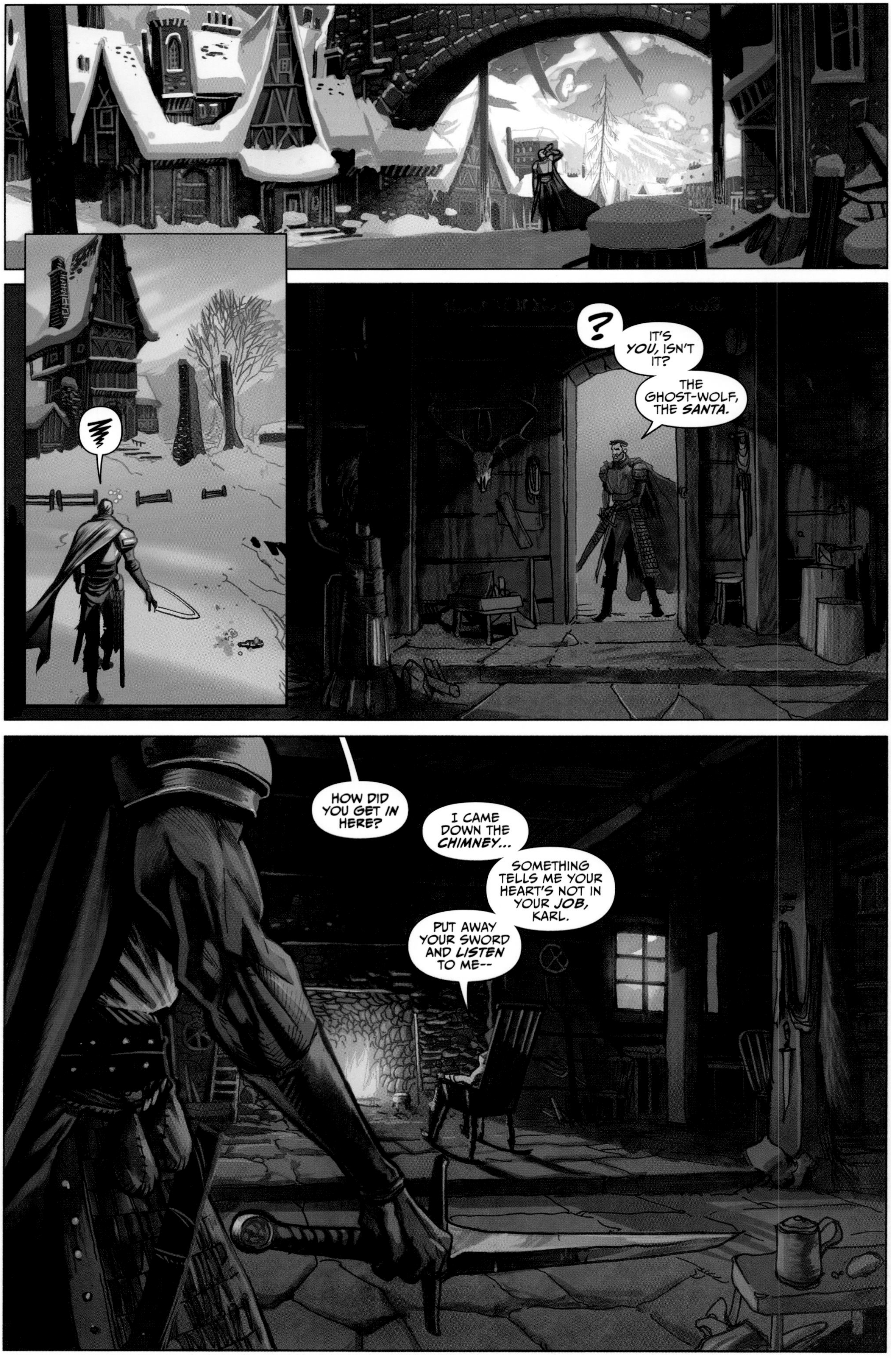
?
IT'S *YOU*, ISN'T IT?
THE GHOST-WOLF, THE *SANTA.*
HOW DID YOU GET *IN* HERE?
I CAME DOWN THE *CHIMNEY...*
SOMETHING TELLS ME YOUR HEART'S NOT IN YOUR *JOB*, KARL.
PUT AWAY YOUR SWORD AND *LISTEN* TO ME--

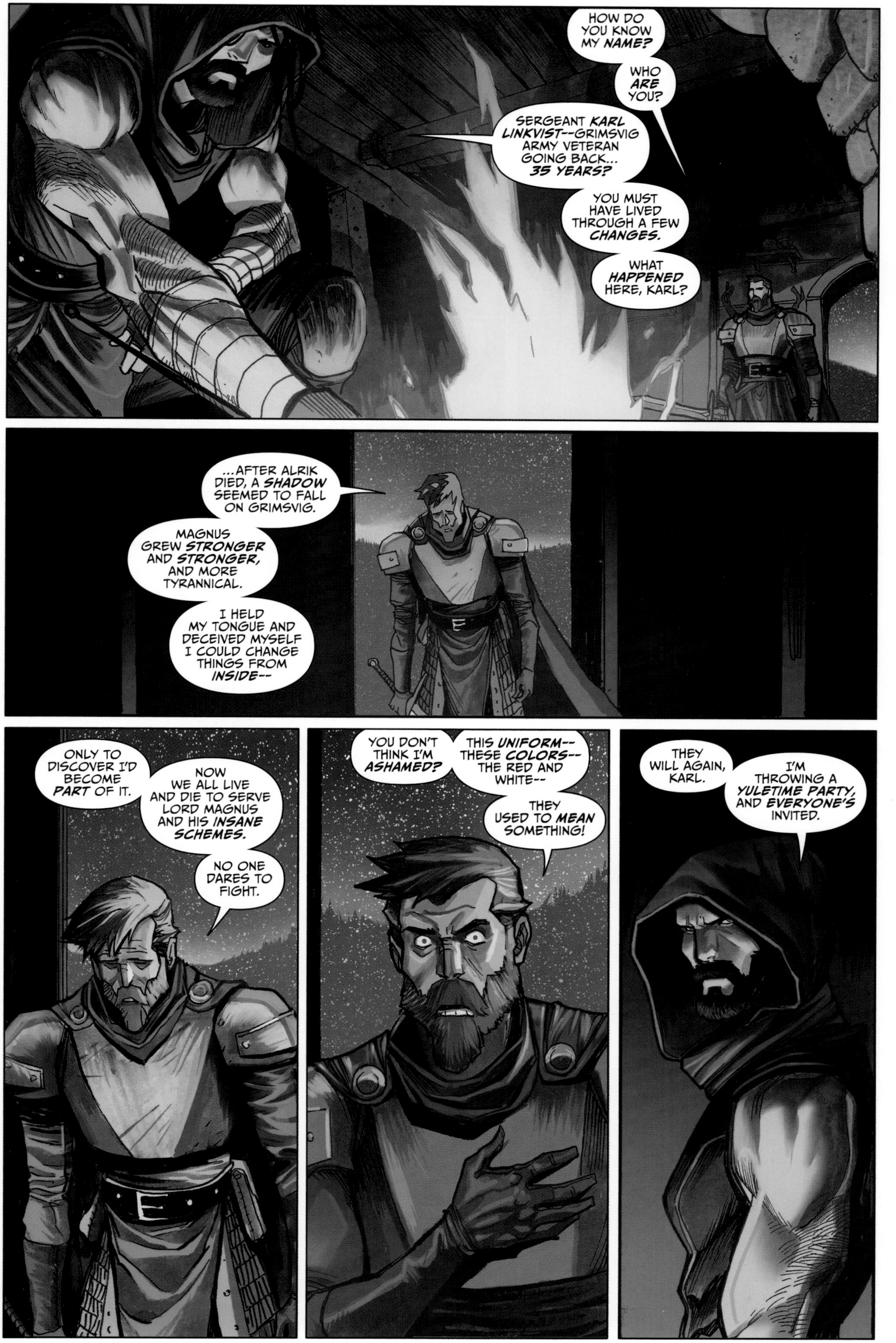

HOW DO YOU KNOW MY NAME?
WHO ARE YOU?
SERGEANT KARL LINKVIST--GRIMSVIG ARMY VETERAN GOING BACK... 35 YEARS?
YOU MUST HAVE LIVED THROUGH A FEW CHANGES.
WHAT HAPPENED HERE, KARL?
...AFTER ALRIK DIED, A SHADOW SEEMED TO FALL ON GRIMSVIG.
MAGNUS GREW STRONGER AND STRONGER, AND MORE TYRANNICAL.
I HELD MY TONGUE AND DECEIVED MYSELF I COULD CHANGE THINGS FROM INSIDE--
ONLY TO DISCOVER I'D BECOME PART OF IT.
NOW WE ALL LIVE AND DIE TO SERVE LORD MAGNUS AND HIS INSANE SCHEMES.
NO ONE DARES TO FIGHT.
YOU DON'T THINK I'M ASHAMED?
THIS UNIFORM-- THESE COLORS-- THE RED AND WHITE--
THEY USED TO MEAN SOMETHING!
THEY WILL AGAIN, KARL.
I'M THROWING A YULETIME PARTY, AND EVERYONE'S INVITED.

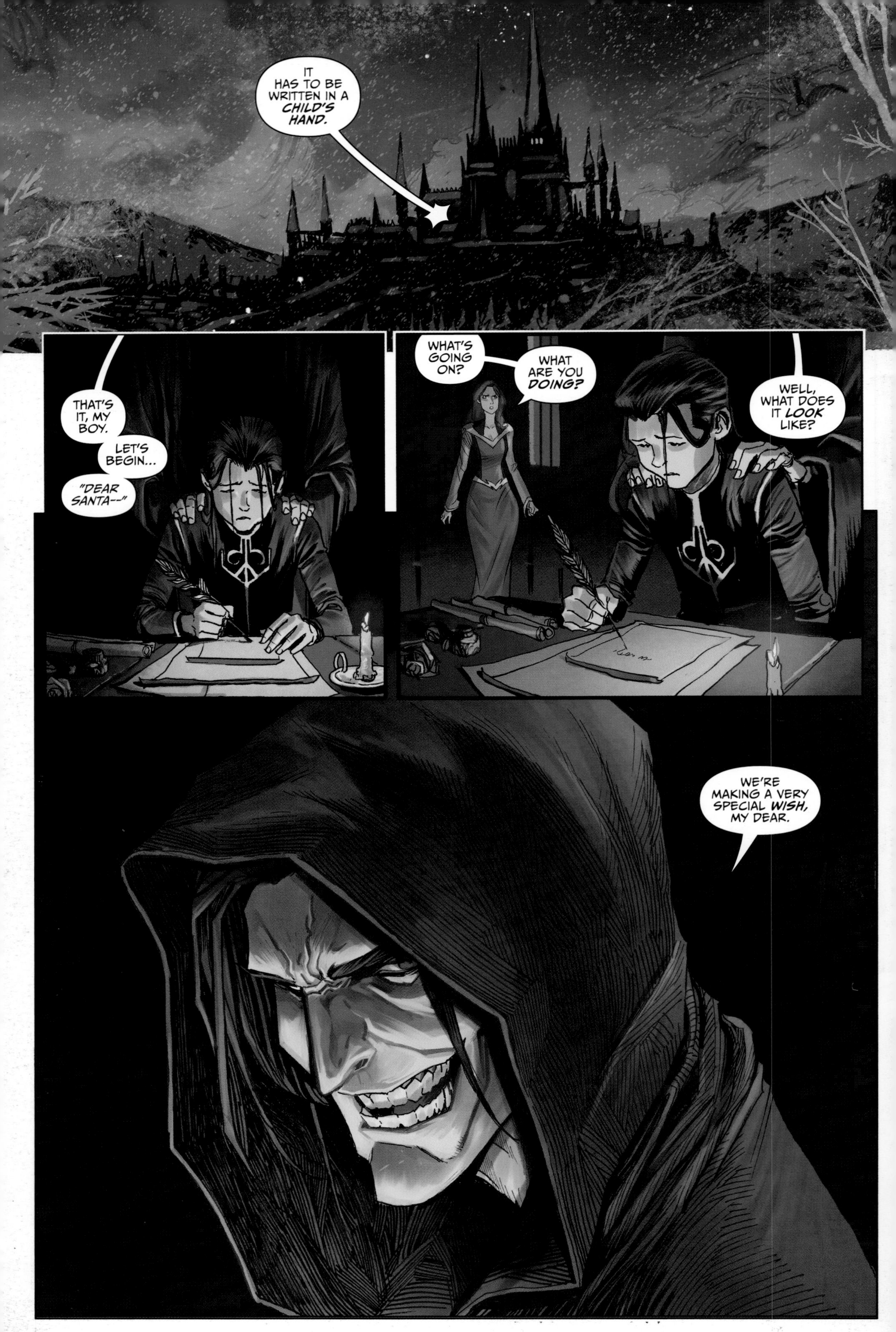
IT HAS TO BE WRITTEN IN A CHILD'S HAND.
THAT'S IT, MY BOY.
LET'S BEGIN...
"DEAR SANTA--"
WHAT'S GOING ON?
WHAT ARE YOU DOING?
WELL, WHAT DOES IT LOOK LIKE?
WE'RE MAKING A VERY SPECIAL WISH, MY DEAR.

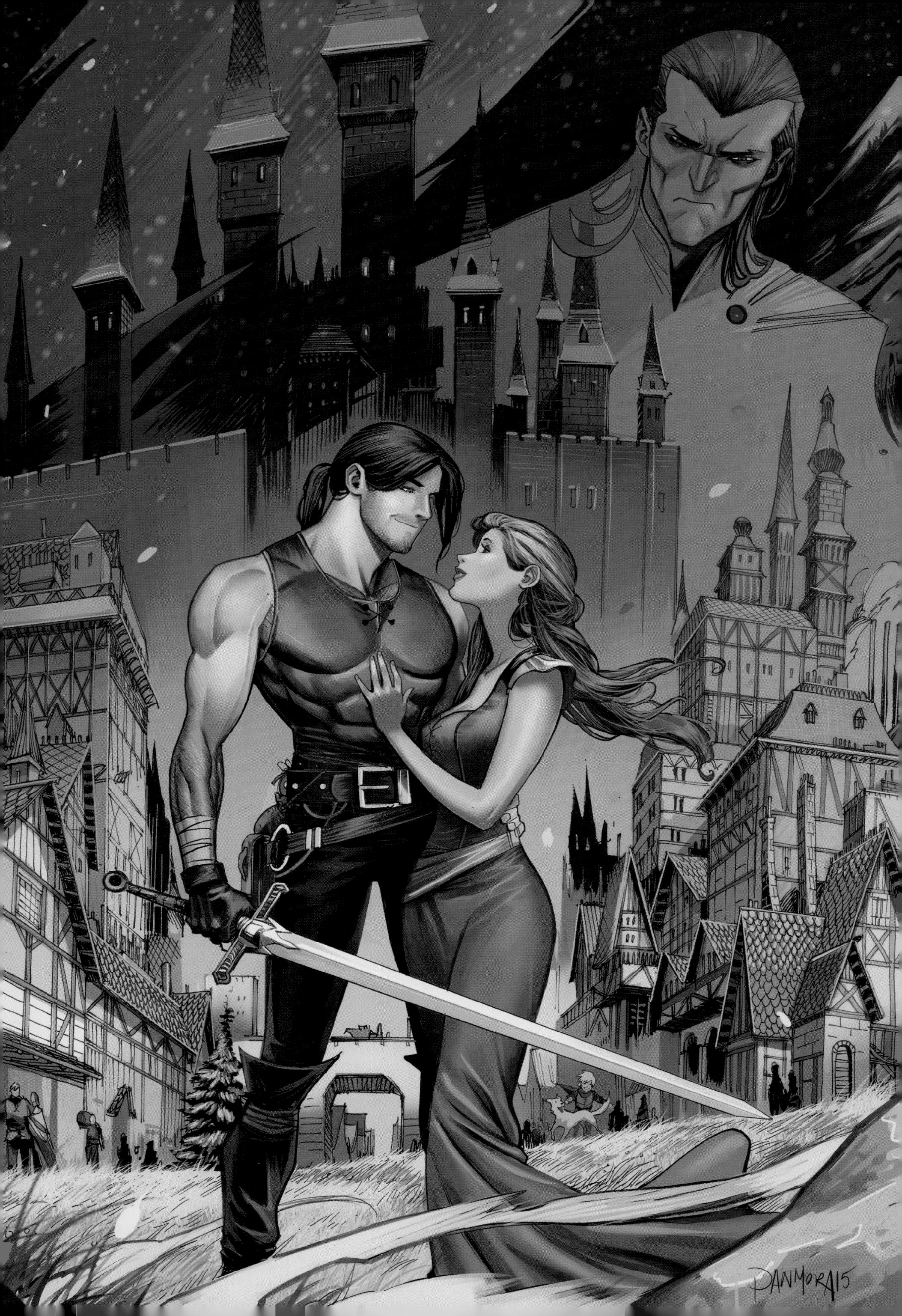
DANMORA15

CHAPTER FIVE

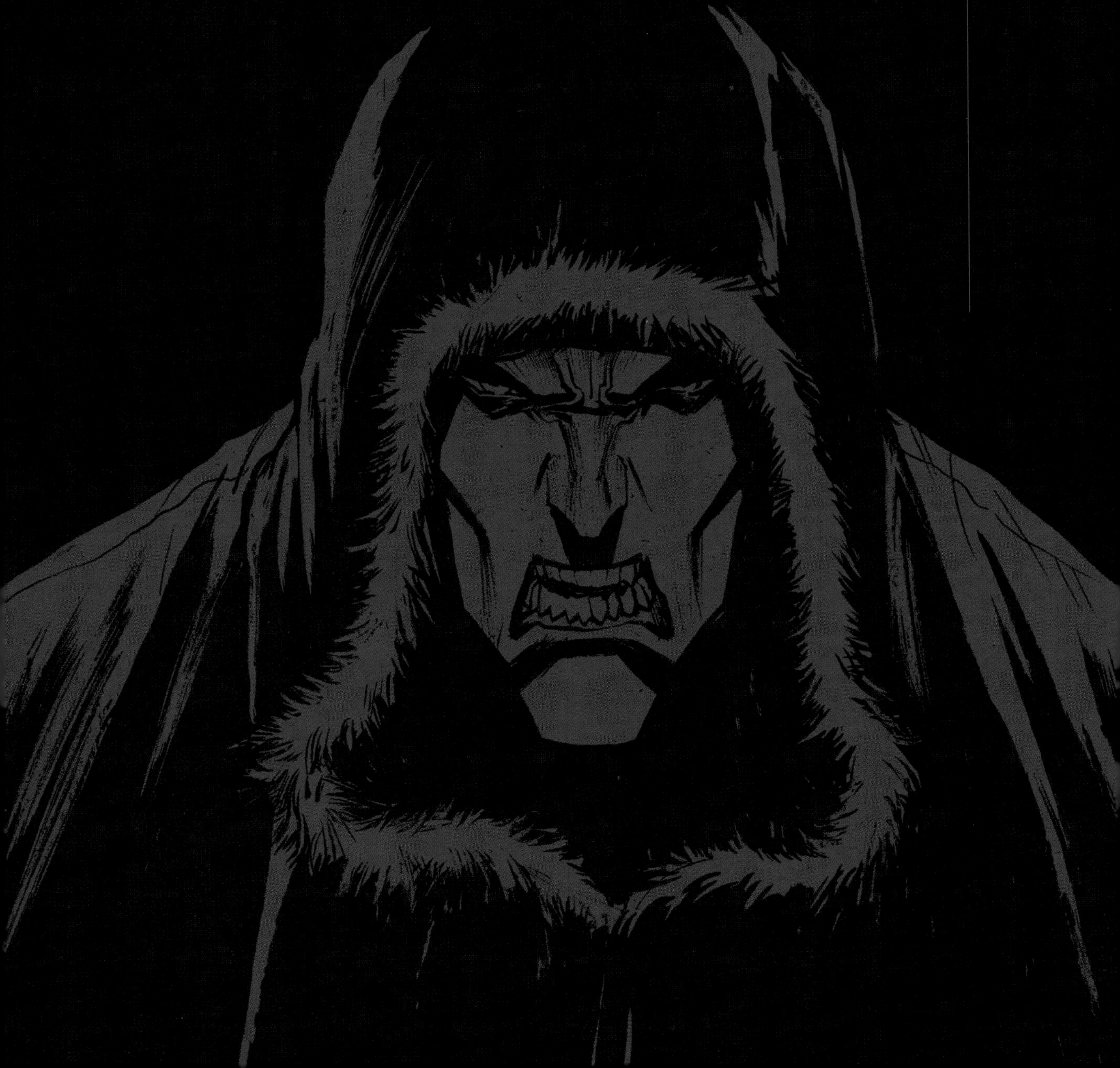

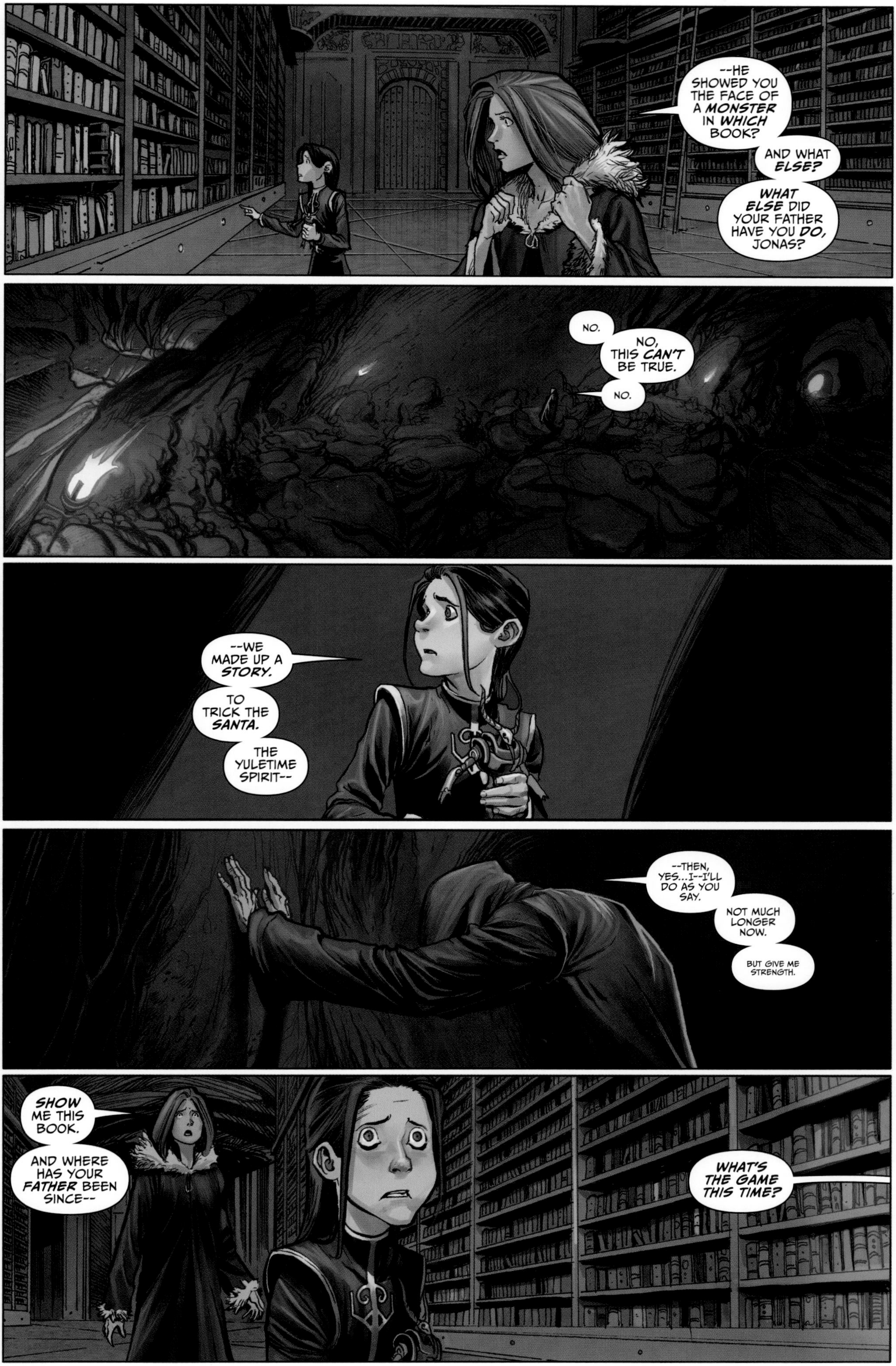
--HE SHOWED YOU THE FACE OF A MONSTER IN WHICH BOOK?
AND WHAT ELSE?
WHAT ELSE DID YOUR FATHER HAVE YOU DO, JONAS?
NO.
NO, THIS CAN'T BE TRUE.
NO.
--WE MADE UP A STORY.
TO TRICK THE SANTA.
THE YULETIME SPIRIT--
--THEN, YES...I--I'LL DO AS YOU SAY.
NOT MUCH LONGER NOW.
BUT GIVE ME STRENGTH.
SHOW ME THIS BOOK.
AND WHERE HAS YOUR FATHER BEEN SINCE--
WHAT'S THE GAME THIS TIME?

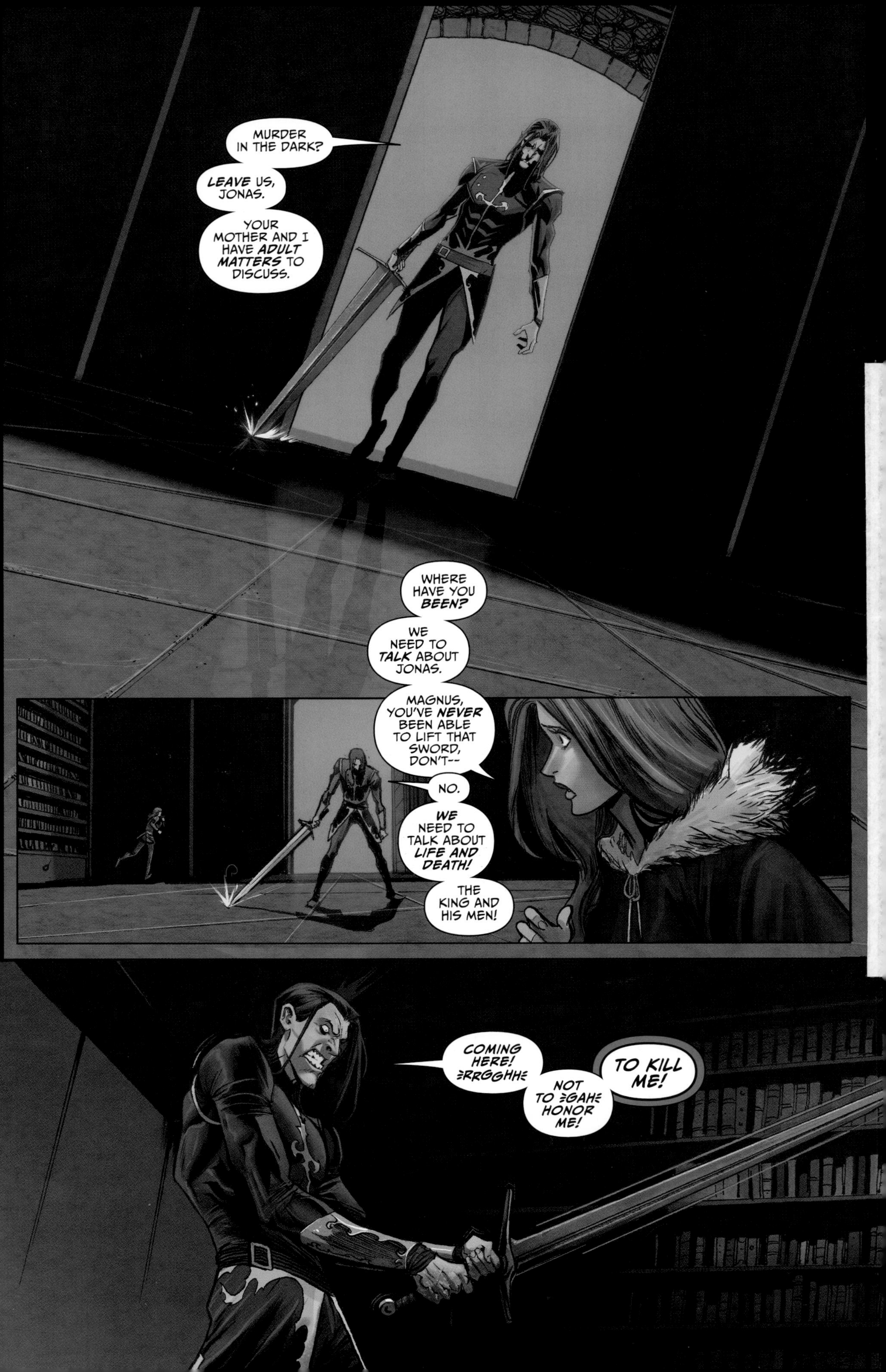
MURDER IN THE DARK?
LEAVE US, JONAS.
YOUR MOTHER AND I HAVE ADULT MATTERS TO DISCUSS.
WHERE HAVE YOU BEEN?
WE NEED TO TALK ABOUT JONAS.
MAGNUS, YOU'VE NEVER BEEN ABLE TO LIFT THAT SWORD, DON'T--
NO.
WE NEED TO TALK ABOUT LIFE AND DEATH!
THE KING AND HIS MEN!
COMING HERE! RRGGHH
NOT TO GAH HONOR ME!
TO KILL ME!

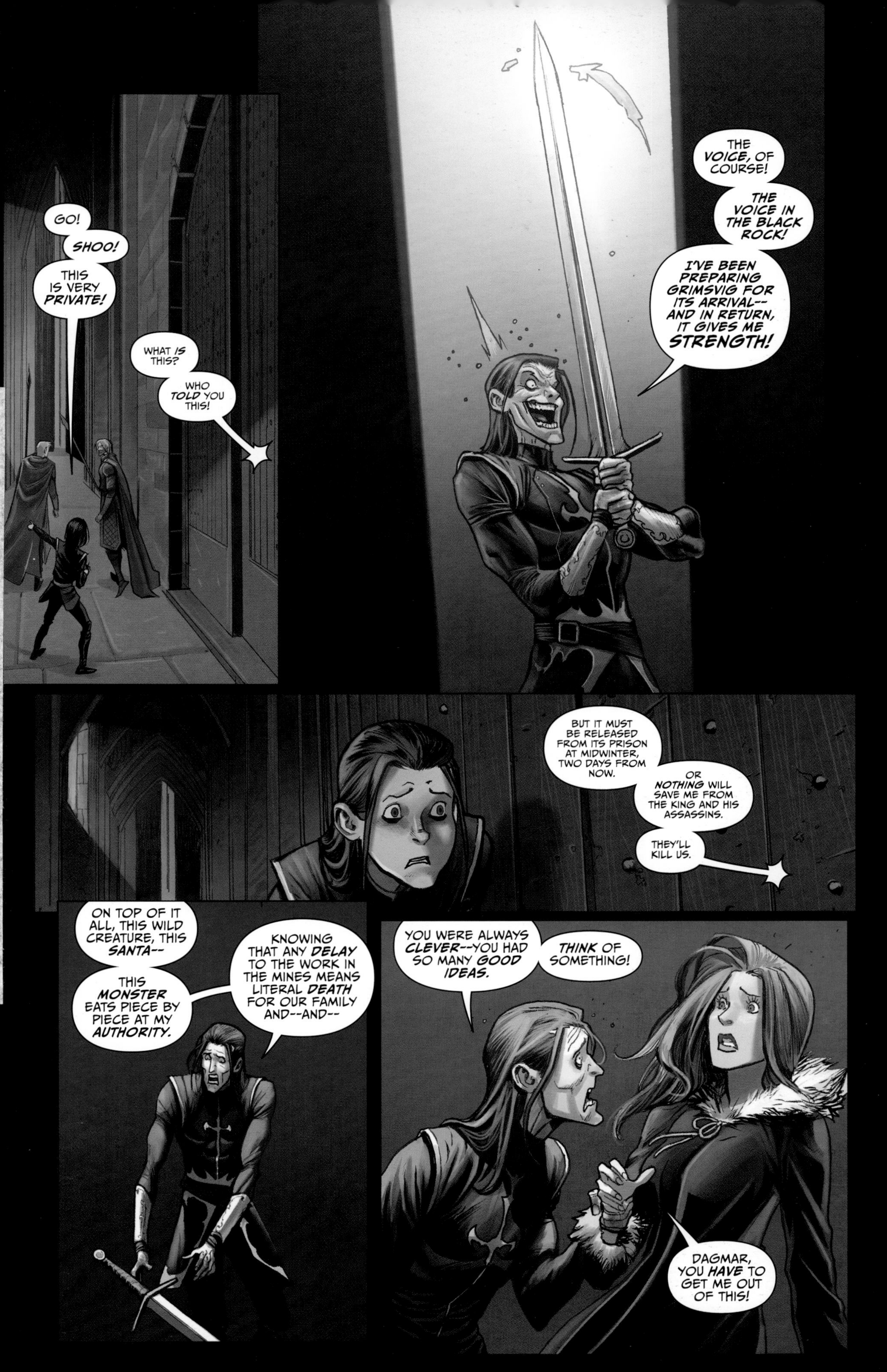
GO!
SHOO!
THIS IS VERY PRIVATE!
WHAT IS THIS?
WHO TOLD YOU THIS!
THE VOICE, OF COURSE!
THE VOICE IN THE BLACK ROCK!
I'VE BEEN PREPARING GRIMSVIG FOR ITS ARRIVAL-- AND IN RETURN, IT GIVES ME STRENGTH!
BUT IT MUST BE RELEASED FROM ITS PRISON AT MIDWINTER, TWO DAYS FROM NOW.
OR NOTHING WILL SAVE ME FROM THE KING AND HIS ASSASSINS.
THEY'LL KILL US.
ON TOP OF IT ALL, THIS WILD CREATURE, THIS SANTA--
THIS MONSTER EATS PIECE BY PIECE AT MY AUTHORITY.
KNOWING THAT ANY DELAY TO THE WORK IN THE MINES MEANS LITERAL DEATH FOR OUR FAMILY AND--AND--
YOU WERE ALWAYS CLEVER--YOU HAD SO MANY GOOD IDEAS.
THINK OF SOMETHING!
DAGMAR, YOU HAVE TO GET ME OUT OF THIS!

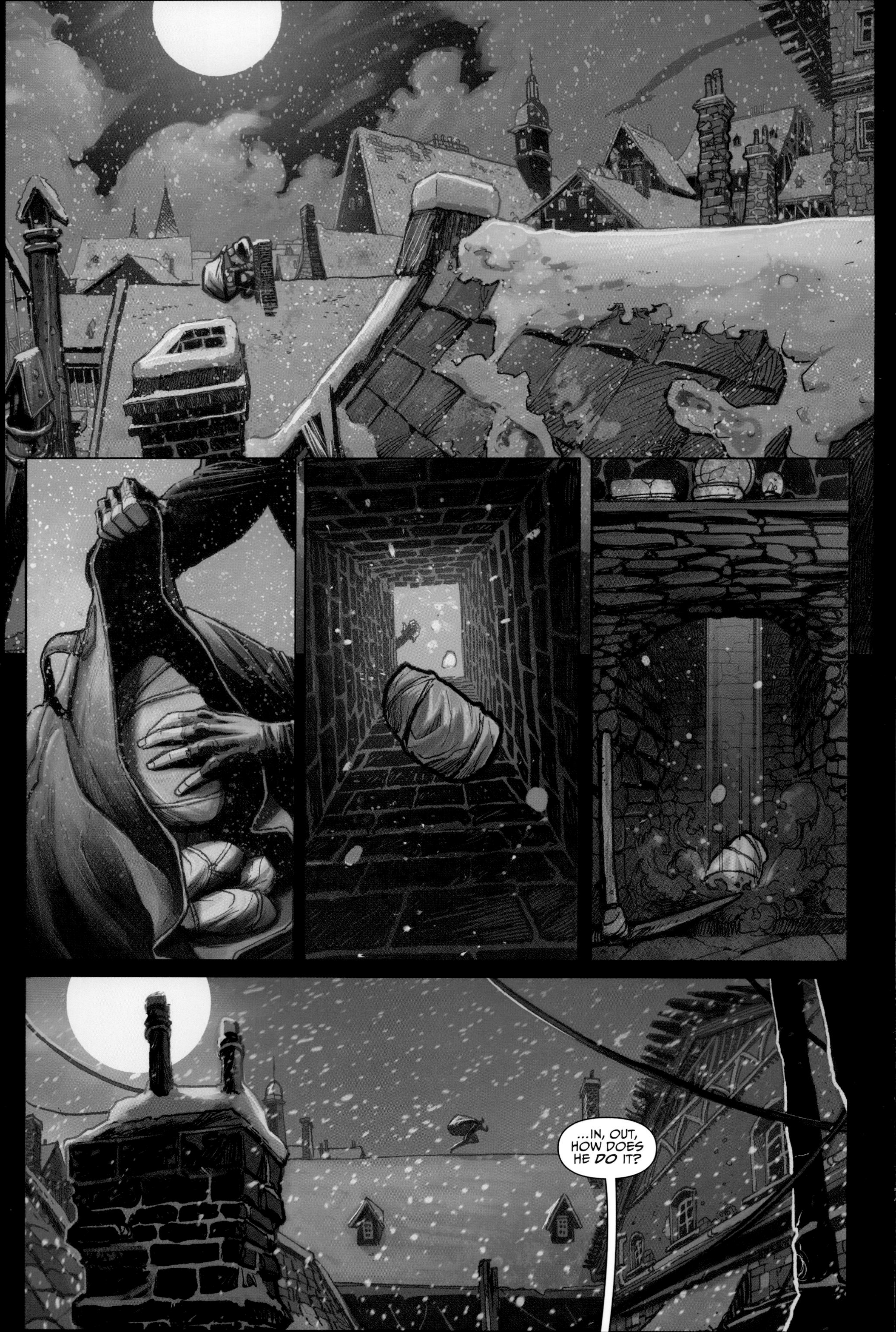
...IN, OUT, HOW DOES HE *DO* IT?

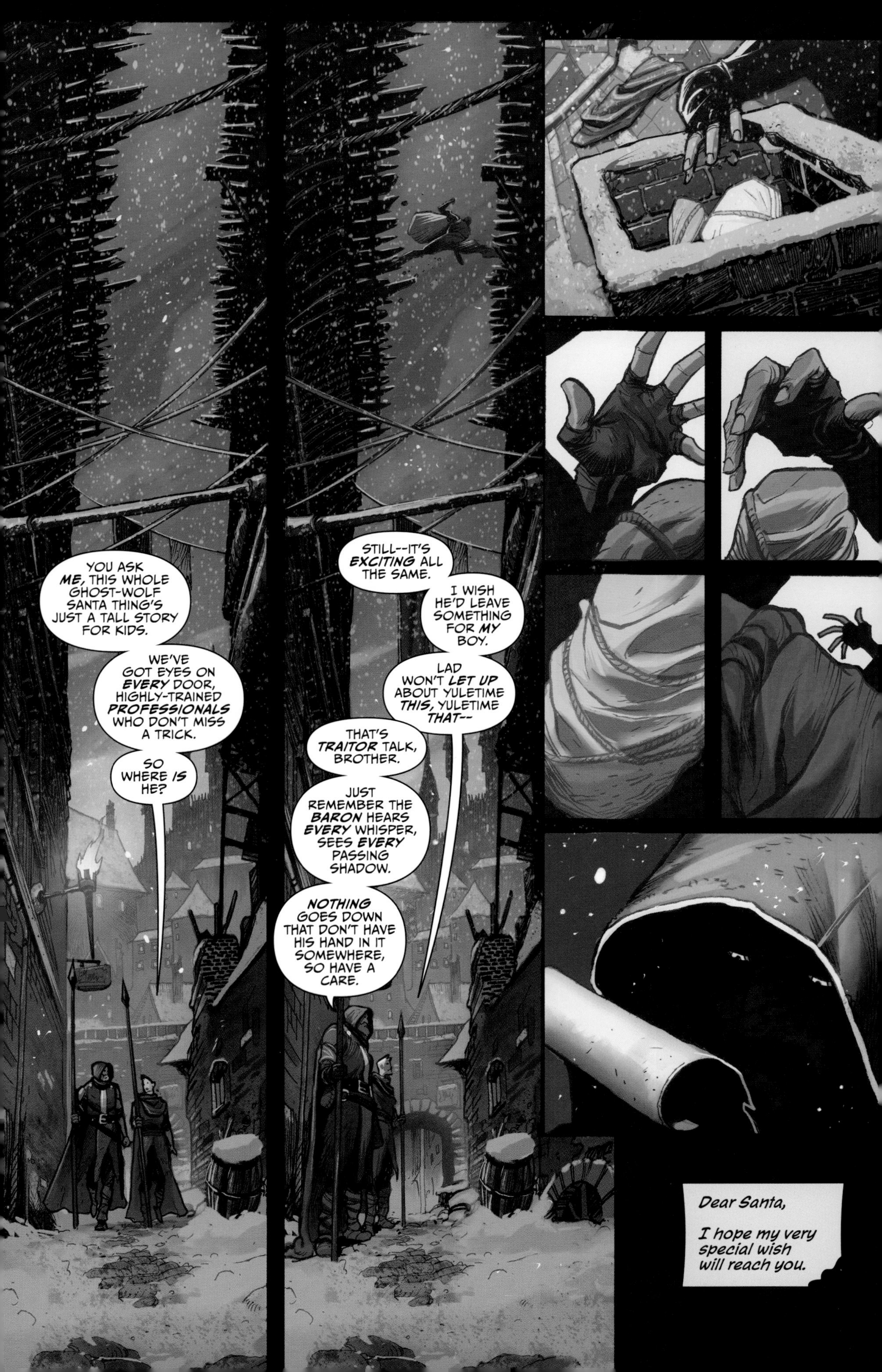

YOU ASK *ME,* THIS WHOLE GHOST-WOLF SANTA THING'S JUST A TALL STORY FOR KIDS.
WE'VE GOT EYES ON *EVERY* DOOR, HIGHLY-TRAINED *PROFESSIONALS* WHO DON'T MISS A TRICK.
SO WHERE *IS* HE?
STILL--IT'S *EXCITING* ALL THE SAME.
I WISH HE'D LEAVE SOMETHING FOR *MY* BOY.
LAD WON'T *LET UP* ABOUT YULETIME *THIS,* YULETIME *THAT*--
THAT'S *TRAITOR* TALK, BROTHER.
JUST REMEMBER THE *BARON* HEARS *EVERY* WHISPER, SEES *EVERY* PASSING SHADOW.
NOTHING GOES DOWN THAT DON'T HAVE HIS HAND IN IT SOMEWHERE, SO HAVE A CARE.
Dear Santa,
I hope my very special wish will reach you.

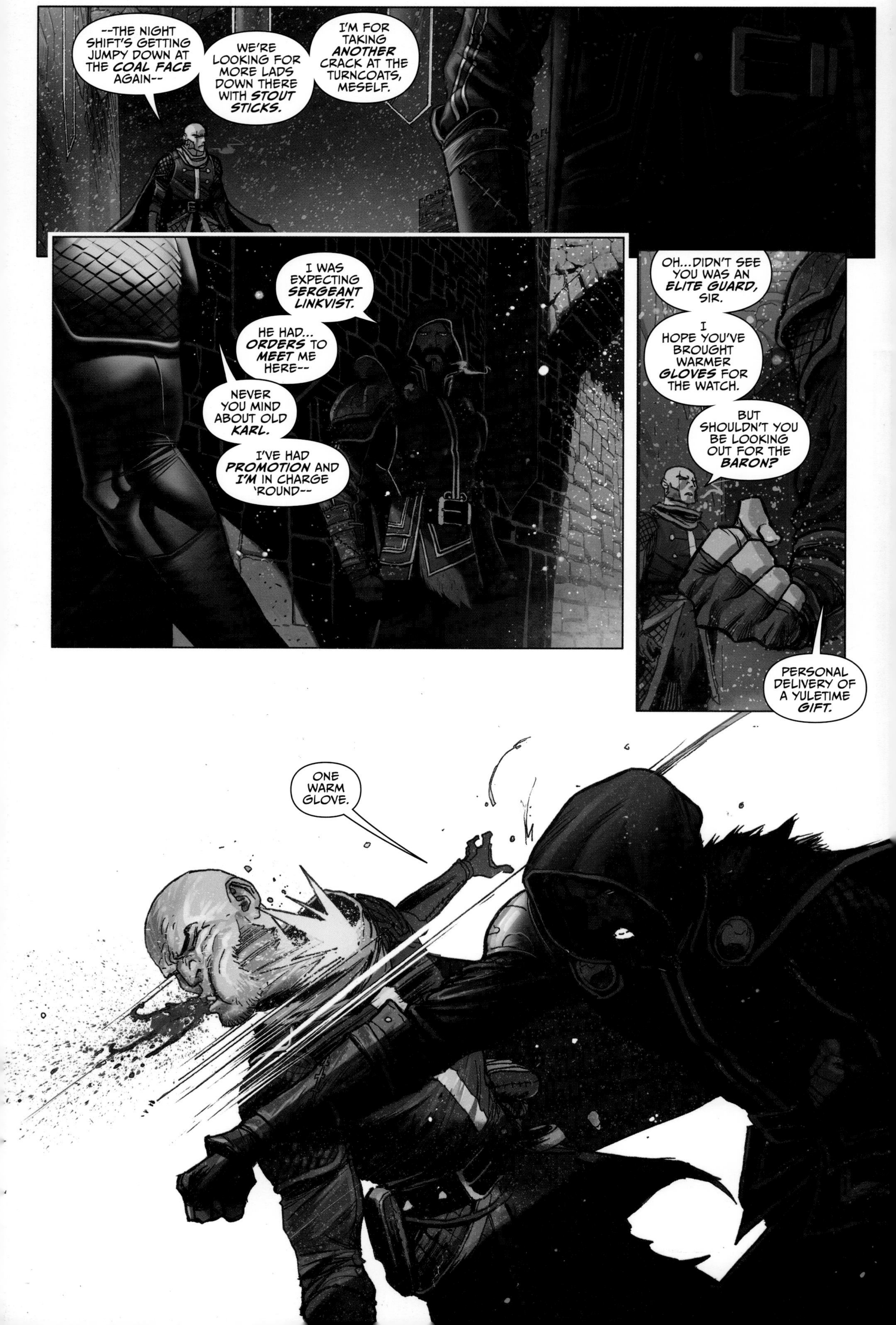
--THE NIGHT SHIFT'S GETTING JUMPY DOWN AT THE COAL FACE AGAIN--
WE'RE LOOKING FOR MORE LADS DOWN THERE WITH STOUT STICKS.
I'M FOR TAKING ANOTHER CRACK AT THE TURNCOATS, MESELF.
I WAS EXPECTING SERGEANT LINKVIST.
HE HAD... ORDERS TO MEET ME HERE--
NEVER YOU MIND ABOUT OLD KARL.
I'VE HAD PROMOTION AND I'M IN CHARGE 'ROUND--
OH...DIDN'T SEE YOU WAS AN ELITE GUARD, SIR.
I HOPE YOU'VE BROUGHT WARMER GLOVES FOR THE WATCH.
BUT SHOULDN'T YOU BE LOOKING OUT FOR THE BARON?
PERSONAL DELIVERY OF A YULETIME GIFT.
ONE WARM GLOVE.

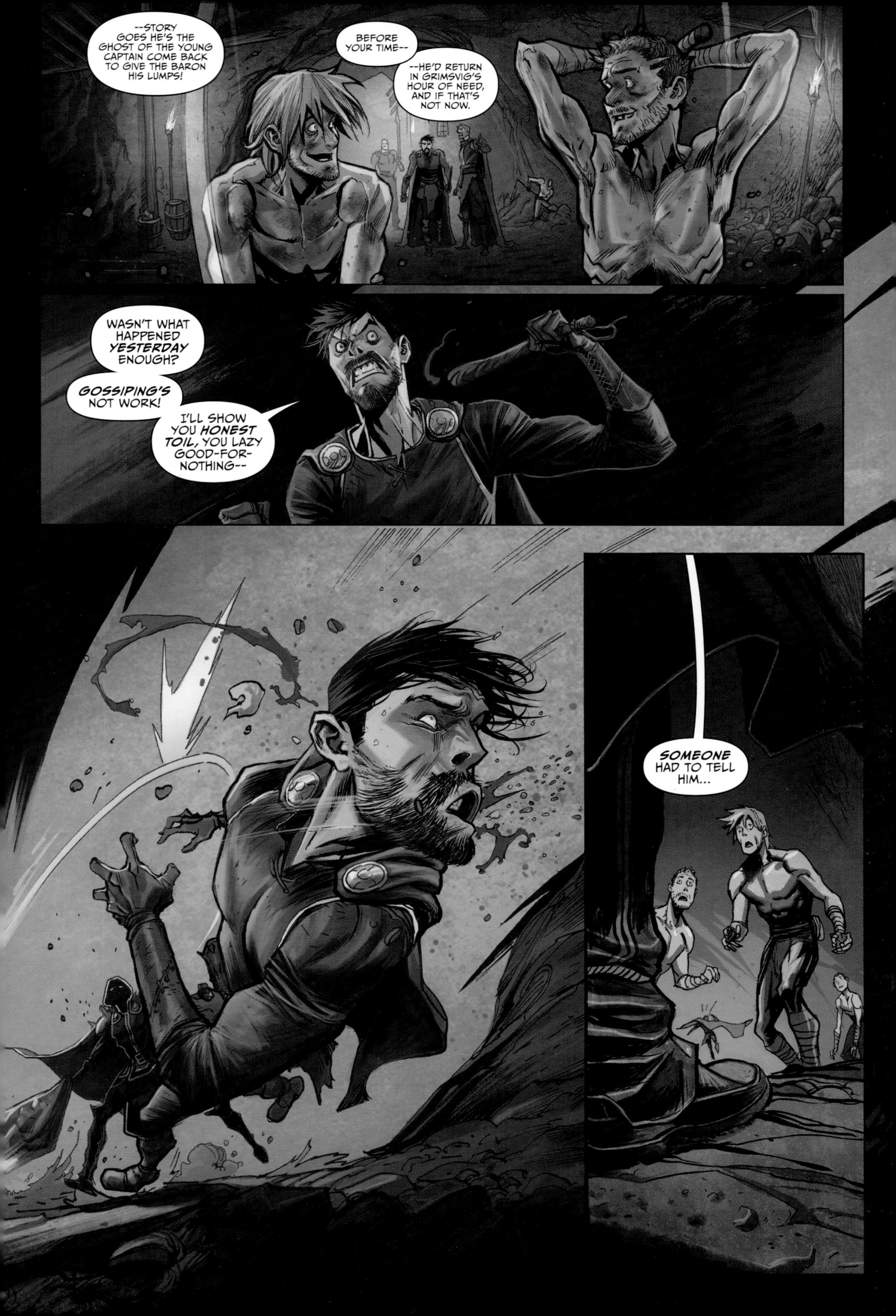
--STORY GOES HE'S THE GHOST OF THE YOUNG CAPTAIN COME BACK TO GIVE THE BARON HIS LUMPS!
BEFORE YOUR TIME--
--HE'D RETURN IN GRIMSVIG'S HOUR OF NEED, AND IF THAT'S NOT NOW.
WASN'T WHAT HAPPENED ***YESTERDAY*** ENOUGH?
GOSSIPING'S NOT WORK!
I'LL SHOW YOU ***HONEST TOIL,*** YOU LAZY GOOD-FOR-NOTHING--
SOMEONE HAD TO TELL HIM...

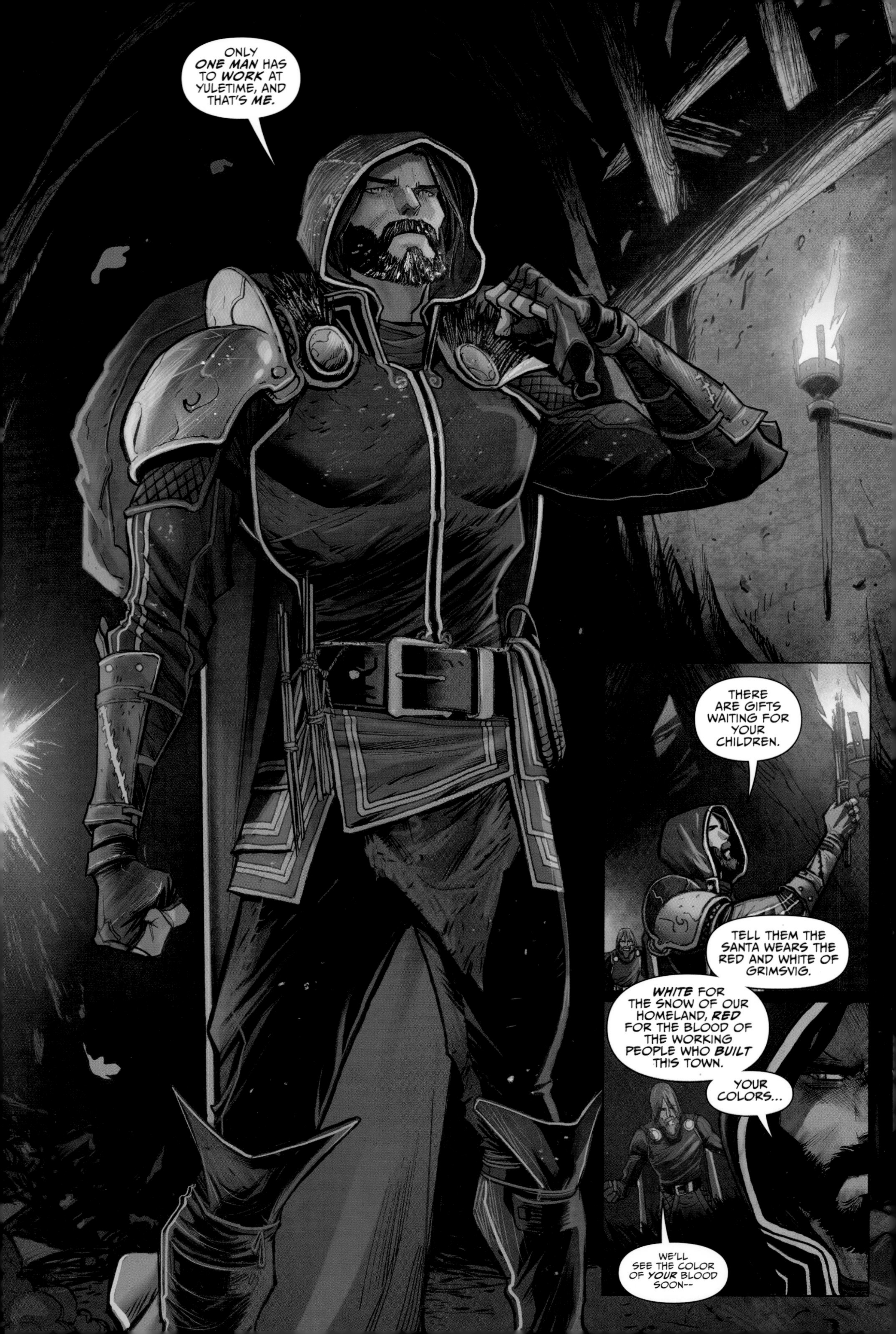
ONLY ONE MAN HAS TO WORK AT YULETIME, AND THAT'S ME.
THERE ARE GIFTS WAITING FOR YOUR CHILDREN.
TELL THEM THE SANTA WEARS THE RED AND WHITE OF GRIMSVIG.
WHITE FOR THE SNOW OF OUR HOMELAND, RED FOR THE BLOOD OF THE WORKING PEOPLE WHO BUILT THIS TOWN.
YOUR COLORS...
WE'LL SEE THE COLOR OF YOUR BLOOD SOON--

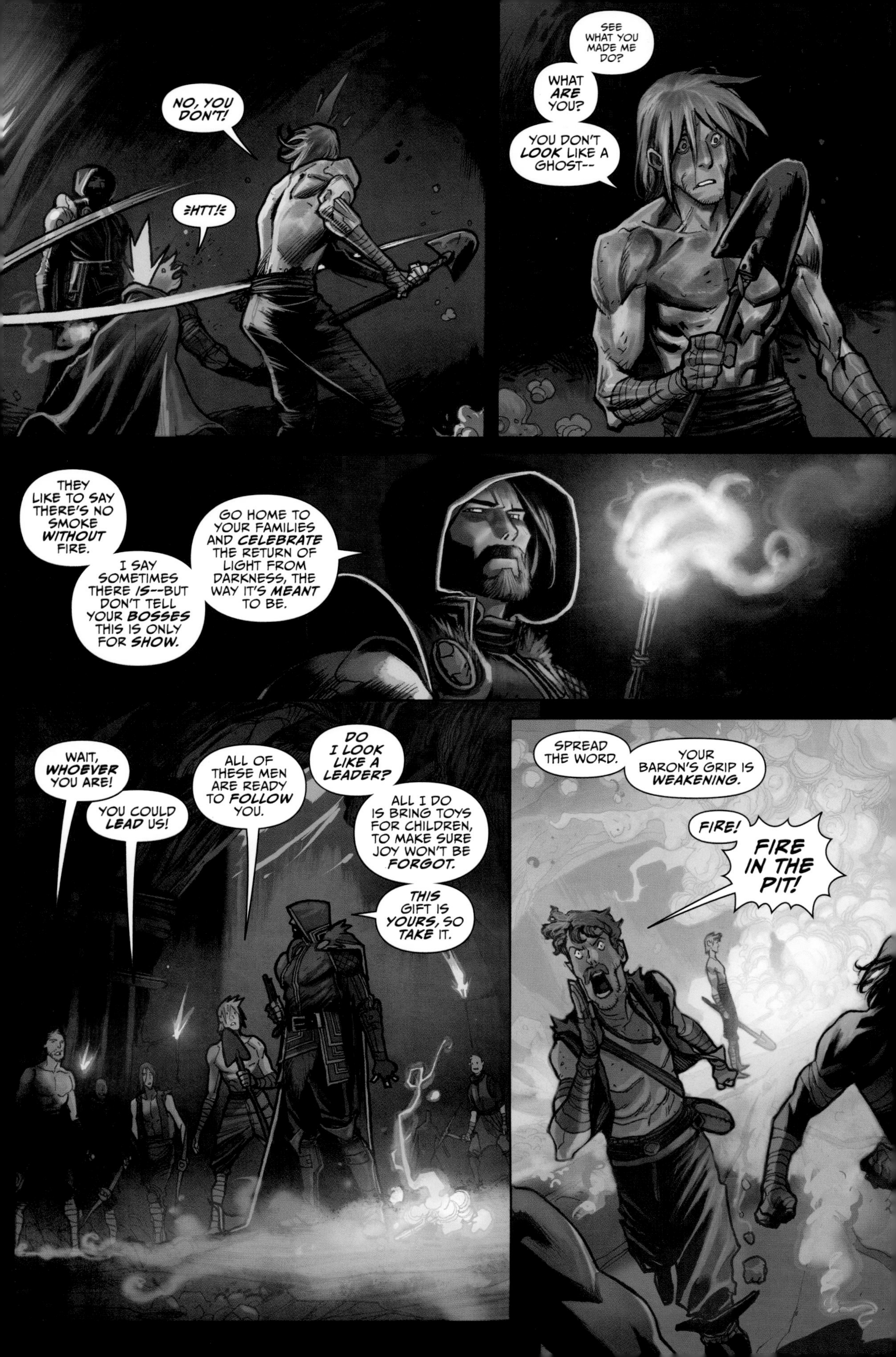
NO, YOU DON'T!
≷HTT!≶
SEE WHAT YOU MADE ME DO?
WHAT ARE YOU?
YOU DON'T LOOK LIKE A GHOST--
THEY LIKE TO SAY THERE'S NO SMOKE WITHOUT FIRE.
I SAY SOMETIMES THERE IS--BUT DON'T TELL YOUR BOSSES THIS IS ONLY FOR SHOW.
GO HOME TO YOUR FAMILIES AND CELEBRATE THE RETURN OF LIGHT FROM DARKNESS, THE WAY IT'S MEANT TO BE.
WAIT, WHOEVER YOU ARE!
YOU COULD LEAD US!
ALL OF THESE MEN ARE READY TO FOLLOW YOU.
DO I LOOK LIKE A LEADER?
ALL I DO IS BRING TOYS FOR CHILDREN, TO MAKE SURE JOY WON'T BE FORGOT.
THIS GIFT IS YOURS, SO TAKE IT.
SPREAD THE WORD.
YOUR BARON'S GRIP IS WEAKENING.
FIRE!
FIRE IN THE PIT!

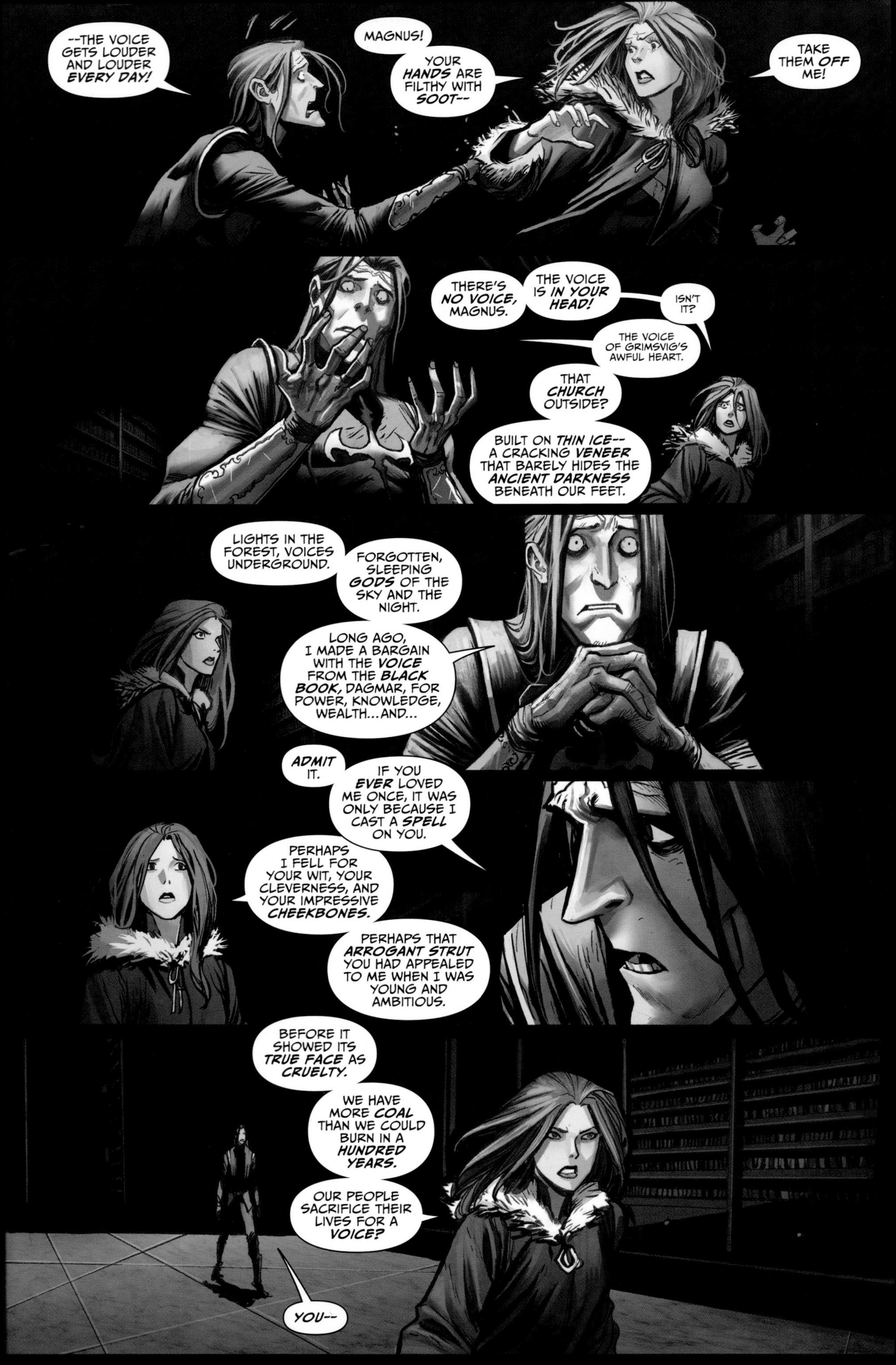
--THE VOICE GETS LOUDER AND LOUDER EVERY DAY!
MAGNUS!
YOUR HANDS ARE FILTHY WITH SOOT--
TAKE THEM OFF ME!
THERE'S NO VOICE, MAGNUS.
THE VOICE IS IN YOUR HEAD!
ISN'T IT?
THE VOICE OF GRIMSVIG'S AWFUL HEART.
THAT CHURCH OUTSIDE?
BUILT ON THIN ICE-- A CRACKING VENEER THAT BARELY HIDES THE ANCIENT DARKNESS BENEATH OUR FEET.
LIGHTS IN THE FOREST, VOICES UNDERGROUND.
FORGOTTEN, SLEEPING GODS OF THE SKY AND THE NIGHT.
LONG AGO, I MADE A BARGAIN WITH THE VOICE FROM THE BLACK BOOK, DAGMAR, FOR POWER, KNOWLEDGE, WEALTH...AND...
ADMIT IT.
IF YOU EVER LOVED ME ONCE, IT WAS ONLY BECAUSE I CAST A SPELL ON YOU.
PERHAPS I FELL FOR YOUR WIT, YOUR CLEVERNESS, AND YOUR IMPRESSIVE CHEEKBONES.
PERHAPS THAT ARROGANT STRUT YOU HAD APPEALED TO ME WHEN I WAS YOUNG AND AMBITIOUS.
BEFORE IT SHOWED ITS TRUE FACE AS CRUELTY.
WE HAVE MORE COAL THAN WE COULD BURN IN A HUNDRED YEARS.
OUR PEOPLE SACRIFICE THEIR LIVES FOR A VOICE?
YOU--

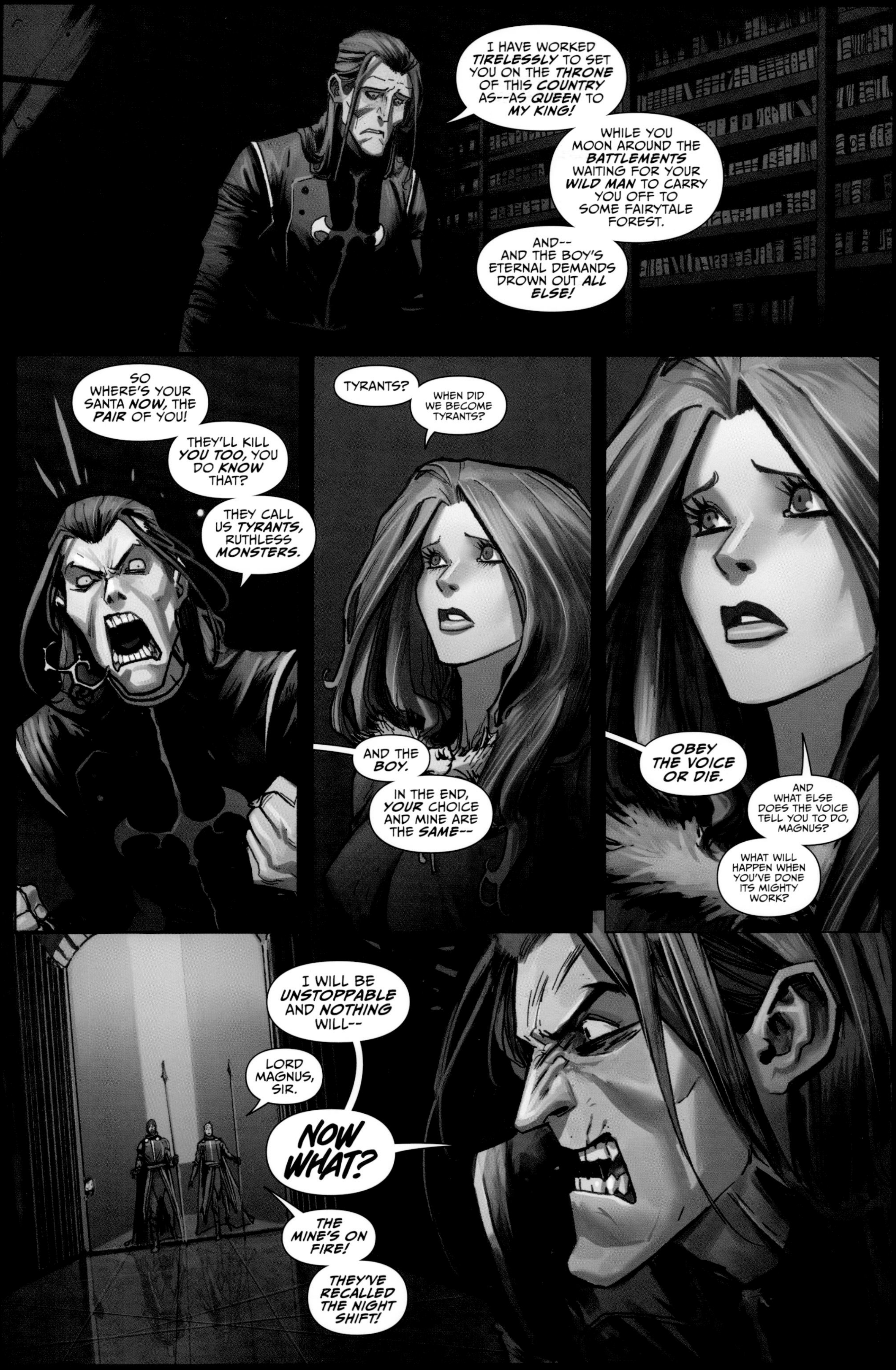
I HAVE WORKED TIRELESSLY TO SET YOU ON THE THRONE OF THIS COUNTRY AS--AS QUEEN TO MY KING!
WHILE YOU MOON AROUND THE BATTLEMENTS WAITING FOR YOUR WILD MAN TO CARRY YOU OFF TO SOME FAIRYTALE FOREST.
AND-- AND THE BOY'S ETERNAL DEMANDS DROWN OUT ALL ELSE!
SO WHERE'S YOUR SANTA NOW, THE PAIR OF YOU!
THEY'LL KILL YOU TOO, YOU DO KNOW THAT?
THEY CALL US TYRANTS, RUTHLESS MONSTERS.
TYRANTS?
WHEN DID WE BECOME TYRANTS?
AND THE BOY.
IN THE END, YOUR CHOICE AND MINE ARE THE SAME--
OBEY THE VOICE OR DIE.
AND WHAT ELSE DOES THE VOICE TELL YOU TO DO, MAGNUS?
WHAT WILL HAPPEN WHEN YOU'VE DONE ITS MIGHTY WORK?
I WILL BE UNSTOPPABLE AND NOTHING WILL--
LORD MAGNUS, SIR.
NOW WHAT?
THE MINE'S ON FIRE!
THEY'VE RECALLED THE NIGHT SHIFT!

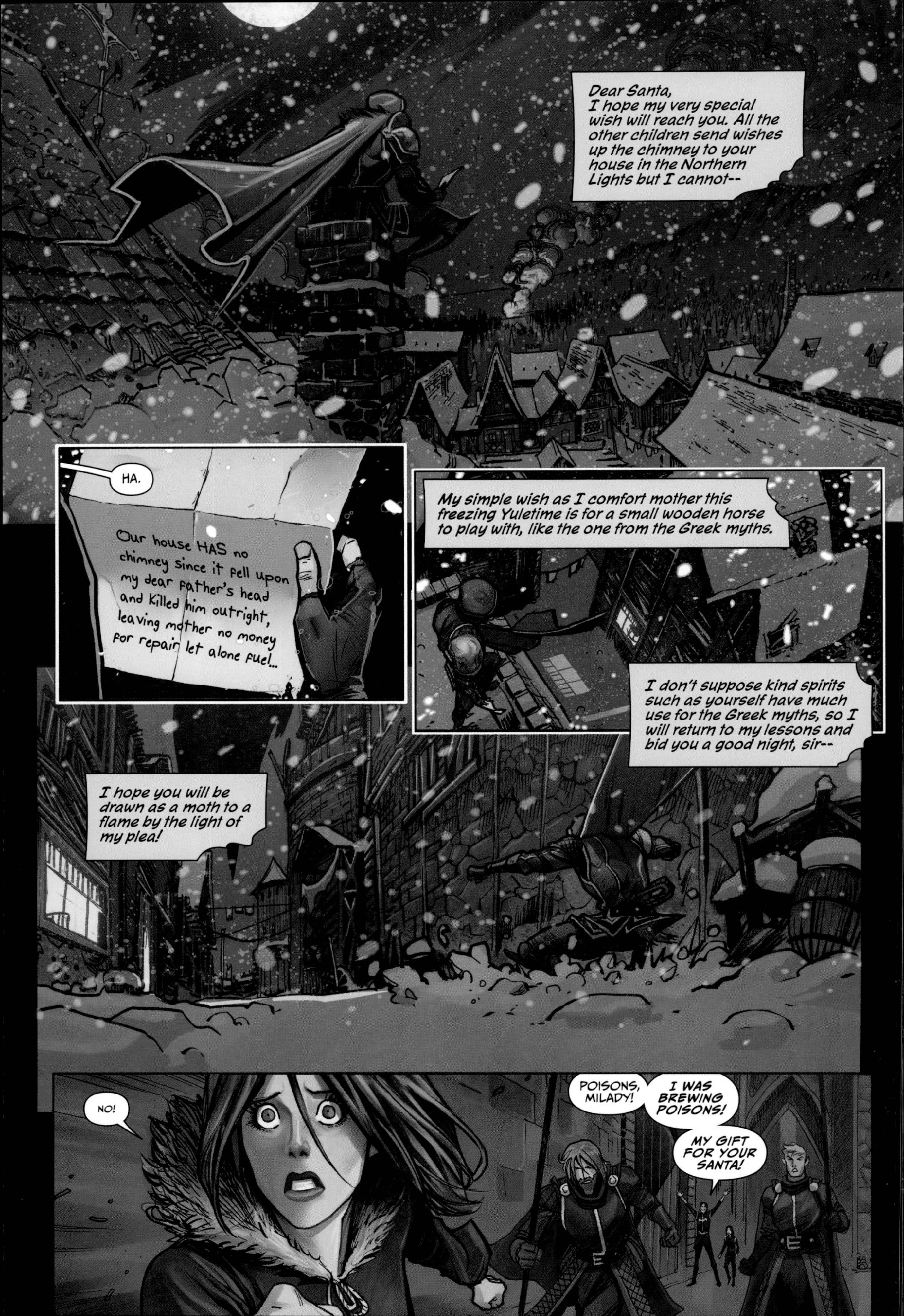

Dear Santa,
I hope my very special wish will reach you. All the other children send wishes up the chimney to your house in the Northern Lights but I cannot--
HA.
Our house HAS no chimney since it fell upon my dear father's head and killed him outright, leaving mother no money for repair let alone fuel...
My simple wish as I comfort mother this freezing Yuletime is for a small wooden horse to play with, like the one from the Greek myths.
I don't suppose kind spirits such as yourself have much use for the Greek myths, so I will return to my lessons and bid you a good night, sir--
I hope you will be drawn as a moth to a flame by the light of my plea!
NO!
POISONS, MILADY!
I WAS BREWING POISONS!
MY GIFT FOR YOUR SANTA!

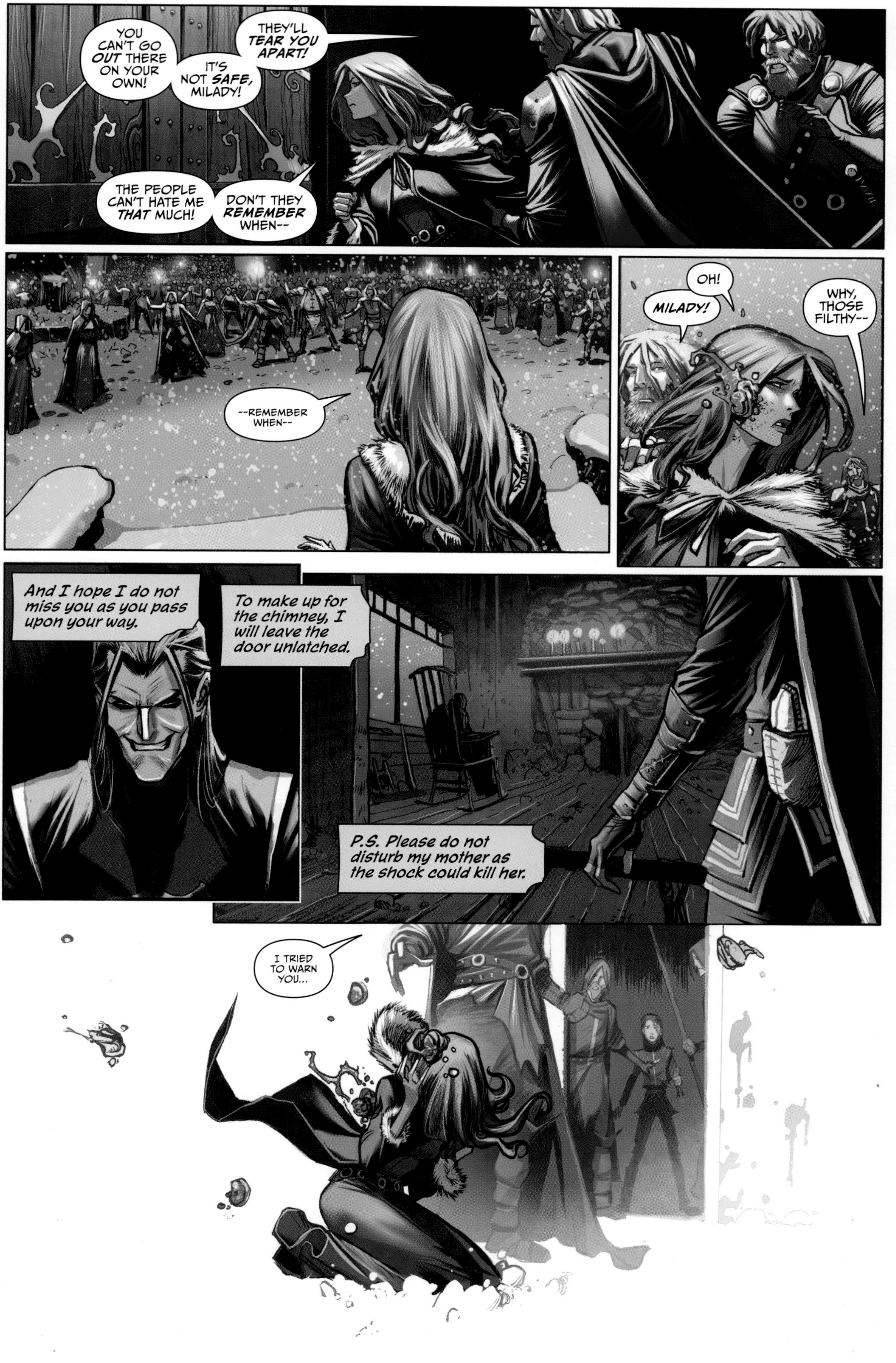

YOU CAN'T GO OUT THERE ON YOUR OWN!
IT'S NOT SAFE, MILADY!
THEY'LL TEAR YOU APART!
THE PEOPLE CAN'T HATE ME THAT MUCH!
DON'T THEY REMEMBER WHEN--
--REMEMBER WHEN--
OH!
MILADY!
WHY, THOSE FILTHY--
And I hope I do not miss you as you pass upon your way.
To make up for the chimney, I will leave the door unlatched.
P.S. Please do not disturb my mother as the shock could kill her.
I TRIED TO WARN YOU...

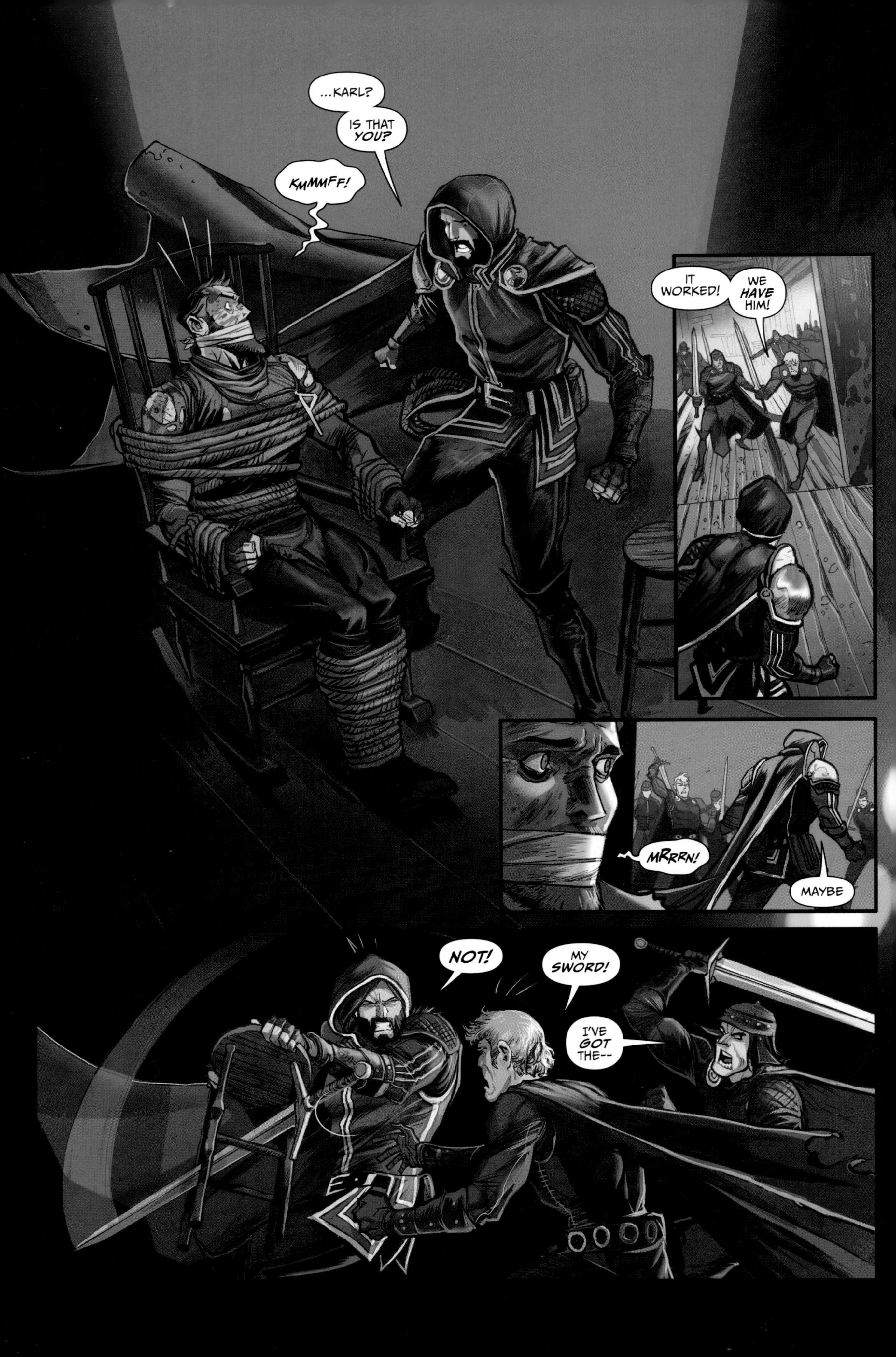
...KARL?
IS THAT YOU?
KMMMFF!
IT WORKED!
WE HAVE HIM!
MRRRN!
MAYBE
NOT!
MY SWORD!
I'VE GOT THE--

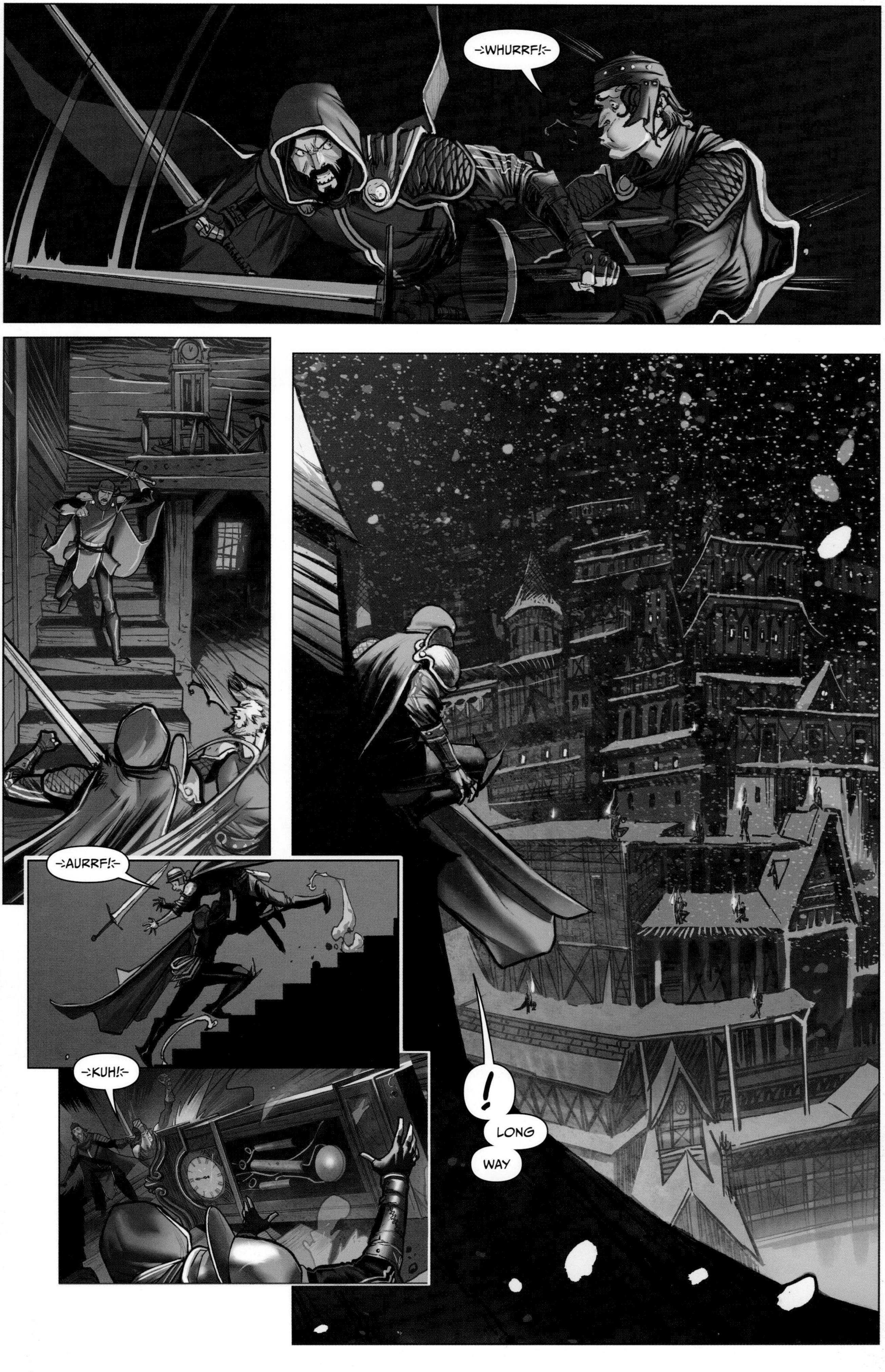

-WHURRF!-
-AURRF!-
-KUH!-
!
LONG
WAY

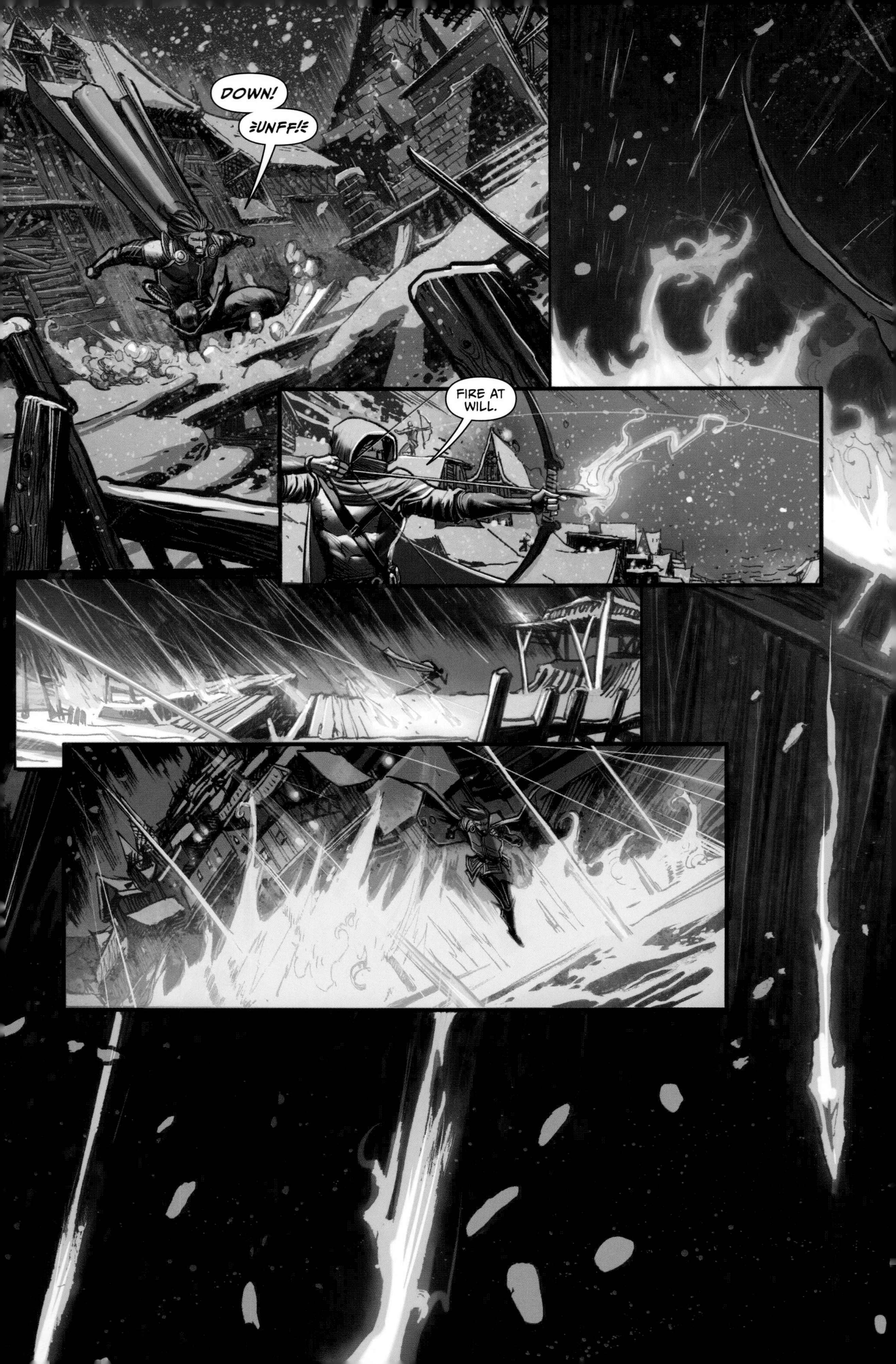
DOWN!
UNFF!
FIRE AT WILL.

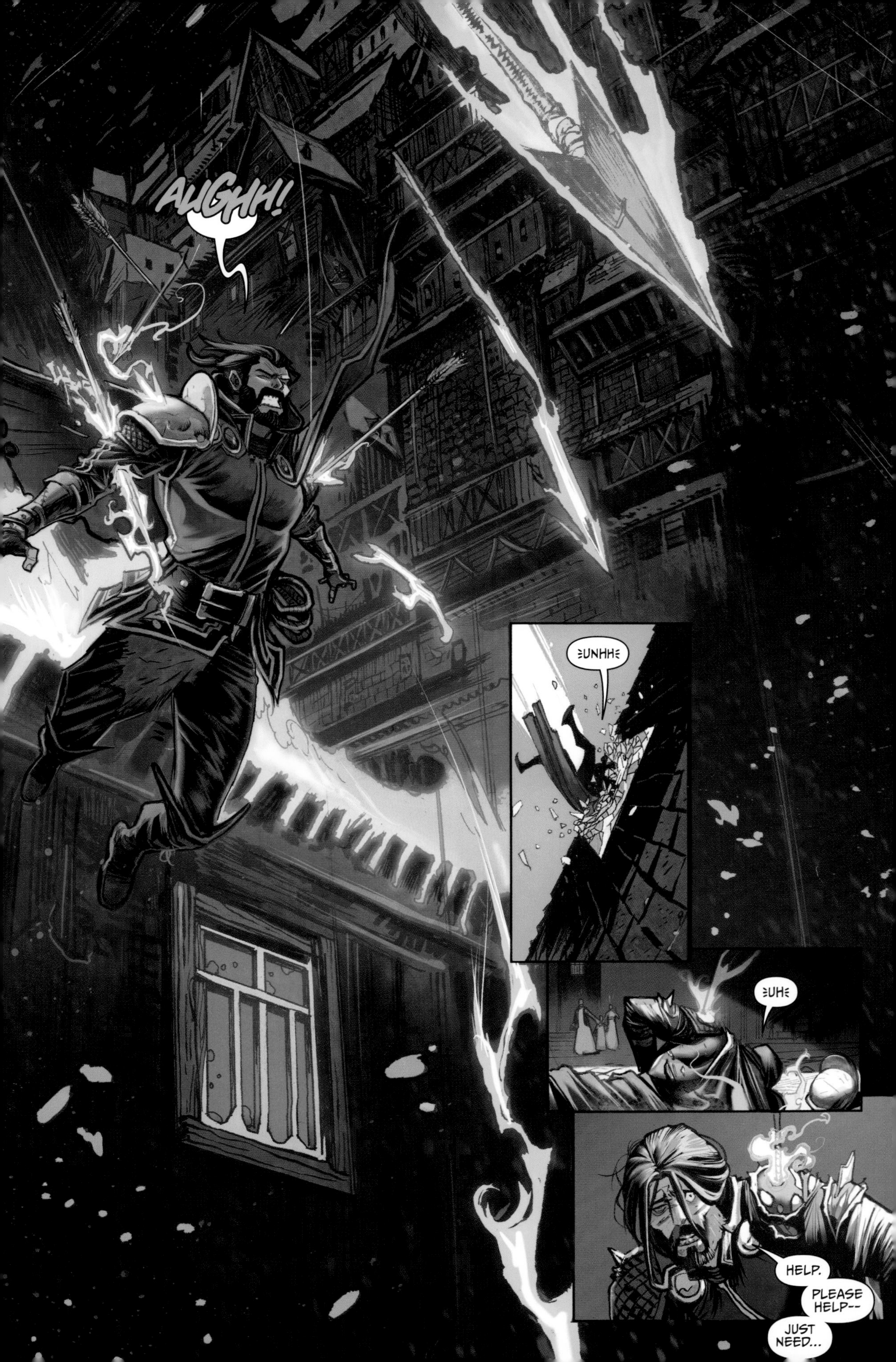
AUGHH!
UNHH
UH
HELP.
PLEASE HELP--
JUST NEED...

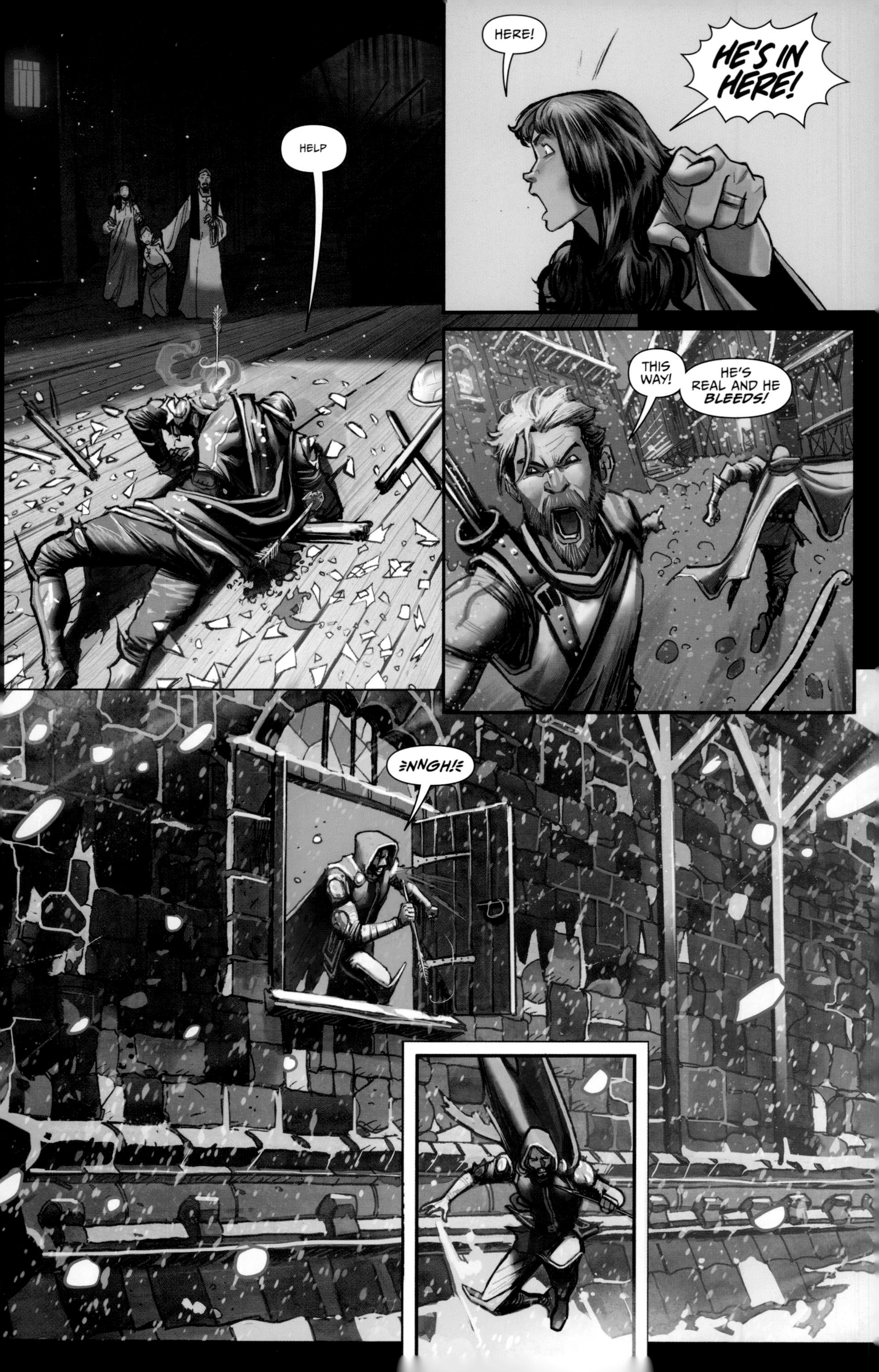
HELP
HERE!
HE'S IN HERE!
THIS WAY!
HE'S REAL AND HE BLEEDS!
NNGH!

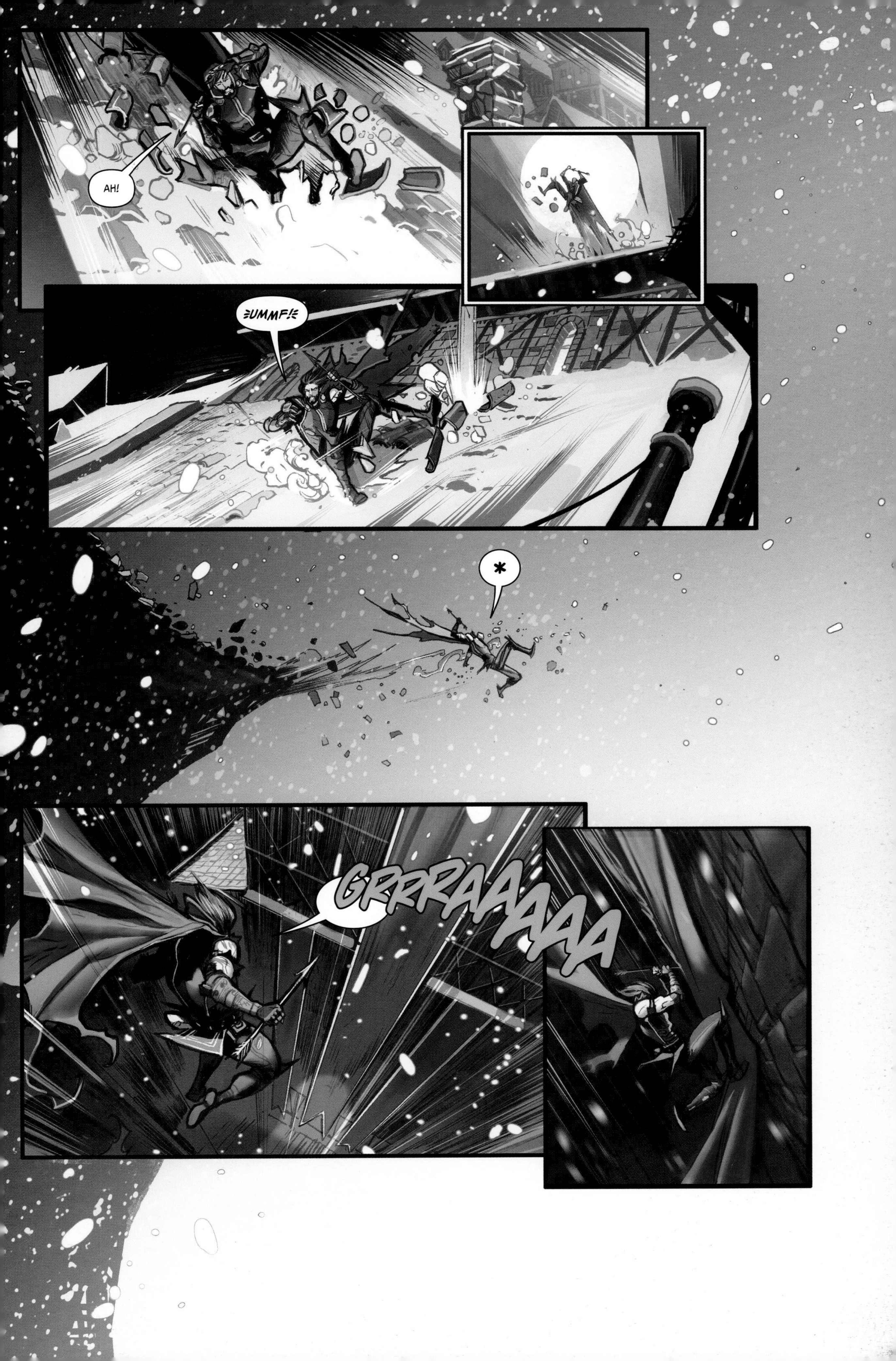
AH!
UMMF!
*
GRRRAAAAAAA

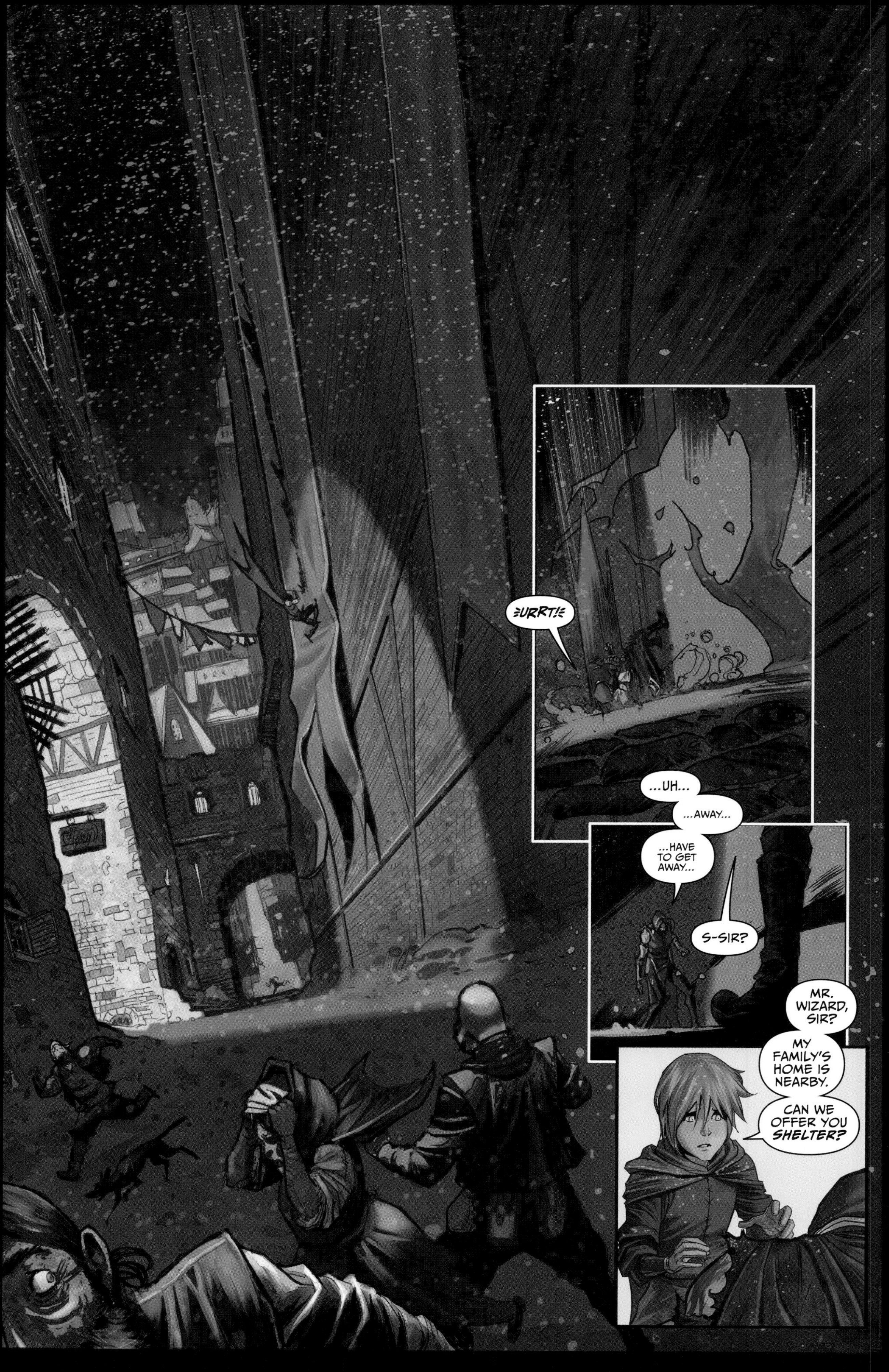
URRT!
...UH...
...AWAY...
...HAVE TO GET AWAY...
S-SIR?
MR. WIZARD, SIR?
MY FAMILY'S HOME IS NEARBY.
CAN WE OFFER YOU *SHELTER?*

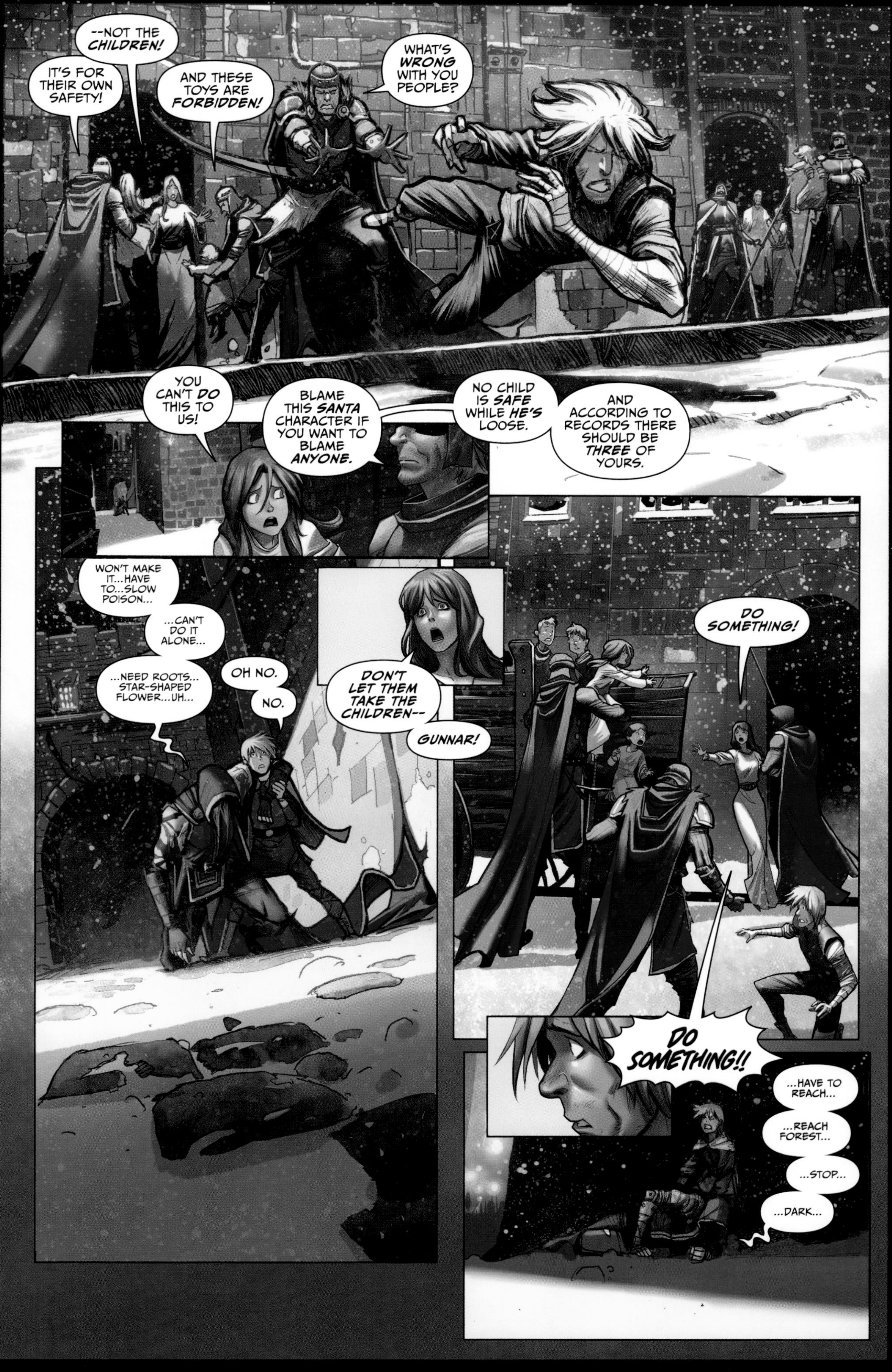

--NOT THE CHILDREN!
IT'S FOR THEIR OWN SAFETY!
AND THESE TOYS ARE FORBIDDEN!
WHAT'S WRONG WITH YOU PEOPLE?
YOU CAN'T DO THIS TO US!
BLAME THIS SANTA CHARACTER IF YOU WANT TO BLAME ANYONE.
NO CHILD IS SAFE WHILE HE'S LOOSE.
AND ACCORDING TO RECORDS THERE SHOULD BE THREE OF YOURS.
WON'T MAKE IT...HAVE TO...SLOW POISON...
...CAN'T DO IT ALONE...
...NEED ROOTS... STAR-SHAPED FLOWER...UH...
OH NO.
NO.
DON'T LET THEM TAKE THE CHILDREN--
GUNNAR!
DO SOMETHING!
DO SOMETHING!!
...HAVE TO REACH...
...REACH FOREST...
...STOP...
...DARK...

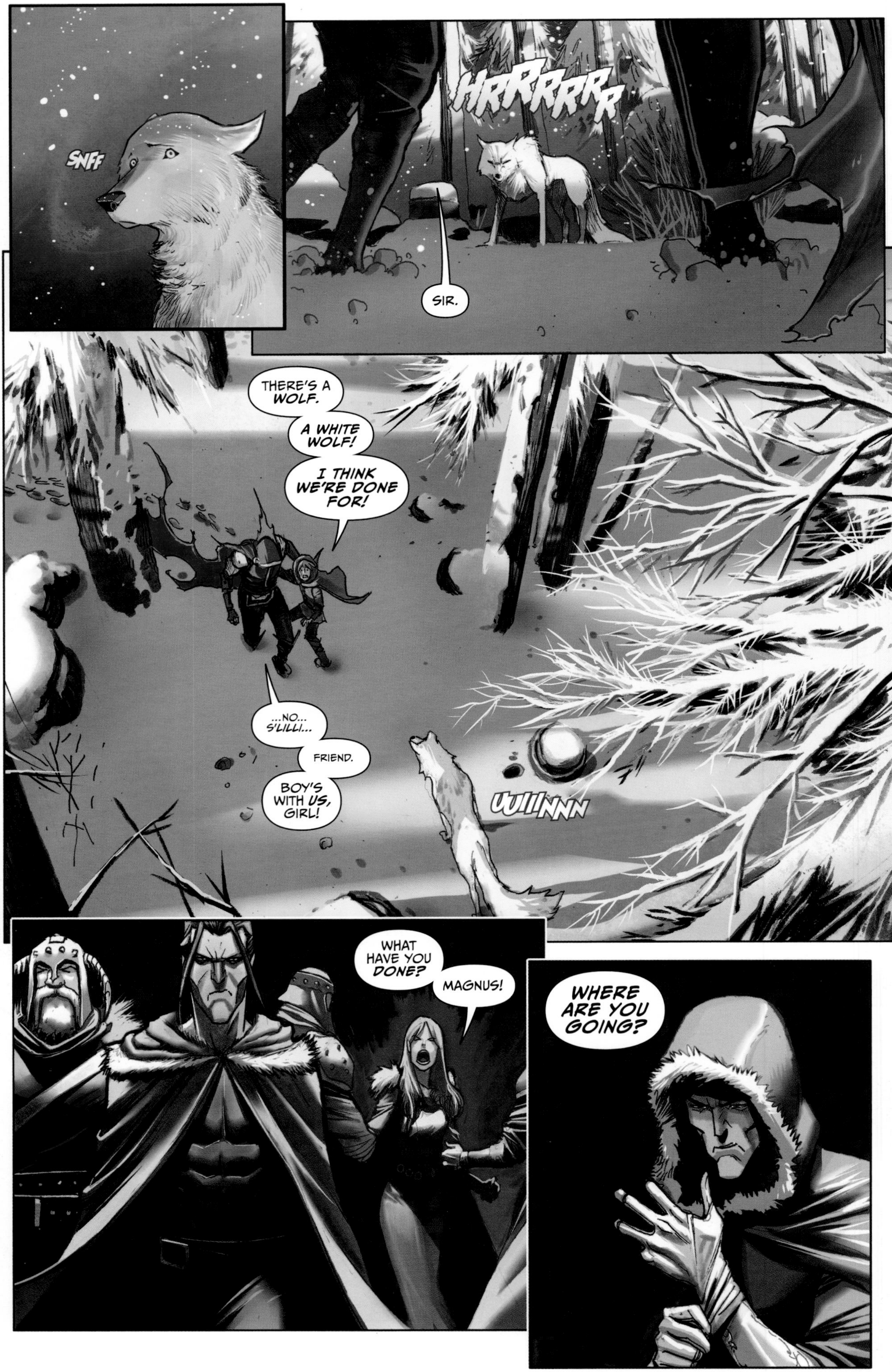
SNFF
HRRRRRR
SIR.
THERE'S A WOLF.
A WHITE WOLF!
I THINK WE'RE DONE FOR!
...NO... S'LILLI...
FRIEND.
BOY'S WITH US, GIRL!
UUIIINNN
WHAT HAVE YOU DONE?
MAGNUS!
WHERE ARE YOU GOING?

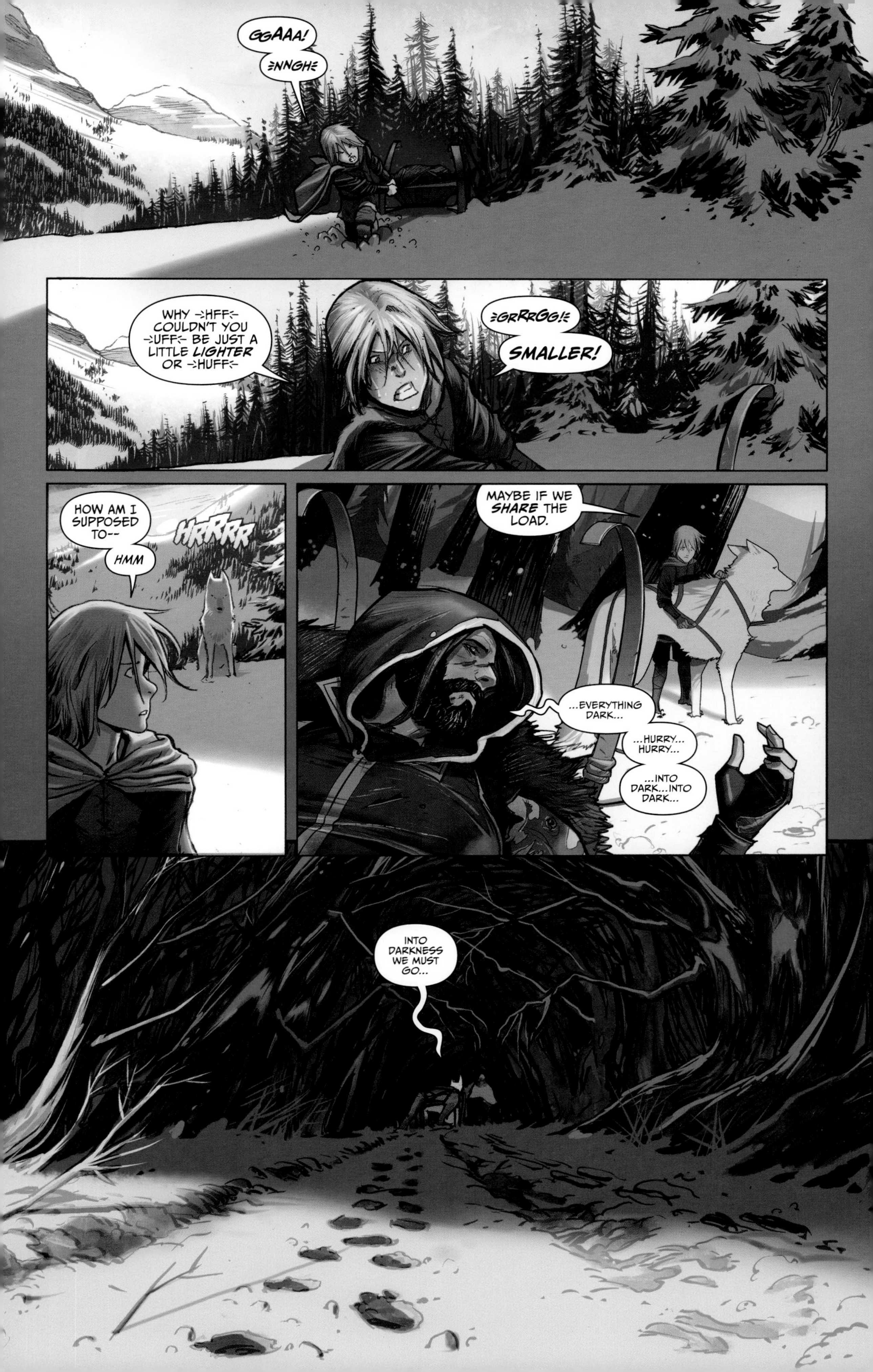
GGAAA!
NNGH
WHY HFF COULDN'T YOU UFF BE JUST A LITTLE *LIGHTER* OR HUFF
GRRRGG!
SMALLER!
HOW AM I SUPPOSED TO--
HRRRR
HMM
MAYBE IF WE *SHARE* THE LOAD.
...EVERYTHING DARK...
...HURRY... HURRY...
...INTO DARK...INTO DARK...
INTO DARKNESS WE MUST GO...

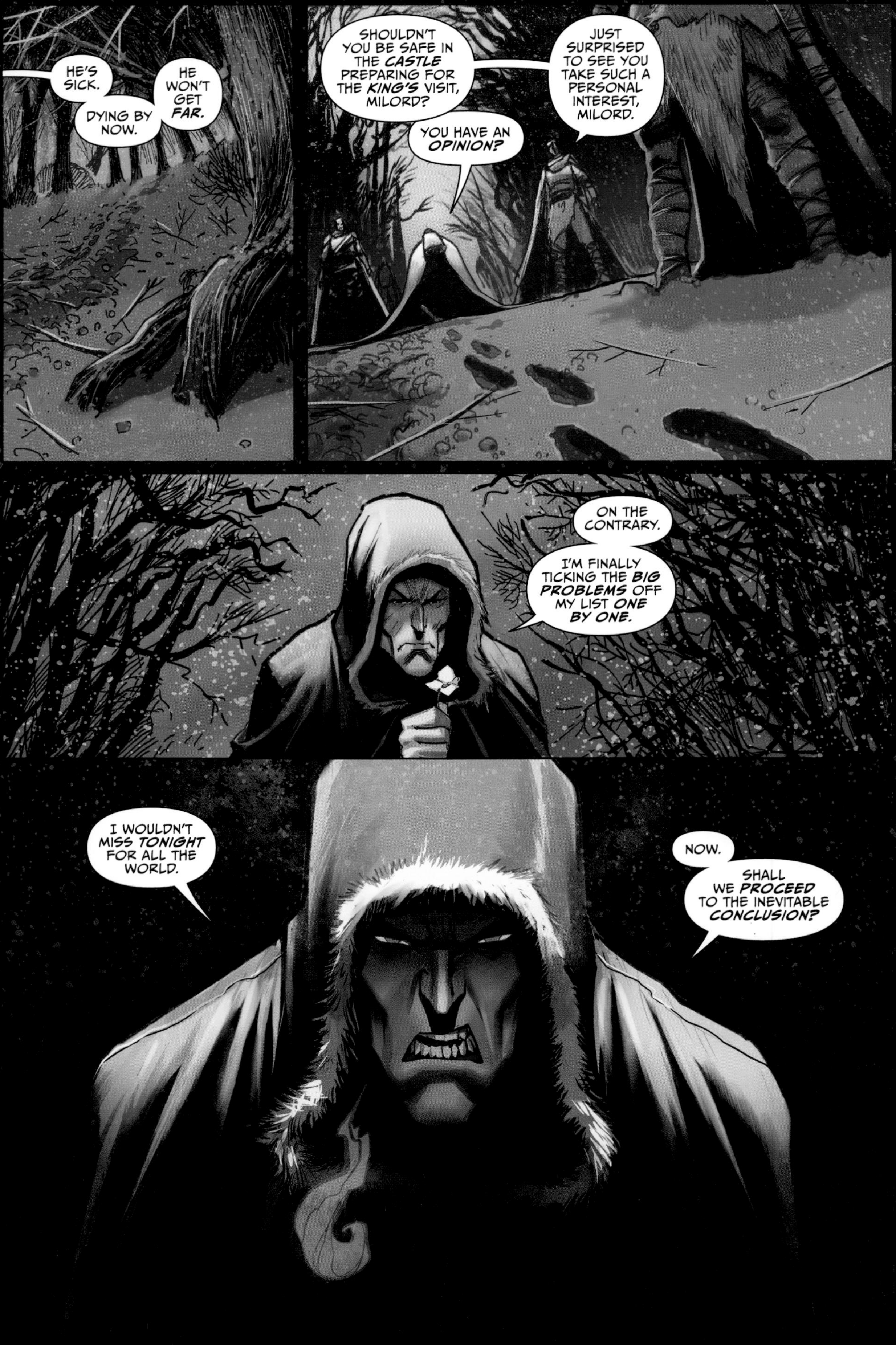
HE'S SICK.
HE WON'T GET FAR.
DYING BY NOW.
SHOULDN'T YOU BE SAFE IN THE CASTLE PREPARING FOR THE KING'S VISIT, MILORD?
YOU HAVE AN OPINION?
JUST SURPRISED TO SEE YOU TAKE SUCH A PERSONAL INTEREST, MILORD.
ON THE CONTRARY.
I'M FINALLY TICKING THE BIG PROBLEMS OFF MY LIST ONE BY ONE.
I WOULDN'T MISS TONIGHT FOR ALL THE WORLD.
NOW.
SHALL WE PROCEED TO THE INEVITABLE CONCLUSION?

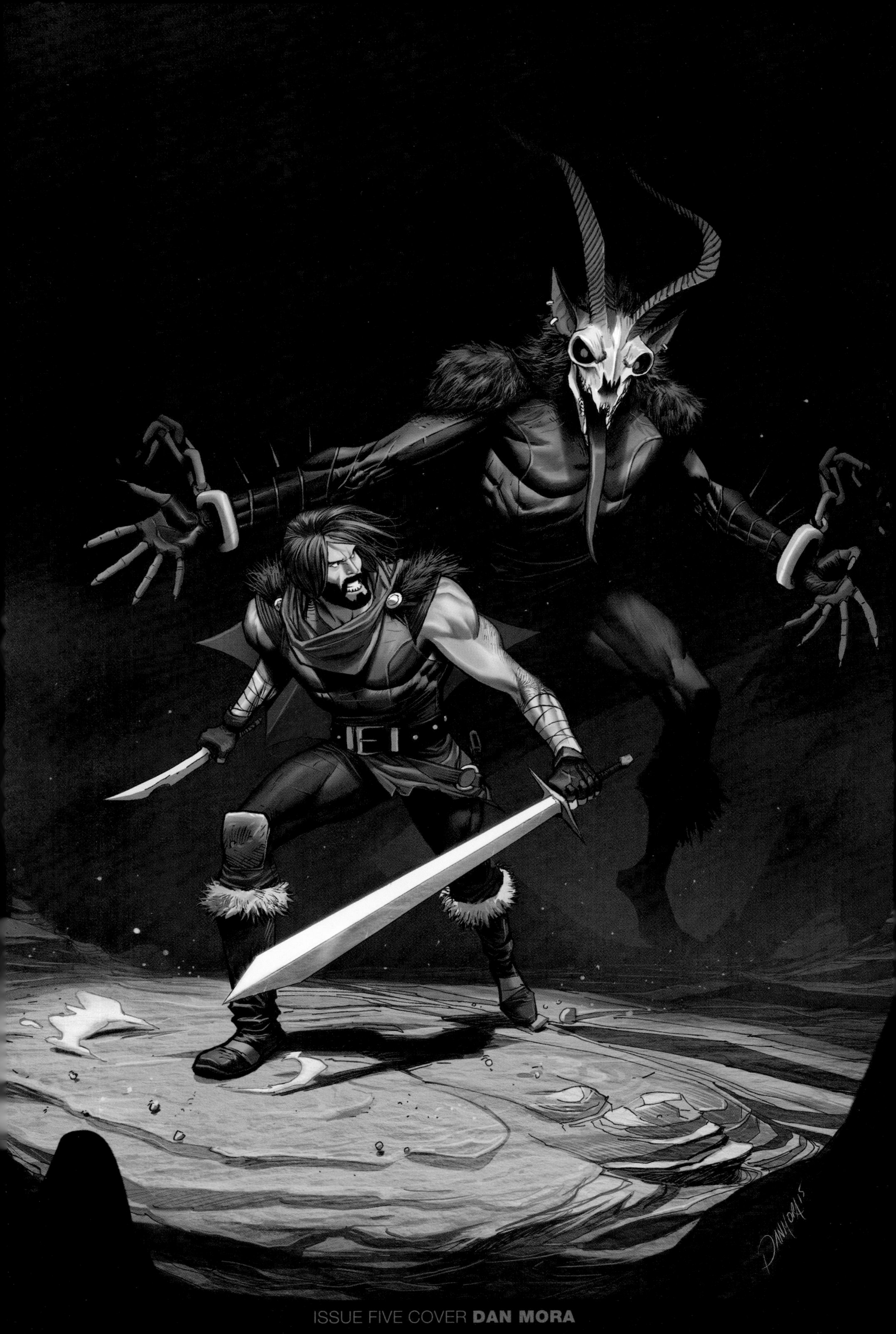

ISSUE FIVE COVER **DAN MORA**

CHAPTER

SIX

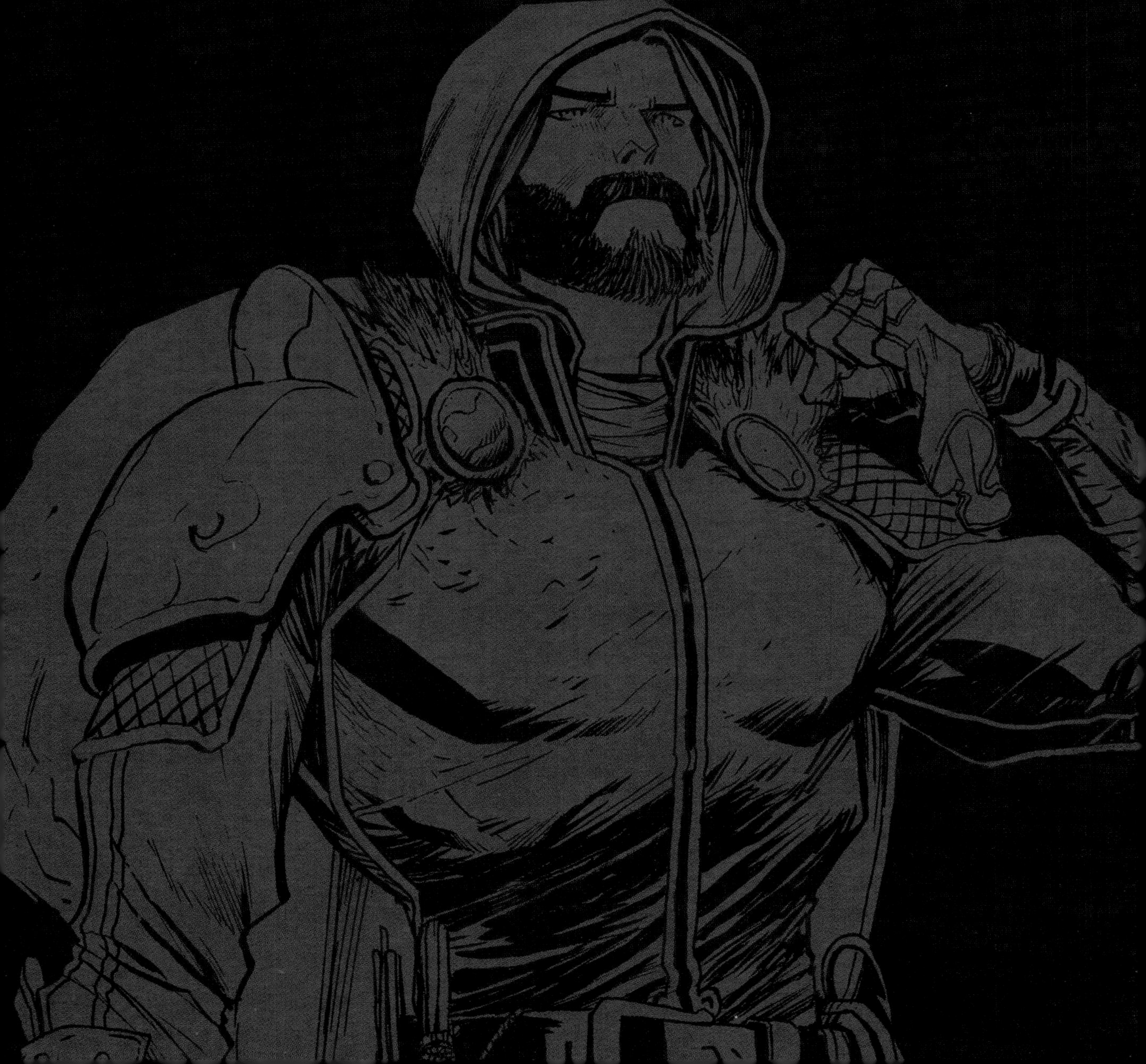

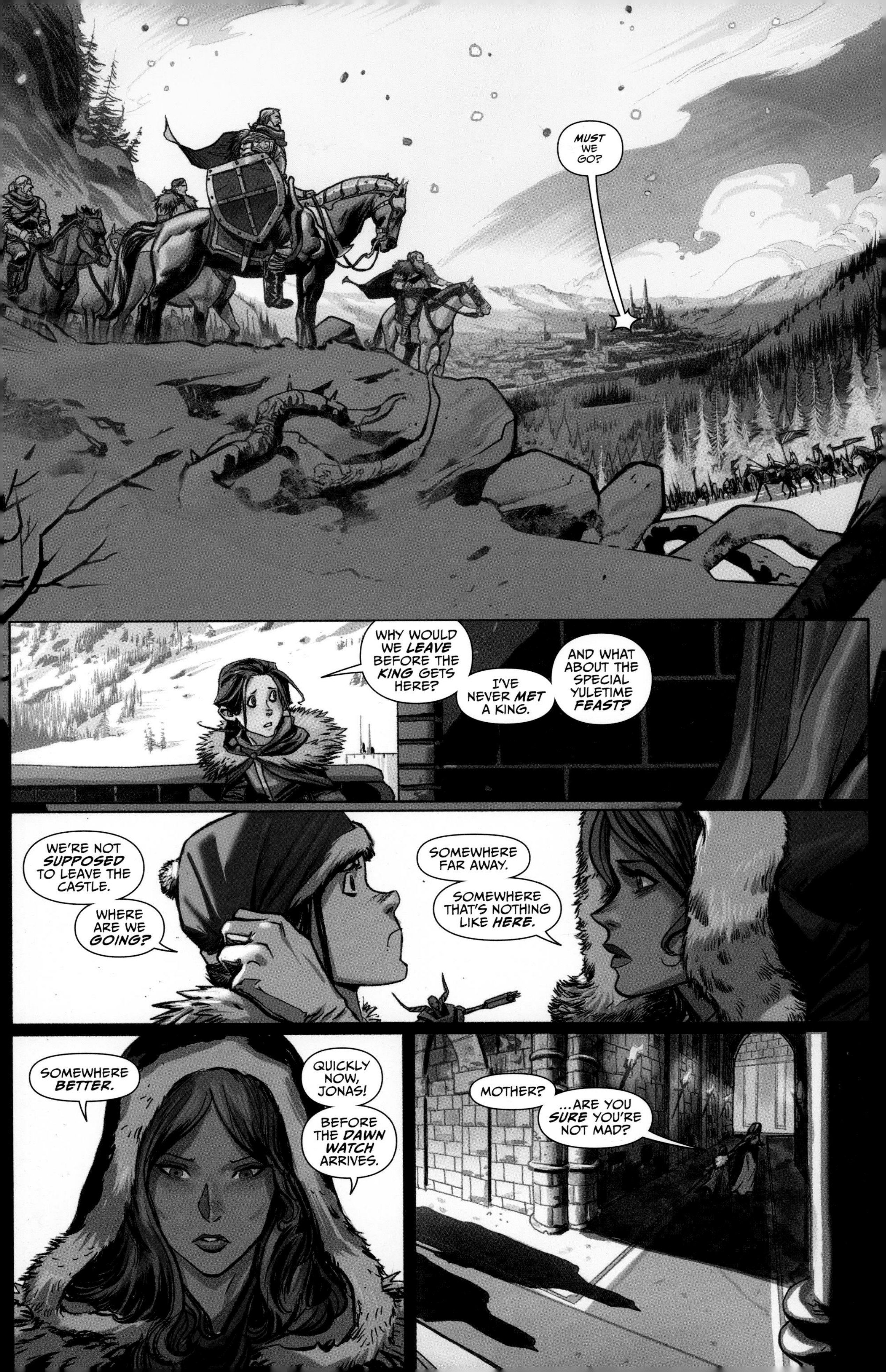
MUST WE GO?
WHY WOULD WE LEAVE BEFORE THE KING GETS HERE?
I'VE NEVER MET A KING.
AND WHAT ABOUT THE SPECIAL YULETIME FEAST?
WE'RE NOT SUPPOSED TO LEAVE THE CASTLE.
WHERE ARE WE GOING?
SOMEWHERE FAR AWAY.
SOMEWHERE THAT'S NOTHING LIKE HERE.
SOMEWHERE BETTER.
QUICKLY NOW, JONAS!
BEFORE THE DAWN WATCH ARRIVES.
MOTHER?
...ARE YOU SURE YOU'RE NOT MAD?

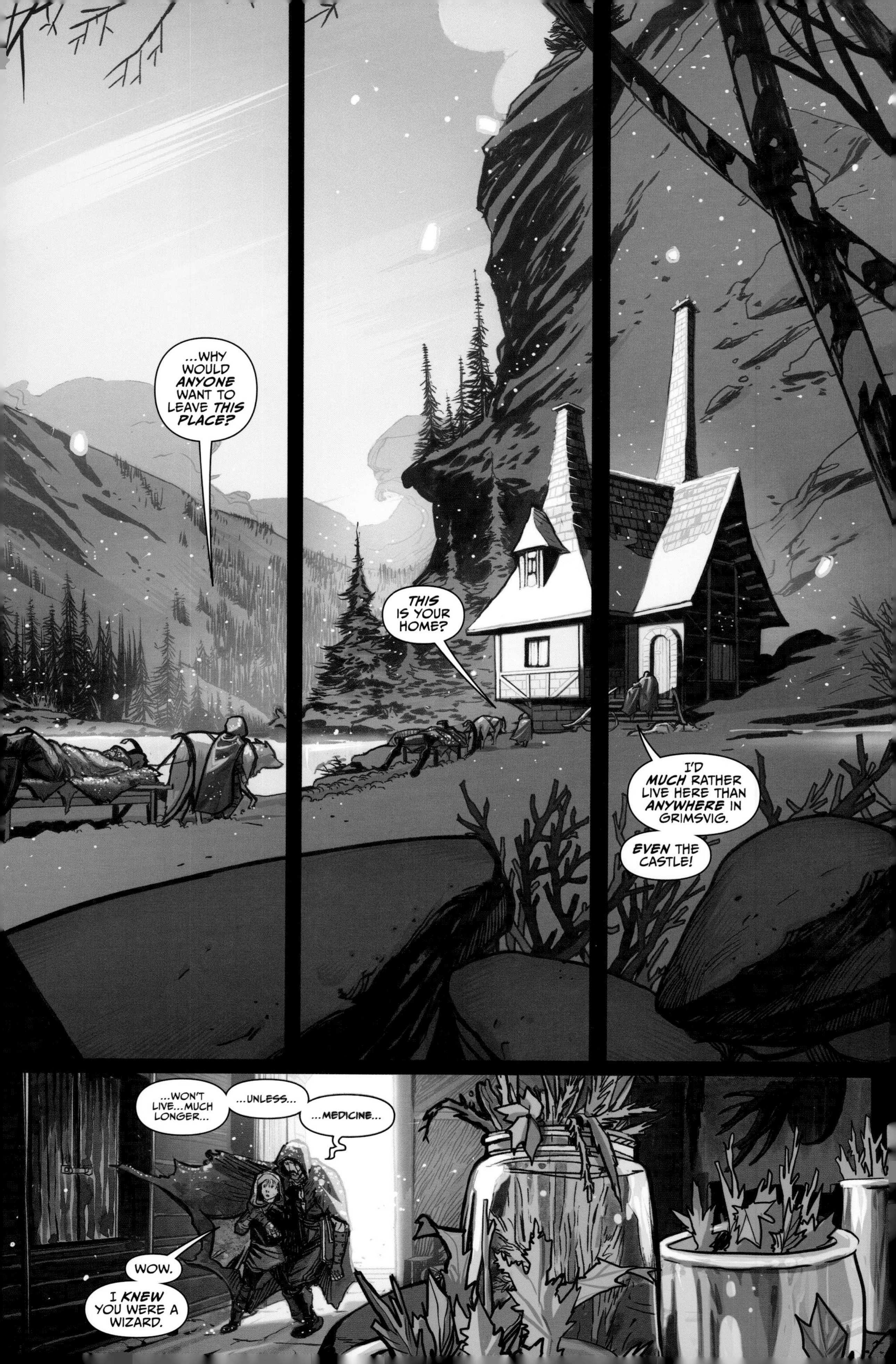
...WHY WOULD ANYONE WANT TO LEAVE THIS PLACE?
THIS IS YOUR HOME?
I'D MUCH RATHER LIVE HERE THAN ANYWHERE IN GRIMSVIG.
EVEN THE CASTLE!
...WON'T LIVE...MUCH LONGER...
...UNLESS...
...MEDICINE...
WOW.
I KNEW YOU WERE A WIZARD.

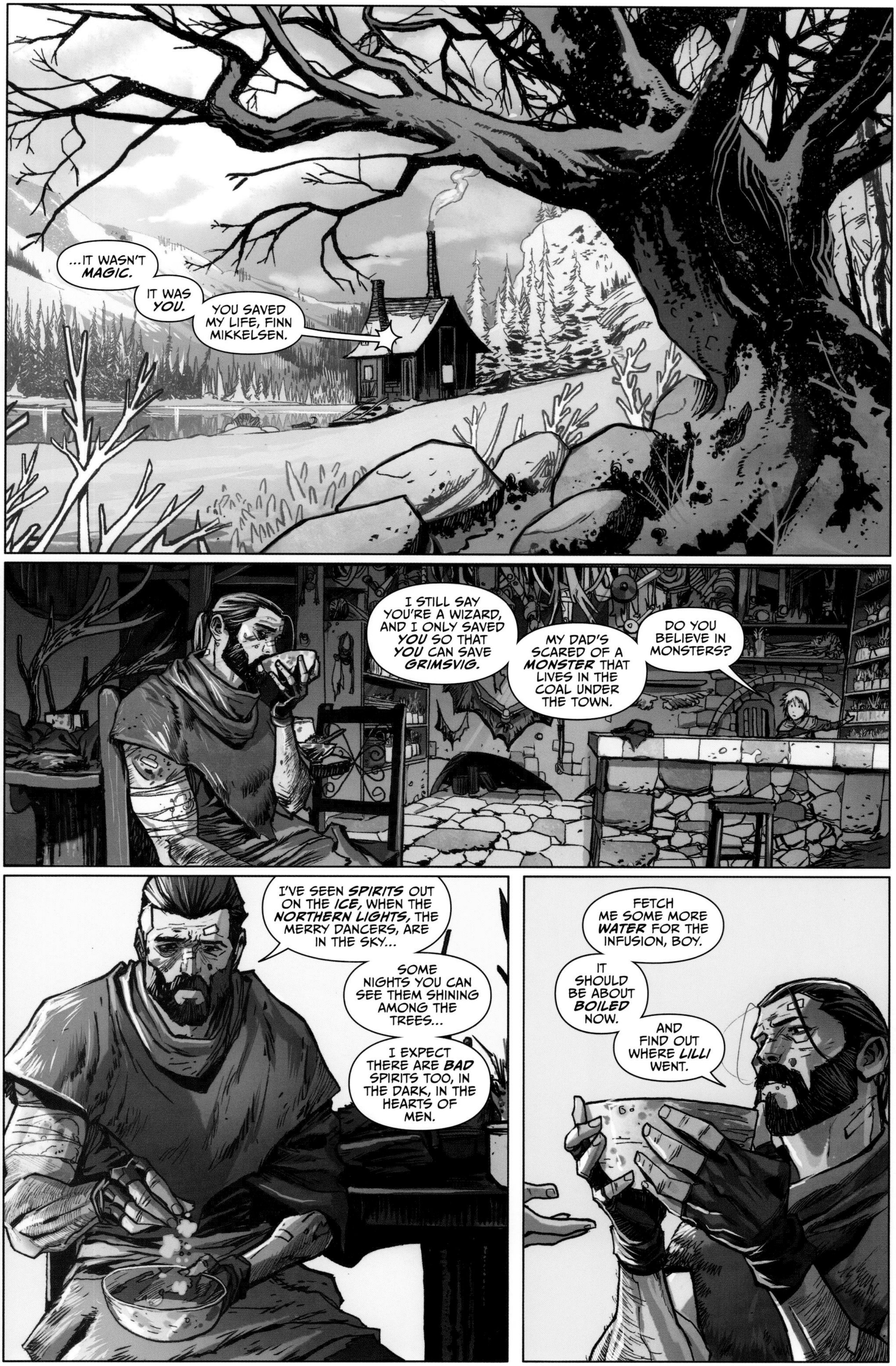

...IT WASN'T MAGIC.
IT WAS YOU.
YOU SAVED MY LIFE, FINN MIKKELSEN.
I STILL SAY YOU'RE A WIZARD, AND I ONLY SAVED YOU SO THAT YOU CAN SAVE GRIMSVIG.
MY DAD'S SCARED OF A MONSTER THAT LIVES IN THE COAL UNDER THE TOWN.
DO YOU BELIEVE IN MONSTERS?
I'VE SEEN SPIRITS OUT ON THE ICE, WHEN THE NORTHERN LIGHTS, THE MERRY DANCERS, ARE IN THE SKY...
SOME NIGHTS YOU CAN SEE THEM SHINING AMONG THE TREES...
I EXPECT THERE ARE BAD SPIRITS TOO, IN THE DARK, IN THE HEARTS OF MEN.
FETCH ME SOME MORE WATER FOR THE INFUSION, BOY.
IT SHOULD BE ABOUT BOILED NOW.
AND FIND OUT WHERE LILLI WENT.

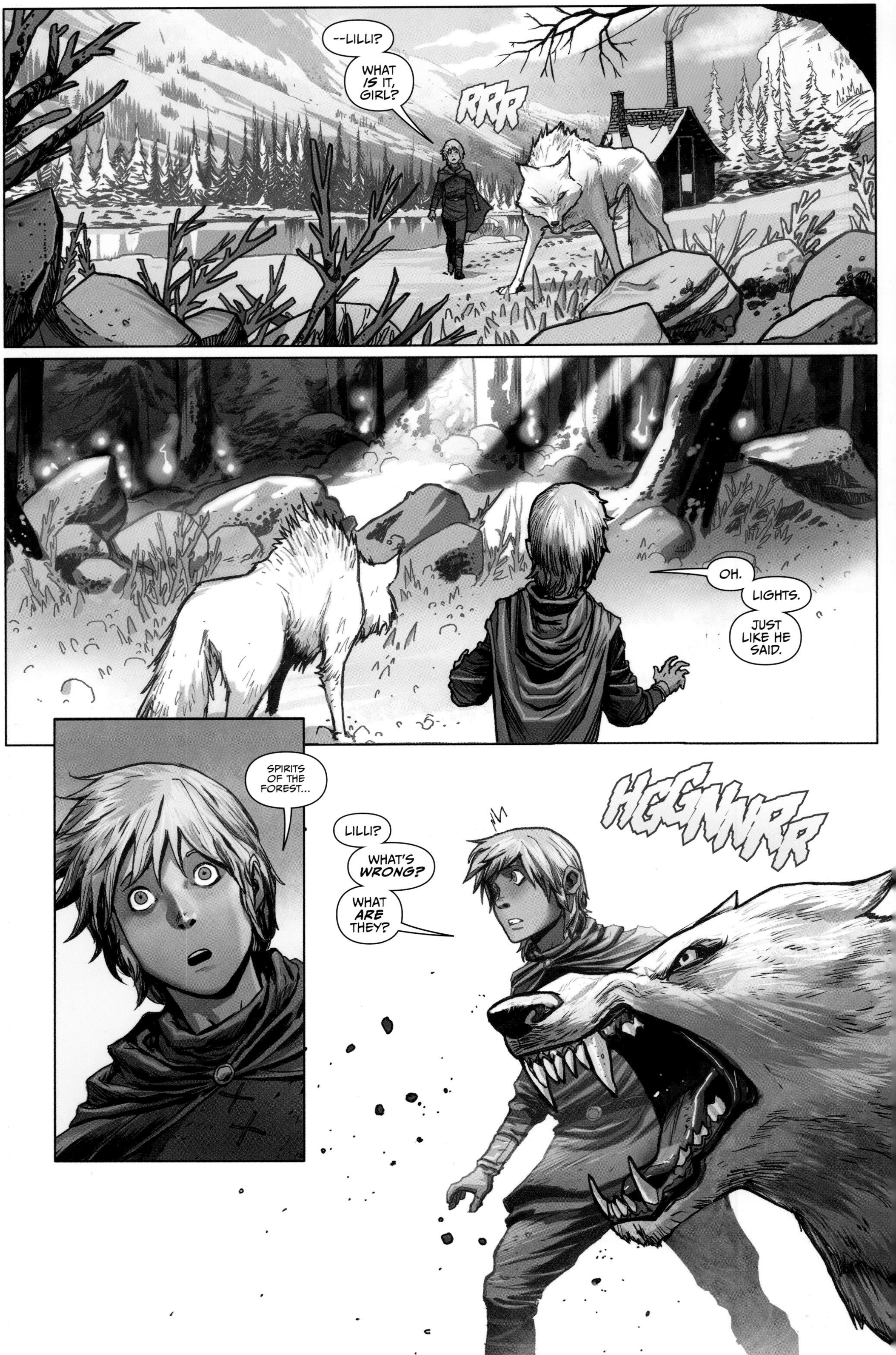
--LILLI?
WHAT *IS* IT, GIRL?
RRR
OH.
LIGHTS.
JUST LIKE HE SAID.
SPIRITS OF THE FOREST...
LILLI?
WHAT'S *WRONG?*
WHAT *ARE* THEY?
HGGNNRR

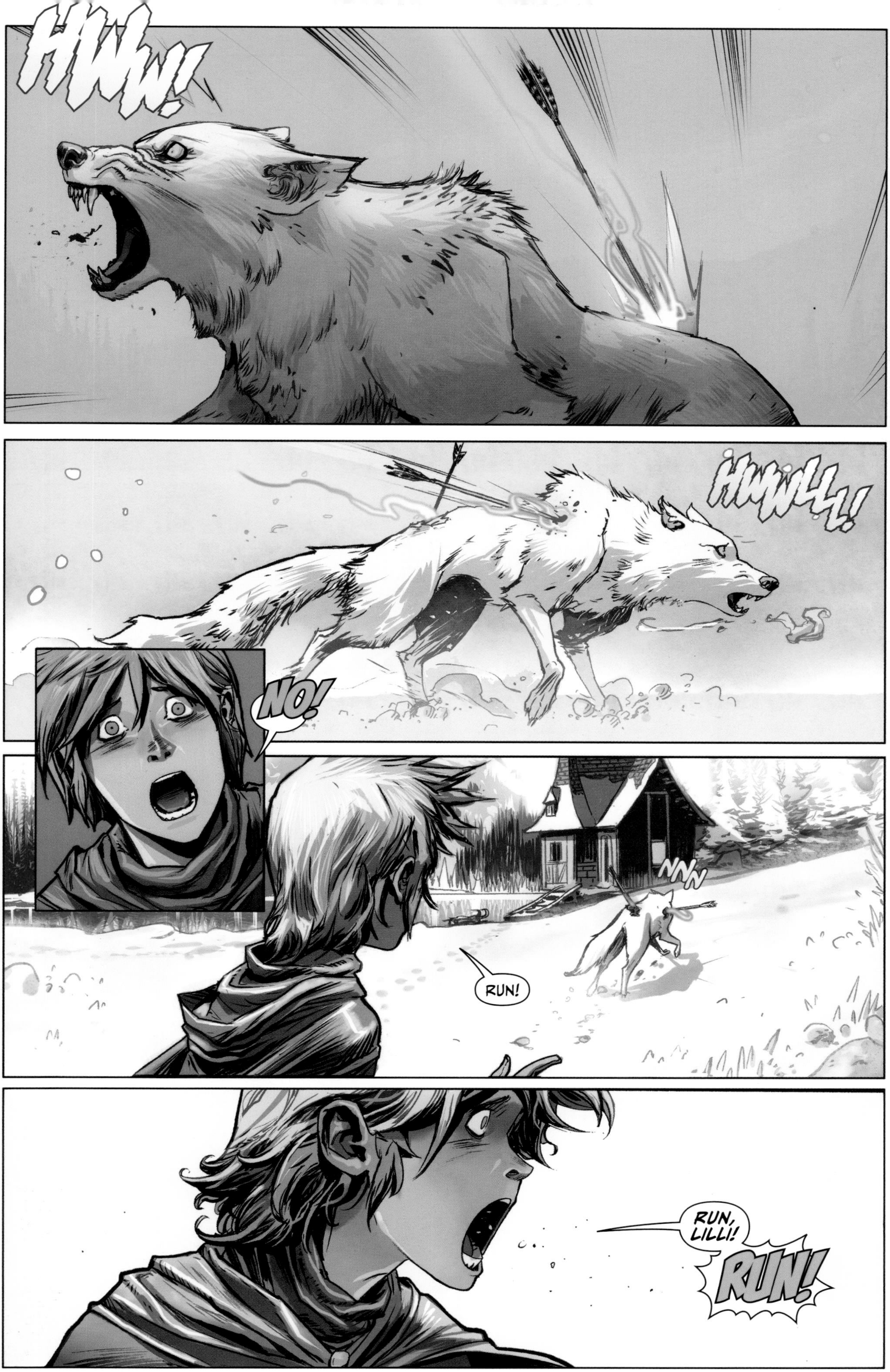
HWW!
HWWLLL!
NO!
NNN
RUN!
RUN, LILLI!
RUN!

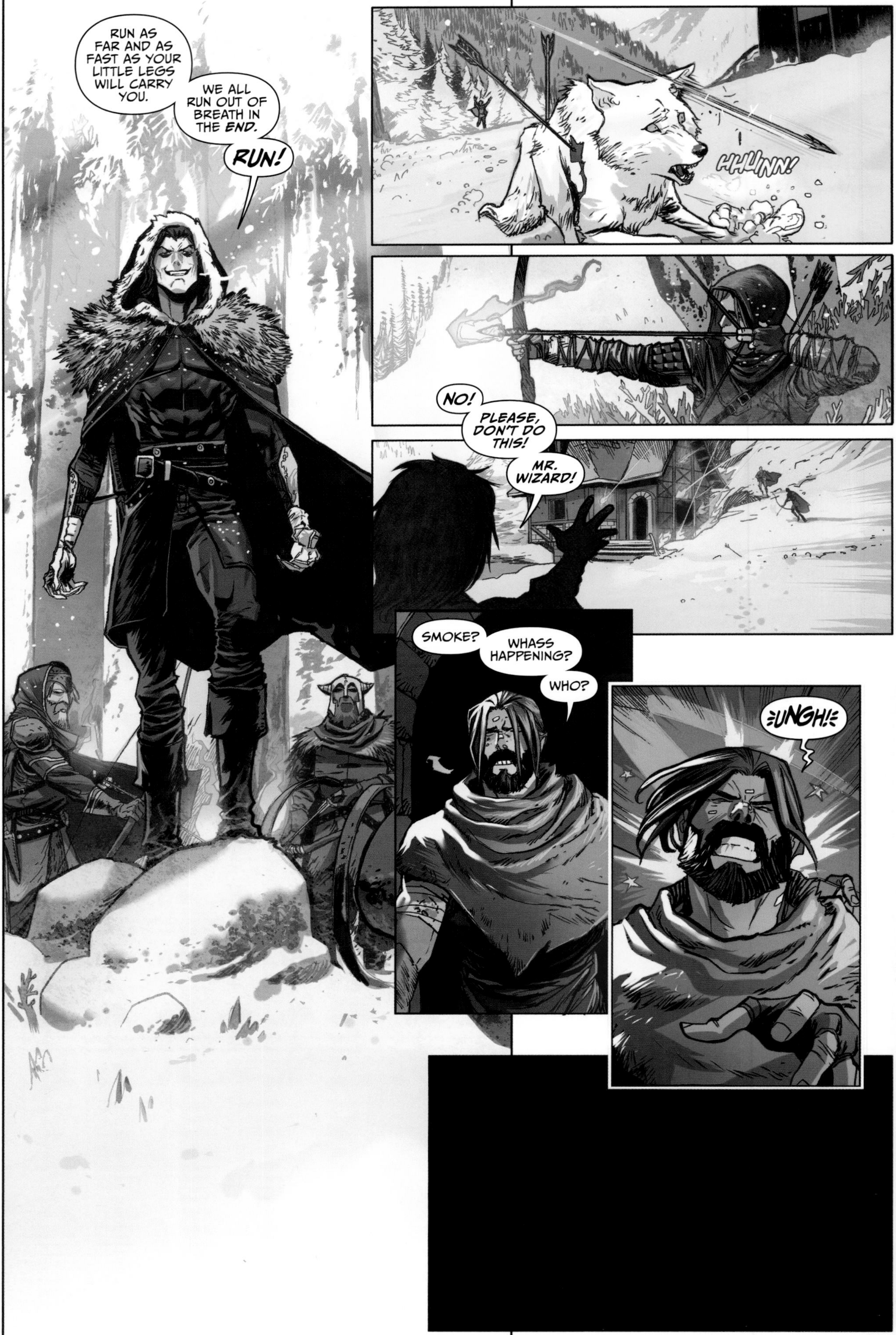

RUN AS FAR AND AS FAST AS YOUR LITTLE LEGS WILL CARRY YOU.
WE ALL RUN OUT OF BREATH IN THE *END.*
RUN!
HHUNN!
NO!
PLEASE, DON'T DO THIS!
MR. WIZARD!
SMOKE?
WHASS HAPPENING?
WHO?
UNGH!

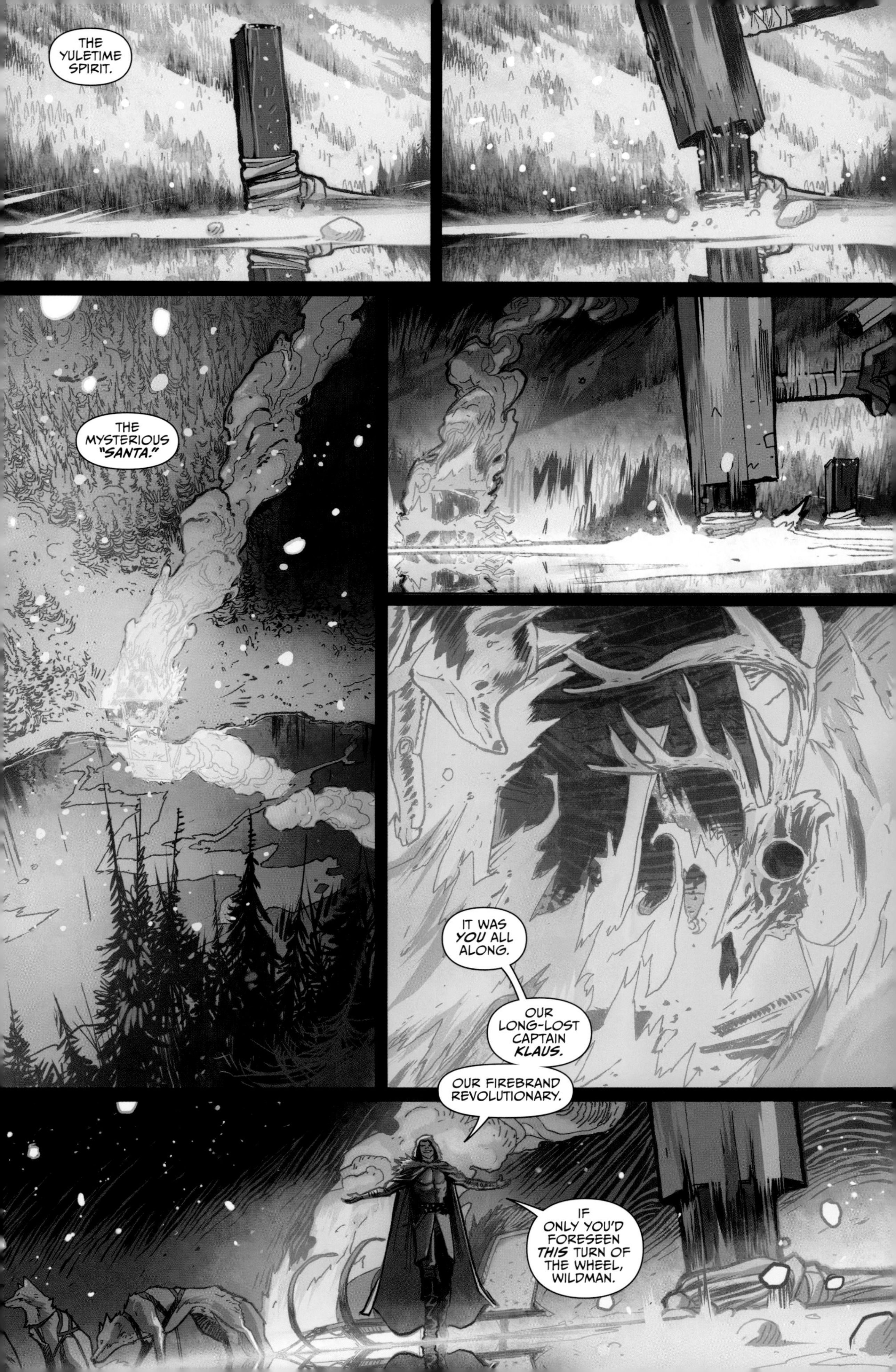
THE YULETIME SPIRIT.
THE MYSTERIOUS "SANTA."
IT WAS YOU ALL ALONG.
OUR LONG-LOST CAPTAIN KLAUS.
OUR FIREBRAND REVOLUTIONARY.
IF ONLY YOU'D FORESEEN THIS TURN OF THE WHEEL, WILDMAN.

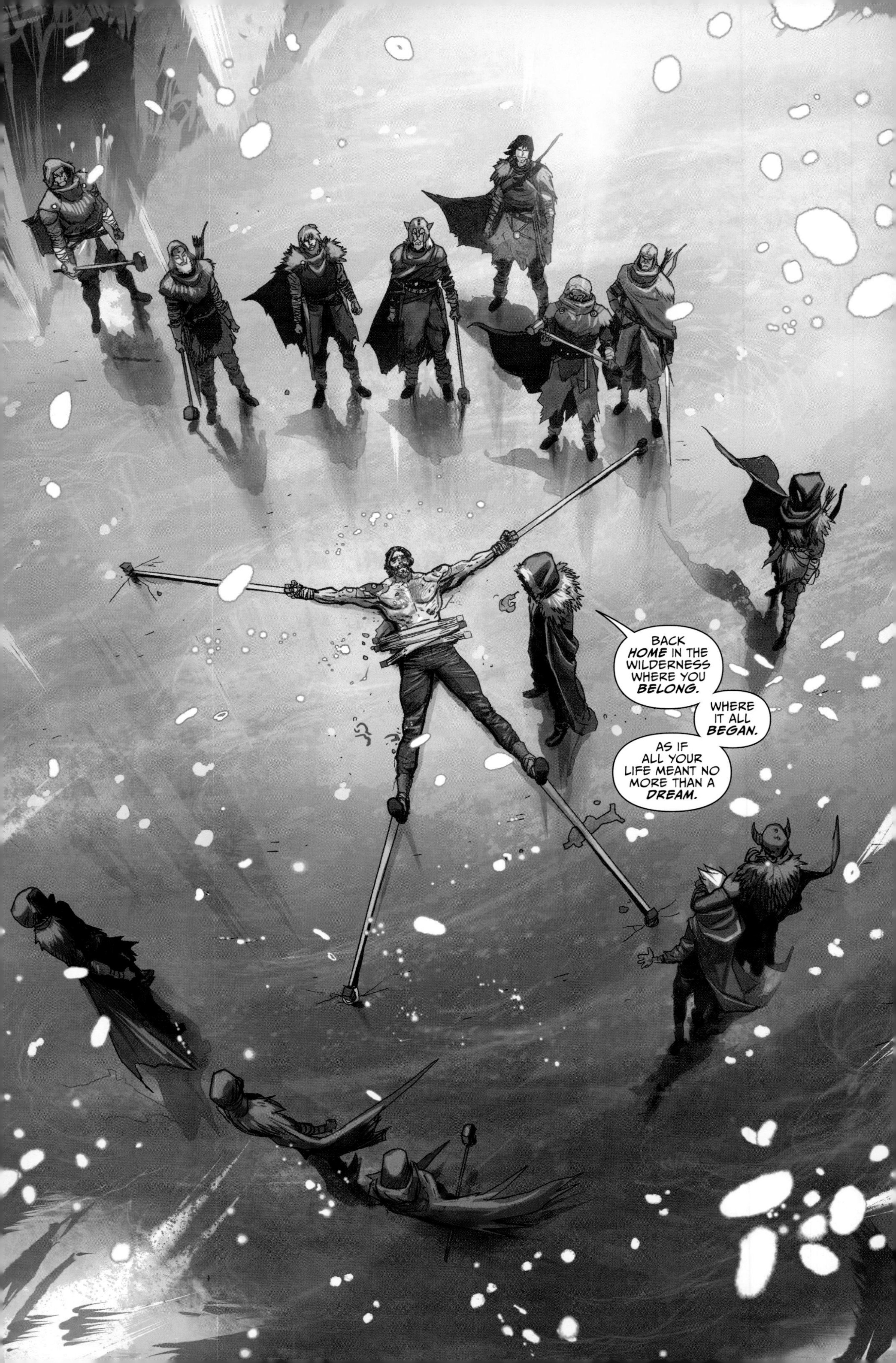
BACK *HOME* IN THE WILDERNESS WHERE YOU *BELONG.*
WHERE IT ALL *BEGAN.*
AS IF ALL YOUR LIFE MEANT NO MORE THAN A *DREAM.*

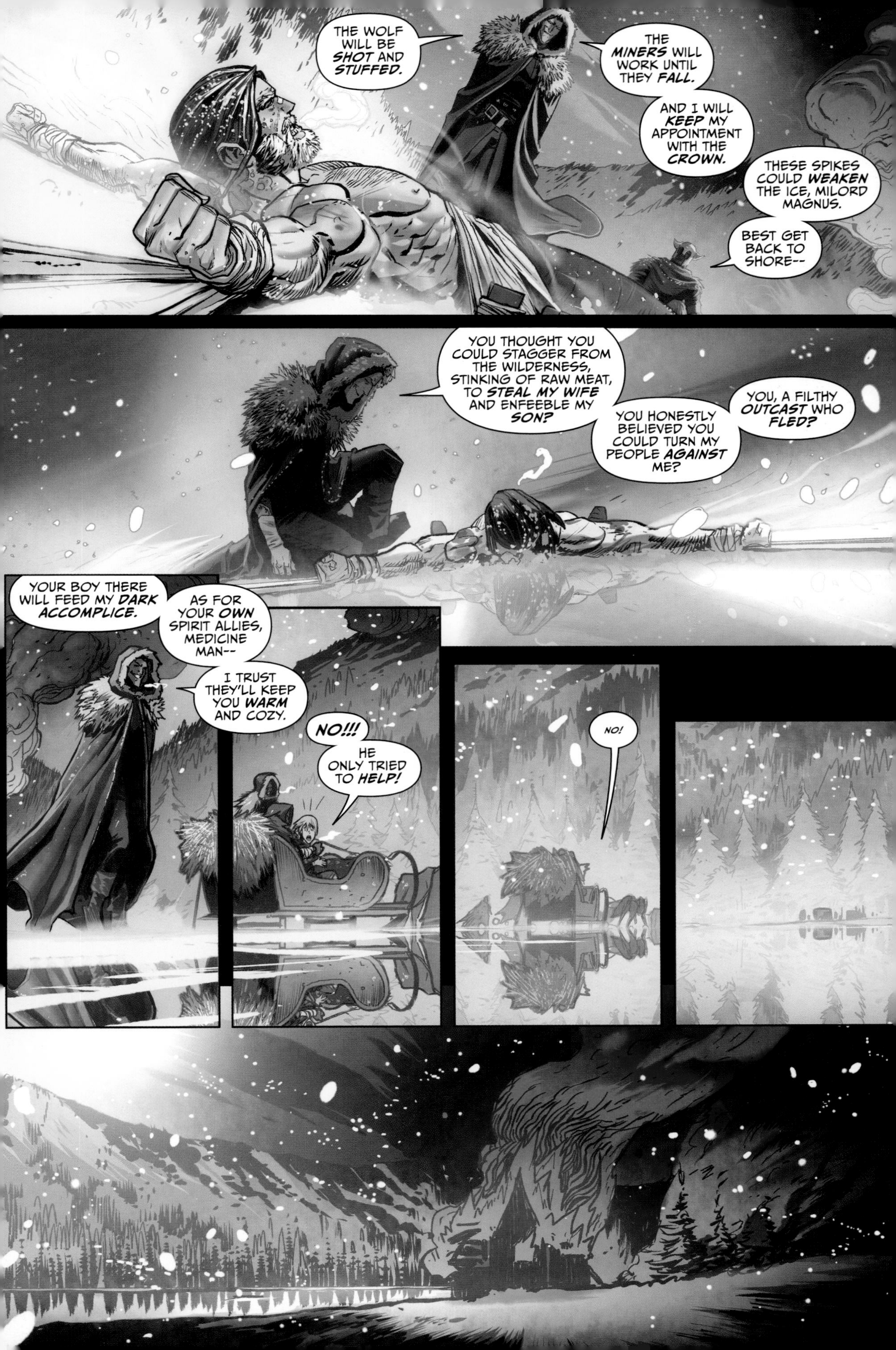
THE WOLF WILL BE SHOT AND STUFFED.
THE MINERS WILL WORK UNTIL THEY FALL.
AND I WILL KEEP MY APPOINTMENT WITH THE CROWN.
THESE SPIKES COULD WEAKEN THE ICE, MILORD MAGNUS.
BEST GET BACK TO SHORE--
YOU THOUGHT YOU COULD STAGGER FROM THE WILDERNESS, STINKING OF RAW MEAT, TO STEAL MY WIFE AND ENFEEBLE MY SON?
YOU HONESTLY BELIEVED YOU COULD TURN MY PEOPLE AGAINST ME?
YOU, A FILTHY OUTCAST WHO FLED?
YOUR BOY THERE WILL FEED MY DARK ACCOMPLICE.
AS FOR YOUR OWN SPIRIT ALLIES, MEDICINE MAN--
I TRUST THEY'LL KEEP YOU WARM AND COZY.
NO!!!
HE ONLY TRIED TO HELP!
NO!

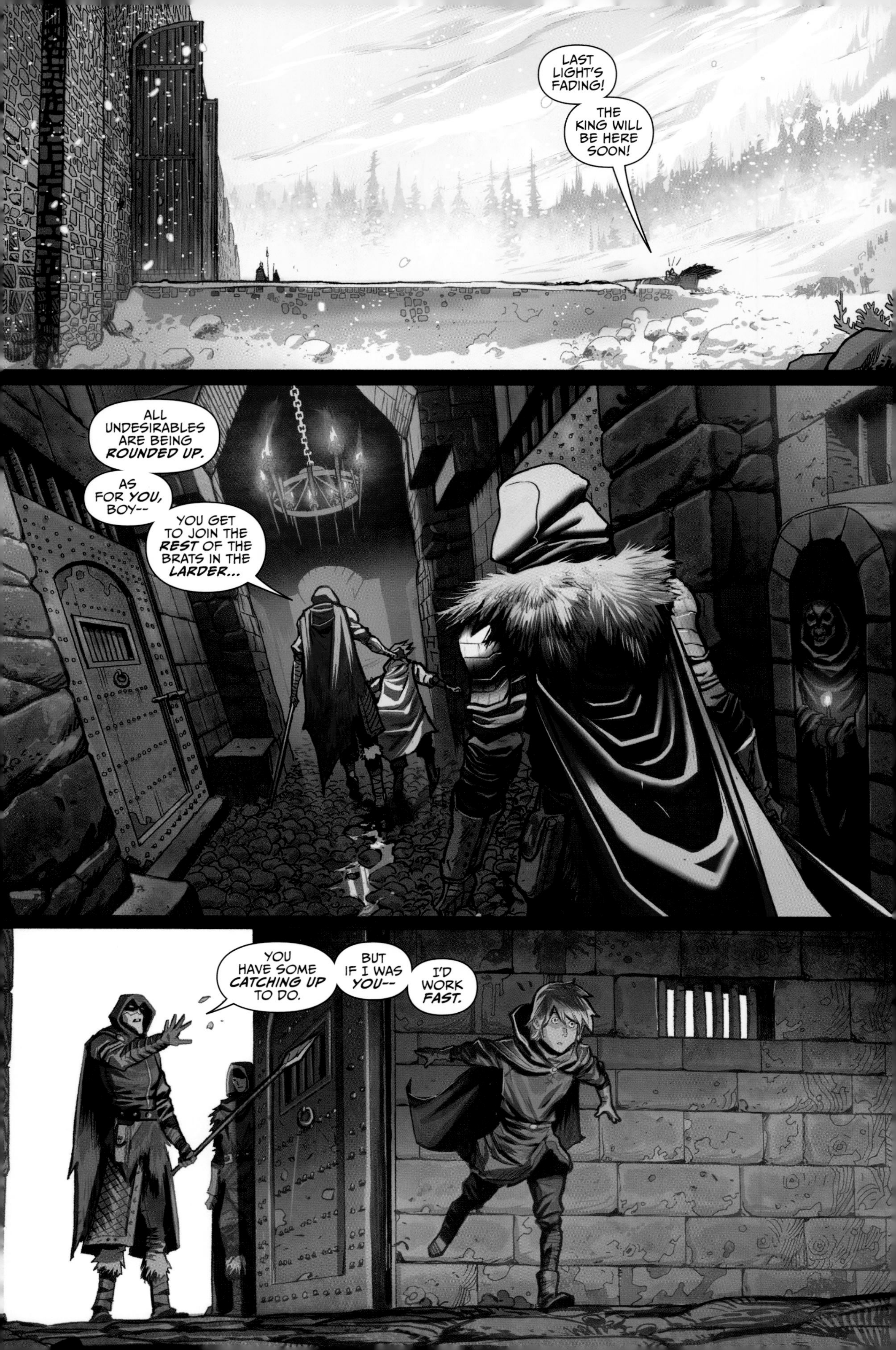
LAST LIGHT'S FADING!
THE KING WILL BE HERE SOON!
ALL UNDESIRABLES ARE BEING *ROUNDED UP.*
AS FOR *YOU,* BOY--
YOU GET TO JOIN THE *REST* OF THE BRATS IN THE *LARDER...*
YOU HAVE SOME *CATCHING UP* TO DO.
BUT IF I WAS *YOU--*
I'D WORK *FAST.*

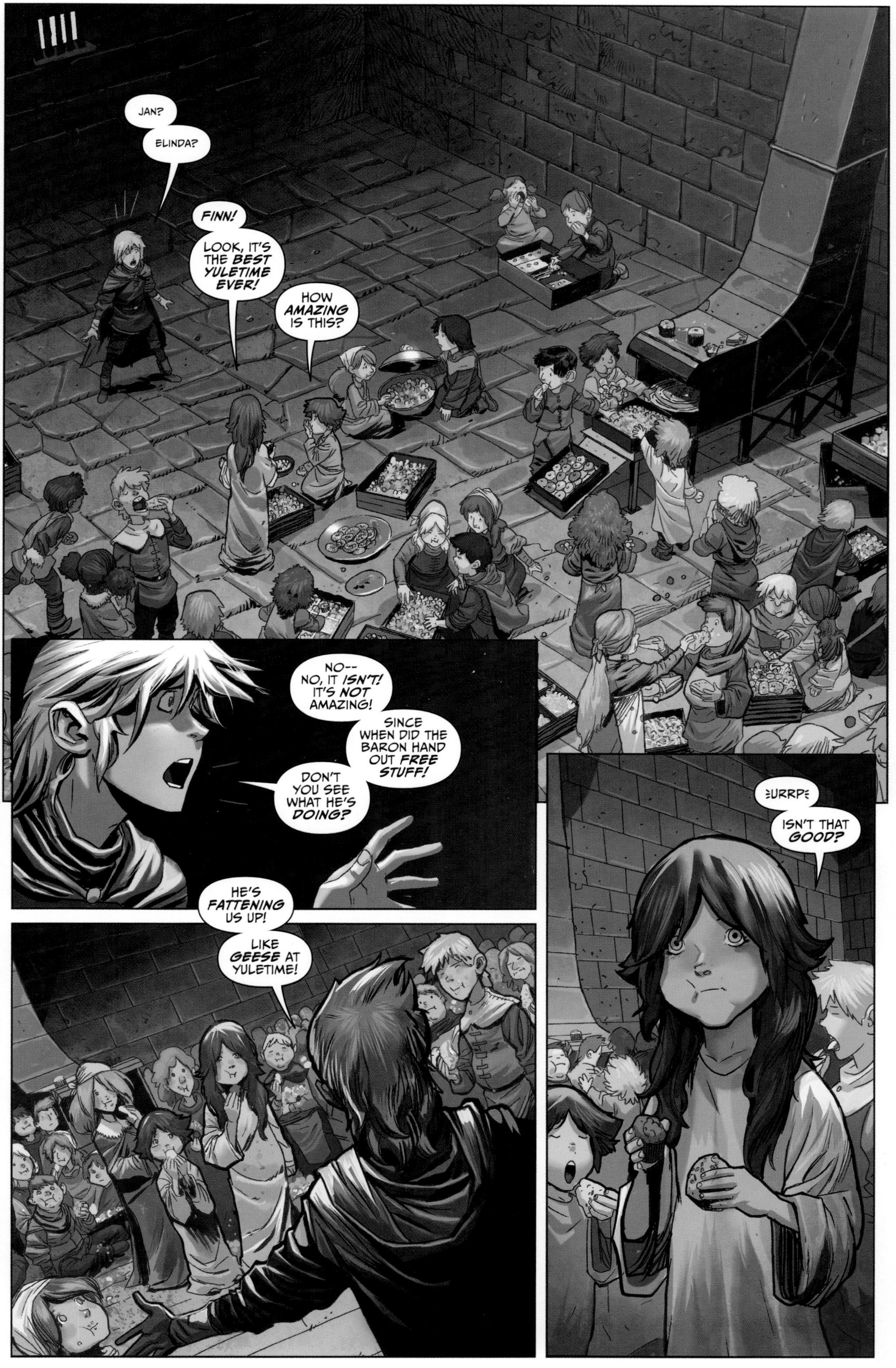
JAN?
ELINDA?
FINN!
LOOK, IT'S THE BEST YULETIME EVER!
HOW AMAZING IS THIS?
NO-- NO, IT ISN'T! IT'S NOT AMAZING!
SINCE WHEN DID THE BARON HAND OUT FREE STUFF!
DON'T YOU SEE WHAT HE'S DOING?
HE'S FATTENING US UP!
LIKE GEESE AT YULETIME!
URRP
ISN'T THAT GOOD?

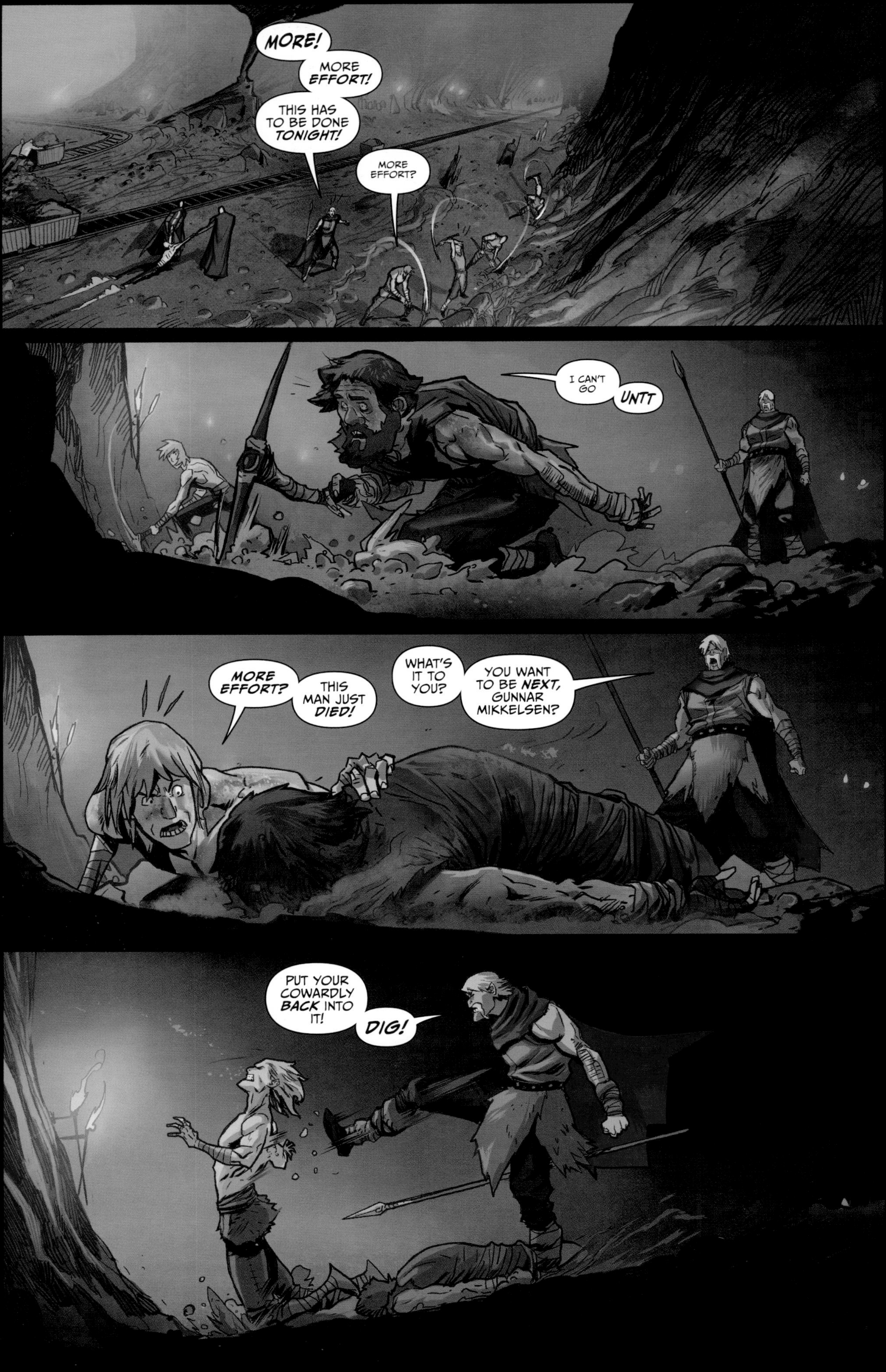
MORE!
MORE EFFORT!
THIS HAS TO BE DONE TONIGHT!
MORE EFFORT?
I CAN'T GO
UNTT
MORE EFFORT?
THIS MAN JUST DIED!
WHAT'S IT TO YOU?
YOU WANT TO BE NEXT, GUNNAR MIKKELSEN?
PUT YOUR COWARDLY BACK INTO IT!
DIG!

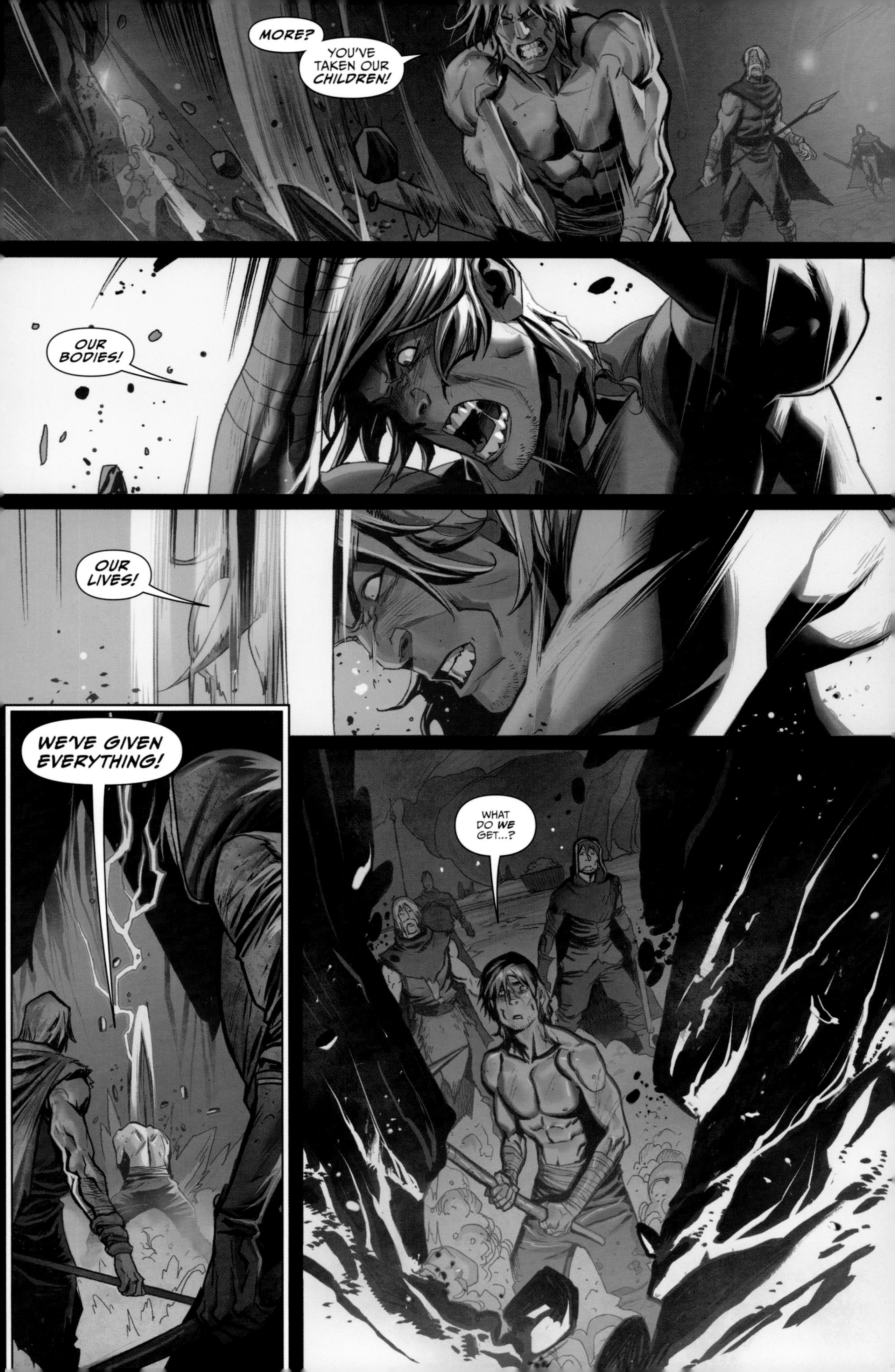
MORE?
YOU'VE TAKEN OUR CHILDREN!
OUR BODIES!
OUR LIVES!
WE'VE GIVEN EVERYTHING!
WHAT DO WE GET...?

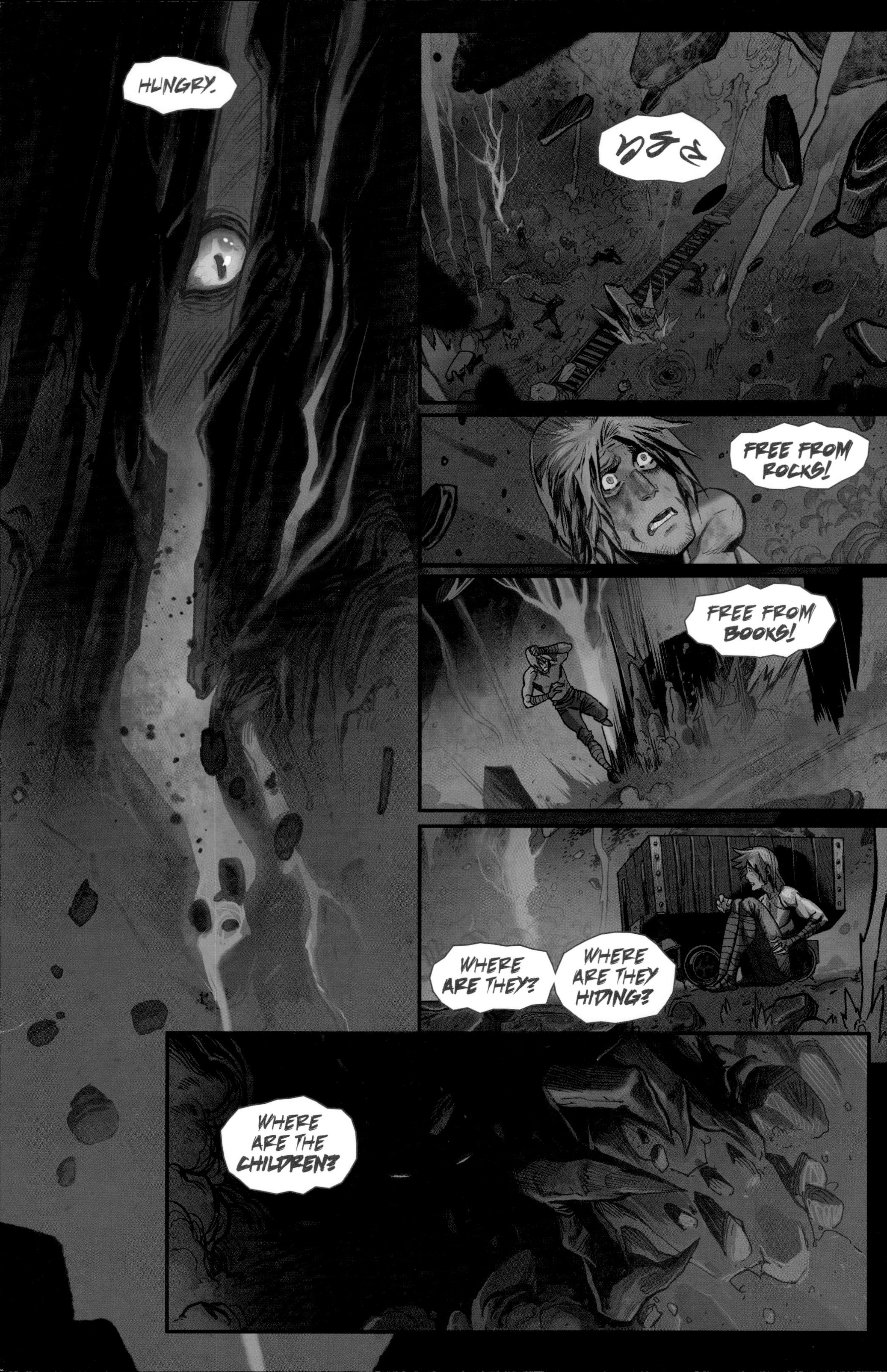
HUNGRY.
FREE FROM ROCKS!
FREE FROM BOOKS!
WHERE ARE THEY?
WHERE ARE THEY HIDING?
WHERE ARE THE CHILDREN?

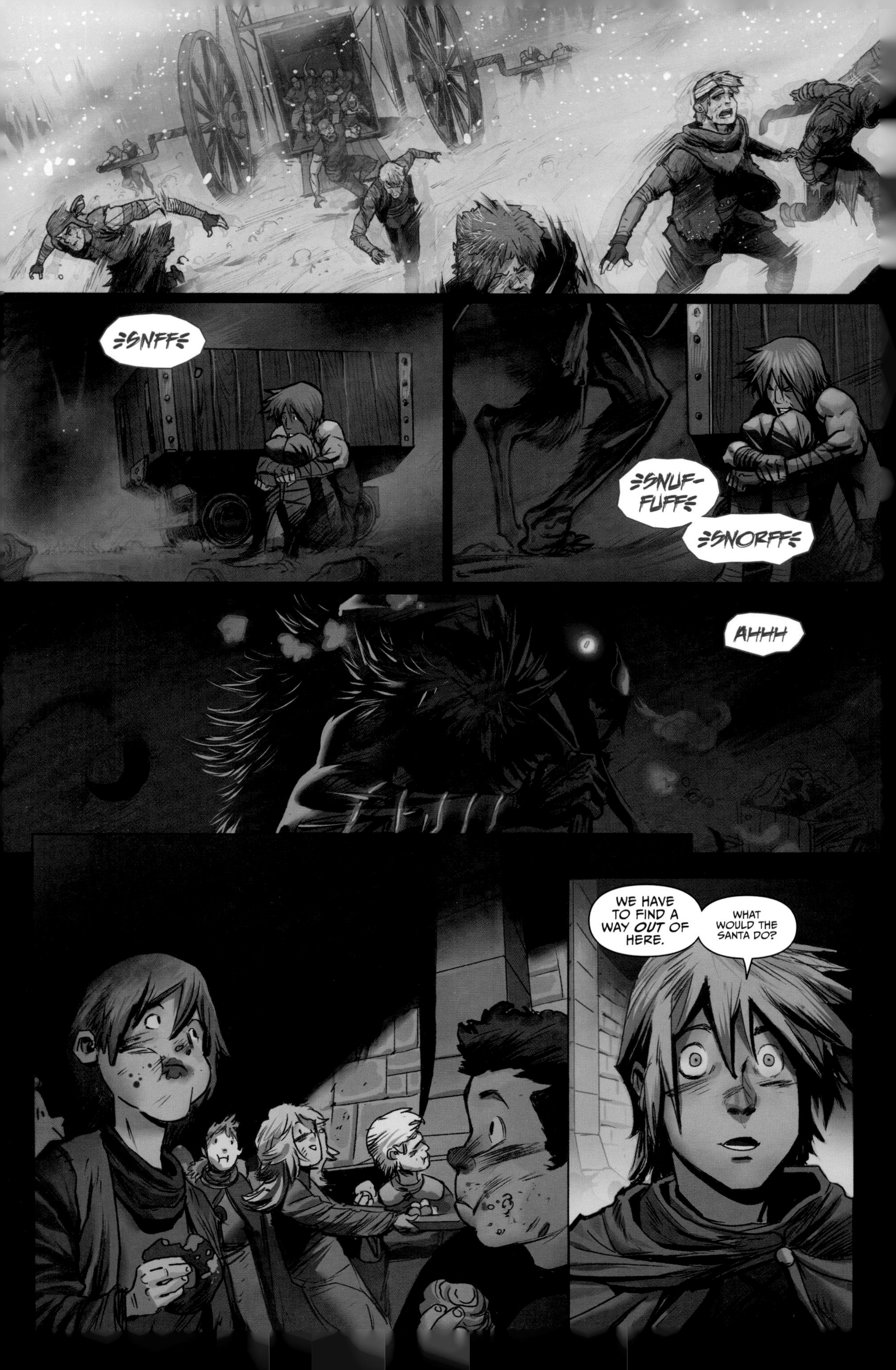
SNFF
SNUF-FUFF
SNORFF
AHHH
WE HAVE TO FIND A WAY OUT OF HERE.
WHAT WOULD THE SANTA DO?

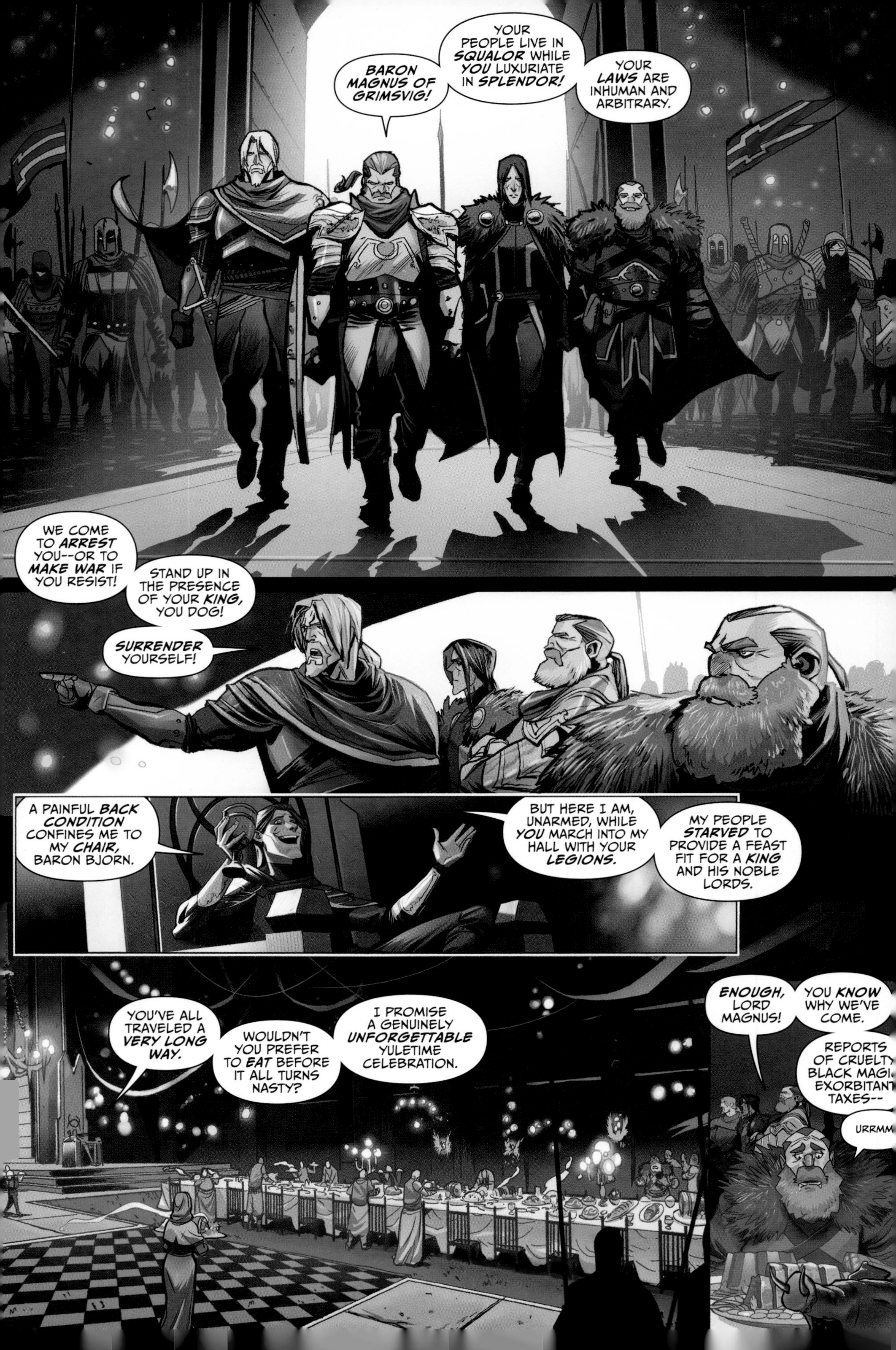
BARON MAGNUS OF GRIMSVIG!
YOUR PEOPLE LIVE IN SQUALOR WHILE YOU LUXURIATE IN SPLENDOR!
YOUR LAWS ARE INHUMAN AND ARBITRARY.
WE COME TO ARREST YOU--OR TO MAKE WAR IF YOU RESIST!
STAND UP IN THE PRESENCE OF YOUR KING, YOU DOG!
SURRENDER YOURSELF!
A PAINFUL BACK CONDITION CONFINES ME TO MY CHAIR, BARON BJORN.
BUT HERE I AM, UNARMED, WHILE YOU MARCH INTO MY HALL WITH YOUR LEGIONS.
MY PEOPLE STARVED TO PROVIDE A FEAST FIT FOR A KING AND HIS NOBLE LORDS.
YOU'VE ALL TRAVELED A VERY LONG WAY.
WOULDN'T YOU PREFER TO EAT BEFORE IT ALL TURNS NASTY?
I PROMISE A GENUINELY UNFORGETTABLE YULETIME CELEBRATION.
ENOUGH, LORD MAGNUS!
YOU KNOW WHY WE'VE COME.
REPORTS OF CRUELTY, BLACK MAGI EXORBITANT TAXES--
URRMM

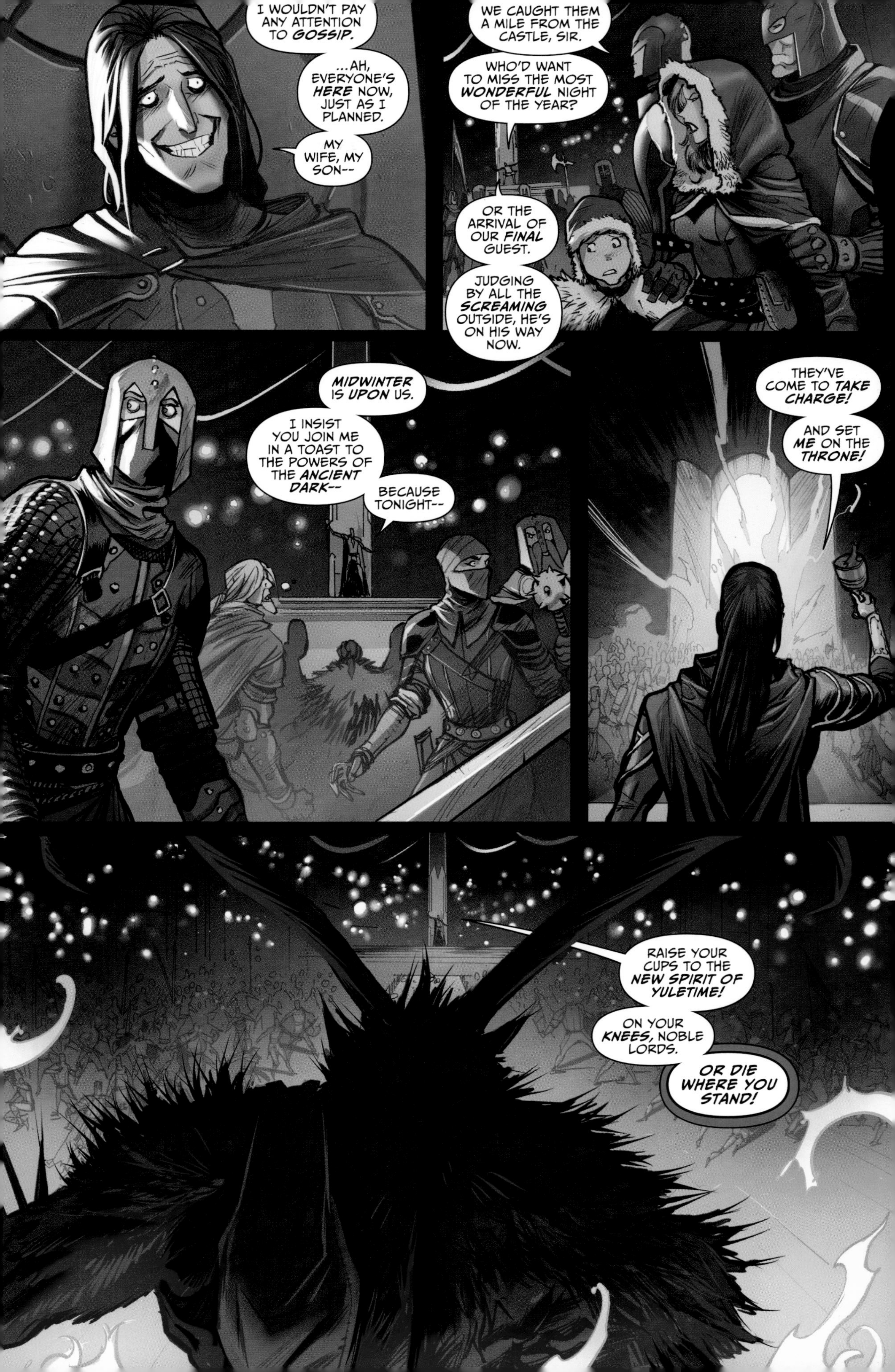
I WOULDN'T PAY ANY ATTENTION TO *GOSSIP.*
...AH, EVERYONE'S *HERE* NOW, JUST AS I PLANNED.
MY WIFE, MY SON--
WE CAUGHT THEM A MILE FROM THE CASTLE, SIR.
WHO'D WANT TO MISS THE MOST *WONDERFUL* NIGHT OF THE YEAR?
OR THE ARRIVAL OF OUR *FINAL* GUEST.
JUDGING BY ALL THE *SCREAMING* OUTSIDE, HE'S ON HIS WAY NOW.
MIDWINTER IS *UPON* US.
I INSIST YOU JOIN ME IN A TOAST TO THE POWERS OF THE *ANCIENT DARK--*
BECAUSE TONIGHT--
THEY'VE COME TO *TAKE CHARGE!*
AND SET *ME* ON THE *THRONE!*
RAISE YOUR CUPS TO THE *NEW SPIRIT OF YULETIME!*
ON YOUR *KNEES,* NOBLE LORDS.
OR DIE WHERE YOU STAND!

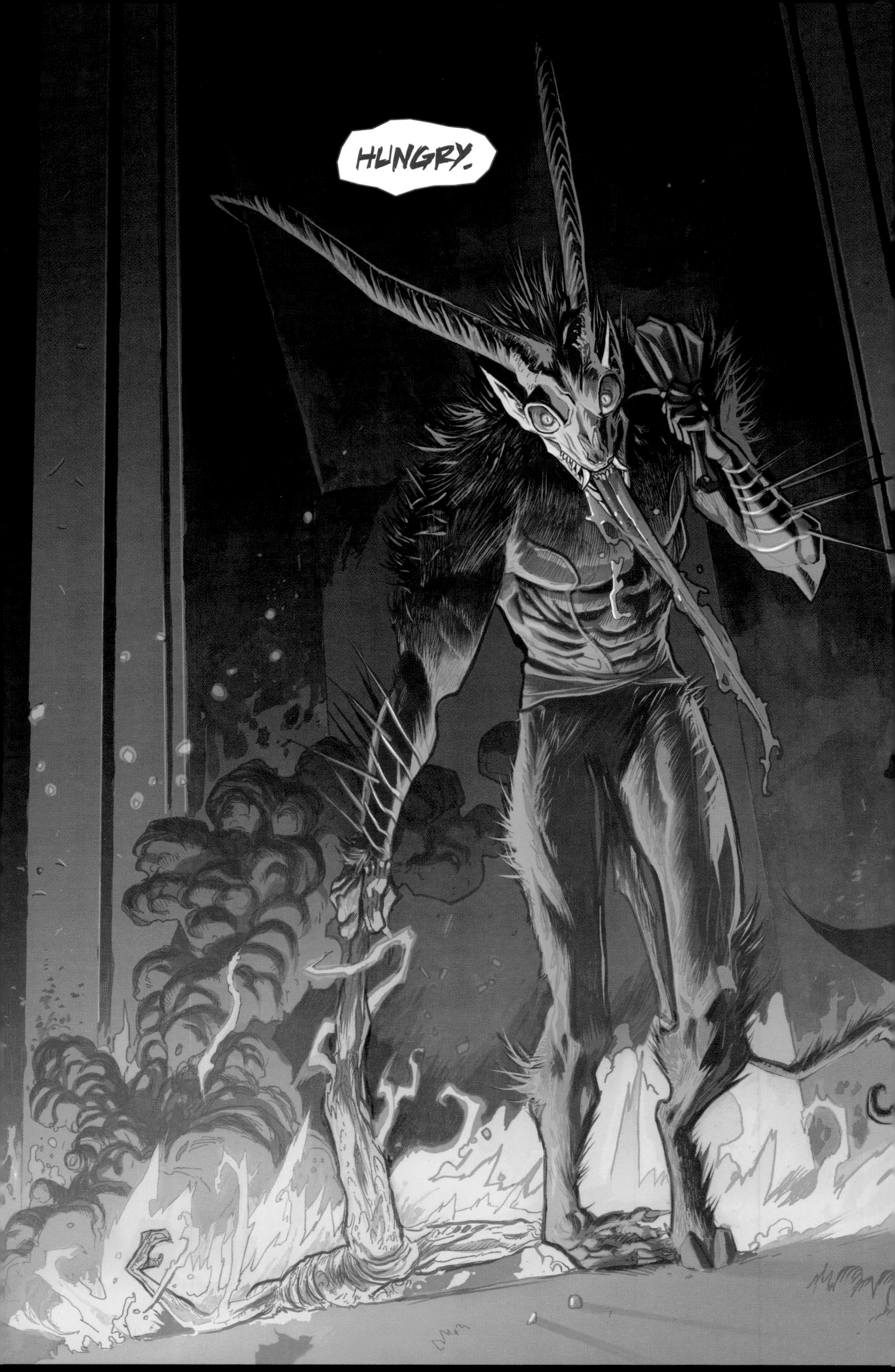
HUNGRY.

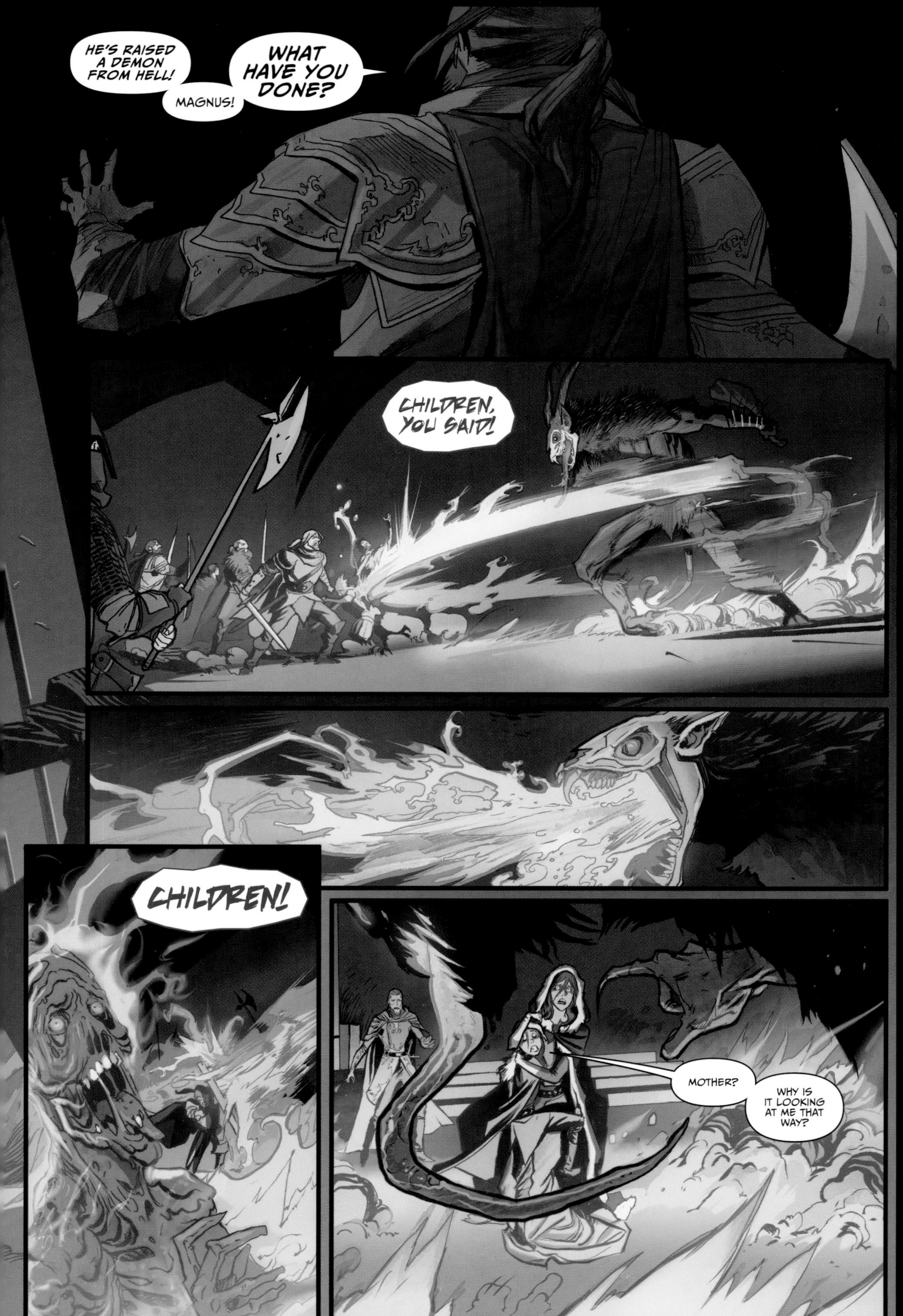
HE'S RAISED A DEMON FROM HELL!
MAGNUS!
WHAT HAVE YOU DONE?
CHILDREN, YOU SAID!
CHILDREN!
MOTHER?
WHY IS IT LOOKING AT ME THAT WAY?

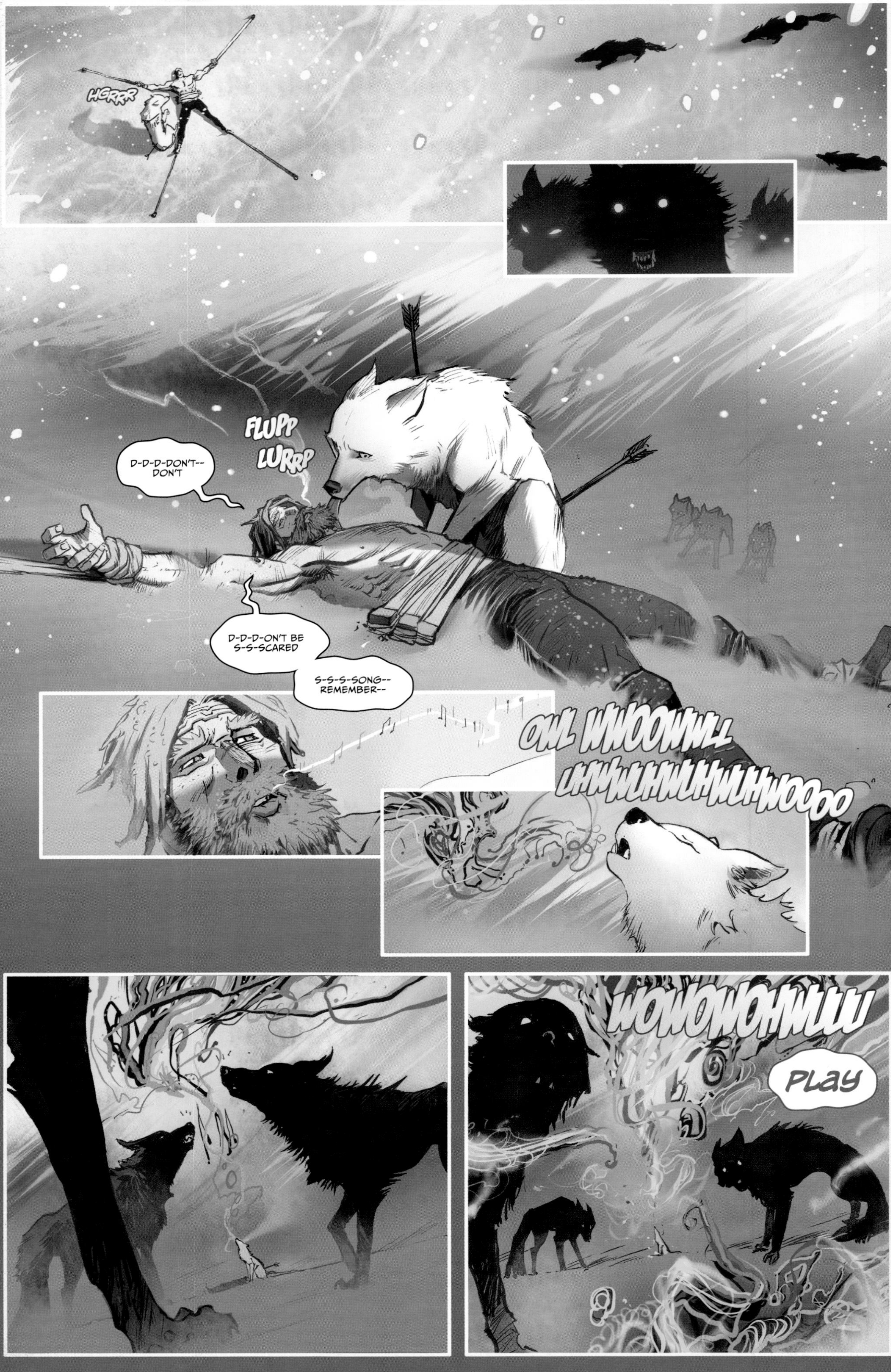
HGRRR
FLUPP
LURRP
D-D-D-DON'T--
DON'T
D-D-D-ON'T BE
S-S-SCARED
S-S-S-SONG--
REMEMBER--
OWL WWOOWWLL
LHHWWHHWHWHHWOOOO
WOWOWOHWUUU
PLAY

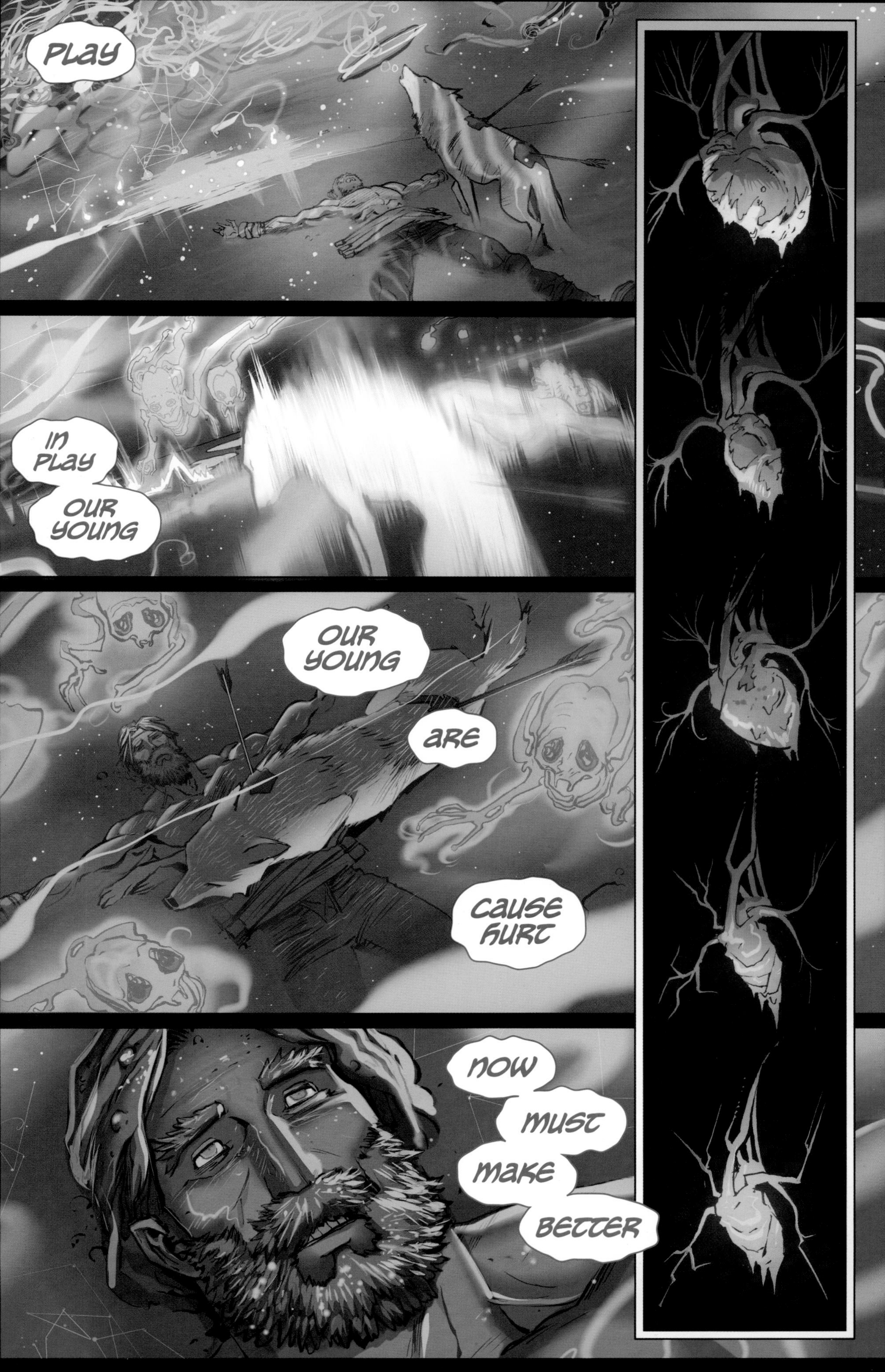
PLAY
IN PLAY
OUR YOUNG
OUR YOUNG
ARE
CAUSE HURT
NOW
MUST
MAKE
BETTER

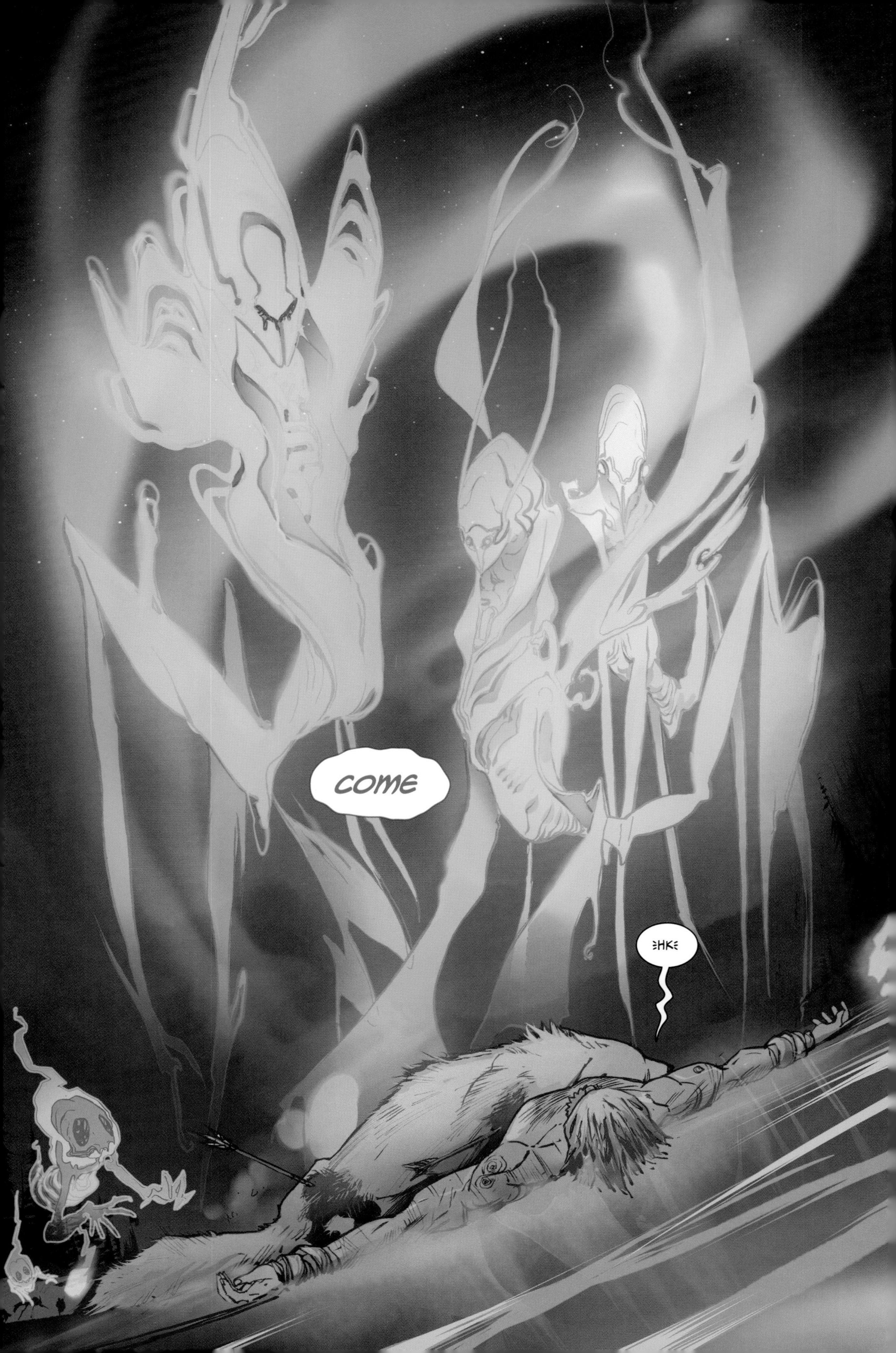
COME
HK

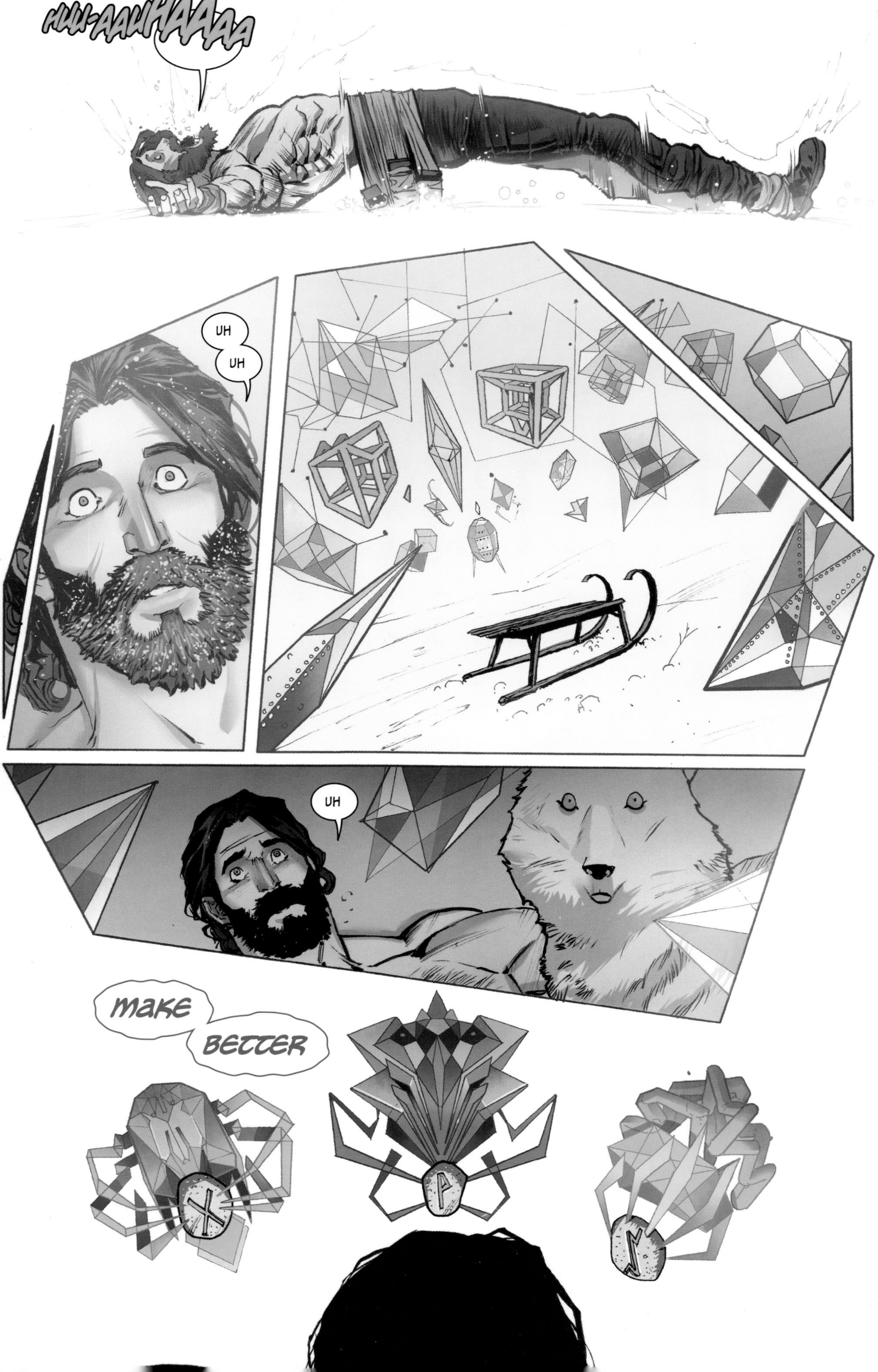
HUU-AAUHAAAAA
UH
UH
UH
MAKE
BETTER

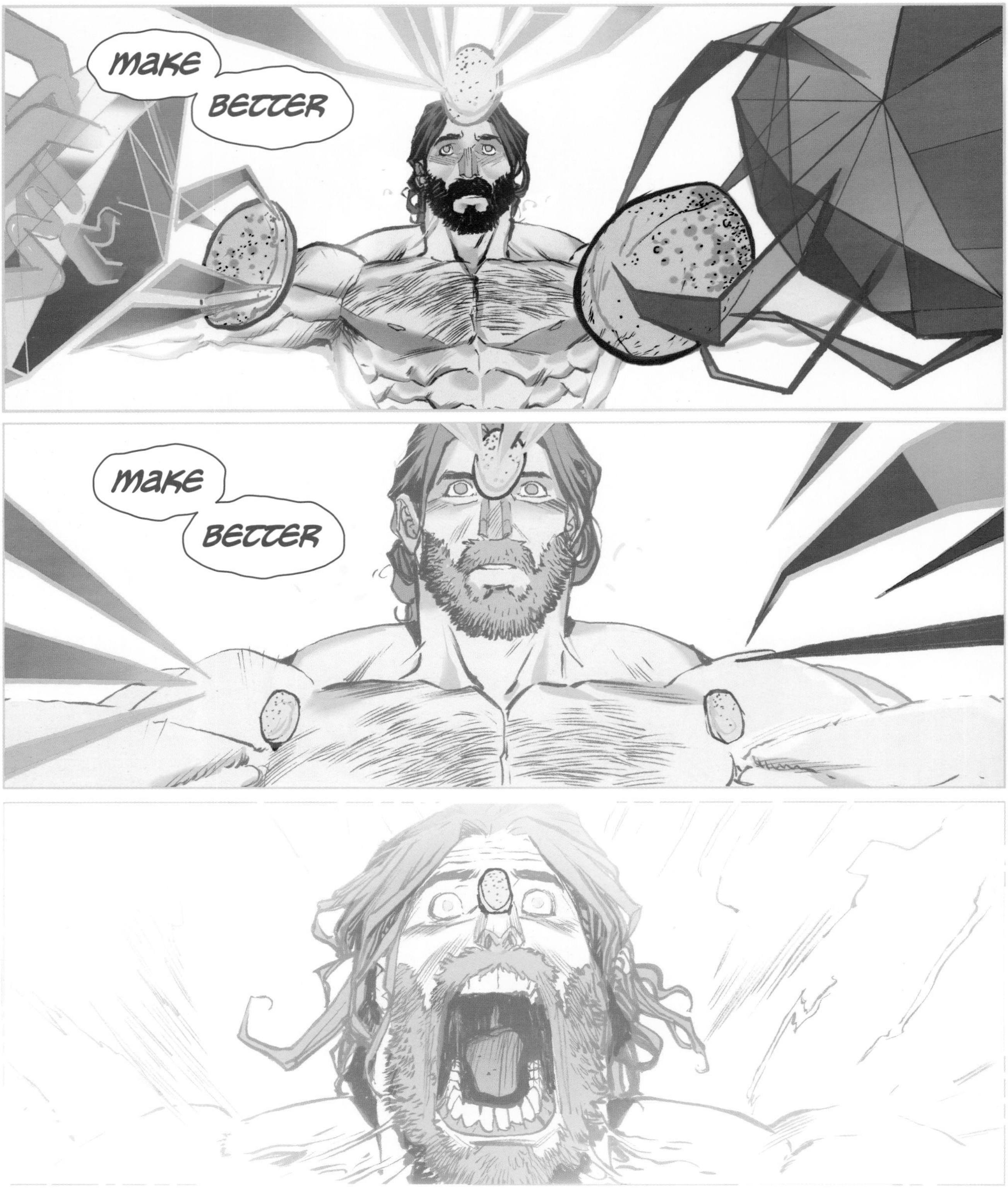
MAKE
BETTER
MAKE
BETTER

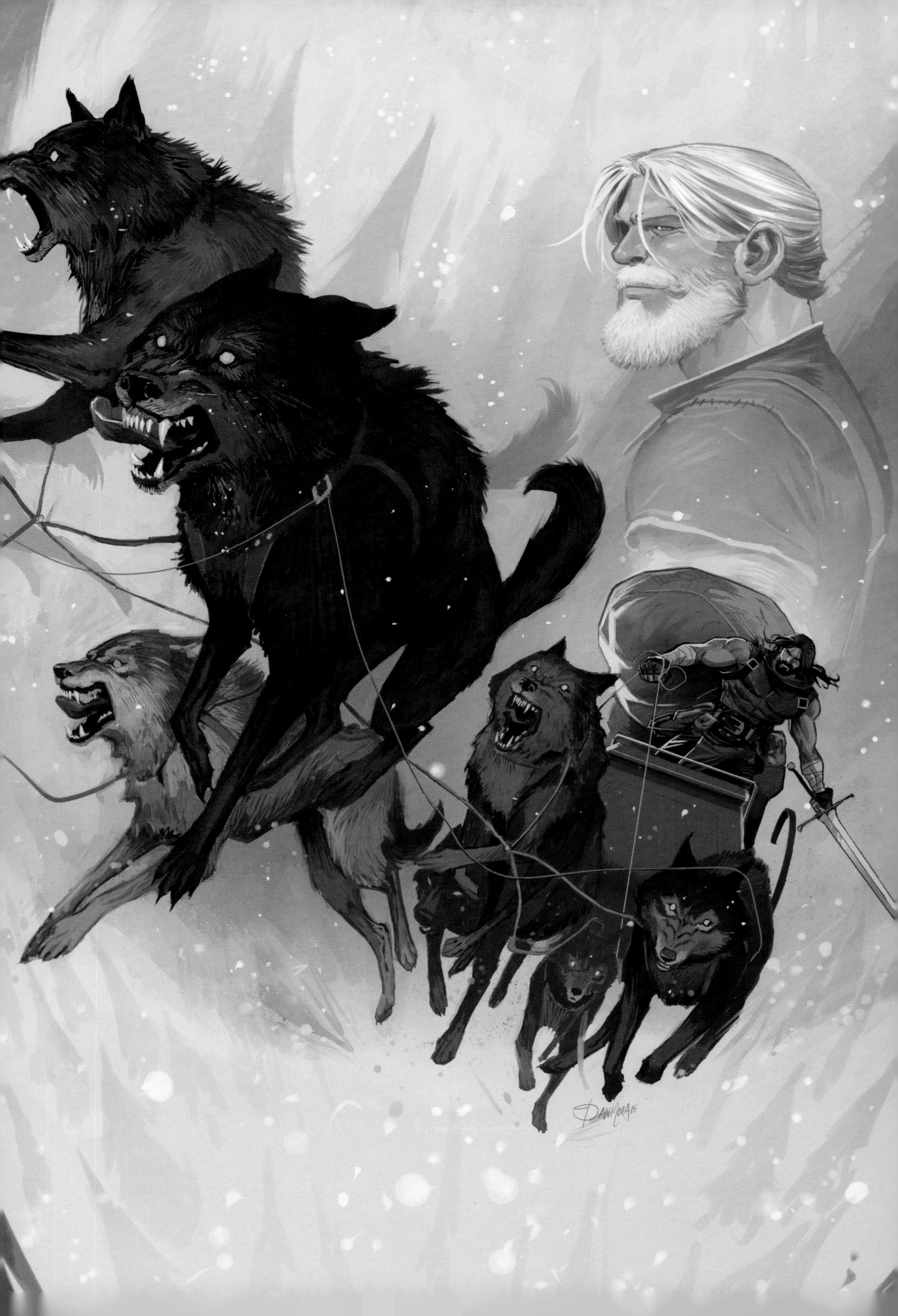

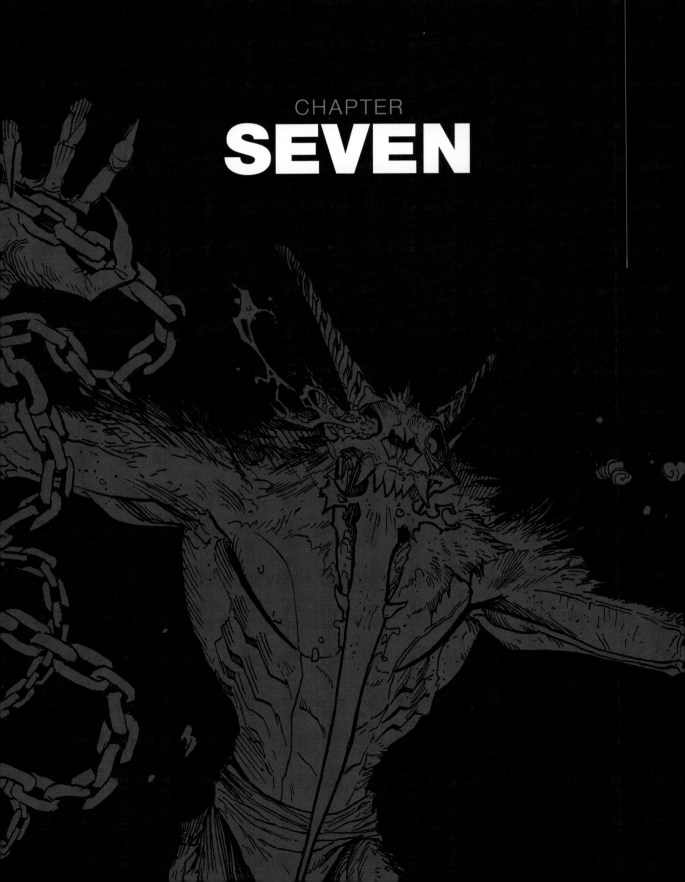

CHAPTER
SEVEN

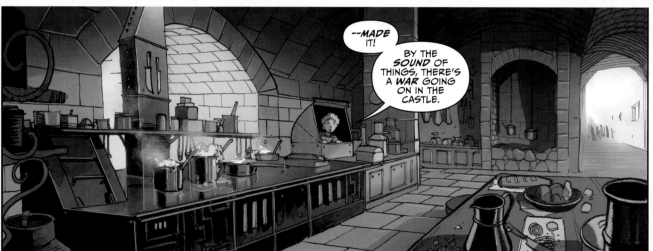

--MADE IT!

BY THE SOUND OF THINGS, THERE'S A WAR GOING ON IN THE CASTLE.

WELL, THERE'S AN EARTHQUAKE DOWN HERE!

HURRY!

YOUR TURN, JAN.

THE SANTA WILL SAVE US, FINN--

--WON'T HE?

THE SANTA'S DEAD.

HE WAS ONLY A MAN.

WE HAVE TO DO THIS OURSELVES.

HOW CAN HE BE DEAD?

IF THERE'S NO GOOD SPIRIT...

...WHO'S GOING TO STOP THE BAD ONE?

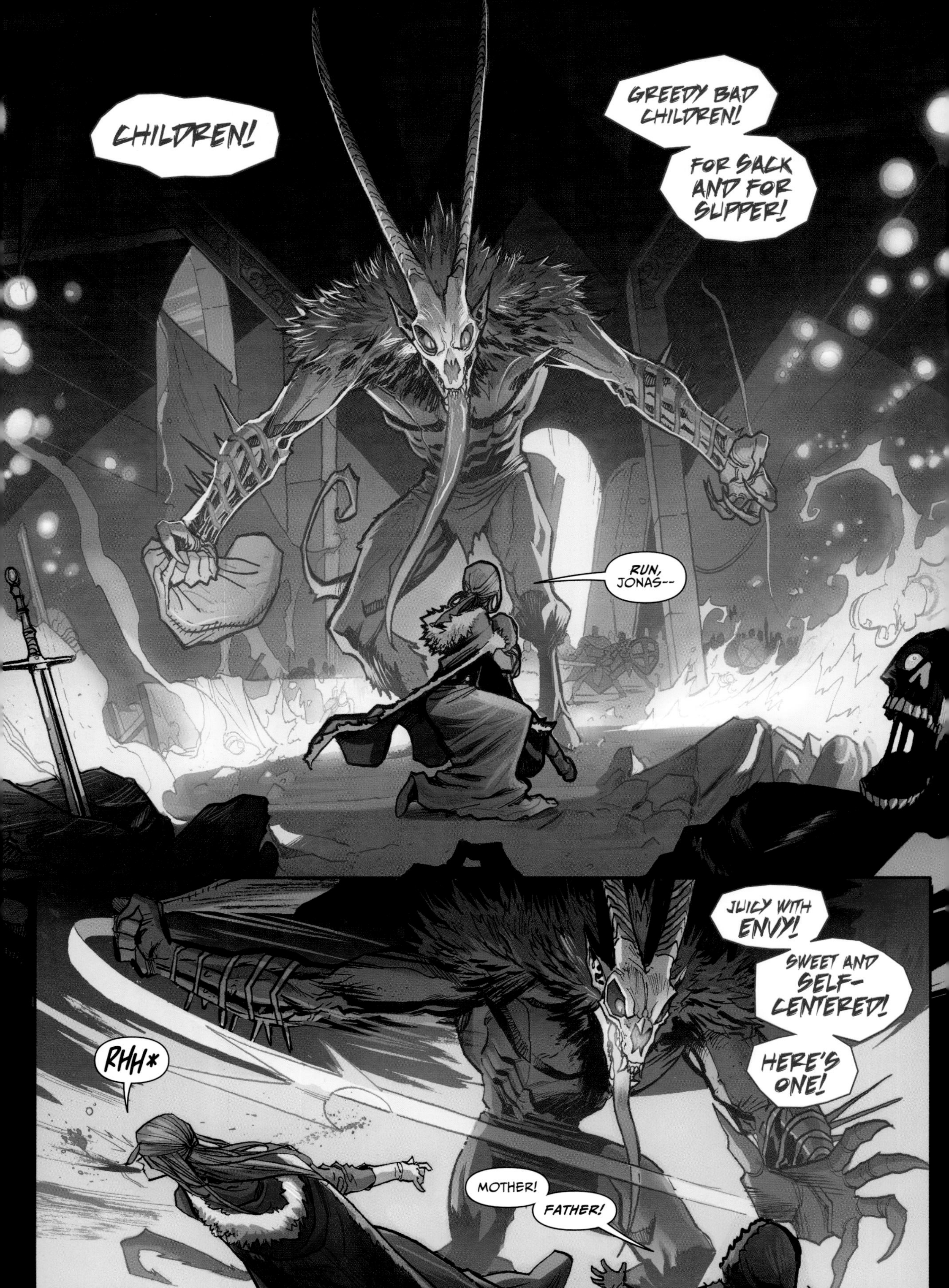
CHILDREN!
GREEDY BAD CHILDREN!
FOR SACK AND FOR SUPPER!
RUN, JONAS--
JUICY WITH ENVY!
SWEET AND SELF-CENTERED!
HERE'S ONE!
RHH*
MOTHER!
FATHER!

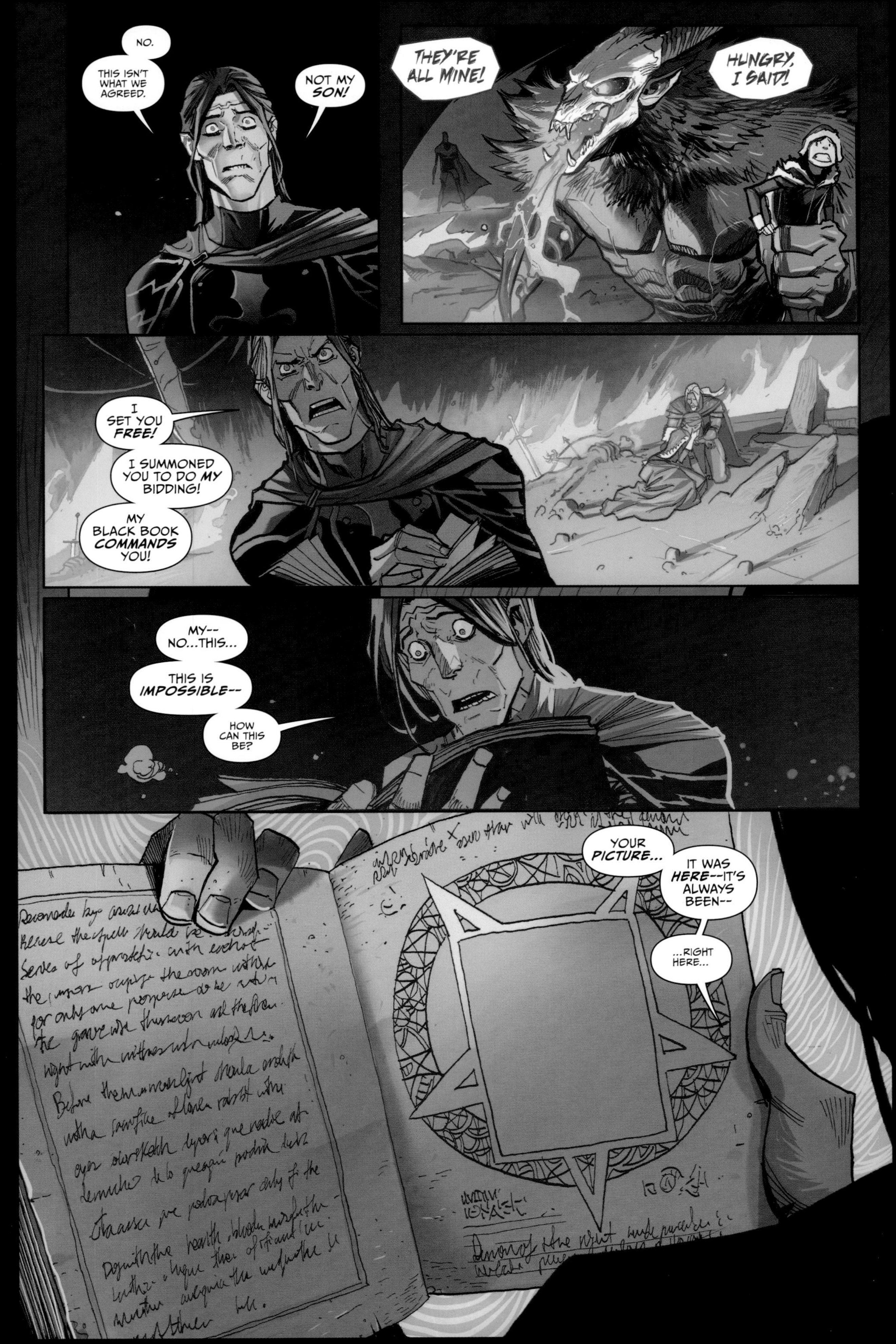
NO.
THIS ISN'T WHAT WE AGREED.
NOT MY SON!
THEY'RE ALL MINE!
HUNGRY, I SAID!
I SET YOU FREE!
I SUMMONED YOU TO DO MY BIDDING!
MY BLACK BOOK COMMANDS YOU!
MY-- NO...THIS...
THIS IS IMPOSSIBLE--
HOW CAN THIS BE?
YOUR PICTURE...
IT WAS HERE--IT'S ALWAYS BEEN--
...RIGHT HERE...

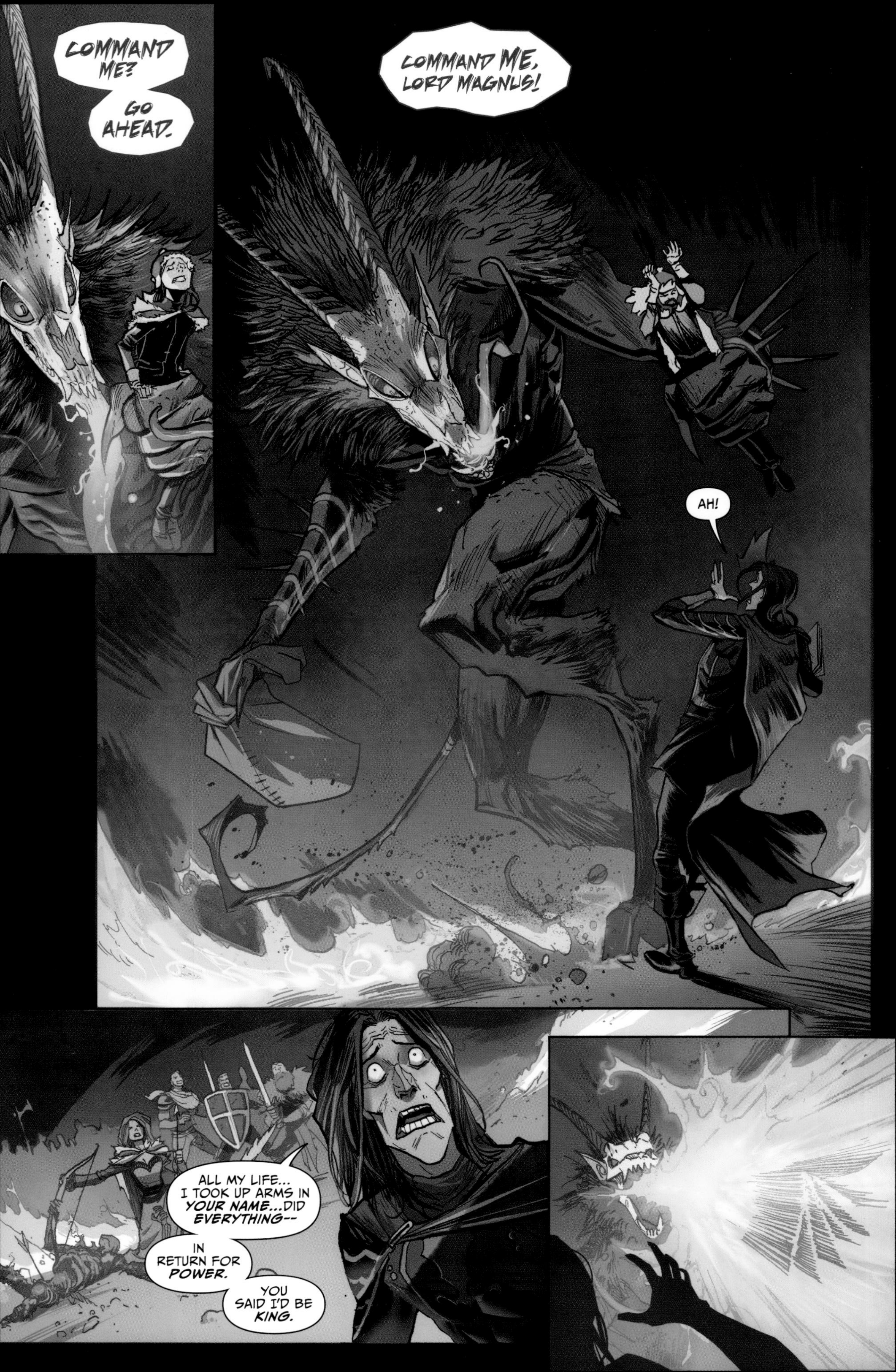
COMMAND ME?
GO AHEAD.
COMMAND ME, LORD MAGNUS!
AH!
ALL MY LIFE... I TOOK UP ARMS IN YOUR NAME...DID EVERYTHING--
IN RETURN FOR POWER.
YOU SAID I'D BE KING.

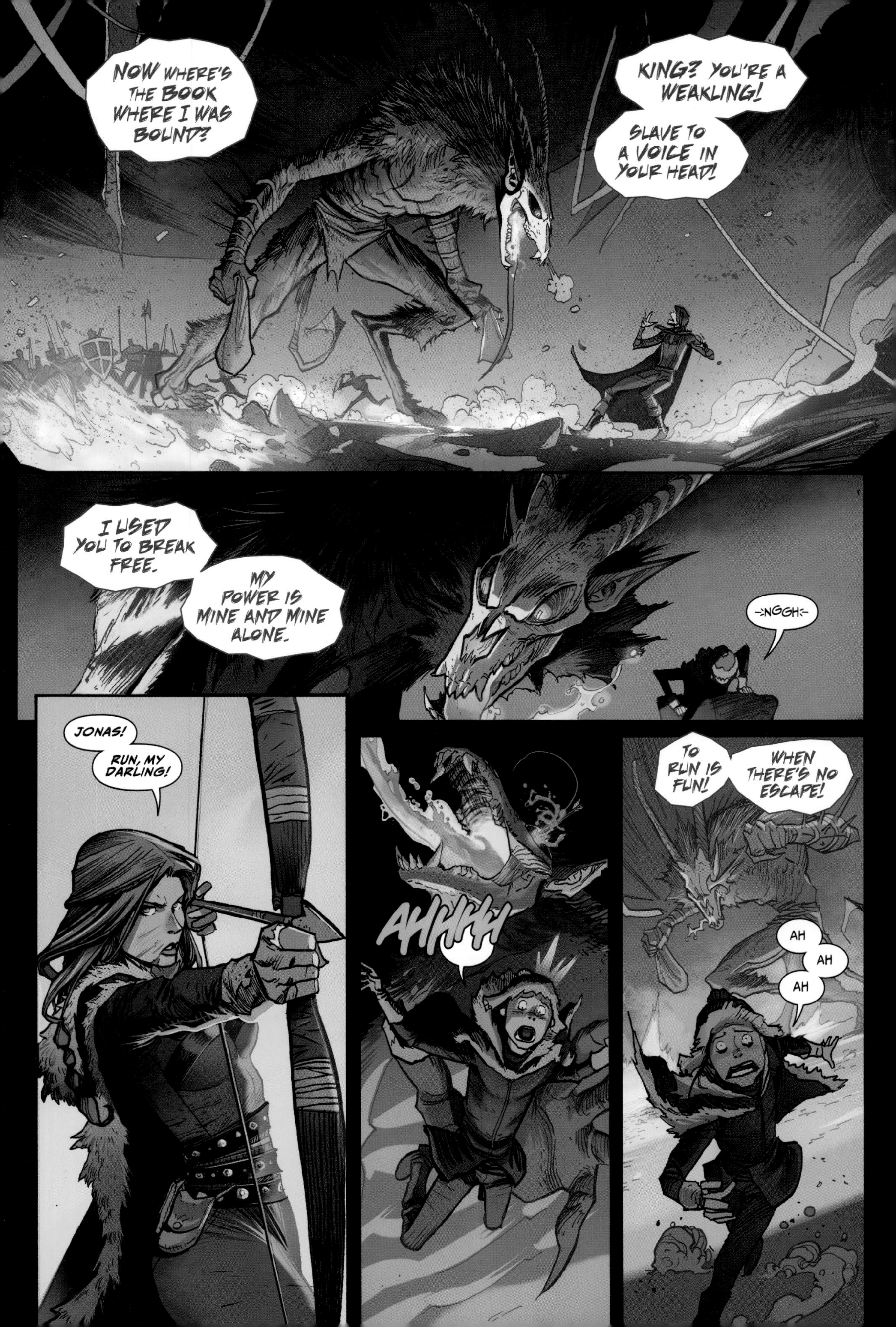
NOW WHERE'S THE BOOK WHERE I WAS BOUND?
KING? YOU'RE A WEAKLING!
SLAVE TO A VOICE IN YOUR HEAD!
I USED YOU TO BREAK FREE.
MY POWER IS MINE AND MINE ALONE.
-NGGH-
JONAS!
RUN, MY DARLING!
AHHHH
TO RUN IS FUN!
WHEN THERE'S NO ESCAPE!
AH
AH
AH

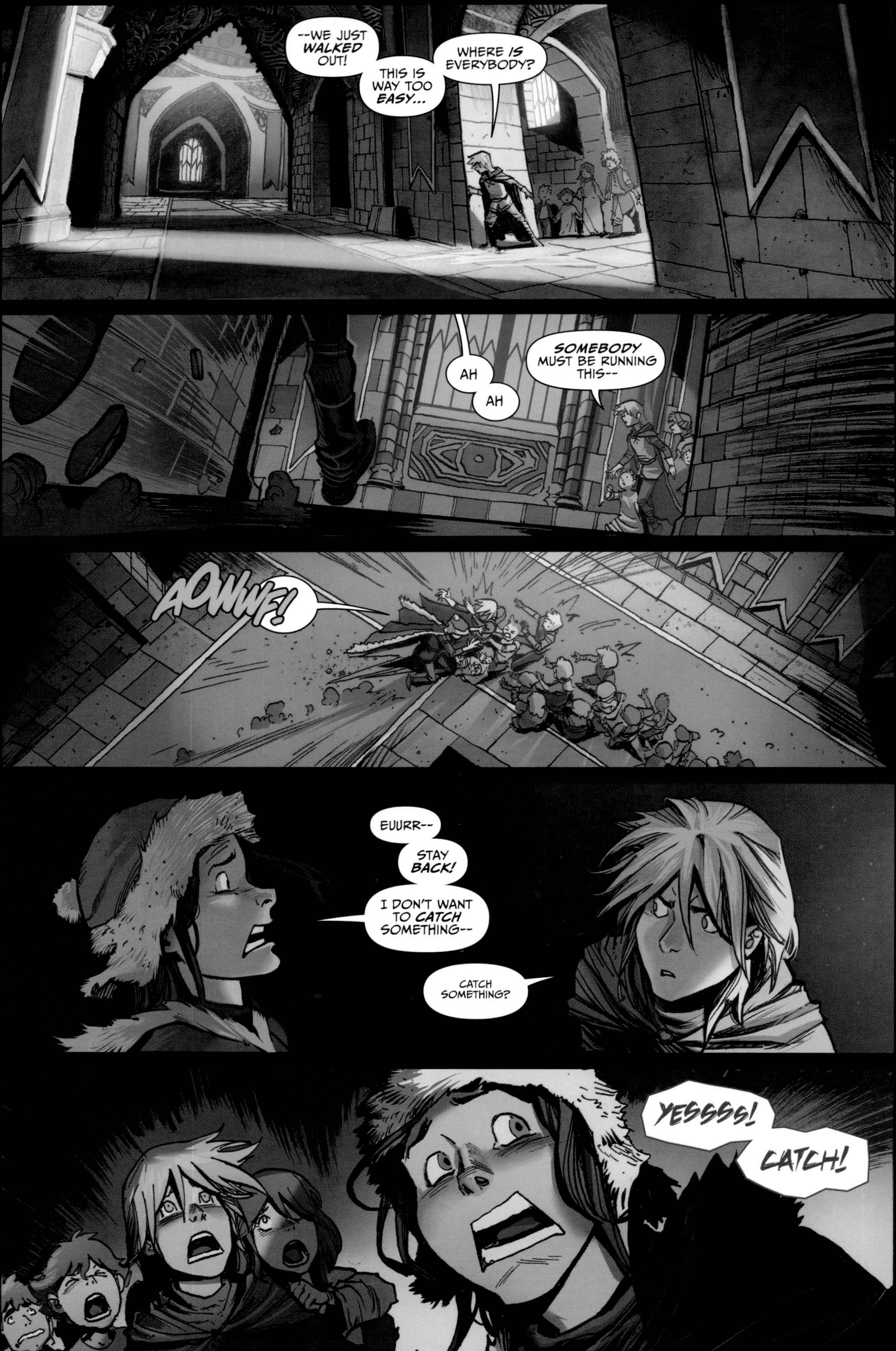
--WE JUST WALKED OUT!
THIS IS WAY TOO EASY...
WHERE IS EVERYBODY?
AH
AH
SOMEBODY MUST BE RUNNING THIS--
AOWWF!
EUURR--
STAY BACK!
I DON'T WANT TO CATCH SOMETHING--
CATCH SOMETHING?
YESSSS!
CATCH!

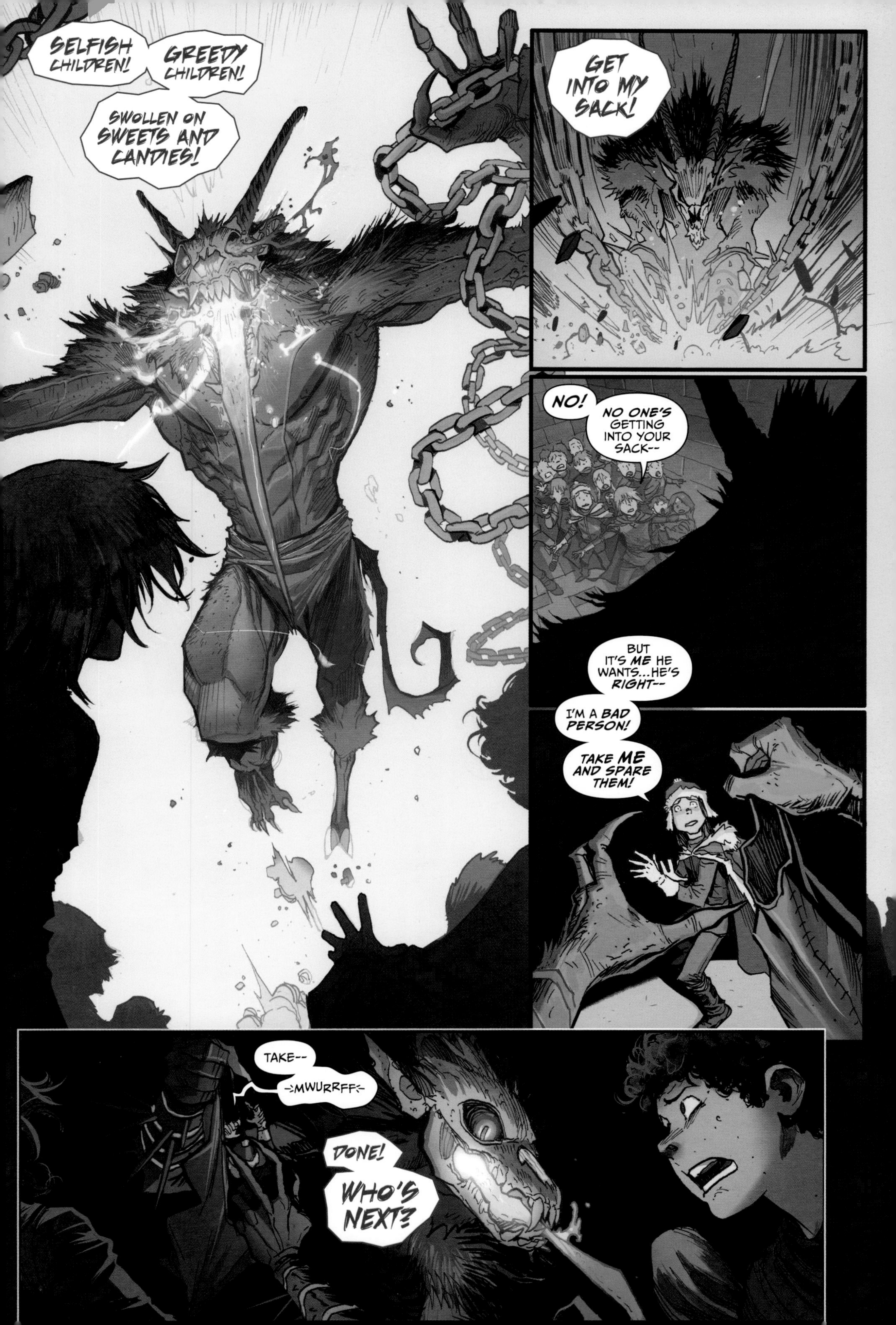
SELFISH CHILDREN!
GREEDY CHILDREN!
SWOLLEN ON SWEETS AND CANDIES!
GET INTO MY SACK!
NO!
NO ONE'S GETTING INTO YOUR SACK--
BUT IT'S ME HE WANTS...HE'S RIGHT--
I'M A BAD PERSON!
TAKE ME AND SPARE THEM!
TAKE--
-MWURRFF-
DONE!
WHO'S NEXT?

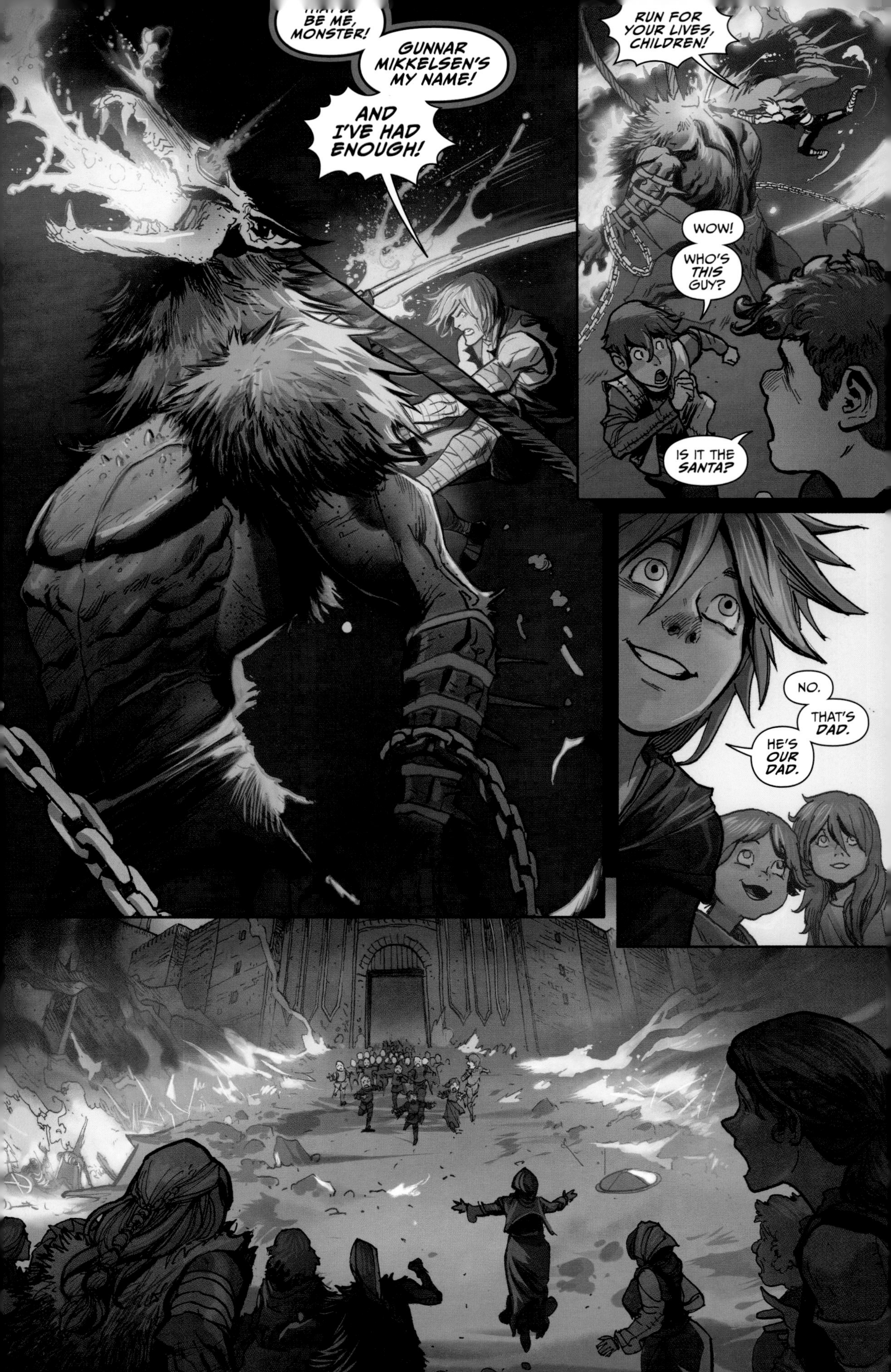
BE ME, MONSTER!
GUNNAR MIKKELSEN'S MY NAME!
AND I'VE HAD ENOUGH!
RUN FOR YOUR LIVES, CHILDREN!
WOW!
WHO'S THIS GUY?
IS IT THE SANTA?
NO.
THAT'S DAD.
HE'S OUR DAD.

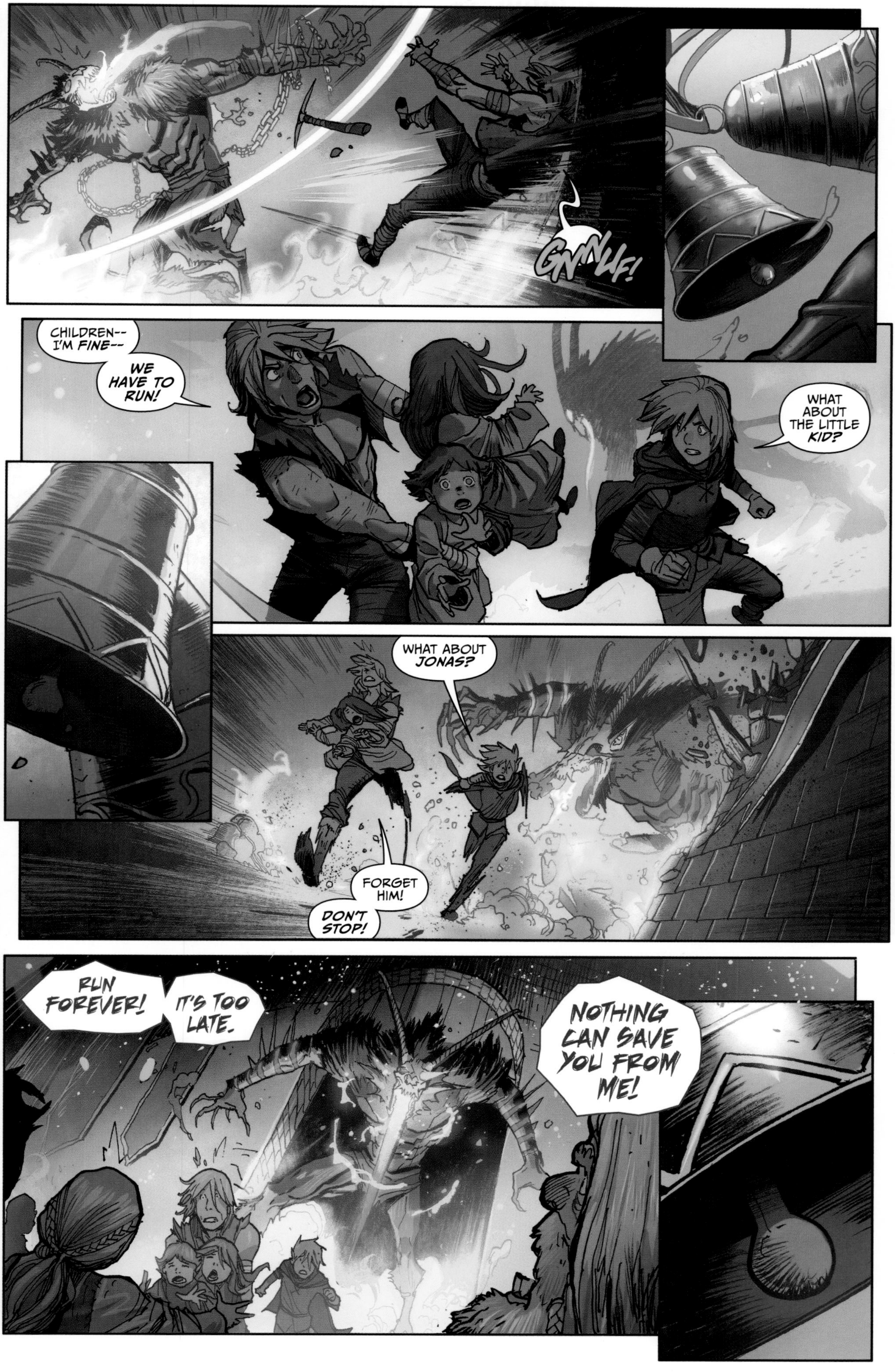
GNNUF!
CHILDREN-- I'M FINE--
WE HAVE TO RUN!
WHAT ABOUT THE LITTLE KID?
WHAT ABOUT JONAS?
FORGET HIM!
DON'T STOP!
RUN FOREVER!
IT'S TOO LATE.
NOTHING CAN SAVE YOU FROM ME!

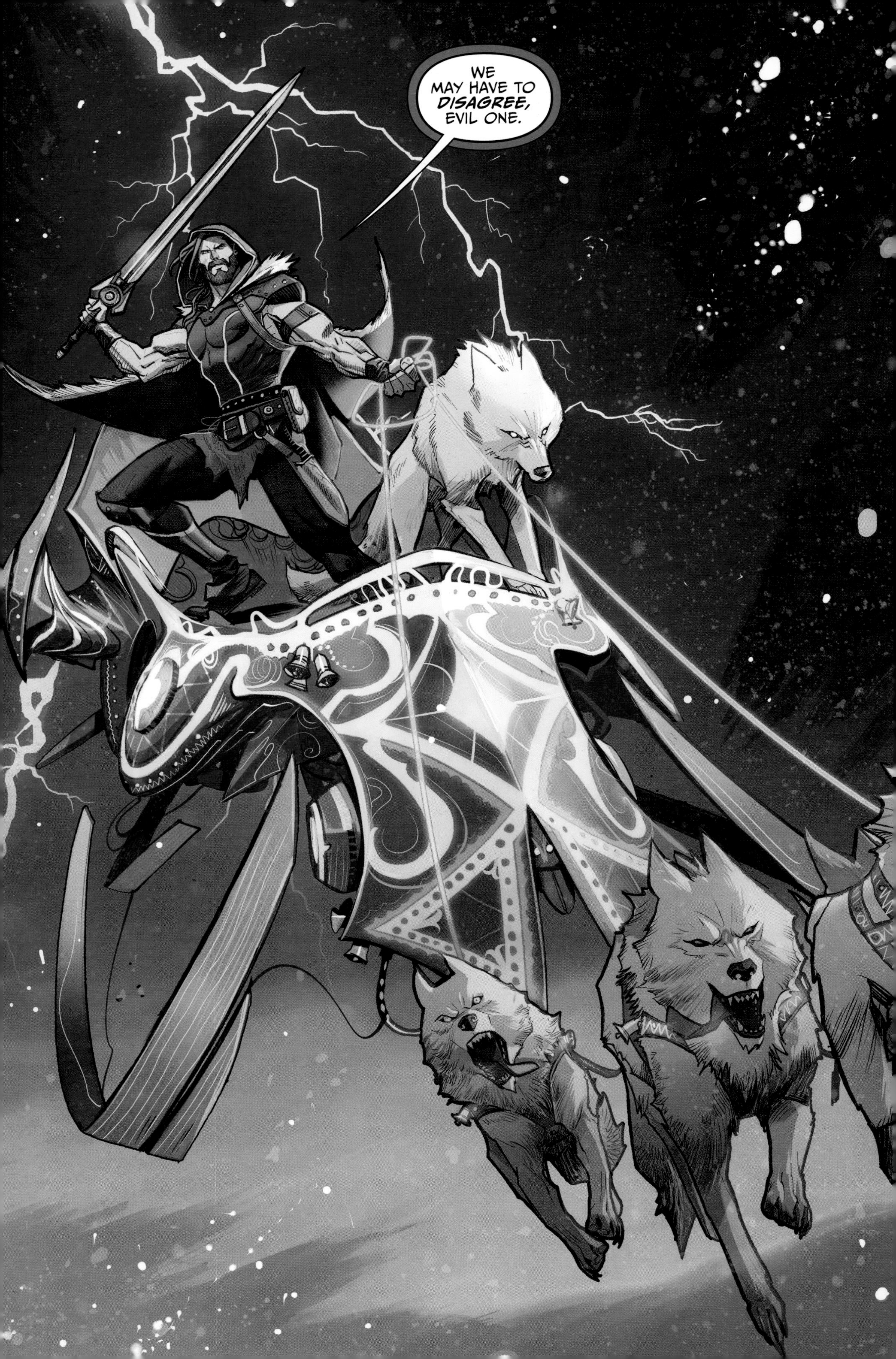
WE MAY HAVE TO DISAGREE, EVIL ONE.

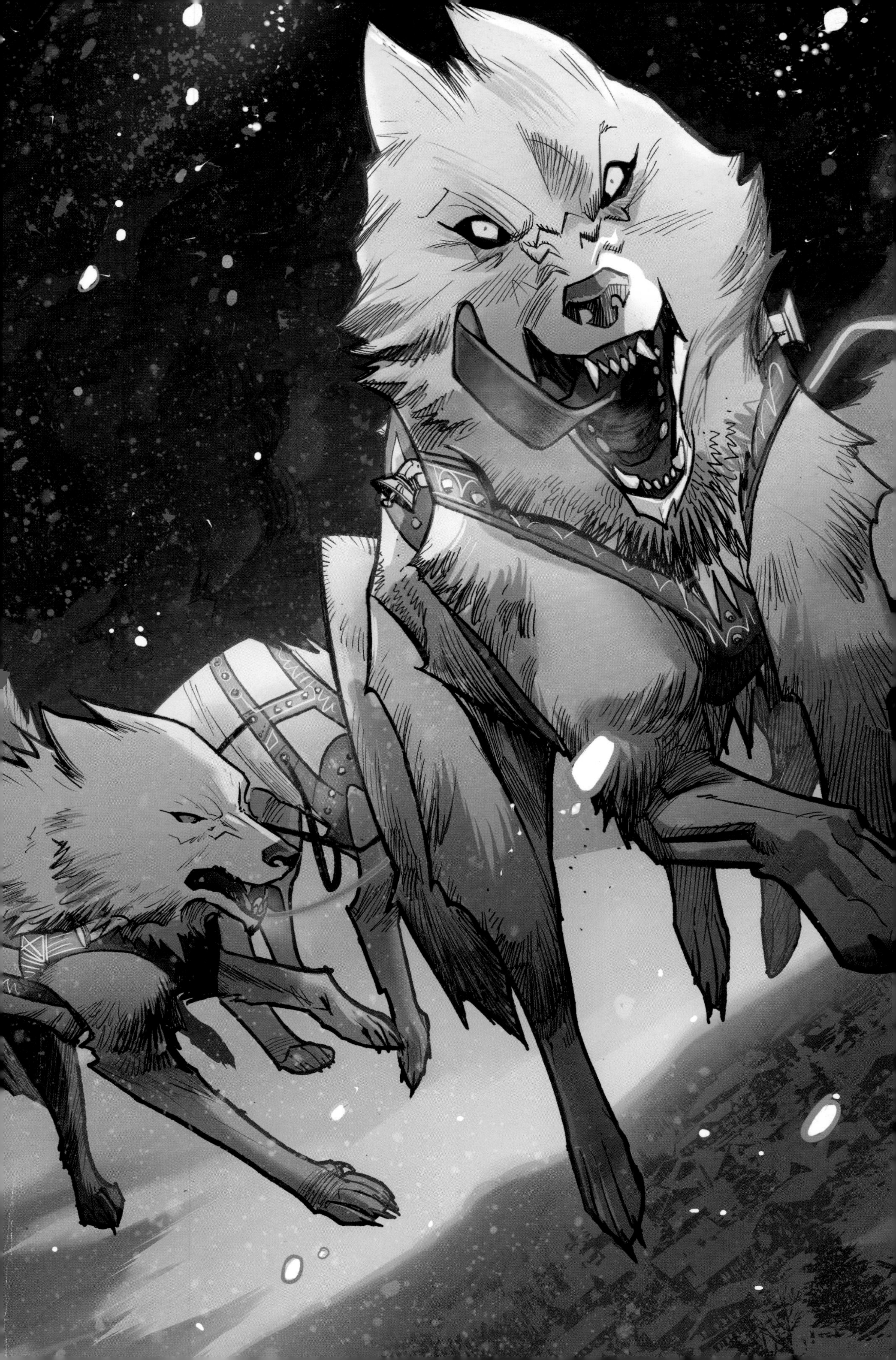

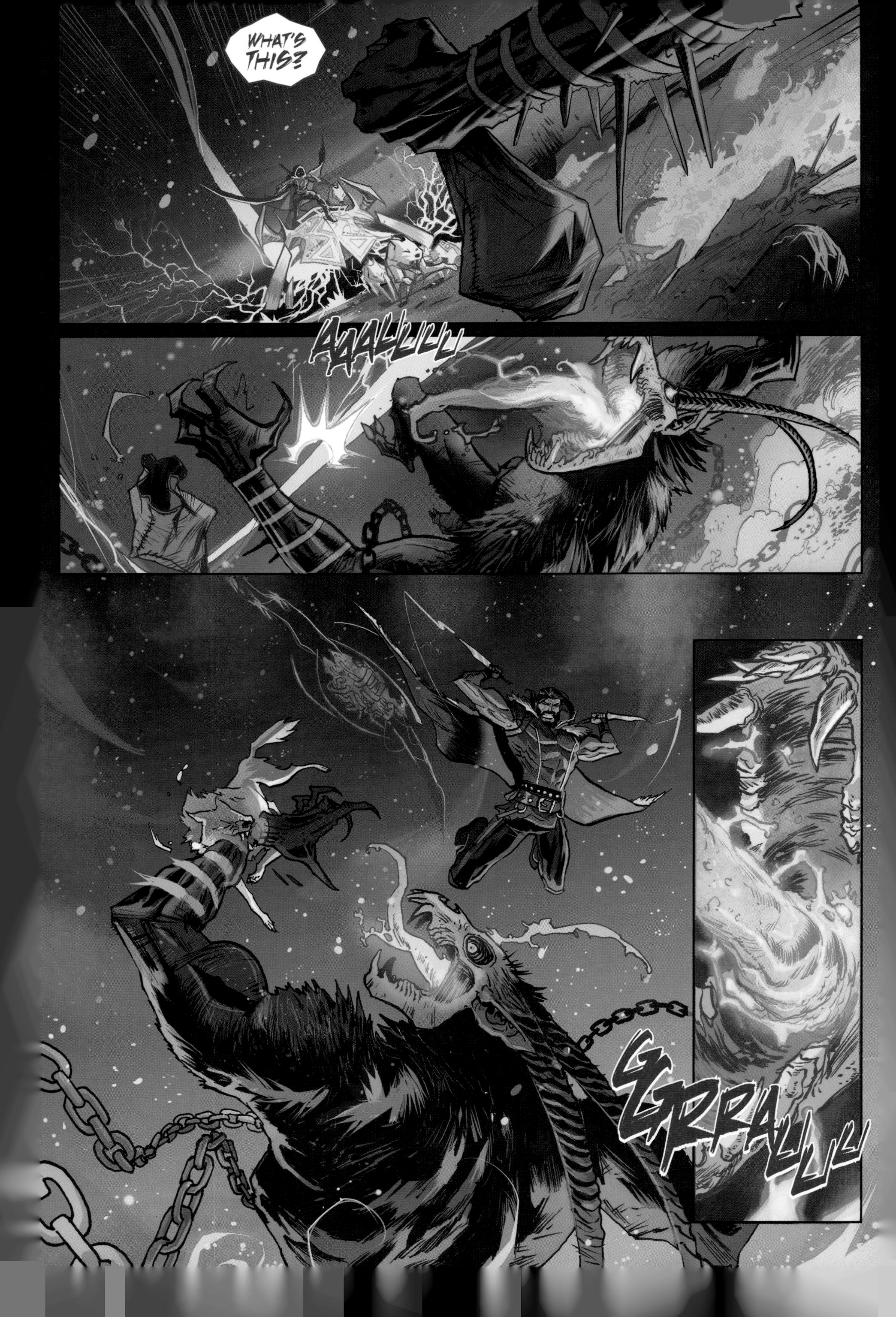
WHAT'S THIS?
AAAALLLLU
GRRALLLU

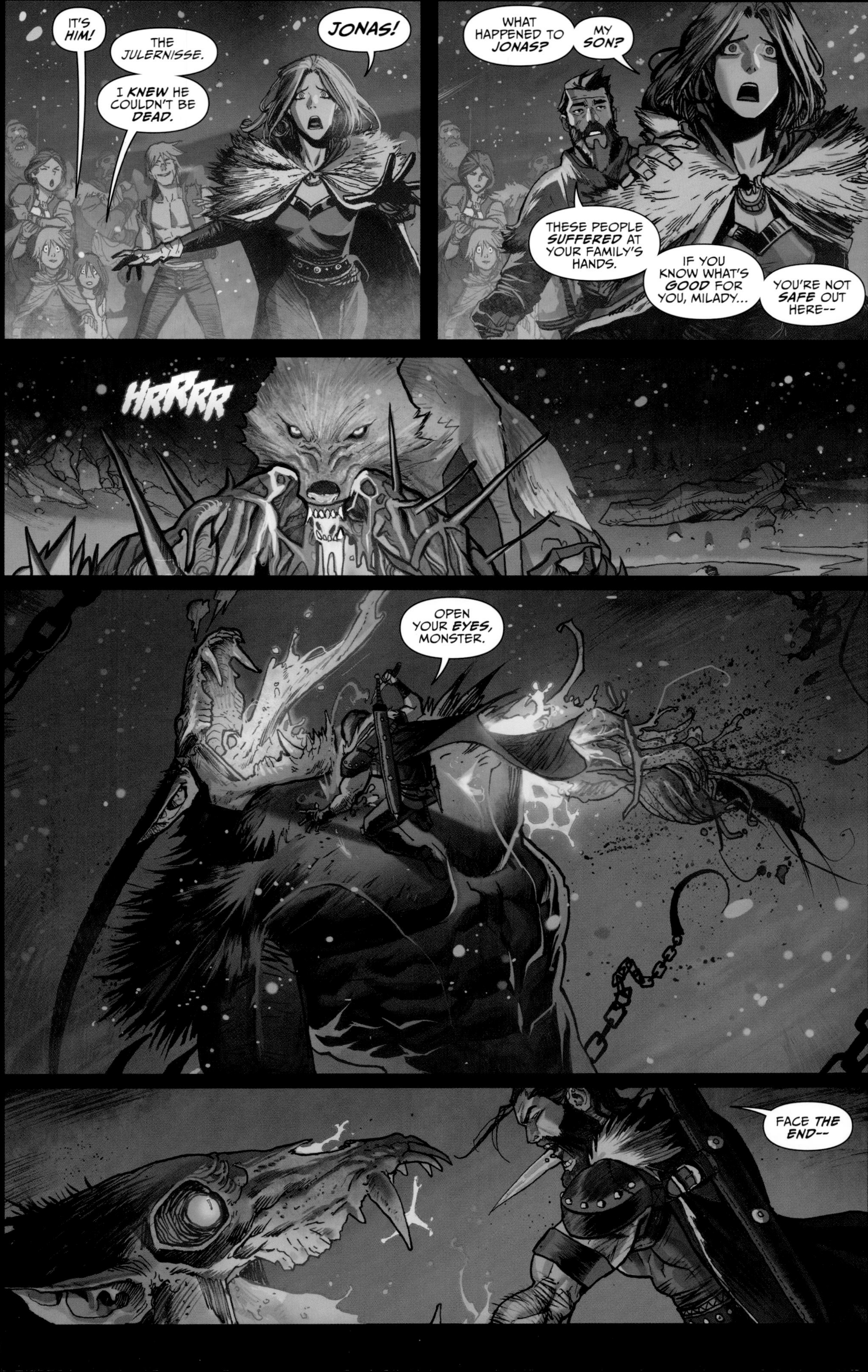

IT'S HIM!
THE JULERNISSE.
I KNEW HE COULDN'T BE DEAD.
JONAS!
WHAT HAPPENED TO JONAS?
MY SON?
THESE PEOPLE SUFFERED AT YOUR FAMILY'S HANDS.
IF YOU KNOW WHAT'S GOOD FOR YOU, MILADY...
YOU'RE NOT SAFE OUT HERE--
HRRRR
OPEN YOUR EYES, MONSTER.
FACE THE END--

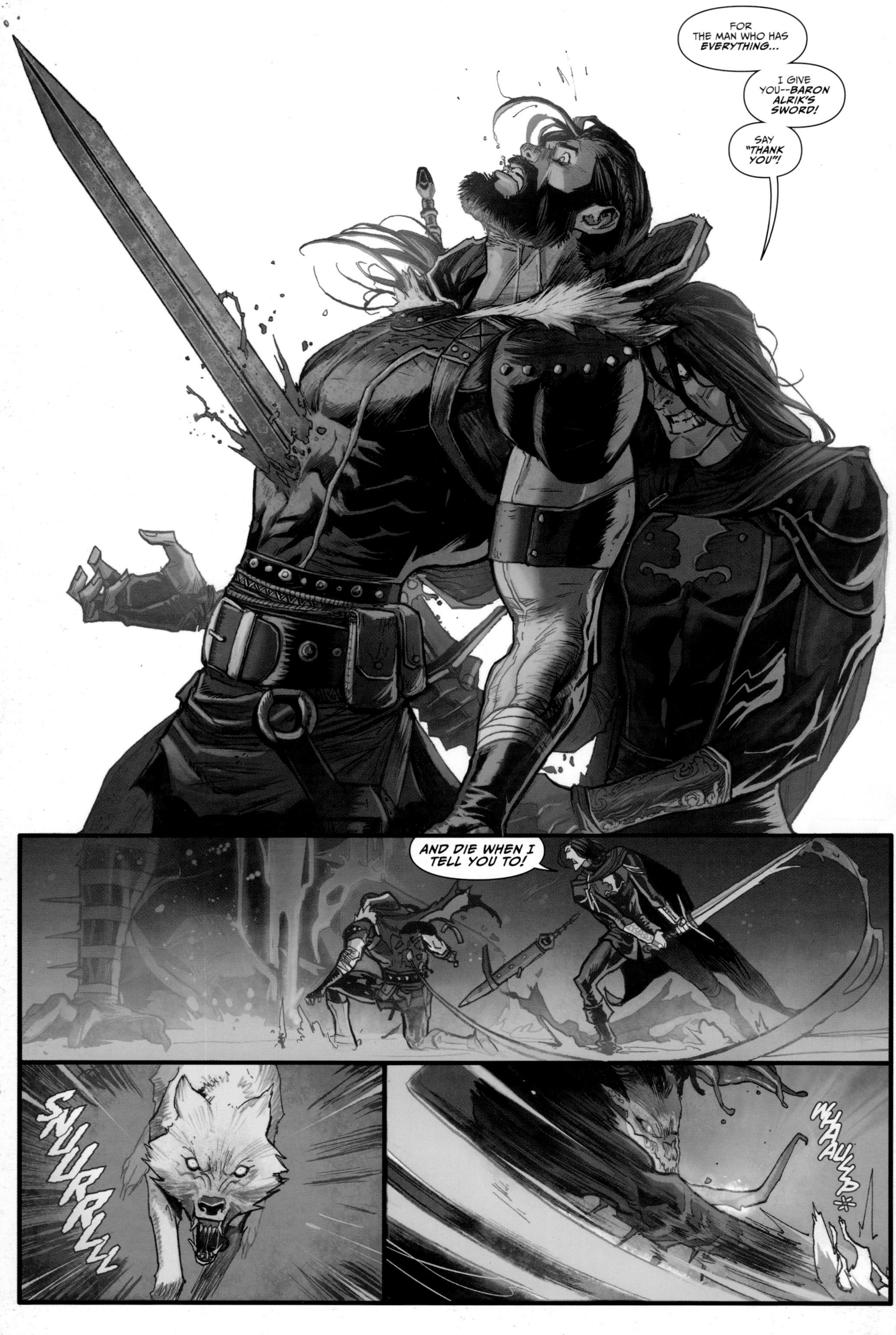
FOR THE MAN WHO HAS EVERYTHING...
I GIVE YOU--BARON ALRIK'S SWORD!
SAY "THANK YOU"!
AND DIE WHEN I TELL YOU TO!
SNURRLL
WHAUUP

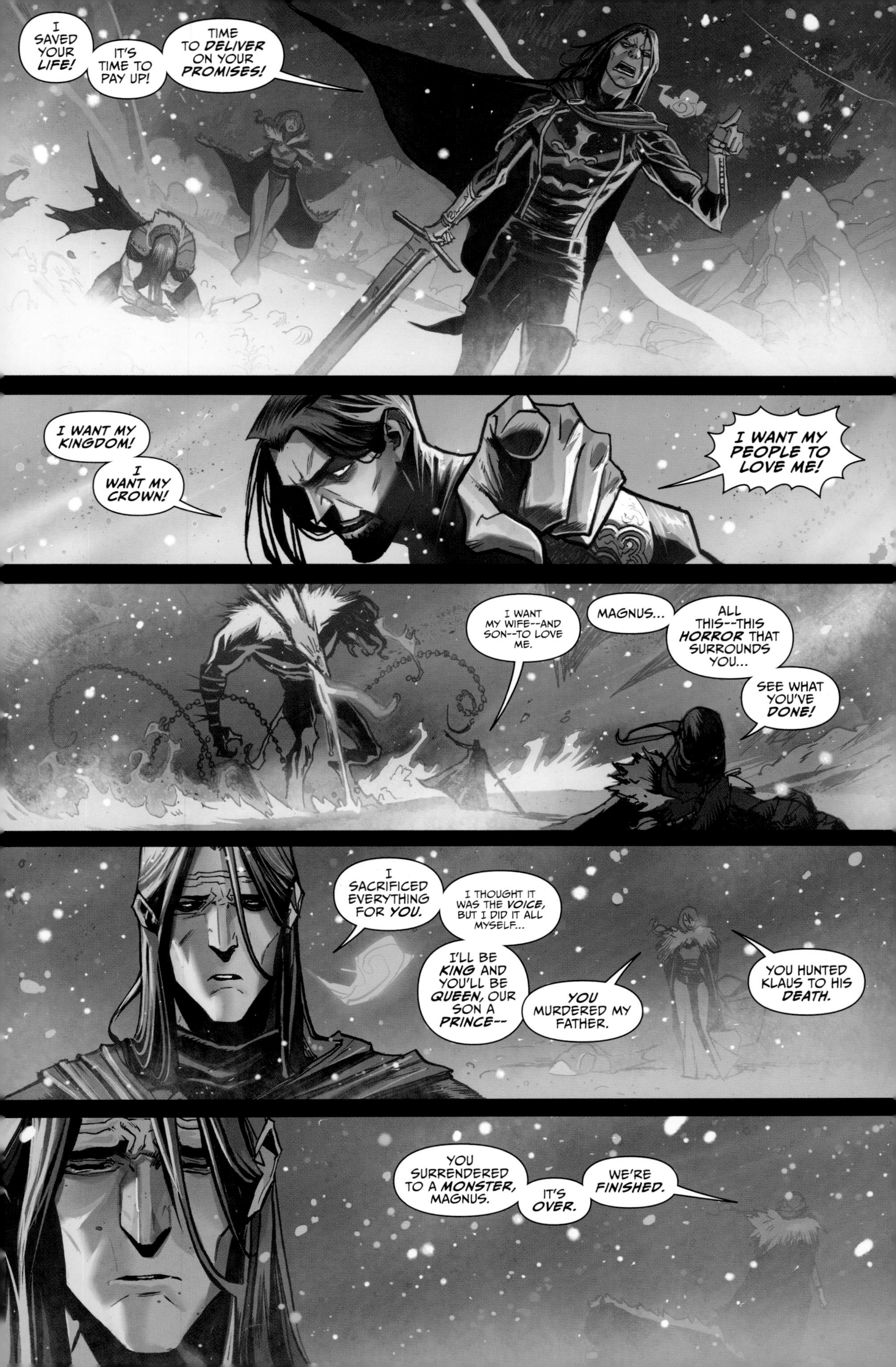
I SAVED YOUR LIFE!
IT'S TIME TO PAY UP!
TIME TO DELIVER ON YOUR PROMISES!
I WANT MY KINGDOM!
I WANT MY CROWN!
I WANT MY PEOPLE TO LOVE ME!
I WANT MY WIFE--AND SON--TO LOVE ME.
MAGNUS...
ALL THIS--THIS HORROR THAT SURROUNDS YOU...
SEE WHAT YOU'VE DONE!
I SACRIFICED EVERYTHING FOR YOU.
I THOUGHT IT WAS THE VOICE, BUT I DID IT ALL MYSELF...
I'LL BE KING AND YOU'LL BE QUEEN, OUR SON A PRINCE--
YOU MURDERED MY FATHER.
YOU HUNTED KLAUS TO HIS DEATH.
YOU SURRENDERED TO A MONSTER, MAGNUS.
IT'S OVER.
WE'RE FINISHED.

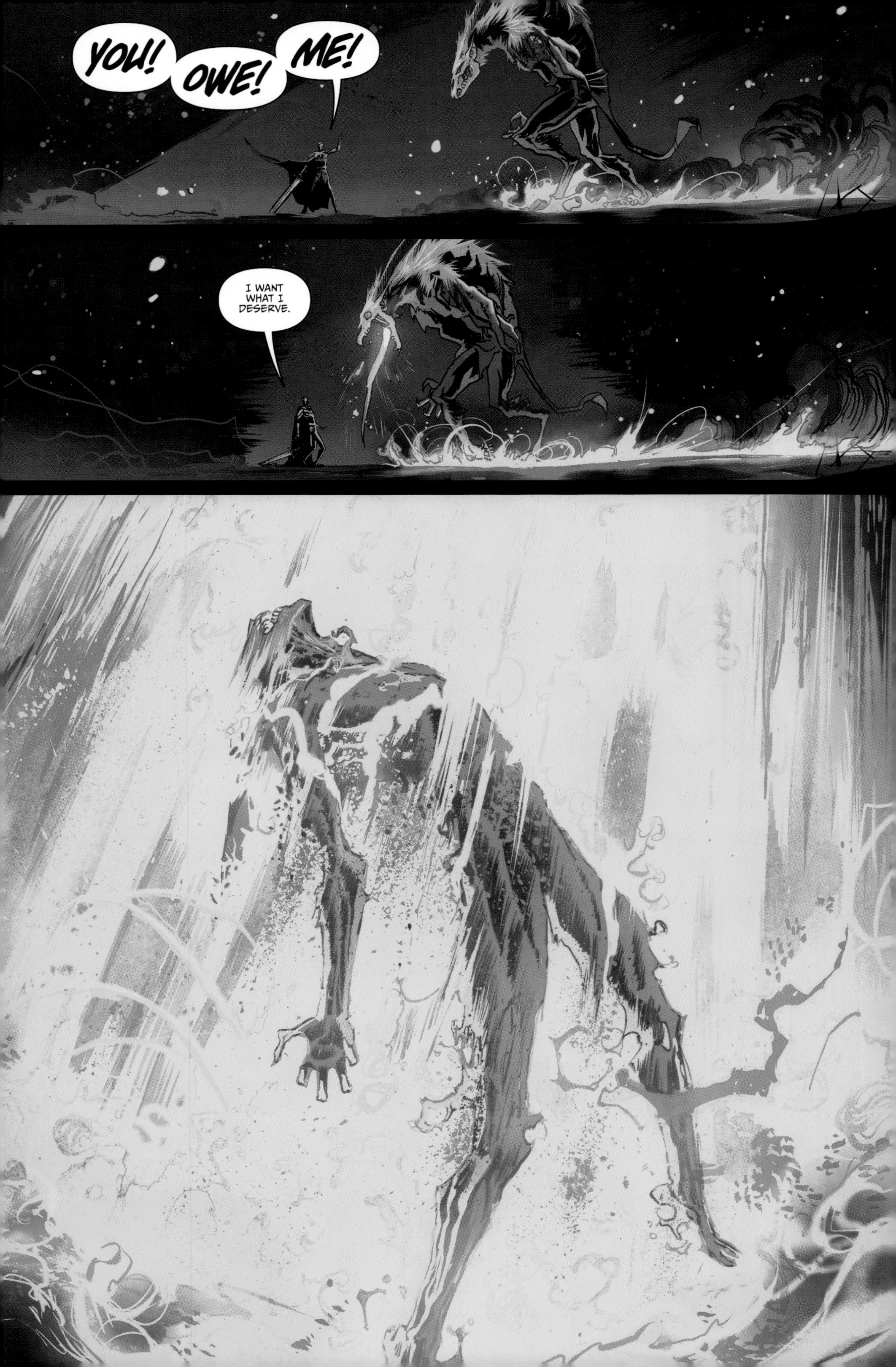
YOU!
OWE!
ME!
I WANT WHAT I DESERVE.

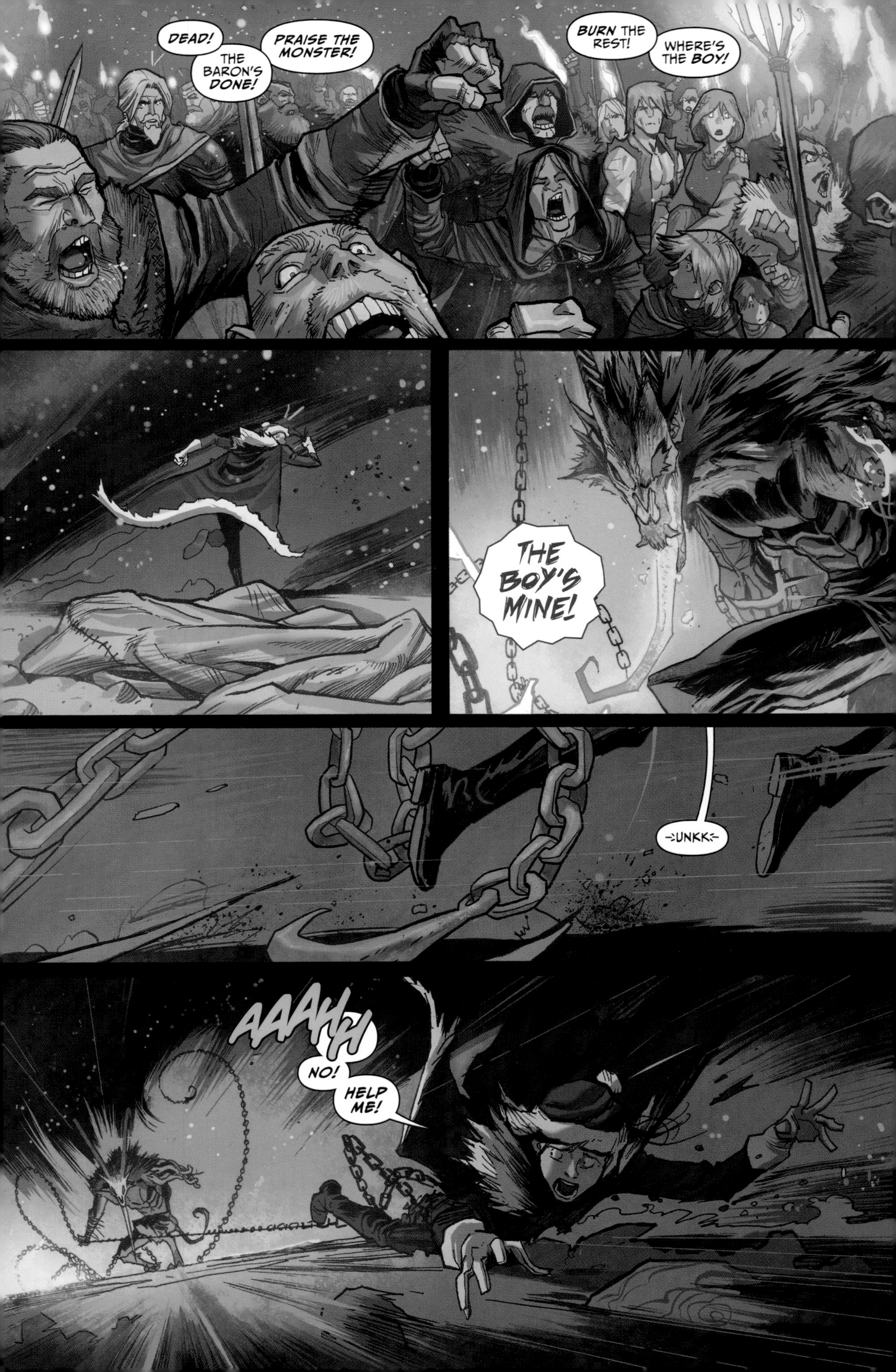

DEAD!
THE BARON'S DONE!
PRAISE THE MONSTER!
BURN THE REST!
WHERE'S THE BOY!
THE BOY'S MINE!
UNKK
AAAHH
NO!
HELP ME!

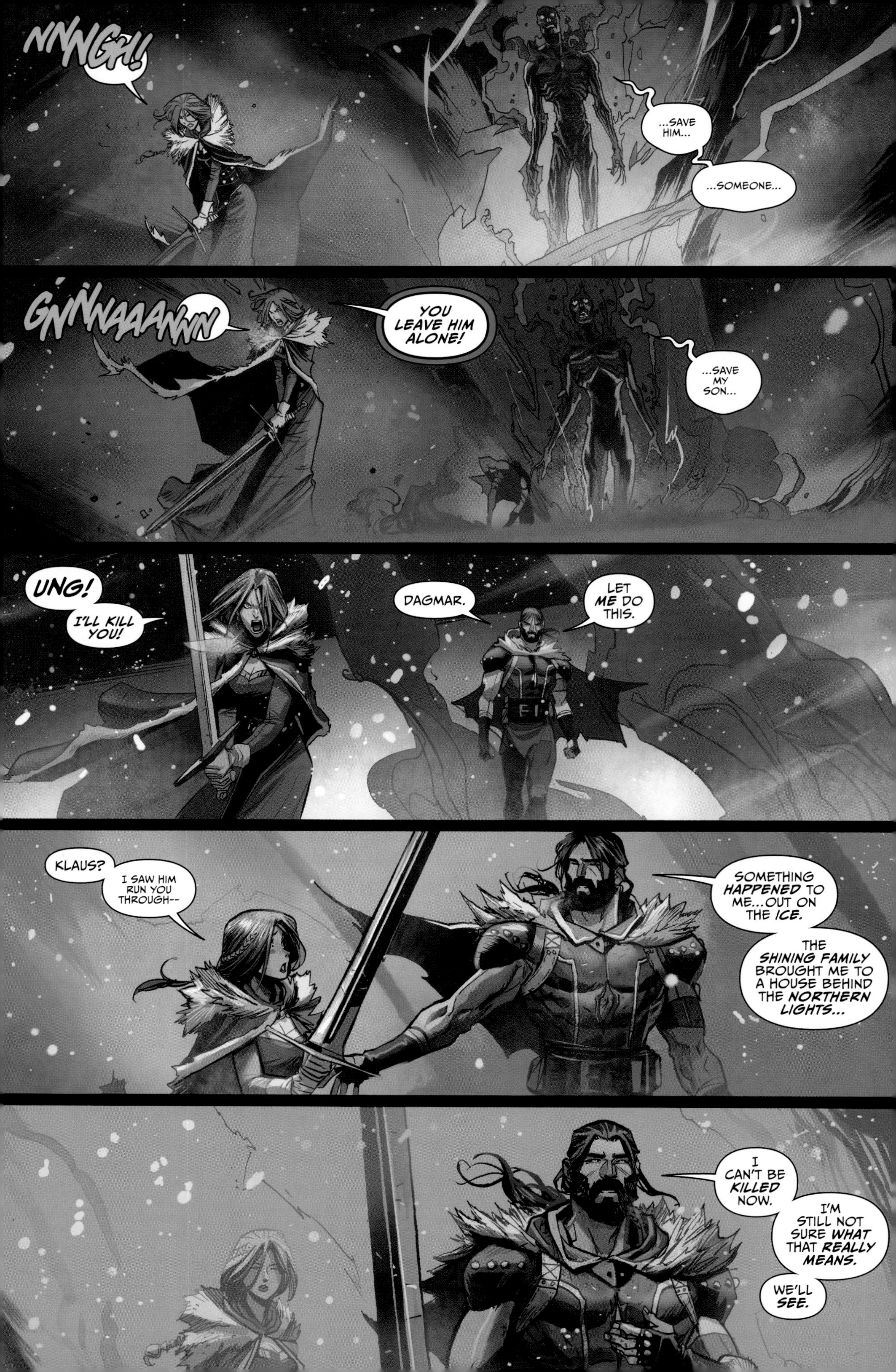
NNNGH!
...SAVE HIM...
...SOMEONE...
GNNWAAANNN
YOU LEAVE HIM ALONE!
...SAVE MY SON...
UNG!
I'LL KILL YOU!
DAGMAR.
LET ME DO THIS.
KLAUS?
I SAW HIM RUN YOU THROUGH--
SOMETHING HAPPENED TO ME...OUT ON THE ICE.
THE SHINING FAMILY BROUGHT ME TO A HOUSE BEHIND THE NORTHERN LIGHTS...
I CAN'T BE KILLED NOW.
I'M STILL NOT SURE WHAT THAT REALLY MEANS.
WE'LL SEE.

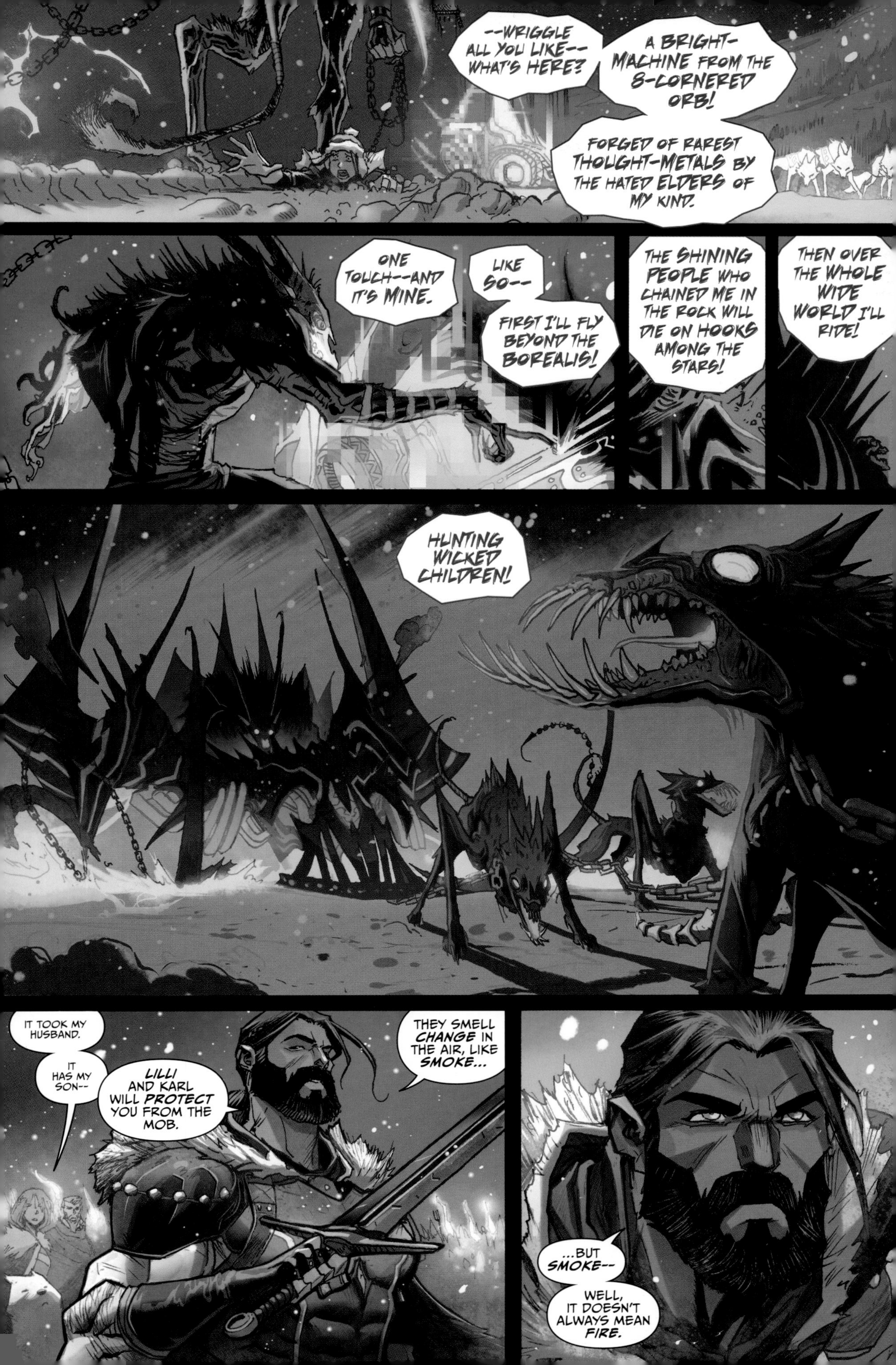
--WRIGGLE ALL YOU LIKE--WHAT'S HERE?
A BRIGHT-MACHINE FROM THE 8-CORNERED ORB!
FORGED OF RAREST THOUGHT-METALS BY THE HATED ELDERS OF MY KIND.
ONE TOUCH--AND IT'S MINE.
LIKE SO--
FIRST I'LL FLY BEYOND THE BOREALIS!
THE SHINING PEOPLE WHO CHAINED ME IN THE ROCK WILL DIE ON HOOKS AMONG THE STARS!
THEN OVER THE WHOLE WIDE WORLD I'LL RIDE!
HUNTING WICKED CHILDREN!
IT TOOK MY HUSBAND.
IT HAS MY SON--
LILLI AND KARL WILL PROTECT YOU FROM THE MOB.
THEY SMELL CHANGE IN THE AIR, LIKE SMOKE...
...BUT SMOKE--
WELL, IT DOESN'T ALWAYS MEAN FIRE.

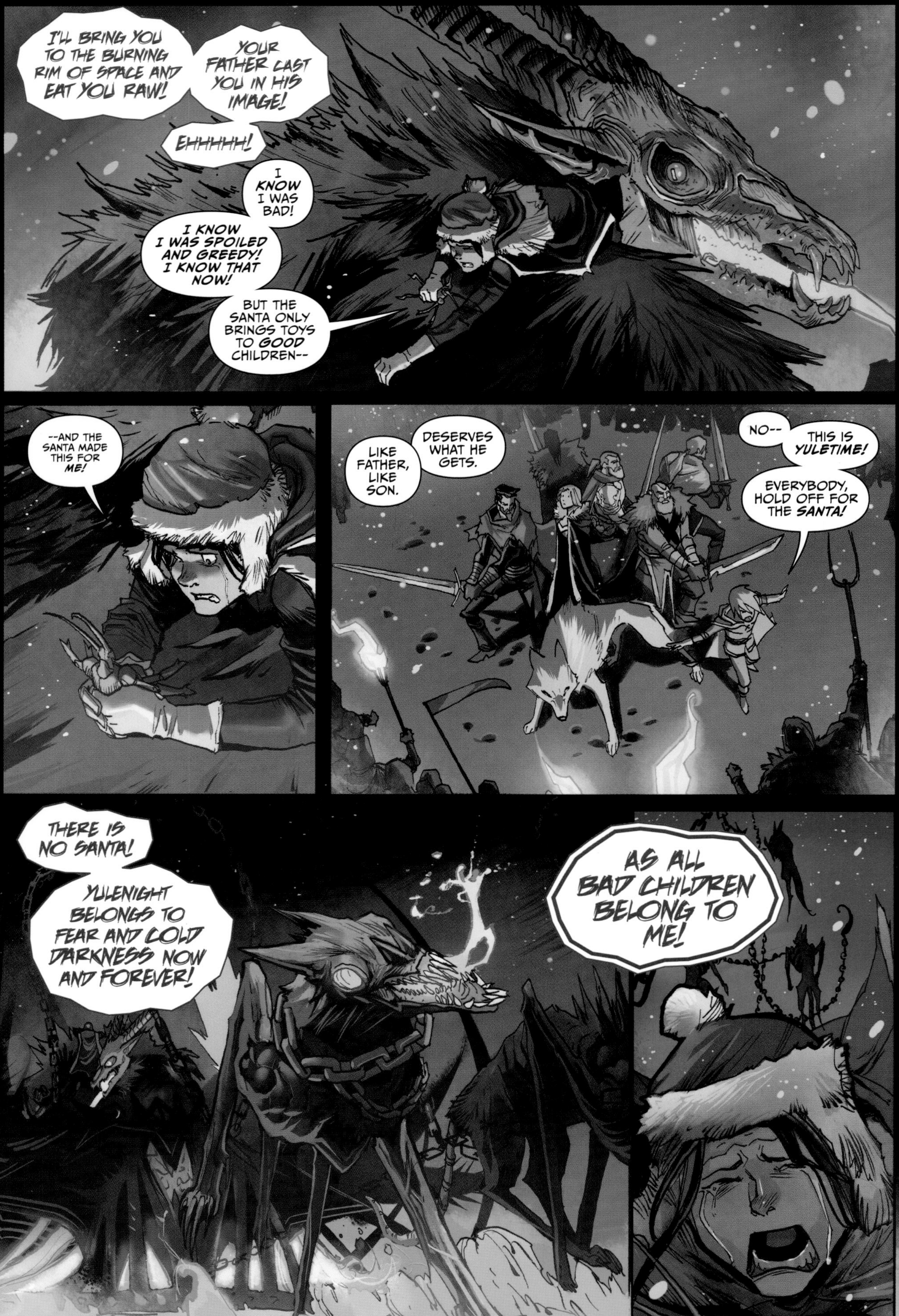
I'LL BRING YOU TO THE BURNING RIM OF SPACE AND EAT YOU RAW!
YOUR FATHER CAST YOU IN HIS IMAGE!
EHHHHH!
I KNOW I WAS BAD!
I KNOW I WAS SPOILED AND GREEDY! I KNOW THAT NOW!
BUT THE SANTA ONLY BRINGS TOYS TO GOOD CHILDREN--
--AND THE SANTA MADE THIS FOR ME!
DESERVES WHAT HE GETS.
LIKE FATHER, LIKE SON.
NO--
THIS IS YULETIME!
EVERYBODY, HOLD OFF FOR THE SANTA!
THERE IS NO SANTA!
YULENIGHT BELONGS TO FEAR AND COLD DARKNESS NOW AND FOREVER!
AS ALL BAD CHILDREN BELONG TO ME!

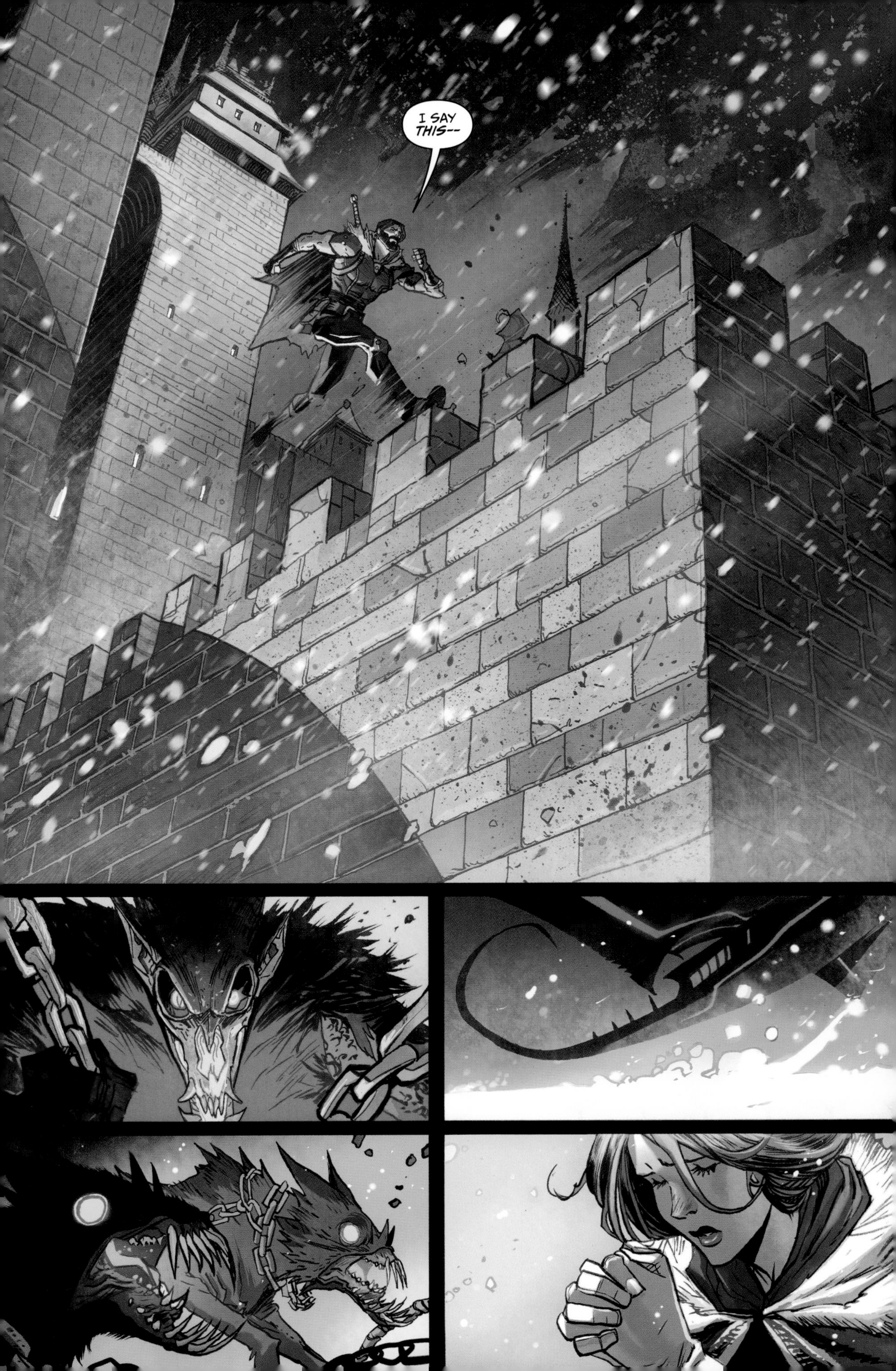
I SAY THIS--

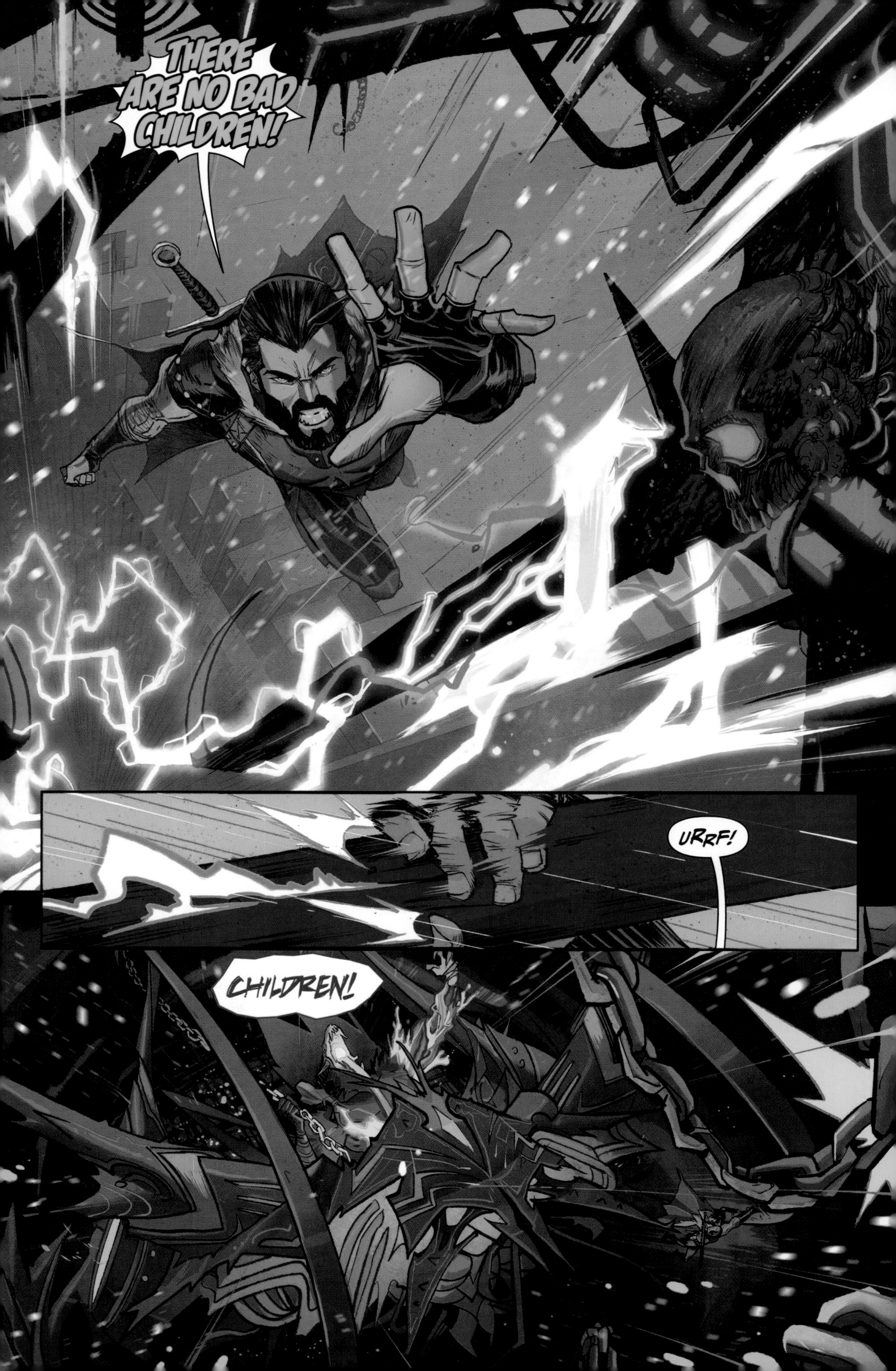
THERE ARE NO BAD CHILDREN!
URRF!
CHILDREN!

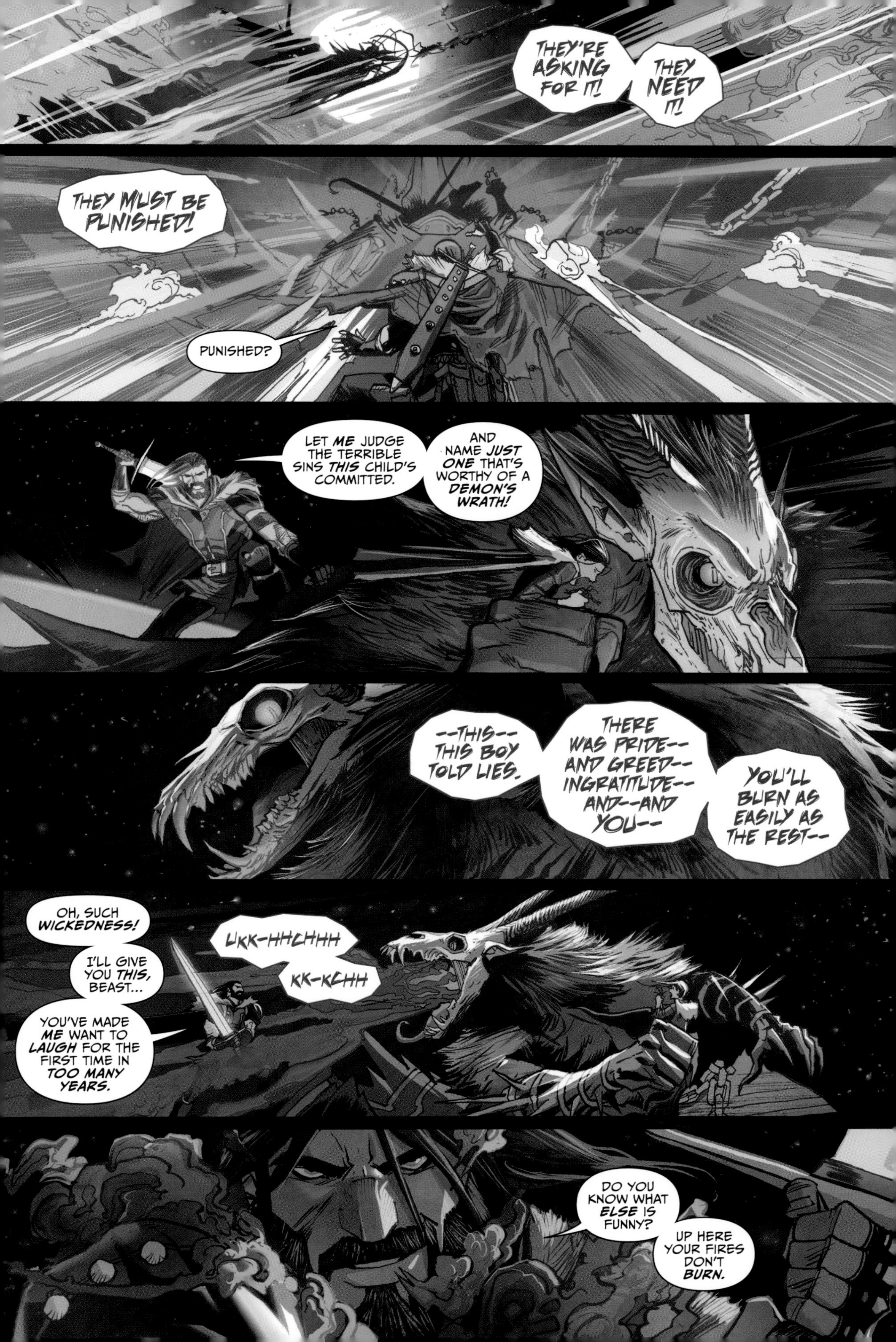
THEY'RE ASKING FOR IT!
THEY NEED IT!
THEY MUST BE PUNISHED!
PUNISHED?
LET ME JUDGE THE TERRIBLE SINS THIS CHILD'S COMMITTED.
AND NAME JUST ONE THAT'S WORTHY OF A DEMON'S WRATH!
--THIS-- THIS BOY TOLD LIES.
THERE WAS PRIDE-- AND GREED-- INGRATITUDE-- AND--AND YOU--
YOU'LL BURN AS EASILY AS THE REST--
OH, SUCH WICKEDNESS!
I'LL GIVE YOU THIS, BEAST...
YOU'VE MADE ME WANT TO LAUGH FOR THE FIRST TIME IN TOO MANY YEARS.
UKK-HHCHHH
KK-KCHH
DO YOU KNOW WHAT ELSE IS FUNNY?
UP HERE YOUR FIRES DON'T BURN.

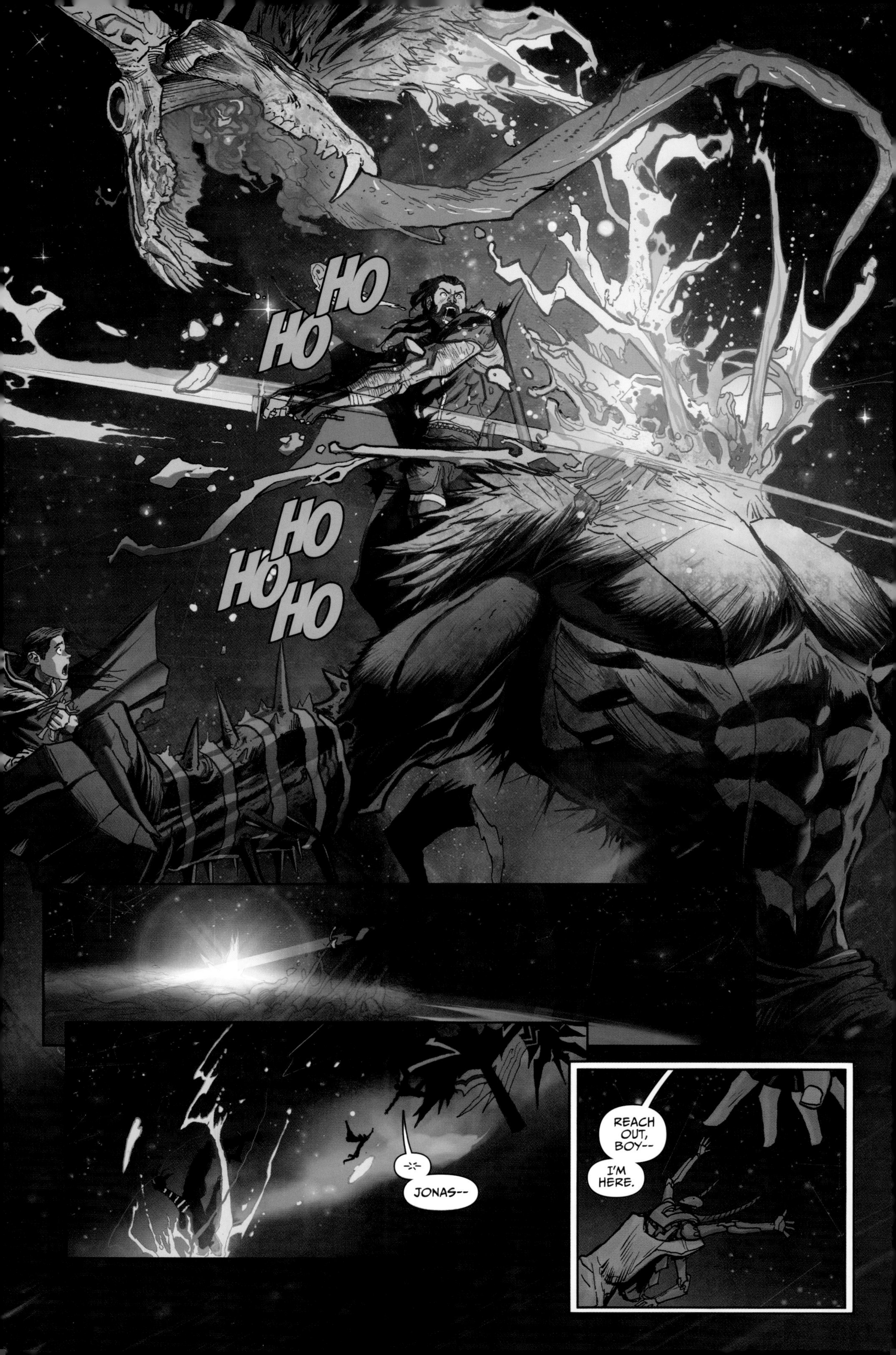
HO HO
HO HO HO HO
-!-
JONAS--
REACH OUT, BOY--
I'M HERE.

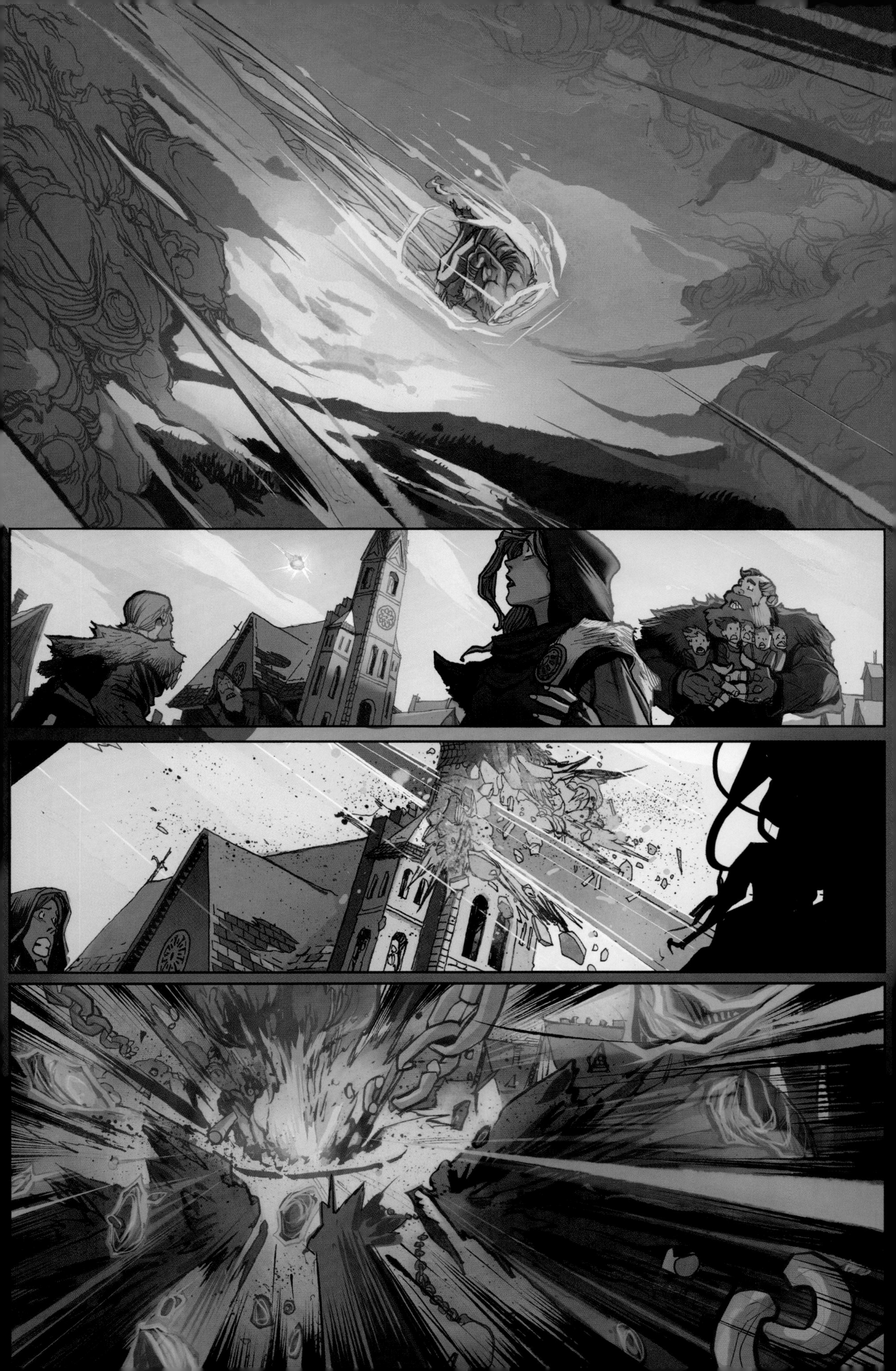

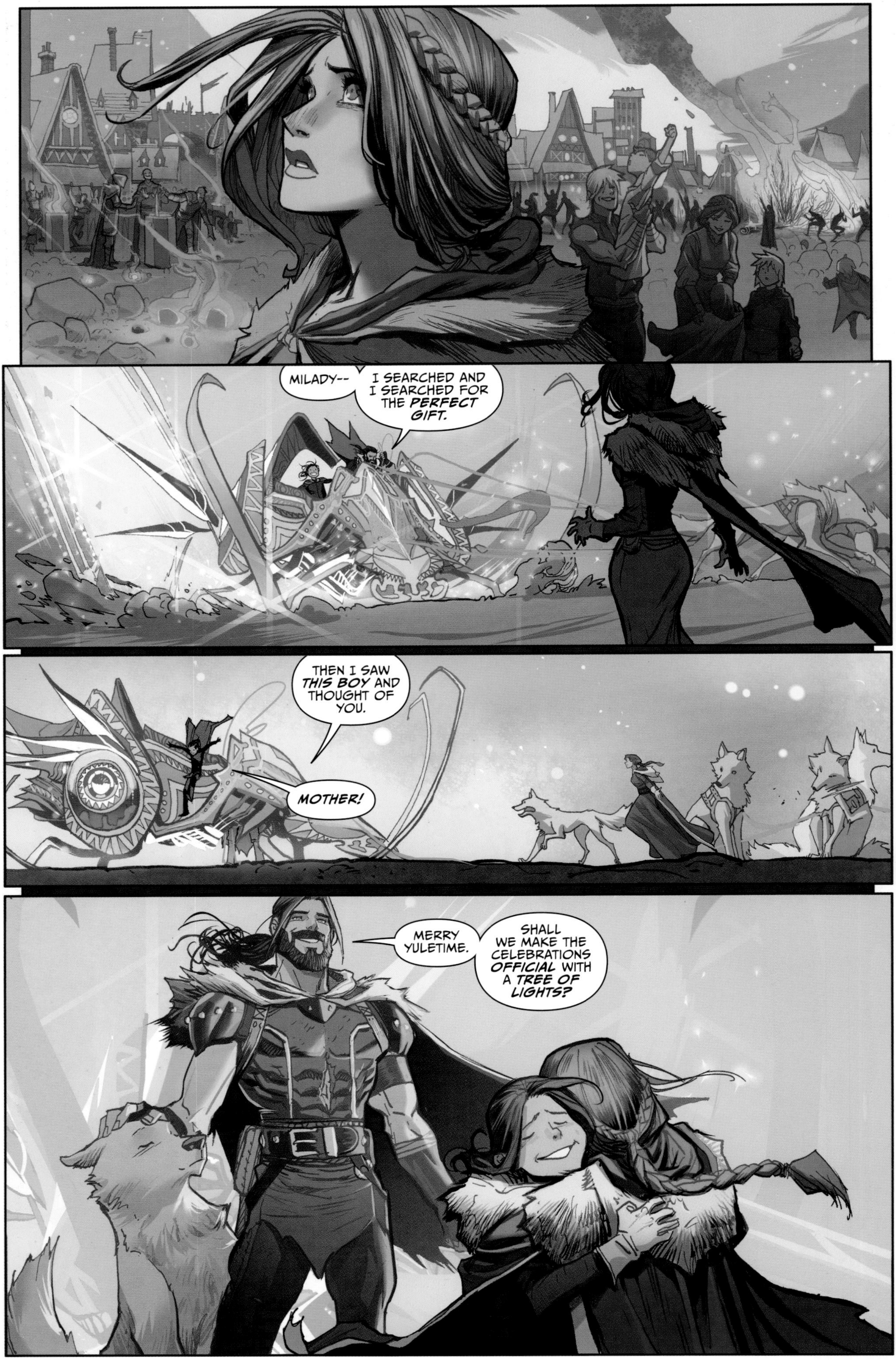
MILADY--
I SEARCHED AND I SEARCHED FOR THE *PERFECT GIFT.*
THEN I SAW *THIS BOY* AND THOUGHT OF YOU.
MOTHER!
MERRY YULETIME.
SHALL WE MAKE THE CELEBRATIONS *OFFICIAL* WITH A *TREE OF LIGHTS?*

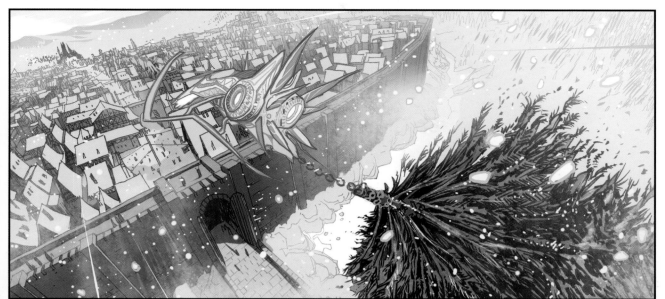

--WITH *KLAUS* AS MY ADVISOR, I VOW TO MAKE AMENDS FOR MY LATE HUSBAND'S DARK MISDEEDS.

THE LORD MAGNUS WAS... UNDER AN EVIL *SPELL*, YOUR MAJESTY.

THINGS WILL *CHANGE* IN GRIMSVIG--

MILADY--

WE WILL ATTEND TO YOUR *PROGRESS* WITH GREAT INTEREST.

NOW... AS REGARDS THIS EPIC *FEAST* YOUR HUSBAND PROMISED...

ONCE UPON A TIME.

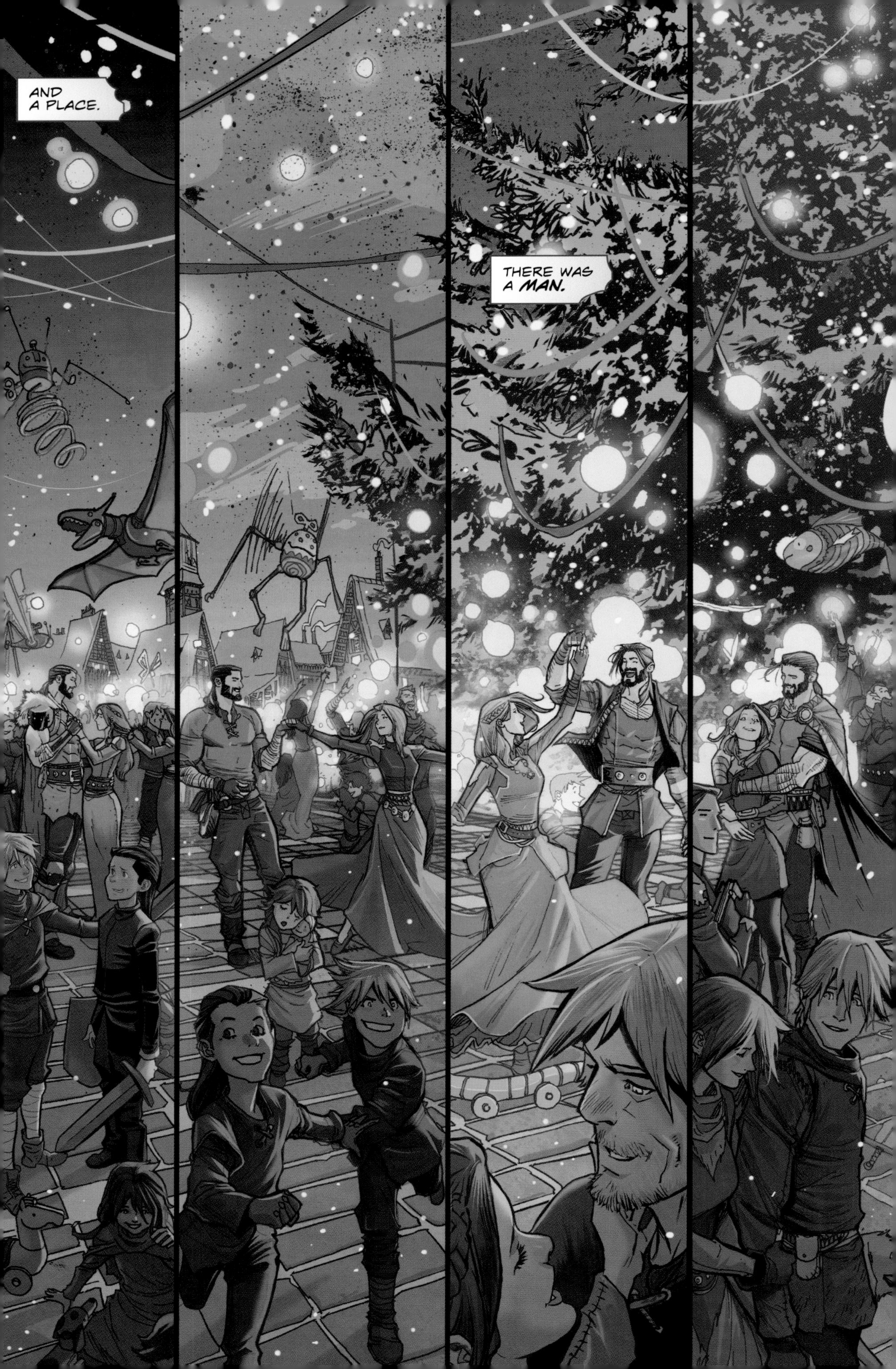
AND A PLACE.
THERE WAS A MAN.

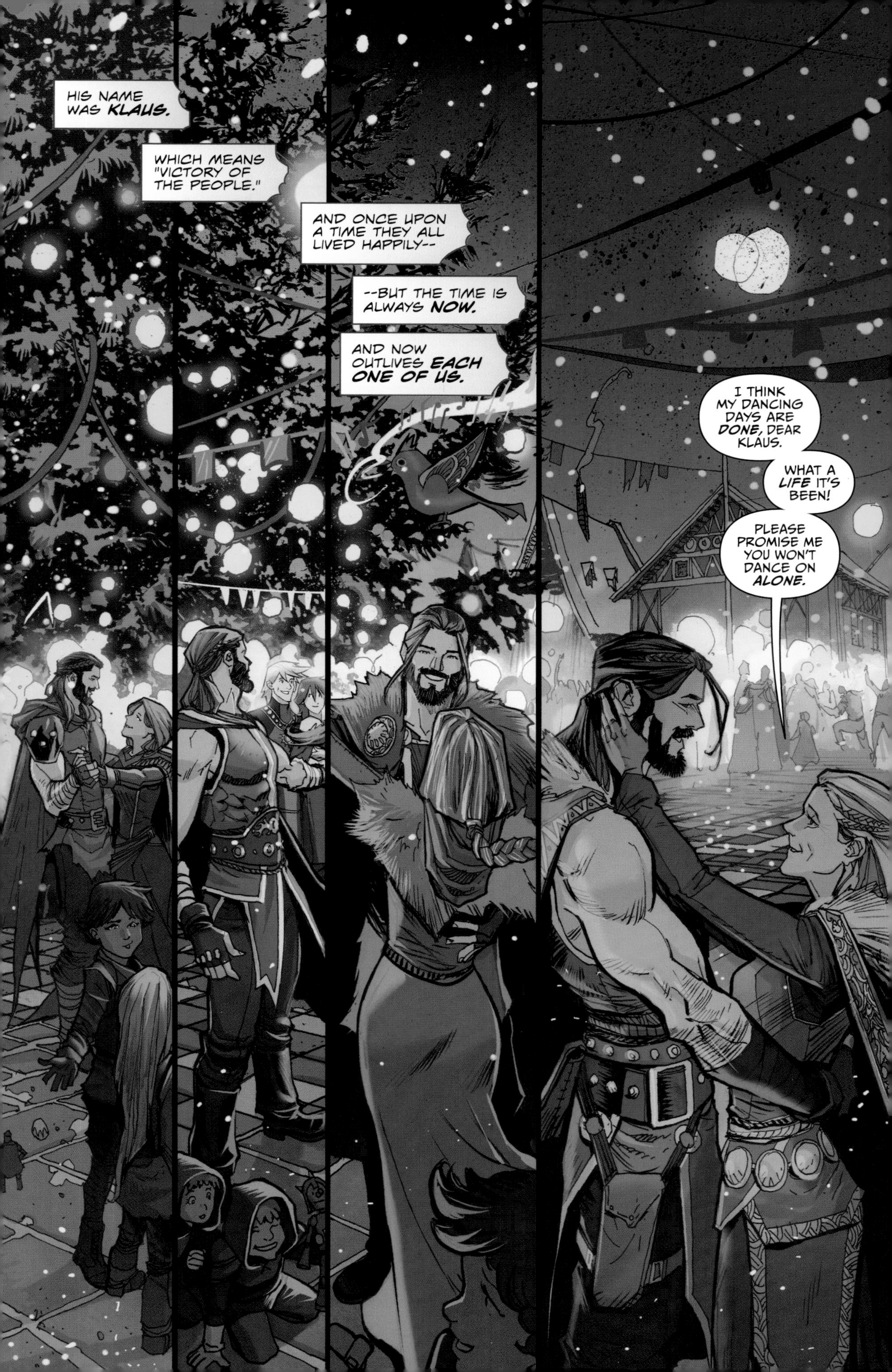
HIS NAME WAS KLAUS.
WHICH MEANS "VICTORY OF THE PEOPLE."
AND ONCE UPON A TIME THEY ALL LIVED HAPPILY--
--BUT THE TIME IS ALWAYS NOW.
AND NOW OUTLIVES EACH ONE OF US.
I THINK MY DANCING DAYS ARE DONE, DEAR KLAUS.
WHAT A LIFE IT'S BEEN!
PLEASE PROMISE ME YOU WON'T DANCE ON ALONE.

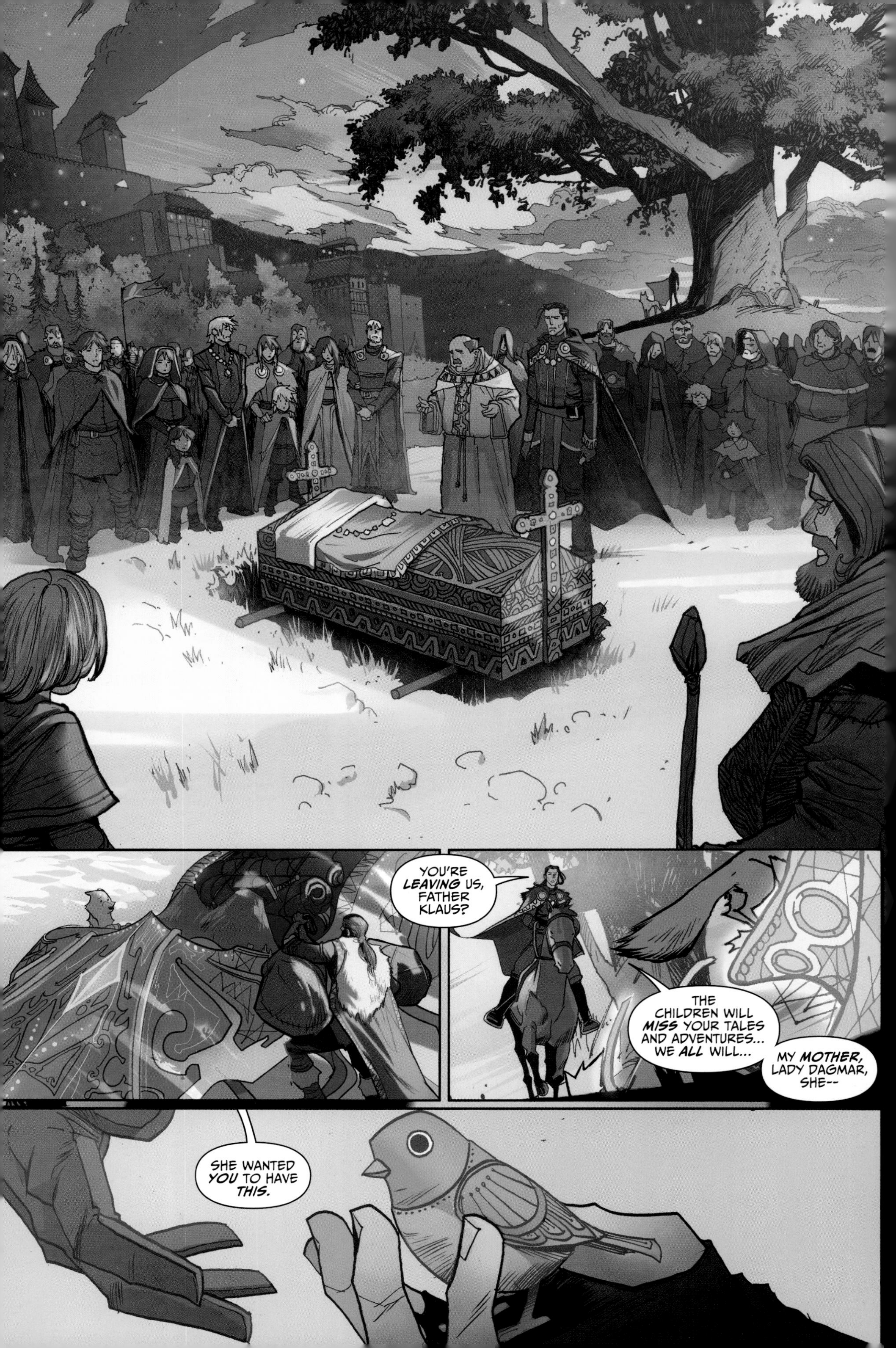
YOU'RE LEAVING US, FATHER KLAUS?
THE CHILDREN WILL MISS YOUR TALES AND ADVENTURES... WE ALL WILL...
MY MOTHER, LADY DAGMAR, SHE--
SHE WANTED YOU TO HAVE THIS.

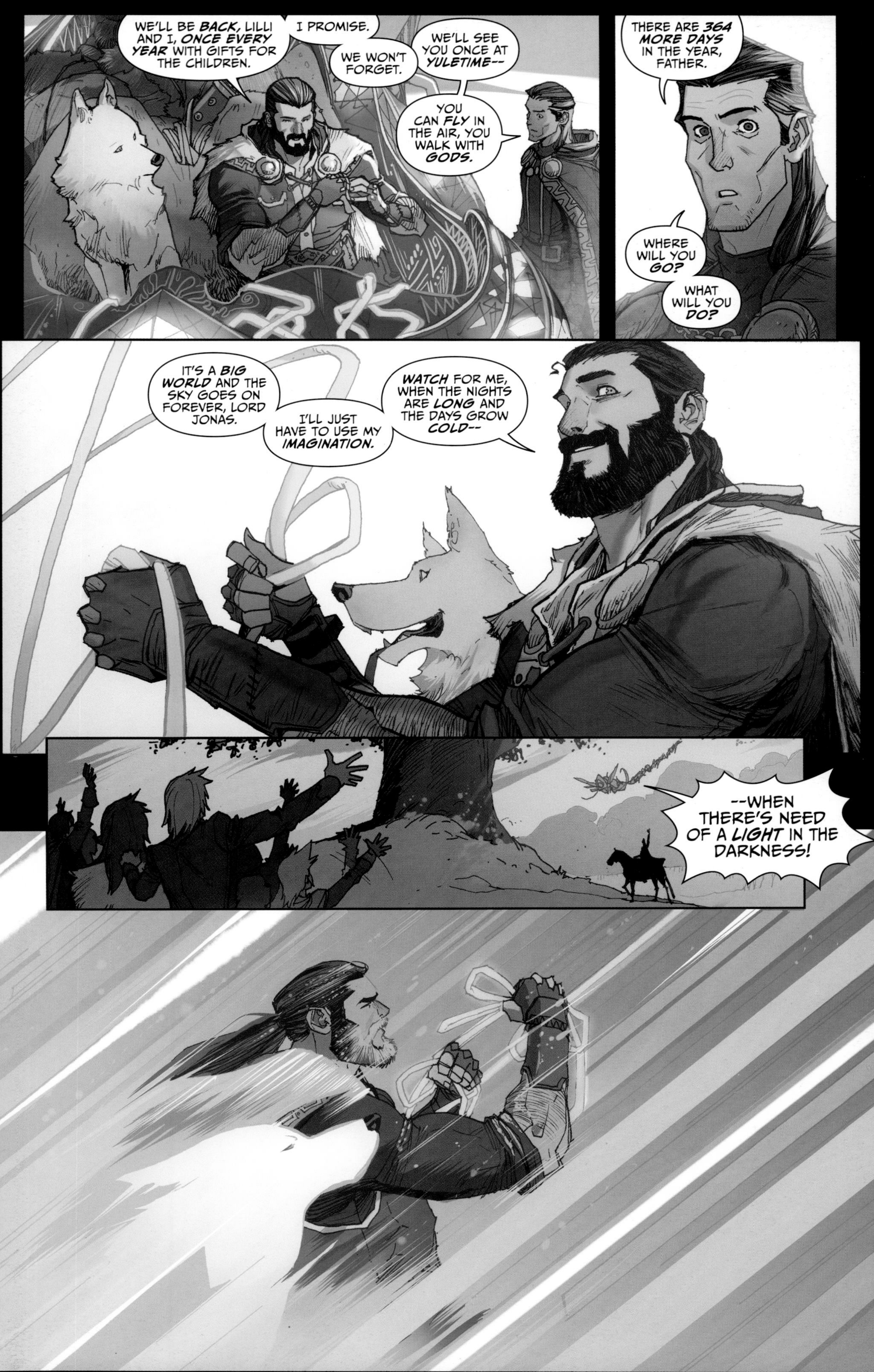
WE'LL BE BACK, LILLI AND I, ONCE EVERY YEAR WITH GIFTS FOR THE CHILDREN.
I PROMISE.
WE WON'T FORGET.
WE'LL SEE YOU ONCE AT YULETIME--
YOU CAN FLY IN THE AIR, YOU WALK WITH GODS.
THERE ARE 364 MORE DAYS IN THE YEAR, FATHER.
WHERE WILL YOU GO?
WHAT WILL YOU DO?
IT'S A BIG WORLD AND THE SKY GOES ON FOREVER, LORD JONAS.
I'LL JUST HAVE TO USE MY IMAGINATION.
WATCH FOR ME, WHEN THE NIGHTS ARE LONG AND THE DAYS GROW COLD--
--WHEN THERE'S NEED OF A LIGHT IN THE DARKNESS!

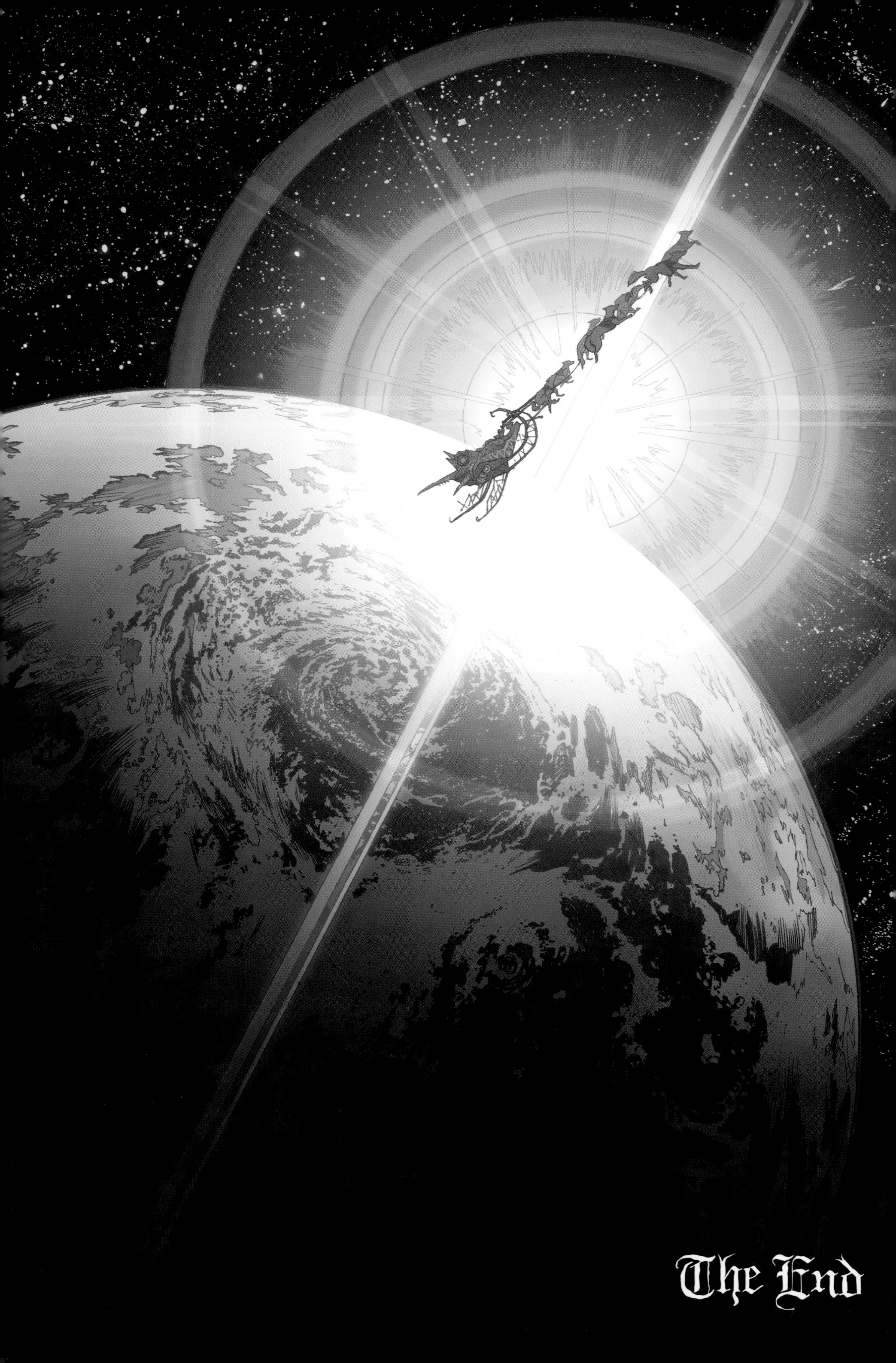
The End

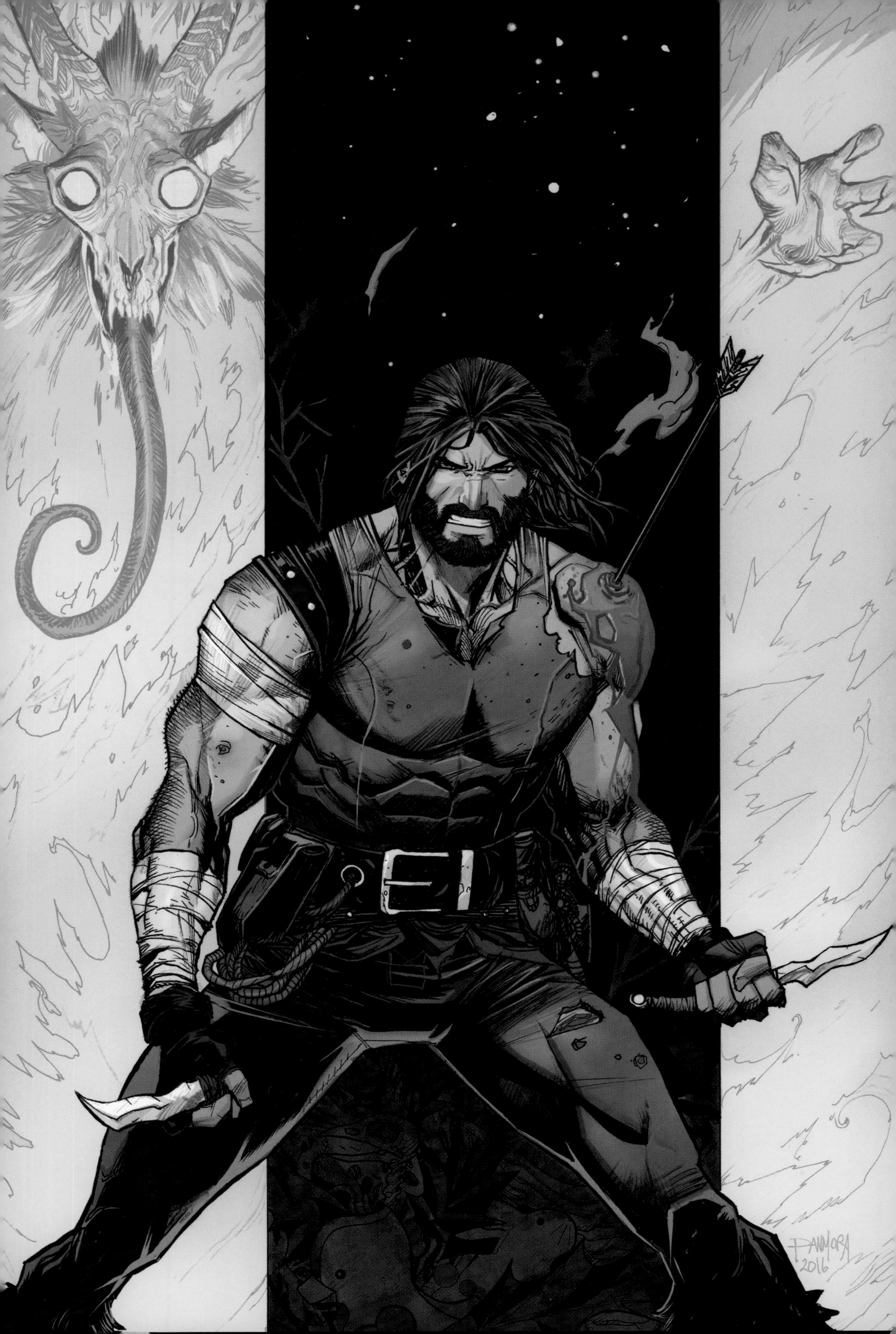
DANMORA
2016

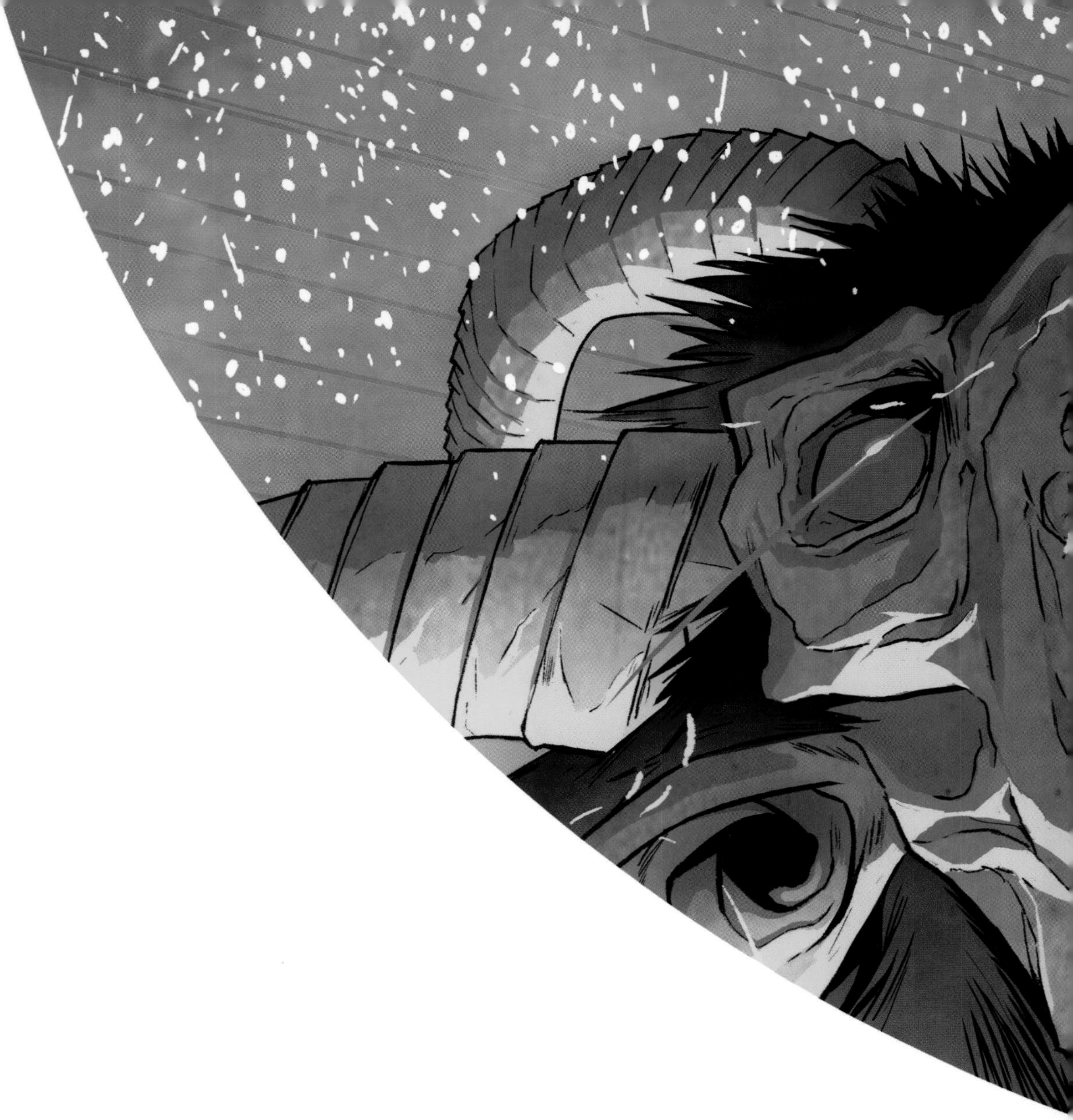

ISSUE ONE BOOM! TEN YEARS VARIANT COVER **FELIPE SMIT**

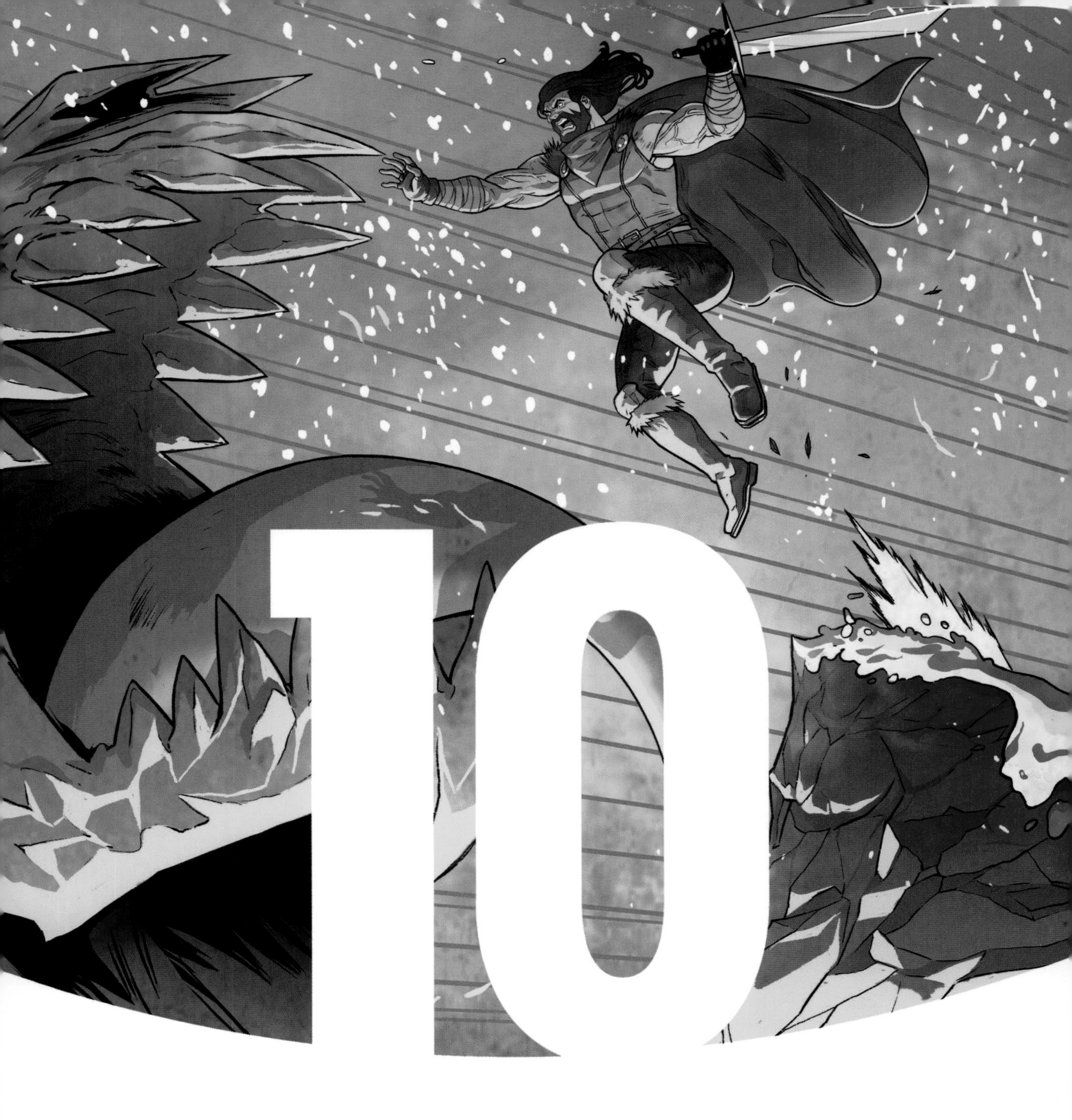

10

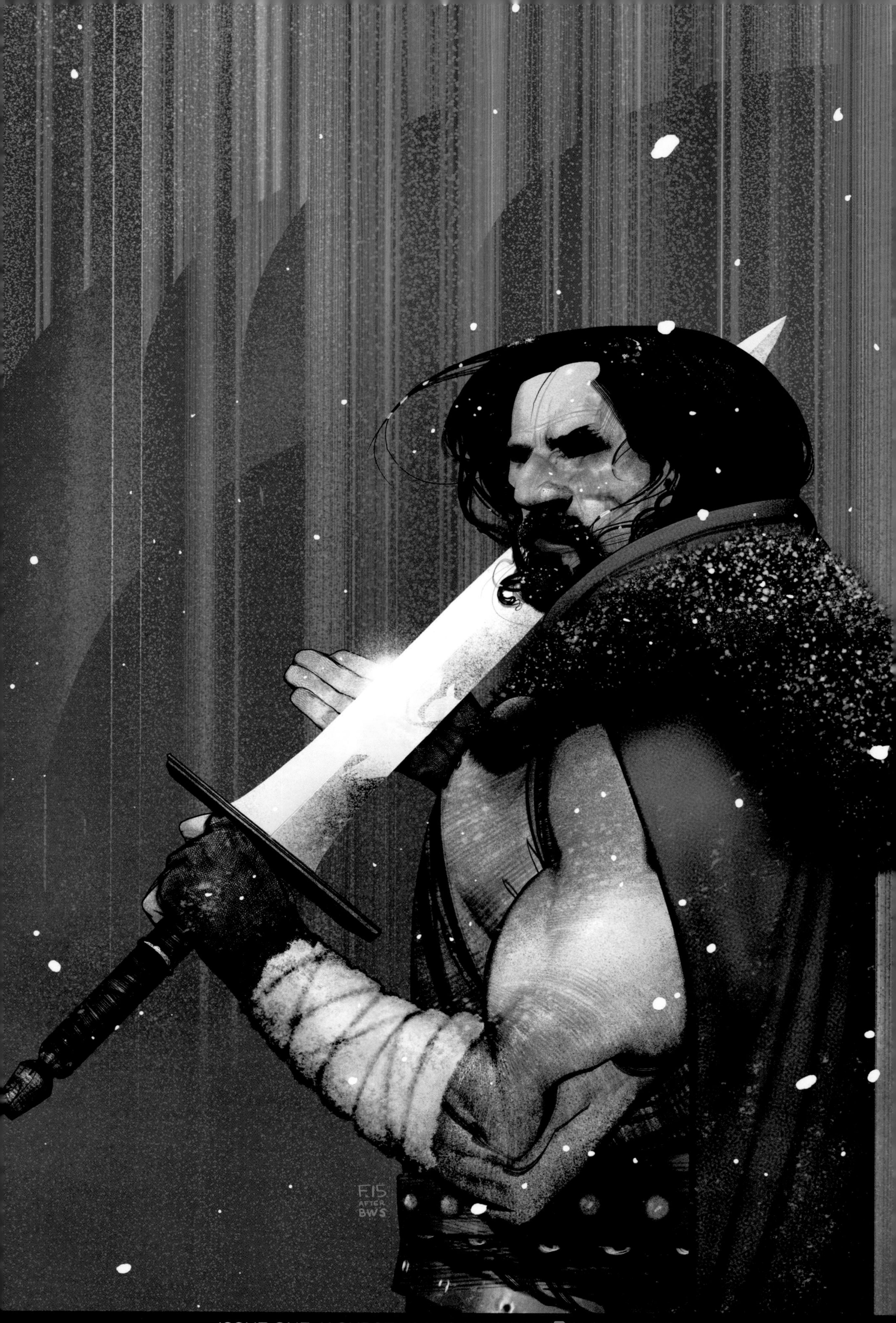
F.15
AFTER
BWS
ISSUE ONE JACKPOT VARIANT COVER FRAZER IRVING

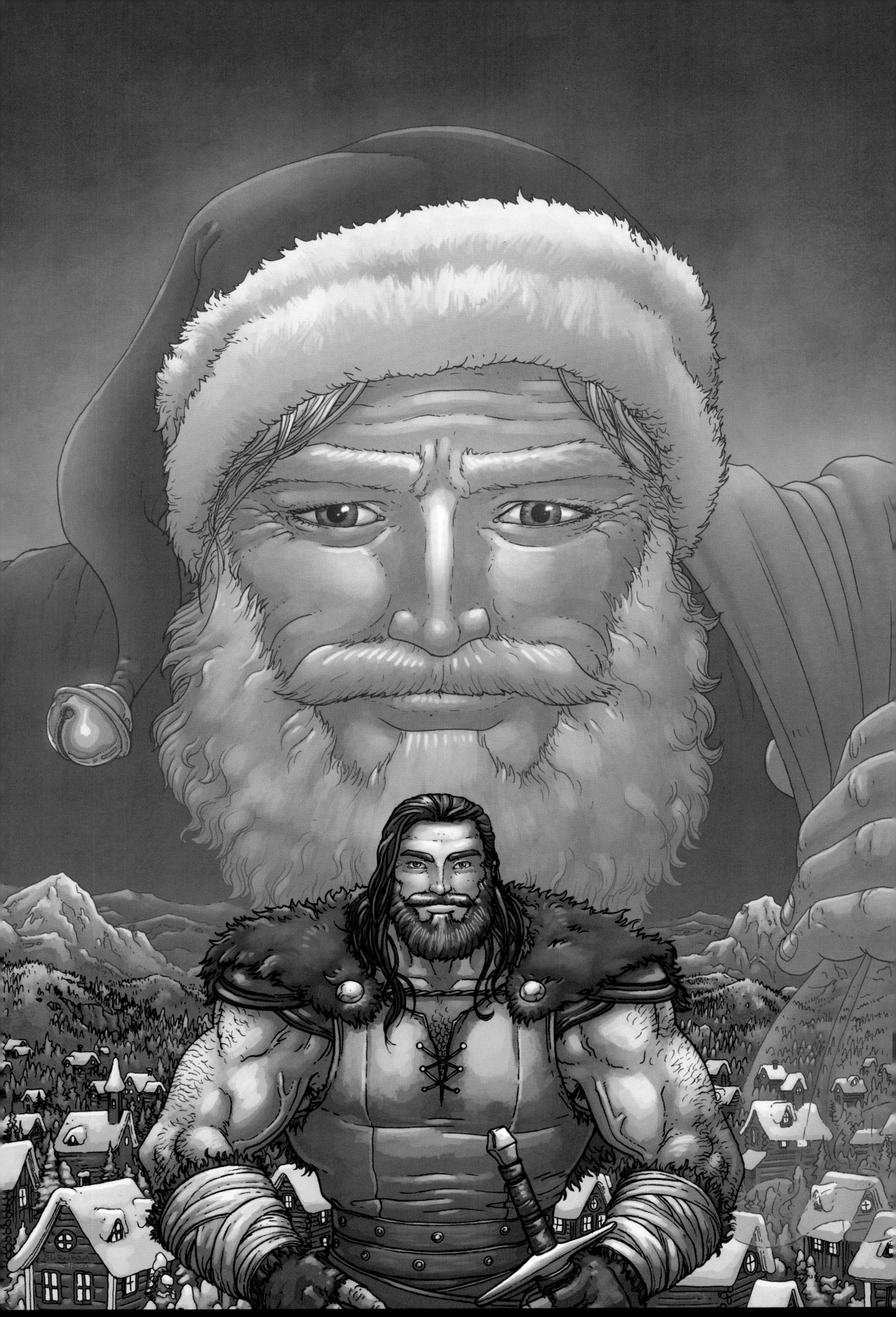

ISSUE ONE VARIANT COVER **CHRIS BURNHAM** COLORS **JORDAN BOYD**

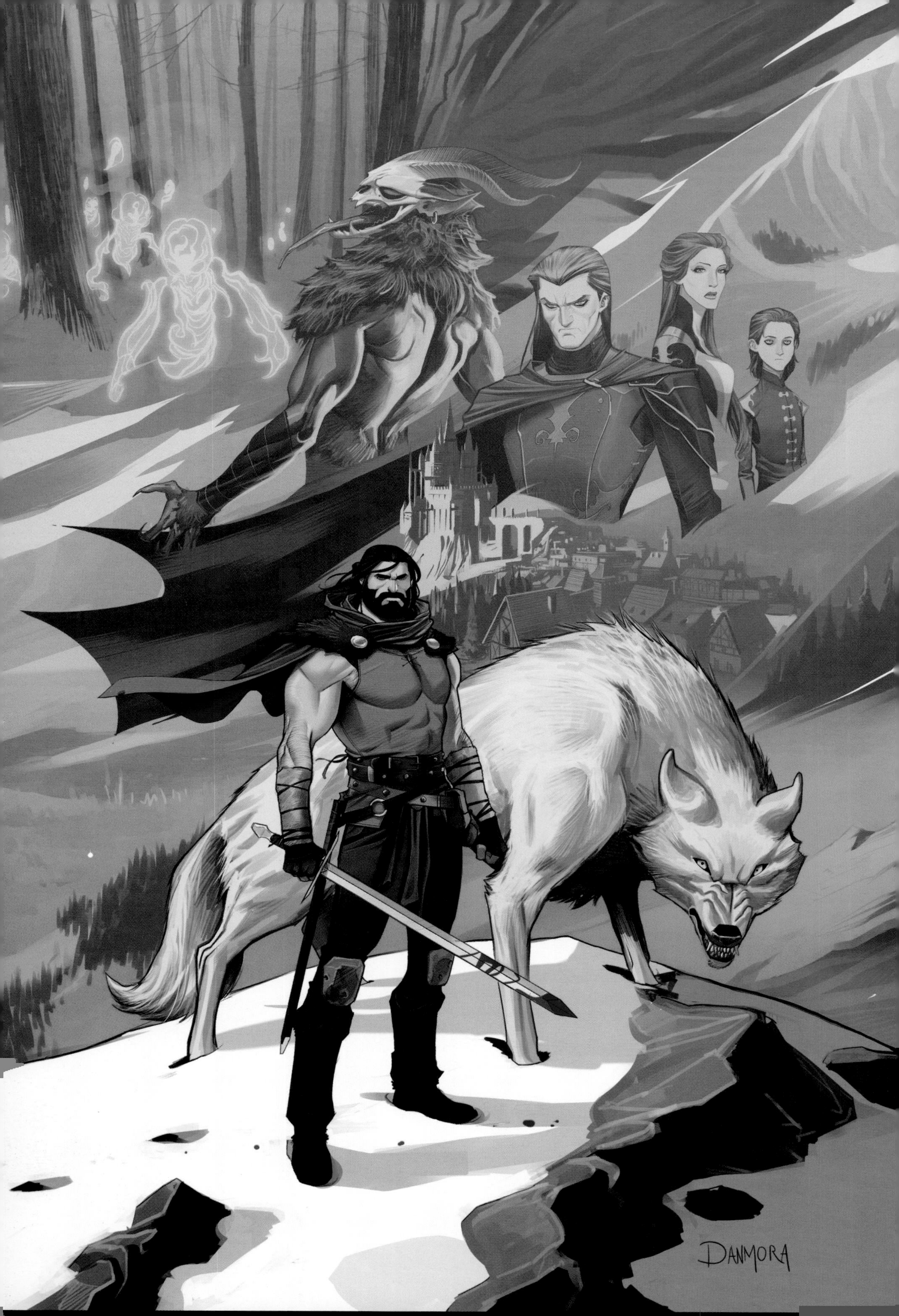
DANMORA

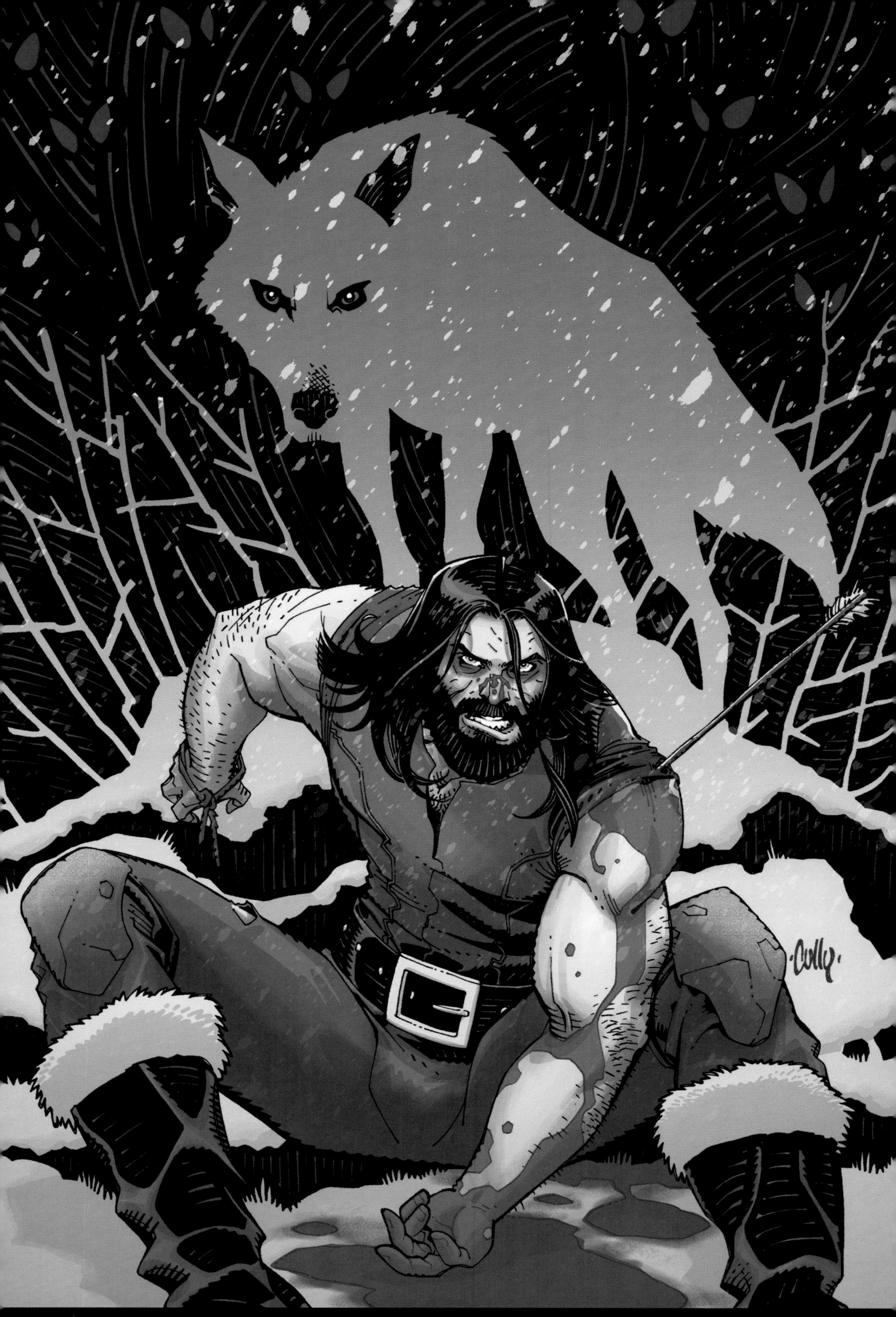
Cully
ISSUE ONE CARDS, COMICS & COLLECTIBLES EXCLUSIVE COVER **CULLY HAMNER**

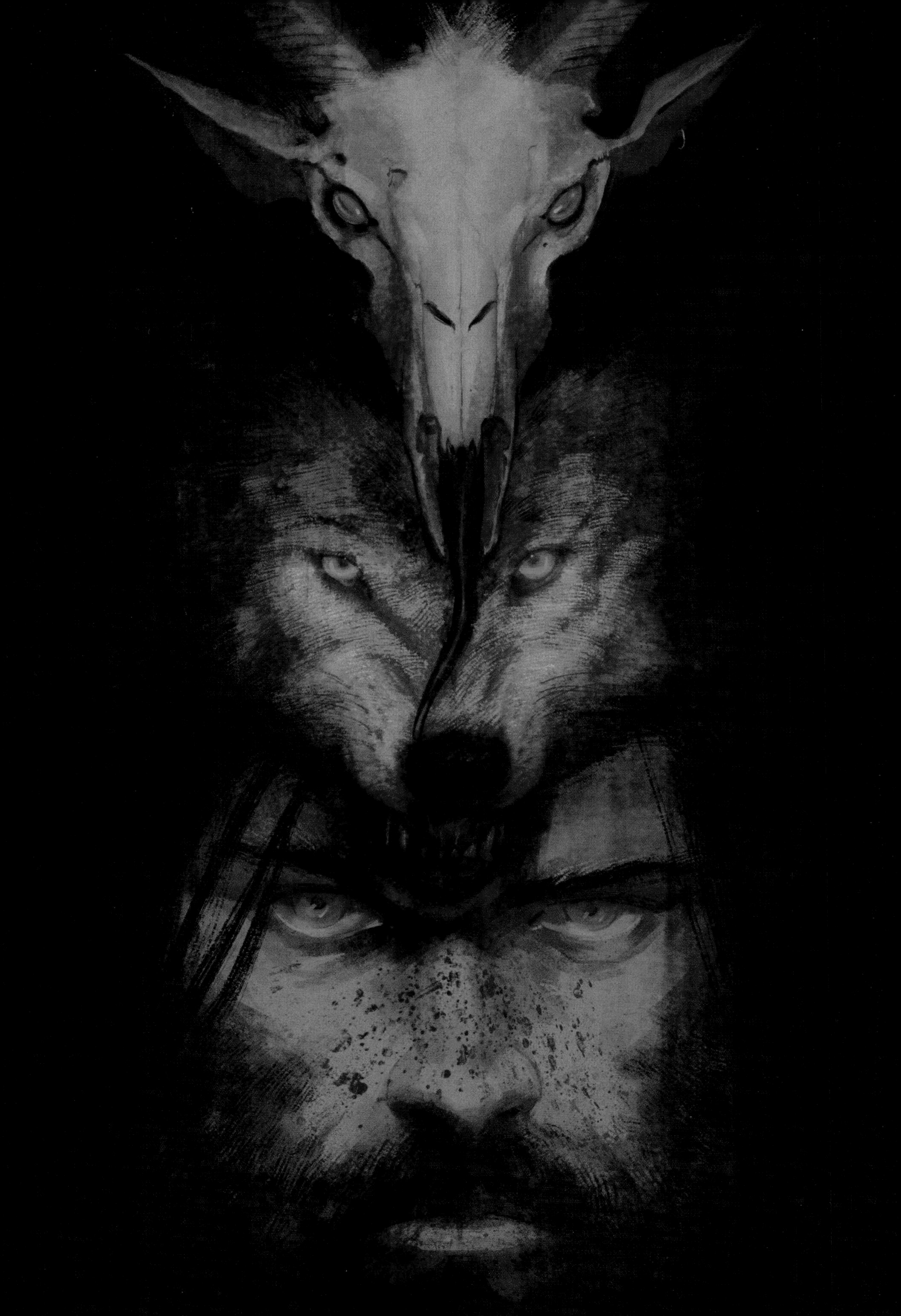

ISSUE ONE NEWBURY COMICS EXCLUSIVE COVER **VANESA R. DEL REY**

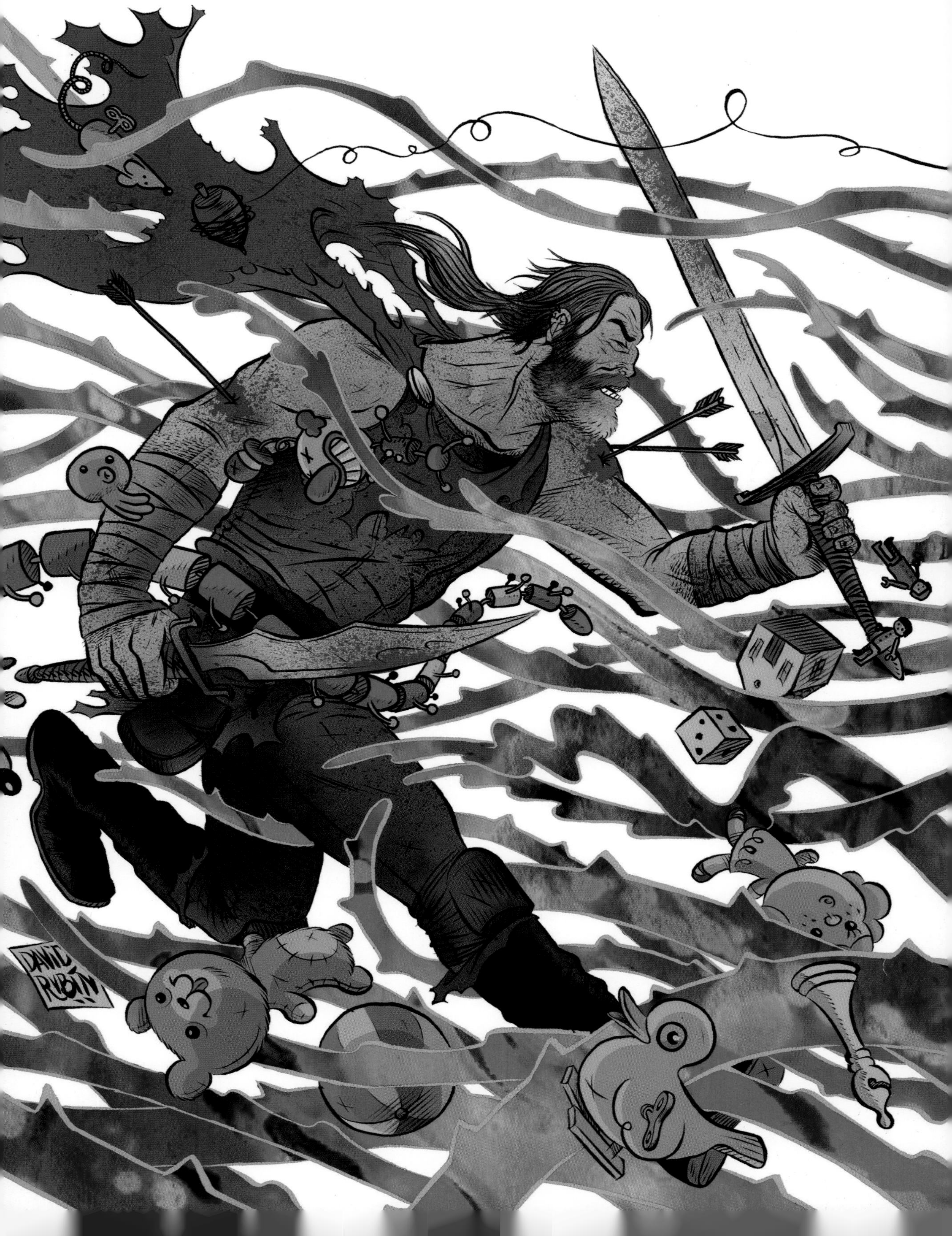
DAVID RUBÍN

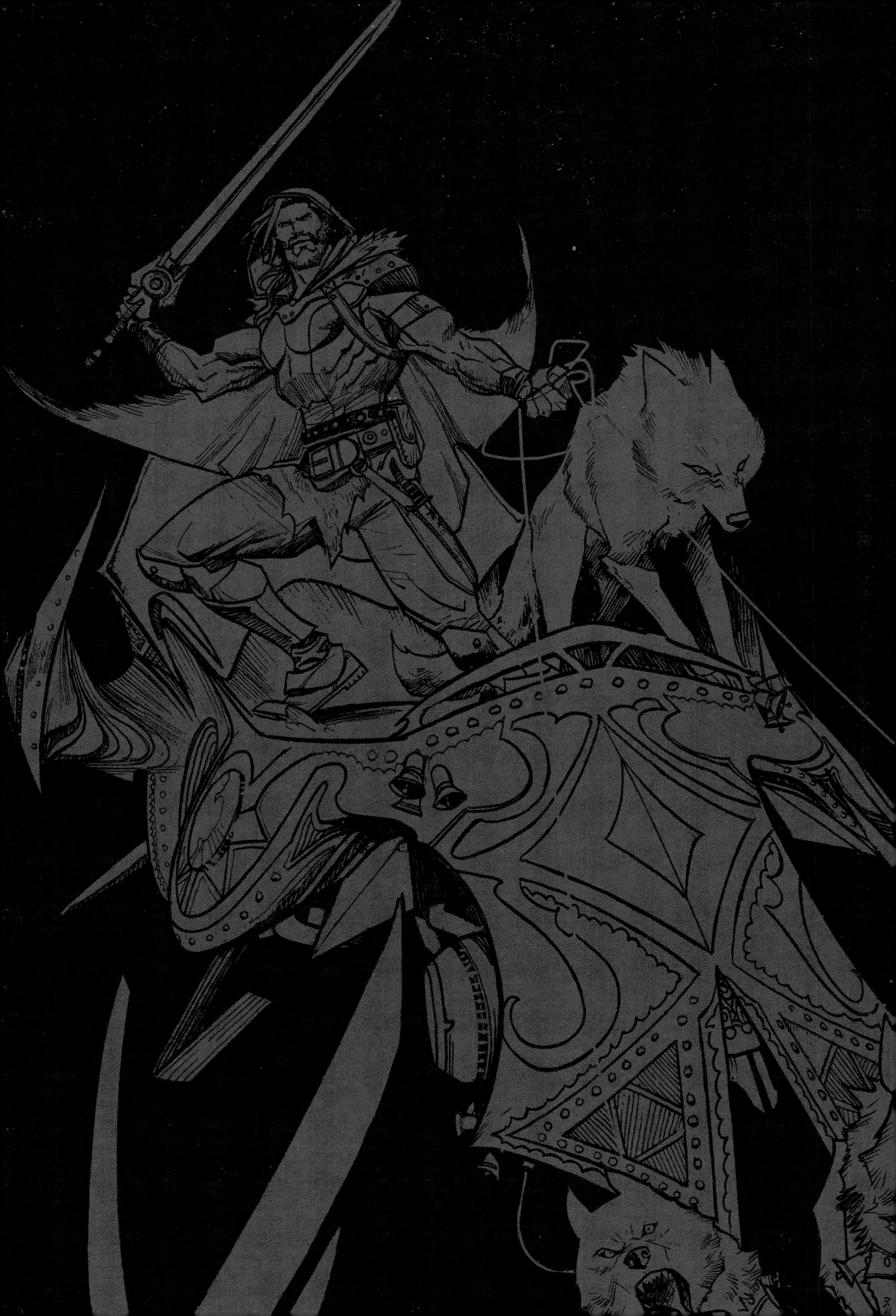

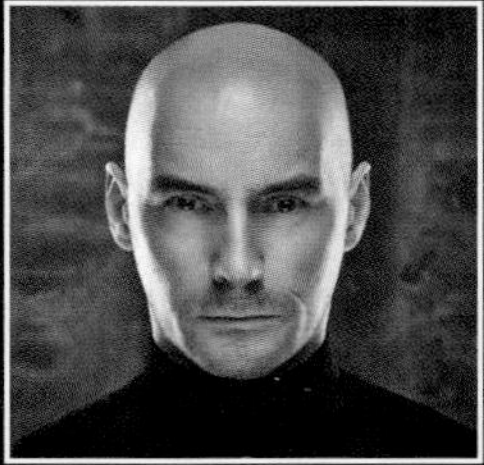

Photo by Allan Amato

GRANT MORRISON

Grant Morrison is one of the most successful and critically-acclaimed writers in the medium of comic books. Credits include *Batman: Arkham Asylum, The Invisibles, The Filth, We3, Happy!, Heavy Metal,* and many more. He has also completed best-selling runs on *Animal Man, Doom Patrol, Batman, Superman, New X-Men,* and *JLA,* and is currently working on a series of *Wonder Woman* graphic novels. Most recently he has been collaborating on film and television adaptations of some of his stories. He is also a prominent Chaos Magician. He spends four months of the year in West Hollywood and the rest of the time in Scotland, with his wife Kristan, two cats, and a menagerie of stray and wild animals which rely on their charity.

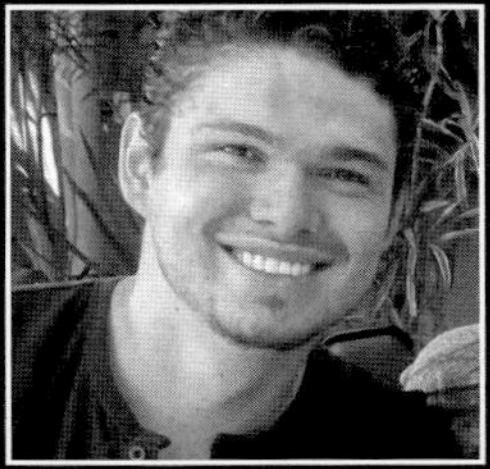

DAN MORA

Dan Mora Chaves was born in 1987. He's been drawing all his life, but was formally trained and graduated from the Fine Arts School at the University of Costa Rica. He has been part of many design, illustrator & animator groups in Costa Rica but got his big break from BOOM! in 2014 on the monthly series *Hexed*. He is married and lives in Alajuela. He was awarded with the 2016 Russ Manning Promising Newcomer Award for his work on ***Klaus***.

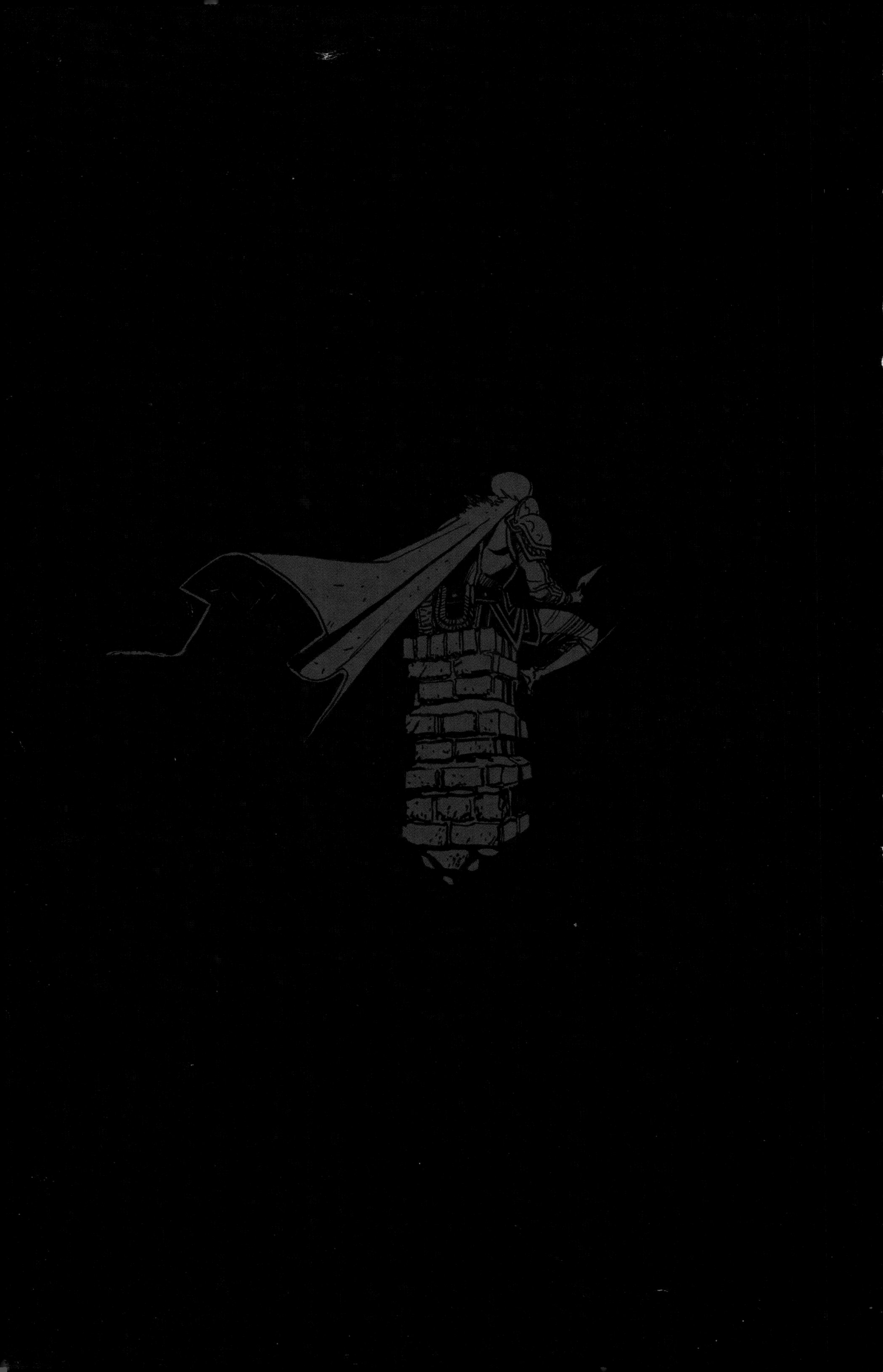